PENGUIN BOOKS

THE SANTE FE TRAIL

David Dary, a native of Manhattan, Kansas, worked for CBS News and NBC News in Texas and Washington, D.C., and for many years taught journalism at the University of Kansas. He then headed the School of Journalism at the University of Oklahoma, from which he recently retired. Dary is the author of eight previous books on the West: *The Buffalo Book*, *True Tales of the Old-Time Plains*, *Cowboy Culture*, *True Tales of Old-Time Kansas*, *More True Tales of Old-Time Kansas*, *Entrepreneurs of the Old West*, *Seeking Pleasure in the Old West*, and *Red Blood and Black Ink*. He is the recipient of a Cowboy Hall of Fame Wrangler Award, two Western Writers of America Spur Awards, and the Westerners International Best Nonfiction Book Award. He lives in Norman, Oklahoma.

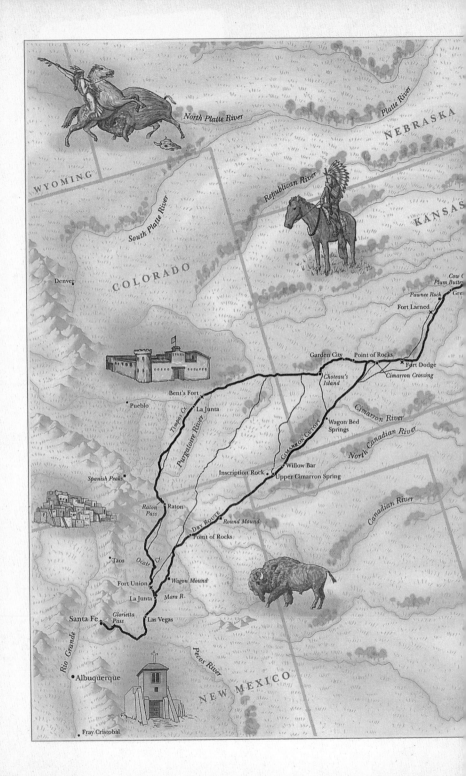

St. Louis

Mississippi River

MISSOURI

Missouri River

Old Franklin

St. Joseph

Atchison

Fort Osage

Fort Leavenworth

Independence

Tipton

Westport Landing

Lawrence

Lone Elm

Topeka

Fort Riley

Willow Springs

Kansas River

Salina

Council Grove

Neosho River

Stone Corral

Arkansas River

ARKANSAS

Wichita

Caldwell

OKLAHOMA

Red River

TEXAS

THE SANTA FE TRAIL

KILOMETERS	
0	150

MILES	
0	150

THE SANTA FE TRAIL

Its History, Legends, and Lore

DAVID DARY

PENGUIN BOOKS

PENGUIN BOOKS
Published by the Penguin Group
Penguin Putnam Inc., 375 Hudson Street,
New York, New York 10014, U.S.A.
Penguin Books Ltd, 80 Strand, London WC2R oRL, England
Penguin Books Australia Ltd, 250 Camberwell Road,
Camberwell, Victoria 3124, Australia
Penguin Books Canada Ltd, 10 Alcorn Avenue,
Toronto, Ontario, Canada M4V 3B2
Penguin Books India (P) Ltd, 11 Community Centre,
Panchsheel Park, New Delhi – 110 017, India
Penguin Books (N.Z.) Ltd, Cnr Rosedale and Airborne Roads,
Albany, Auckland, New Zealand
Penguin Books (South Africa) (Pty) Ltd, 24 Sturdee Avenue,
Rosebank, Johannesburg 2196, South Africa

Penguin Books Ltd, Registered Offices:
Harmondsworth, Middlesex, England

First published in the United States of America by Alfred A. Knopf,
a division of Random House 2000
Published in Penguin Books 2002

1   3   5   7   9   10   8   6   4   2

Copyright © David Dary, 2000
Map and illustration copyright © David Lindroth, Inc., 2000
All rights reserved

THE LIBRARY OF CONGRESS HAS CATALOGED
THE HARDCOVER EDITION AS FOLLOWS:
Dary, David.
The Santa Fe Trail: its history, legends, and lore / by David Dary.
p.   cm.
ISBN 0-375-40361-2 (hc.)
ISBN 0 14 20.0058 2 (pbk.)
1. Santa Fe Trail—History.   I. Title.
F786.D37 2000
978—dc21   00-023276

Printed in the United States of America
Set in ITC New Baskerville
Designed by Robert C. Olsson

To the memory of
John Shelby Masterman
friend, colleague, and westerner,
who was fascinated with
the Santa Fe Trail

Ever since that moment when two individuals first lived upon this earth, one has had what the other wanted, and has been willing for a consideration to part with his possession.

—H. Gordon Selfridge

Contents

Acknowledgments

THE BIBLIOGRAPHY and notes list the names of many writers whose works were consulted in researching this book. To each I am indebted for blazing different aspects of the trail's story. I owe thanks to others, including Mark Gardner, an accomplished historian in Cascade, Colorado, for letting me pick his mind on matters relating to the wagons used in the Santa Fe trade; and Robert White at the Smithsonian Institution, Washington, D.C. Thanks also to John Mark Lambertson, director and archivist at the National Frontier Trails Center in Independence, Missouri; Gordon Julich at the beautifully restored Fort Osage, Missouri; and the friendly people at the Missouri Tourism Department in Jefferson City. Others who were of great help include John Lovett, librarian at the Western History Collection, University of Oklahoma Libraries, and Don DeWitt, curator, in Norman; Arthur O'Leavis and Richard Rodeasil of the photo archives of the Museum of New Mexico; Al Regensberg, senior archivist for the State Records Center and Archives in Santa Fe; and Nancy Sherbert of the Kansas State Historical Society, Topeka. Thanks also to George Miles, curator, Western Americana Collection, the Beinecke Rare Book and Manuscript Library, Yale University, for helpful advice. A special note of thanks to my editor, Ann Close, at Alfred A. Knopf, who molded the completed manuscript and illustrations into the final product.

—*David Dary*

Introduction

THE SANTA FE TRAIL has a romantic place in American history not only because it was a pioneer road or highway linking Missouri to New Mexico, especially the fabled town of Santa Fe, and continuing south to Old Mexico, but because of the humans who crossed the desolate prairie and plains and mountains, most in search of profitable trade.

The Indians, and later Spaniards and Anglo-Americans, undoubtedly followed a multiplicity of old trails first made by buffalo that eventually became known as the Santa Fe Trail. The route was not as long as the Oregon Trail, over which emigrants traveled to make their homes in the promised land, and, unlike those who followed the Oregon Trail, the people who used the Santa Fe Trail engaged primarily in commerce. Many of them traversed the trail many times between Missouri and New Mexico carrying thousands upon thousands of tons of merchandise for a waiting market. For those traveling west on the trail, there was also the appeal of Santa Fe and its different customs, its different languages and dress, and of seeing people whose lives were unlike those at the eastern end of the trail. For traders returning to Missouri with their profits, it was a journey home to their families, friends, and relatives, who were anxiously awaiting the traders' safe return. Hispanic traders had similar experiences as they headed east over the trail to enjoy the benefits of capitalism. Those leaving their homes in Santa Fe or Chihuahua probably found Missouri and cities in the East as exciting and different as Missourians found Santa Fe and Chihuahua.

My interest in the Santa Fe Trail goes back at least half a century to my childhood, when on summer Sunday drives my parents would often follow gravel roads nearly forty miles south of Manhattan, Kansas, my hometown, to Council Grove, once a stopping point on the old trail.

There my father would point out the old buildings, still standing, where merchants catered to travelers following the trail to Santa Fe and other historic sites. Those visits instilled in me an interest that has never died. After I had traveled the entire route of the old trail from Missouri to Santa Fe several times, it was only natural to acquire books, pamphlets, maps, and other materials relating to the trail. Today my Santa Fe Trail collection fills several bookshelves.

Hundreds of popular and scholarly books, pamphlets, and articles have been written about the Santa Fe Trail. Most focus on a particular aspect of its history or the characters associated with one time period or another. This work is different. It seeks to compress in one volume the trail's full story—from the arrival of the Spanish to their explorations and settlement of New Mexico, the founding of Santa Fe in 1610, the city's subsequent development as a trading center, the arrival of the first French and American traders, the establishment of the Santa Fe Trail, and what happened to it after its glory days ended. Throughout I have sought to capture the romance, flavor, and color associated with the trail.

May your journey over the trail on the pages that follow be as enjoyable as its history.

—*David Dary*
Along Imhoff Creek
Norman, Oklahoma

THE SANTA FE TRAIL

ONE

---◆---

From Conquest to de Oñate, 1492-1610

He who would bring home the wealth of the Indies
must carry the wealth of the Indies with him.

—*Spanish proverb*

IT IS LESS THAN nine hundred miles from the eastern terminus of the old Santa Fe Trail at the site of Franklin, Missouri, to Santa Fe, New Mexico. Today you can leisurely drive that distance in three days following highways laid out on or near the old trail, and you can still capture some of the romance and adventure that must have been experienced by the traders and other travelers who traversed the trail during the nineteenth century. There are portions of the route where the terrain has changed little since freight wagons lumbered over the trail. The gently rolling country of western Missouri, a few hundred feet above sea level, still gives way to the rolling hills and valleys of eastern Kansas, which in turn become rolling plains broken occasionally by steep hills, rock outcrops, canyons, and valleys in central and western Kansas. If you follow the Cimarron or dry route across the Oklahoma Panhandle into northeastern New Mexico, you see bluffs, hills, mesas, canyons, and upland slopes. If you follow the mountain route across southeastern Colorado into northeastern New Mexico, you cross the high plains, skirting the southern Rocky Mountains on gentle upland slopes that soon rise from five to seven thousand feet above sea level at Raton Pass and then drop to the gently rolling land of northeastern New Mexico. Where both routes come together near Fort Union, the trail

3

gently rolls on across the land, with scenic mountains to the west that rise to thirteen thousand feet near Santa Fe.

In several places the ruts of the old trail and many of the landmarks used by early travelers as navigational guideposts still can be seen. Cities, towns, and the modern roads and highways linking the communities frequently detract from the historic scenery, as do the rural houses that dot the landscape and the ever-present barbed-wire fences behind which cattle instead of buffalo now graze; but along many stretches of the trail it is not difficult to imagine what the early travelers must have experienced, including the thrill of anticipation they must have felt as they neared the village of Santa Fe nestled below the Sangre de Cristo Mountains. With its Spanish charm, atmosphere, and architecture, Santa Fe is a magnet for modern travelers much as it was for traders from Missouri during the nineteenth century. But to understand why and how the Santa Fe Trail came to be, one must go back in time before the founding of Santa Fe.

LONG BEFORE THE American West was penetrated from the east by the French and English, the Spanish had already explored portions of present-day Alabama, Arizona, Arkansas, California, Colorado, Florida, Georgia, Kansas, Mississippi, Nevada, New Mexico, Oklahoma, Texas, and Utah. From Florida to California, Spaniards established settlements, tried to pacify natives by converting them to Christianity, and searched for gold, silver, and other riches. Santa Fe was central.

To fully grasp its importance, one must go back to 1492, when the Italian-Spanish navigator Christopher Columbus, while searching for a route to Asia, found the New World. Spaniards had settled modern-day Puerto Rico, Jamaica, Cuba, and other islands in the West Indies by the early sixteenth century. In 1519, Hernán Cortés set out from the West Indies and succeeded in conquering Mexico, which the Spanish thereafter duffed "New Spain." Meantime, other Spaniards explored Central and South America, where during the early 1530s Francisco Pizarro overthrew the Inca empire in Peru. These conquests were made in the name of God, country, and gold, not necessarily in that order.

The prospect of finding riches whetted the appetites of the Spanish explorers and conquistadores, most of whom came from proud but poor families and who instinctively sought wealth and power. The Spanish Crown, lacking sufficient resources to meet its growing responsibilities as it claimed more and more territory in the Americas, began to grant private contracts to explore, conquer, and generate revenues from resources found in the New World. In this way the Crown did not risk a single peso but stood to profit by demanding a fifth of all bullion and precious stones discovered by its explorers and conquistadores.

Even before Columbus sailed westward in 1492 seeking the rich Indies, there was a legend of seven rich cities located somewhere to the west of Spain across what was called the Sea of Darkness. The legend can be traced back to the Middle Ages, when seven Christian bishops supposedly fled Portugal ahead of the Moors to escape persecution during the Muslim conquest. Tradition says the bishops and a small group of followers sailed westward until they landed on an island they named Antilia, whose streams were filled with gold. There they built seven gold cities, one for each bishop. From "Antilia" the Spaniards derived the name they gave a group of islands in the West Indies, the Antilles, although they found no gold there. Still, many Spaniards believed in the legend, speculating that the seven cities were located on the mainland or along the "Strait of Anian," the waterway they thought cut through North America. Even the English had heard the legend. It was rumored that the explorer John Cabot was searching for the seven cities when he sailed to the New World in 1497, reaching Labrador, Newfoundland, and the New England coasts, and sailing again in 1498 as far south as Chesapeake Bay along the east coast of North America.

When the Spanish first arrived, Montezuma, ruler of the Aztec empire, influenced by a series of prophecies, believed Hernán Cortés to be the Aztec god-king Quetzalcoatl and gave him a gold necklace set with emeralds and hung with pearls, a disk of gold representing the sun that was as large as a wagon wheel, and numerous other objects of gold and silver. Francisco Pizarro, a cousin of Cortés, exploring the Andes Mountains of South America, was given a room full of gold and another of silver as ransom for releasing an Inca chief. Having found such riches in Central and South America, the Spaniards expected North America would yield similar wealth, perhaps even the fabled seven cities.

The Spanish conquistador Nuno de Guzmán went in search of the seven cities in northern New Spain in 1530, taking an expedition up the west coast of modern Mexico into unexplored areas after an Indian named Tejo, the son of a dead trader, told Guzmán how he had accompanied his father on trading trips far to the north. There, Tejo claimed, they found towns as large as Mexico City, and in seven of them there were streets given over to shops and workers in the precious metals. Tejo said that the cities were forty days' travel across barren desert lands to the north. Thereupon Guzmán, a cruel and greedy man, went north at the head of an expedition of five hundred Spaniards and several thousand friendly Indians. He did not find seven rich cities, but he did conquer new territory for the Crown along the northwest coast of what is now Mexico, and he established the Spanish settlement of Culiacán in 1531, a hundred years before the founding of Boston. Guzmán also captured and sold into slavery at least ten thousand Indians. He crucified and hanged men who opposed his will. Once, when a Spaniard cursed him, Guzmán had the man nailed to a post by his tongue.

Next came the revelations of Cabeza de Vaca, a Spaniard who was thought dead. On a bright spring day in April 1536, four Spaniards on horseback hunting for Indians to sell as slaves were traveling along the rugged coastal plain between the Sierra Madre mountains and the rich blue waters of the Gulf of California in the region earlier claimed for Spain by Guzmán. The Spaniards suddenly came upon a sight more strange and unexpected than the footprints seen by Robinson Crusoe on his desert island. Ahead of them was a small party of Indians following three almost nude white men with long tangled hair and beards, and a black man. The four Spaniards were speechless as they sat on their horses staring at the group, until one of the white men spoke to them in Spanish. The man said he was Álvar Núñez Cabeza de Vaca, age forty-six, and that he had been on a royal expedition. He said he wanted to see their captain. The Spaniards escorted Cabeza de Vaca and his companions to their commander, who conducted them to the new settlement of Culiacán. There they rested for several days before being escorted farther south to Compostela to meet with Nuno de Guzmán, governor of the province. Guzmán gave them new clothing from his own wardrobe, but Cabeza de Vaca found the clothes uncomfortable. He also chose to sleep on the bare floor instead of on a bed, something he had not had for eight years.

Cabeza de Vaca told Guzmán how eight years earlier he had been second in command of Pánfilo de Narváez's Spanish expedition of four hundred men and eighty horses sent from Cuba to colonize Florida. It was Spain's first major expedition to North America. The expedition landed near the entrance to Tampa Bay on the west coast of Florida in 1528. The ships that had transported them were instructed to sail along the coast until the expedition was ready to leave. Once ashore, the expedition met friendly Indians who soon persuaded the red-bearded Narváez to move to the northwest—there, they said, the Spaniards would find much gold. They found none, however, after exploring an area extending to near the site of present-day Tallahassee. Hostile Indians, sickness, and harsh conditions took a terrible toll on the Spaniards, who eventually discarded their heavy metal armor. Narváez then decided to leave the region, and sent Cabeza de Vaca and a small party to the coast

In this illustration, the artist Frederic Remington envisions Cabeza de Vaca in the desert trying to make his way to New Spain. It appeared in Collier's Weekly, *October 14, 1905. Three years later, for reasons not known, Remington destroyed the original.* (Author's Collection)

to locate the ships. But they were nowhere to be found. On Cabeza de Vaca's return with this news, Narváez moved the whole expedition to the coast near the mouth of St. Marks River at Apalachee Bay, hoping to meet up there with the ships. But they never showed. The men of the expedition survived by killing horses and cooking their meat. Discouraged, Narváez decided to sail across the Gulf of Mexico to the east coast of New Spain. He ordered his men to kill the remaining horses and build five large horsehide boats, each capable of holding forty-five men. A forge was set up, and the Spaniards made nails and tools out of the metal items they carried. They used as boat riggings ropes made from the manes and tails of the dead horses, and made sails of hides and clothing.

Late in 1528, the expedition of about 225 men set sail for the east coast of New Spain in the five boats. The men were inexperienced sailors, however, and they hugged the coasts of modern Florida, Alabama, Mississippi, Louisiana, and Texas. Thirst, starvation, attacks by Indians when the Spaniards went ashore for food and water, and storms all took their toll, and many men died. Some, including Narváez, drowned. Three of the boats were lost, and the remaining two washed up on low-lying islands off the Texas coast. Cabeza de Vaca's boat probably was wrecked on Galveston Island, where he and the others were made slaves by Indians. During the next few years most of Cabeza de Vaca's companions died or escaped, only to be killed by Indians. Cabeza de Vaca survived by accepting and adapting to the Indians' way of life. He became something of an Indian medicine man, using the sign of the cross and oral prayers as cures; he gained the reputation of a man of peace and acquired much freedom of movement, becoming the first European trader in what is now Texas. Cabeza de Vaca would trade red ochre, an iron ore used as a pigment, and animal skins from the interior for conch shells and mesquite beans on the coast.

During his travels Cabeza de Vaca came across three other survivors from the expedition—Alonso del Castillo Maldonado, Andres Dorantes de Carrance, and an Arab slave from Morocco owned by Dorantes and called Estéban, who had learned the Indian languages and helped to cure sick Indians. Determined to reach New Spain, the four men started walking westward across what is now Texas late in 1534. Their fame as medicine men spread before them, and they were welcomed, fed, and housed by the Indians they met. Exactly what route they followed is not known, but they probably crossed the Rio Grande somewhere between modern Laredo and Brownsville in Texas, and then traveled westward across portions of the present-day Mexican states of Chihuahua, Durango, Sonora, and Sinaloa, and perhaps into what is now southern Arizona. In 1536, two years after setting out, they met the Spanish soldiers near Culiacán. This was some seventy years before Captain John Smith saw the coast of Virginia.

Cabeza de Vaca and his companions told their story to Guzmán, and later to Antonio de Mendoza, the new viceroy of New Spain, who had taken up residence in Mexico City about a year earlier. Cabeza de Vaca spoke of seeing people living in large houses (pueblos) wearing cotton clothing and cultivating rich valleys, raising maize, squash, and beans. He told how these people sometimes dressed in leather from what he called humpbacked cows—buffalo—living in the region, and that emeralds, turquoises, and pearls were plentiful. He said he had observed signs

This nineteenth-century drawing shows Cabeza de Vaca crossing barren country, perhaps in Texas, during the 1530s, in his attempt to reach New Spain. The illustration appeared in Harper's New Monthly Magazine, *July 1880.* (Author's Collection)

of gold, iron, copper, and other valuable metals, and that Indians had told him of still greater riches farther to the north in a region he had not visited. Viceroy Mendoza closely questioned Cabeza de Vaca and his companions and had them describe their travels in writing and also draw a map of the country they had visited.

There were then no reliable maps of the country through which Cabeza de Vaca and his companions had traveled. Such maps as existed contained mostly imagined details, and Spaniards and other Europeans had many misconceptions about the geography of the New World. For instance, because everyone talked about the imagined waterway from Europe to Asia through the New World as though such a thing existed, they drew the "Strait of Anian" on their maps. The cartographer Orontius Fine produced a map in 1531 showing North America as no more than a land extension of Asia, with the Gulf of Mexico opposite the Bay of Bengal. Cuba was portrayed as an island off Asia. If one believed the map, and many Spaniards did, it should have been possible to travel northward from New Spain and reach the fabulous empire of Cathay or Catay (as China was then called). Another map produced a few years later showed *Novus Orbis*—New World, meaning North America—as a large island rather than a continent, with a narrow sea separating it from India. Because the Spanish had very little accurate information concerning the country to the north of New Spain, Mendoza and others gave credence to the stories relayed by Cabeza de Vaca and his companions about great riches in that region.

After Cabeza de Vaca's report was sent to Spain, where it was published, Viceroy Mendoza received permission from the Crown to explore the lands to the north. Following several delays, he selected Fray Marcos

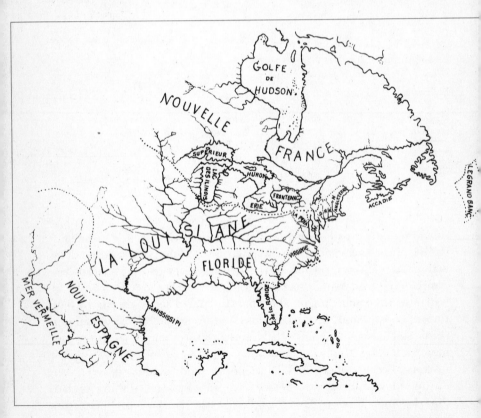

Fraquelin, a young French engineer, drew this map at Quebec in what is now Canada in 1684 using information obtained from La Salle, who had just explored the Mississippi River and claimed Louisiana for France. (Author's Collection)

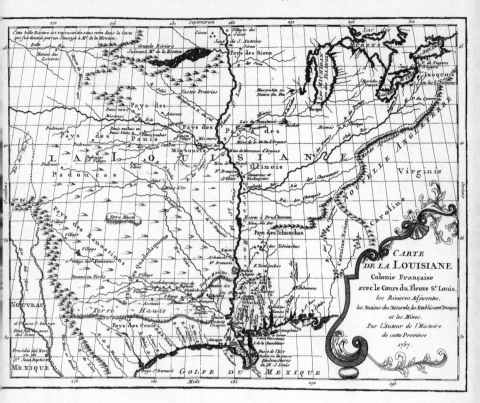

This 1757 map of Louisiana Territory was published in London and appeared in History of Louisiana, *a book by Lee Page du Pratz. Santa Fe is identified (far left center). (Courtesy Library of Congress)*

de Niza, a Franciscan, to lead this new expedition. Fray Marcos had arrived in the New World in 1531 as a missionary on the island of Hispaniola. Later, he went to Guatemala and then to South America, and he was with Francisco Pizarro when he conquered the Inca empire and divided the fabulous Inca spoils. Fray Marcos possessed the qualities of the best modern-day politician. Every inch an optimist, he was a promoter with the ability to dramatize everything in which he became involved. He also possessed physical stamina and imagination.

Mendoza gave the responsibility of supervising preparations for Fray Marcos's expedition to twenty-eight-year-old Francisco Vásquez de Coronado, who had arrived in New Spain in 1535. After gaining Mendoza's favor, Coronado married the wealthy daughter of Alonso de Estrada, the deceased treasurer of New Spain and the reputed bastard son of King

A portion of a map drawn by Herman Moll, an English geographer, published in London about 1710. California is depicted as an island. Santa Fe is identified (left of center), and a portion of the eastern boundary of Mexican territory is labeled "North River" (Rio Grande). The area north of California is labeled "Parts Unknown." (Author's Collection)

Ferdinand. In 1539, Coronado became governor of the province of Nueva Galicia, which covered much of the modern Mexican states of Zacatecas, Aguascalientes, and Jalisco.

Fray Marcos and Coronado met to plan the expedition, but their meeting was interrupted when Coronado left to put down an Indian uprising in Culiacán with soldiers. He put the Indian chief who had started the uprising on trial, and the chief was found guilty and sentenced to death. Coronado then had him quartered in public—his body cut into four pieces while he was still alive—in the accurate belief that this action would stabilize and subdue the Indians who had revolted. Coronado then rejoined Marcos, and they completed plans for the expedition. It was from Culiacán that Fray Marcos, dressed in a sober habit of gray Zaragoza cloth, started north in March 1538. At Coronado's request, Fray Marcos carried with him samples of gold, pearls, and precious stones to show the Indians he met to see if such treasures were known to them. With him went another Franciscan, Brother Onarato, a party of friendly Indians, and the slave Estéban, who had since become the property of Mendoza. Estéban was to guide Fray Marcos northward to the lands he, Cabeza de Vaca, and others had seen.

Fray Marcos and his party walked north along the west coast of modern Mexico. When they reached what is now Sinaloa in western New Spain, Fray Onarato became ill and a few Indians took him back to Culiacán. Fray Marcos continued on and sent Estéban and a small group of Indians ahead of the main party, telling him that if he learned of a country of importance, he should send back a messenger with a small cross one palm in length. If it was of great importance, two palms in length; and if the country was larger and better than New Spain, a very large cross. A few days later a messenger reached Fray Marcos bearing a huge cross as high as a man. The messenger reported that in thirty days' travel there was a land called Cíbola with seven cities, the first of which was the smallest. This apparently was the first time a Spaniard heard the name *Cíbola* associated with tales of the seven cities.

When Fray Marcos met the friendly Indians who had told Estéban of the seven cities, some of them agreed to lead Fray Marcos and the others to Cíbola. The expedition continued northward, entering what is now Arizona, and then turned east until it neared Indian villages in what is now western New Mexico. There Estéban, who was ahead of Fray Marcos with a large party of friendly Indians, was killed, as were most of the Indians with him. News of the tragedy reached Fray Marcos shortly before he reached the high ground from which he could see what his Indian guides described as the first of the seven cities in Cíbola. Fray Marcos decided not to enter the settlement for fear he too would be killed. Instead, he turned and with his party rapidly retraced his steps to Culiacán.

By the time Fray Marcos reached Mexico City, he had embellished his story, perhaps to please the viceroy. Those hearing him added further details, until people believed Fray Marcos had seen walled and gated cities where people wore belts of gold. North America suddenly appeared to be another El Dorado, and Spanish explorers began competing for the chance to go in search of the riches. Viceroy Mendoza selected Coronado to put together a large expedition to find Cíbola, and he ordered Fray Marcos to guide Coronado. Mendoza and Coronado funded the expedition, which consisted of more than three hundred Spaniards, six Franciscans including Marcos, more than a thousand friendly Indians, and about fifteen hundred horses and pack animals plus sheep and cattle to feed everyone. There were at least three women in the expedition; Señora Caballero, wife of Lope de Caballero; Francisca de Hozes, wife of Alonso Sánchez; and María Maldonado, wife of a tailor named Juan de Paradinas, who would nurse sick soldiers and mend their garments.

Mendoza ordered Coronado to treat gently the friendly Indians in the expedition and those met on their journey. Mendoza said Indians should not be molested by the Spaniards, nor their food or other belongings taken from them without compensation. Mendoza's order was in keeping with a new directive from the Crown to correct the injustices perpetrated by earlier Spanish explorers.

Soon the expedition gathered at Compostela, capital of the province governed by Coronado, on the west coast of Mexico. On February 23, 1540, it set out, with the Franciscans leading the long procession. Next came Coronado and his soldiers, followed by the pack animals and their handlers, the Indians, and then the herdsmen driving horses, sheep, and cattle. One can only imagine the sight of more than thirteen hundred humans and nearly two thousand animals moving northward following trails that had been used by Indians perhaps for centuries. The procession was at least two miles long.

Since there were no horses in the New World until the Spanish brought them, the sight of them caused wonder and amazement among Indians. When Cortés brought the first horses to Mexico in 1519, Indians feared them and called them "big dogs"; some Indians believed that man and beast were one. The Spaniards quickly realized that horses were something special, and that they could retain their dominance if they kept horses from the Indians.

Coronado's expedition followed the coastal plain between the Gulf of California and the Sierra Madre north to the present southern border of Arizona and then turned east, traveling over well-worn Indian trails that Fray Marcos claimed led to the seven cities of Cíbola. But Coronado did not find the first great city Marcos had described, only pueblos housing perhaps a hundred poor Hopi Indians. The pueblos were located northwest of present-day Zuñi, New Mexico. The disappointed Coronado ordered Fray Marcos back to Mexico City and sent word to Viceroy Men-

Frederic Remington's depiction of "Coronado's March," drawn late in the nine-teenth century. The illustration appeared in Henry Inman's The Old Santa Fe Trail, *published in 1897.* (Author's Collection)

doza that Marcos had lied about everything except the names of the cities and the large houses.

Coronado did not turn back. He sent Pedro de Tovar and a party with Indian guides to explore the region to the west. They visited Hopi vil-lages in what is now northeastern Arizona. One of Tovar's men, García López de Cárdenas, and a small scouting party became the first Euro-peans to see the Grand Canyon of the Colorado River. Meantime, Coro-nado moved his main force from Zuñi to the Rio Grande in what is now New Mexico. From there he sent another scouting party led by Hernando de Alvarado, who had been with Cortés in the conquest of Mexico, to explore the Pueblo region along the Rio Grande from near modern Albuquerque north to what is today the Taos pueblo. Alvarado's party then moved eastward to the Pecos pueblo, where the Spaniards followed a pass through the Sangre de Cristo Mountains onto the plains. The pass was of strategic importance, since Indian trading and hunting parties used it to travel between the Great Plains and the land of the pueblos.

At the Pecos pueblo, Alvarado and his party rested. Alvarado then asked his Indian guide to show him the strange "cattle" (actually buffalo) that Cabeza de Vaca had seen on the plains to the east. The guide sent two recent captives who knew the area to guide Alvarado to where the animals could be found. One captive was from somewhere far to the east and wore something like a turban on his head. Because Alvarado thought he looked like a Turk, that is what he called him. The other slave was called Ysopete and came from the land of Quivira to the northeast.

With Turk and Ysopete as guides, Alvarado and his party moved onto the plains until they reached what apparently was the Canadian River, which begins in northeastern New Mexico and flows south and then east across the Texas Panhandle north of present-day Amarillo and on into what is now western Oklahoma. Near the Canadian River the Spaniards saw buffalo, and it was there, for the first time in history, that men hunted buffalo from horseback, something that would become commonplace decades later, after Plains Indians acquired the horse. It was apparently after the hunt that Turk told Alvarado he should go northeast to the land called Quivira, where they could find metal and everything else the Spaniards sought. Alvarado took Turk's statements to mean there was gold and silver in the land to the north. But instead of going northeast as Turk had suggested, Alvarado took his party along with Turk and Ysopete and rejoined Coronado's main army wintering near the site of present-day Albuquerque. Before Coronado could consider Turk's stories, Pueblo Indians revolted against the Spaniards, who had demanded their submission to the authority of the king of Spain. Coronado's chief lieutenant, García López de Cárdenas, took soldiers and destroyed the pueblo of Arenal. He had his soldiers burn many of the Indians alive to set an example of what would happen to the other natives if they did not cease their resistance. An uneasy peace resulted.

By spring, Coronado decided to go in search of Quivira. For weeks he had listened to Turk describe the wonders to be found to the north. On April 23, 1541, Coronado took a large expedition and traveled onto the plains of what are today the panhandles of Texas and Oklahoma, where he saw more buffalo. Led by Turk, the expedition turned northward, crossed the Canadian River and then the Arkansas River, traveling into what is now central Kansas in search of Quivira. Coronado found no riches, only villages of poor Indians, but he did take note of the fertility and beauty of the land, which some of the Spaniards said resembled their homeland. Indians told Coronado of a large river to the northeast, probably the Missouri, but he never went in search of it. At the time Coronado did not know that about three hundred miles to the southeast

Hernando de Soto was then exploring what is now Arkansas. One wonders how history might have been changed if they had met.

Believing that Turk had been dishonest, Coronado questioned him closely. Turk admitted he had lied because Pueblo people had urged him to take the Spaniards onto the plains and lead them astray, so that their supplies would be used up and their horses would starve to death. How Turk could have believed these things is a mystery, since the plains provided much grass for the horses and game to feed the Spaniards. Although Coronado opposed putting Turk to death, other Spaniards secretly executed him by putting a rope around his neck, twisting it with a garrote, and choking him to death. He was then buried nearby.

After about a month in what is now Kansas, Coronado and his expedition headed back to New Mexico. While there is no way to tell what route Coronado followed, he probably used Indian trails that had first been made by buffalo, who have a knack for choosing the easiest grades and the path of least resistance. So it is entirely possible that on his return to New Mexico, Coronado traveled over portions of the route that more than two centuries later would become the Santa Fe Trail between New Mexico and Missouri.

Coronado spent the winter along the Rio Grande, where he began to plan another trip to the plains and beyond for the next spring. But when he was injured while riding a horse, he decided to end the expedition. The following spring he returned to New Spain and reported to Viceroy Mendoza. Having failed to find any riches, he was coolly treated by Mendoza and other Spanish officials in Mexico City. Men who had accompanied Coronado north in hopes of finding riches were also unhappy. They complained about his management of the expedition, noting that the Crown's new laws designed to protect Indians had been violated. Coronado was removed as governor, and officials began a lengthy investigation. In failing health and living quietly with his family in Mexico City, he was finally absolved of all charges. He died there on September 22, 1554.

Coronado lived long enough to learn that what is now Mexico was naturally rich in minerals. Silver deposits were discovered in 1546 at Zacatecas and at Guanajuato in 1554. The rich mines distracted the Spaniards, who seemingly forgot about the Pueblo Indians discovered by Fray Marcos and Coronado to the far north. It was three decades before the Spaniards renewed their interest in the lands to the north of New Spain and the Indians who cultivated corn, lived in multistory houses, and wore cotton clothing. Their renewed interest came only after a party of three Franciscans headed by Fray Agustín Rodríguez and seven soldiers supported by the Crown made their way up the Conchos River in 1581 to the Rio Grande and north to the pueblos. The following year Antonio de Espejo received permission to go north, supposedly to assist Fray Rodríguez and his party. In truth, Espejo sought riches, exploring as far west as present-day Arizona and east to the plains but finding none. He did learn that Fray Rodríguez and a companion had been murdered by Indians. When Espejo returned to New Spain with the survivors of Fray Rodríguez's party, new, embellished stories about the area caused the Crown in 1583 to direct the viceroy to send someone north to conquer the potentially rich region.

But before the viceroy could do so, Gaspar Castano de Sosa, an over-enthusiastic lieutenant governor of Nuevo León, the most northeasterly province of New Spain, took an unofficial party of 170 men, women, and children northward in 1590 and established a settlement in the land of the pueblos. The following year the viceroy sent soldiers to arrest Castano and his colonists and return them to Mexico City. Castano was found guilty of invading the lands of peaceable Indians, and exiled to the Philippines. The Crown seemed intent on protecting the native people by requiring royal permission to travel beyond the frontier of New Spain.

The viceroy moved slowly in selecting someone to go and claim the region for Spain. When reports were received telling of English explorers along the Pacific coast, fear of English competition prodded the viceroy to act. The forty-five-year-old Juan de Oñate was appointed governor of New Mexico and ordered to colonize the region. De Oñate came from a distinguished and wealthy family, his father having been one of the discoverers of the rich silver mines at Zacatecas. Juan de Oñate had married the great-granddaughter of Montezuma, who was also the granddaughter of Hernán Cortés. The Crown, however, did not provide de Oñate with financial support; the responsibility of funding the colonization of New Mexico fell to him.

Juan de Oñate, like other Spaniards, underestimated distances in the New World. He believed the continent of North America to be narrow. In fact, he thought New Mexico was close to both the Pacific and Atlantic Oceans and could be supplied by ship from either. Not knowing this was impossible, the Crown gave de Oñate permission to bring two supply ships annually to New Mexico. After numerous delays, de Oñate set out for New Mexico in the spring of 1598. The caravan included eighty wagons or oxcarts, two luxury coaches drawn by mules, three small pieces of artillery, and about seven thousand head of livestock—horses, spare oxen, beef cattle, donkeys, pack mules, sheep, and goats.

A Chihuahua cart outside the entrance to the reconstructed Bent's Old Fort near La Junta, Colorado. (Author's Collection)

The oxcarts used by de Oñate became known as Chihuahua carts (*carretas*). Each was drawn by at least three yoke, or pairs, of oxen. One source describes these carts:

There were three sections to a wheel, the two outer ones semicircular in shape, the center one made from a square timber that was cut away on two sides to join and match the other pieces. The three parts were held together by two wooden pins that passed through the section. A hub was bored in the center of the square section to receive a spindle tapered to the outer end. A long wooden pin, the linchpin, set into a slot cut into the axle spindle, held the wheel on. These wheels varied in size and detailed according to their maker's whim, but the basic design was the same for all. The superstructure on a Chihuahua [cart] was about thirty inches wide, seven feet long, and from four to five feet high. A long center pole—eighteen feet or so—extended back over the axletree to the rear crosstie, which, like the one in the rear, was cut out to fit over both pole and side beams. Cleats mortised into the side beams supported the floor boards. Six to eight upright stakes were fitted into the side beams, the front and end stakes on each side passing through the bolsters as well as the beam. The uprights were connected by a top rail that ran lengthwise of the she-bang, and there was a cross rail at each end. The side beams were doweled to the axletrees.

De Oñate's party included about 500 colonists plus nearly 130 soldiers; their wives, children, servants, and slaves; and ten Franciscans, whose expenses were paid by the Crown. The caravan pushed northward through the sand dunes of Chihuahua, camped on the banks of the Rio Grande below modern Ciudad Juárez, and claimed New Mexico in the name of the Crown.

Crossing the Rio Grande where it flows between two mountain ranges at present-day El Paso, Texas, de Oñate and his party moved slowly northward following the river to the pueblo of San Juan, located on a rich floodplain near where the Rio Chama flows into the Rio Grande. There, on the west side of the Rio Grande, de Oñate and his colonists moved into the pueblo. The Spaniards found living conditions tight, and de Oñate persuaded Indians living in the pueblo called Yunge on the east side of the Rio Grande to move to San Juan. He then moved the colonists across the river to Yunge, remodeled the pueblo, began construction of a church, and gave the pueblo the Christian name of San Gabriel, the first Spanish settlement and the first capital of New Mexico.

Before the first year ended, eleven Spanish soldiers, including de Oñate's nephew, were killed in a surprise attack by Indians living in the high mesa pueblo of Acoma many miles west of San Gabriel. After consulting with Franciscans and believing that Spanish law permitted him to punish the Indians, de Oñate sent Vicente de Zaldivar and a force of about seventy soldiers to attack the pueblo. The Spaniards killed about eight hundred Indians—men, women, and children—and took about eighty men and five hundred women captive. This action resulted in an uncertain peace in New Mexico.

In June 1601, de Oñate took an expedition of seventy men, the Spaniards wearing armor, several hundred miles northeast to Quivira, in what is now Kansas, in search of riches to help finance his colony. On his journey he used eight wooden carts pulled by mules and oxen to carry supplies. As far as is known, these were the first wheeled vehicles on what would later be a portion of the Santa Fe Trail. De Oñate's party found many bison and hunted them for food. Near what is now called the Arkansas River, they met the Escanjaques, possibly Arkansas Indians, who had come up the river to hunt buffalo. They were friendly to the Spaniards.

De Oñate continued on to Quivira, where he and his men found friendly Quivirans (Wichita Indians) living in grass huts in what is now south-central Kansas. Quivirans told de Oñate that there were even more Indians living to the north, but that they were hostile. De Oñate noticed that some of the Indians were wearing seashells as ornaments on their foreheads and concluded that they could only have come from the North Sea (Atlantic Ocean), which must therefore be close by. De Oñate then took his expedition farther north, but his men soon became discouraged and wanted to return to San Gabriel; it was October, and winter was approaching. De Oñate ended his exploration and started home. As the party retraced its steps, however, the once-friendly Escanjaques challenged the Spaniards. De Oñate ordered his men to don armor and put it on their horses as well, and then moved against perhaps fifteen hundred Indians. Arrows rained down on the armored horsemen, but the Spaniards suffered only minor wounds in a battle lasting about two hours. De Oñate and his party then withdrew and resumed their journey without further difficulty. On November 24, 1601, fifty-nine days after leaving, they returned to San Gabriel.

During the next three years, life was difficult for the New Mexico colonists, who lacked supplies and experienced frequent Indian troubles. De Oñate did take a small expedition westward in hopes of finding the South Sea (Pacific Ocean), where he could establish a port to receive supplies, but he was not successful, nor was another expedition he sent west the following year. De Oñate finally succeeded in crossing Arizona and going down the Colorado River to the mouth of the Gulf of California, which he called the South Sea, but it obviously was too far from New Mexico to establish a port. On his return trip, de Oñate stopped at El Morro, a huge sandstone rock formation located between Acoma and Zuñi pueblos. There de Oñate, or perhaps one of his men, chiseled an inscription in the sandstone that is still visible. It reads: THERE PASSED THIS WAY THE ADELANTADO DON JUAN DE OÑATE, FROM THE DISCOVERY OF THE SOUTH SEA, ON THE 16TH OF APRIL, 1605. This was fifteen years before the Pilgrims landed at Plymouth Rock.

Having used much of his wealth and that of friends and relatives in colonizing New Mexico, and disillusioned that he had not found riches or anything he considered significant, de Oñate sent a letter of resignation to the viceroy in August 1607. If he hoped this step would gain additional support for New Mexico from the Crown, it failed. Unbeknownst to him, the Crown had already decided to replace him as governor and was in fact thinking of recalling the colonists and abandoning New Mexico to the Indians. When the Franciscans in Mexico City learned this, they hurriedly sent a representative north to New Mexico who baptized many Indians so that they could then claim them as Christian converts, which on the surface suggested that the missionaries were having success.

The Crown canceled plans to abandon New Mexico, but de Oñate's resignation was accepted. One of his men was appointed acting governor and told to remain on good terms with de Oñate until a new governor arrived. Apparently with the approval of the acting governor, de Oñate selected the site of a new capital located in a narrow valley about twenty miles south of San Gabriel. The unoccupied, arable land, which had plenty of water, was more defensible than San Gabriel. It was also easily accessible from the north via Española Valley, and from the south via Chichito Creek, or the Santa Fe River, as it is now often called, as well as to the west and east. De Oñate then apparently encouraged some of the Spanish colonists to move their homes from San Gabriel to this valley, which he called Santa Fe, possibly after the historic town of Santa Fe located near Granada in Spain. In 1610, ninety-one years after Cortés began the conquest of New Spain, Pedro de Peralta, the new governor, arrived in New Mexico and soon moved the capital from San Gabriel to Santa Fe—La Villa Real de Santa Fé de San Francisco, meaning "The Royal City of the Holy Faith of St. Francis"—which was destined to become the chief trading center of Spain's vast northern province.

TWO

The Attraction of Santa Fe, 1610-1762

*A land without ruins is a land without memories,
a land without memories is a land without history.*

—*Abram Joseph Ryan*

MUCH ABOUT EARLY Santa Fe remains a mystery. The Spaniards probably used Indian labor to construct their first adobe houses, including an official residence for Governor Pedro de Peralta in 1610, when Santa Fe became the capital of New Mexico. The Palace of the Governors, as it is called today, was completed in 1612 and still stands on the north side of the tree-covered Plaza, but the building does not look much like it did nearly four hundred years ago. It is, to begin with, much smaller now; it originally extended much farther north and west. It housed the governor's private apartments, official reception rooms and offices, military barracks, stables, servants' quarters, and an arsenal. Vegetable gardens were planted in a central patio that was about ten acres in size. The original palace also had defense towers constructed on each corner of the building's front facing the Plaza. When completed, the Palace of the Governors probably looked like a large mud hut. Like other structures in Santa Fe, it was built of adobe blocks—sun-dried bricks—made from clay soil mixed with straw and water, cut into the desired sizes, and baked in the sun for several days. Its dirt floor was mixed with animal blood to pack it and produce a sheen.

Just south of the palace is the Plaza, which was laid out as the usual *plaza mayor* in Spain. Originally it was about two blocks in length, stretching twice as far to the east as it does today, and was the setting for daily markets, cockfights, and other social gatherings, as well as for public floggings and the public stocks. If any trees had stood where the Plaza was laid out, they may have been cut down and used in the construction of houses or for firewood during Santa Fe's early years.

Aside from the Palace of the Governors and the Plaza, the rest of early Santa Fe evolved in a haphazard manner with the piecemeal building of one-story, flat-roofed adobe houses. Narrow streets wound between the structures. Santa Fe probably looked like piles of earth-colored bricks when seen from a distance, the view broken only by Chichito Creek, a small tributary of the Rio Grande, flowing through the town past small groves of little crooked piñon pines and perhaps a few small clusters of cottonwood trees, or *bosques,* as the Spaniards came to call them.

By the time Santa Fe was founded, the Crown realized that decades-old legends of vast riches in the region were false. New Mexico was not a land of great mineral wealth or of much agricultural potential. Still, Spain sought to hold on to it in order to claim the vast country to the north and northeast as France and England challenged Spain's control in the New World. But being twelve hundred miles from Mexico City, Santa Fe suffered from poor communications, a feeling of isolation, and military weakness. Growth was very slow because it was difficult to attract settlers. There was also conflict between the Spanish authorities and the Franciscans, who had been given New Mexico as their exclusive field. Each group was jealous of the other's power. Emblematic of this split was Santa Fe's status as the only official town in New Mexico until 1695, with the religious center established in the pueblo of Santo Domingo. In practice the Spanish governor could award his followers the right to tribute from the Indians, and if the Indians failed to supply it in goods, the Spaniards could take it in the form of labor. The Franciscans resented this since their missions relied on such labor from Indian converts, who were needed to tend the crops of wheat, corn, and beans, and peaches and apricots from orchards planted near the missions. Perhaps the only area of agreement between the Franciscans and the civil authorities was in their encouragement of trade among the Indians.

Trade between Pueblo Indians and the nomadic Apaches in fact existed well before the Spaniards arrived. Each summer the Apaches roamed the peripheries of the pueblos, hunting, gathering, and growing some crops. They arrived with their dog trains at the pueblos of Taos, Pecos, and Picuris to trade hides, meat, tallow, and salt for cotton blankets, pottery, maize, turquoise, and breadstuffs produced by the pueblos. With the arrival of Juan de Oñate and his colonists, the Spaniards began trading with the Indians, adding grains, fruits, livestock, and a few manufactured items such as hardware, axes, and spears they had brought north.

About a year before Santa Fe became the capital of New Mexico, supplies for the missions began arriving by mule train and later by mule-drawn wagons over the trail de Oñate blazed from Mexico. The trail followed his route through Zacatecas, Durango, Parral, and then along the Rio Grande. It became known as the Camino Real—the Royal or King's Highway. A caravan service subsidized by the Crown was required to take supplies from Mexico City to New Mexico over this route, a distance of fifteen hundred miles, every three years. A round-trip took eighteen months: six months to travel from Mexico City to Santa Fe, another six months to distribute supplies in New Mexico and to rest, and another six months to return to Mexico City.

The wagons used on the Camino Real were not the primitive oxcarts used by de Oñate when he first brought colonists to New Mexico. Rather, they were large, rather crudely constructed heavy-service wagons with four iron-tired wheels, each pulled by a team of eight mules. Every wagon, capable of carrying about four thousand pounds, had arched hoods covered by forty yards of coarse woolen fabric. Each caravan usually consisted of thirty-two wagons equally divided between two sections. Each section was supervised by a *mayordomo*, or wagon master. Because of the long journey, each caravan also carried spare axles, extra wagon spokes and tires (each weighing twenty-seven pounds), tallow to use as lubrication, and many pounds of extra cord for repairing wagon hoods and cargo coverings. Each caravan usually had a large herd of beef cattle and extra mules to be used as draft replacements. A captain and at least a dozen mounted soldiers usually escorted a caravan, providing security to and from Santa Fe.

When the caravan service began, it was intended to supply only the missions with materials for the altars, clothing for the friars, and hardware, and to carry Franciscans to and from their missions, but since the wagon trains were the only regular link between Mexico City and New Mexico, they soon carried new settlers and officials to Santa Fe along with baggage, mail, royal decrees, and trading merchandise. The contractors hired to organize the caravans began to bring goods to satisfy the wants of Spaniards in New Mexico. In 1665, Franciscans complained to Spanish officials that the contractors of the previous caravan had placed their missions' three-year supplies in only one section of the wagon train and had sold space in the other sections to merchants shipping commercial freight and passengers. Wagons carrying mission supplies were overloaded, the friars complained, and en route to Santa Fe the caravan was often delayed because it stopped frequently to take on or to unload unauthorized commercial goods. Instead of enforcing the law, however, the Crown amended it in 1668 so as to legalize many of the till now illegal practices of caravan contractors, and in 1674 the padres were authorized to buy their own wagons and mules and contract their own supplies.

The wagon trains from Mexico City usually arrived in Santa Fe after the harvest in late October and early November to pack off the year's production, which included corn, beans, wheat, pine nuts, livestock, textiles such as stockings and blankets, and small amounts of jewelry, animal pelts, and brandy produced by the missions from the fruits that were grown nearby. The trains delivered goods the colonists wanted, which included sugar, chocolate, indigo, jewelry, cloth, hats, hard liquor, and manufactured items such as playing cards and gunpowder. Merchants had to have licenses to sell most items. These trains also carried mail and provided the primary communication link between New Spain and New Mexico.

Almost everything was subject to taxes. There was even taxation of taxes because the Crown needed the income. As early as 1650, the Crown prohibited trade with outsiders except when express permission was granted, a restriction that stifled the new colony's growth. Because the governors of New Mexico were poorly paid by the Crown, they regularly sold public offices to the highest bidder and frequently augmented their income by engaging in trade. Even though this was against the law, governors did not seek to hide their involvement in trade. In 1638, for example, Governor Luis de Rosas sold to merchants in Parral on consignment 2,000 yards of coarse woolen dress fabric, 46 drapes, 70 other hangings, 408 blankets, 24 cushions, 8 overskirts, 79 assorted doublets and jackets, 124 painted buffalo hides, 207 antelope skins, 900 candles, and 57 bushels of pine nuts, all of which were apparently obtained from Indians.[1]

To add still more to his income, Governor Rosas, a soldier with a reputation for ruthlessness, also engaged in slaving. Until he became governor, little attention had been paid to the Apaches who wandered the country outside the pueblos. Although Indian slavery was prohibited by the Crown, Rosas forced Apaches to produce cotton blankets in a workshop he established at Santa Fe. He then sold other Apaches to Spanish miners in northern New Spain, to tobacco farmers in Cuba, and to plantation owners in Yucatán. Rosas resented the power of the padres and the church, who also sought to control New Mexico. The padres in turn resented Rosas and his raids into Apache territory to capture slaves. These raids soon brought fierce retaliation by the Apaches, who a few years earlier had begun to acquire horses and were becoming proficient mounted warriors. By 1639, Apaches were raiding many pueblos over a wide area, burning corn, killing or stealing livestock, and generally disrupting trade in the Pecos, Taos, and Picuris pueblos. The Pueblo Indians and the Spanish colonists blamed Governor Rosas for the problems, as did the padres, who knew that enslaving the Indians would make the task of converting them to Christianity even more difficult. Someone eventually assassinated Rosas, perhaps with the approval of the padres, but the practice of enslaving Apaches and forcing Pueblo Indians to perform labor continued, along with the quarrels between the padres and the colonists.

Indians had rebelled against the Spanish at various pueblos as early as 1597. The Spanish managed to crush most of the revolts because each pueblo was an independent political entity acting on its own without allies; the pueblos were, moreover, culturally diverse, and few of them shared a common language. Indian suffering through forced labor, tribute, slavery, and the repression of their religions was compounded in the 1660s and 1670s, when drought and warmer-than-usual temperatures occurred. Many Indians died of hunger because crops failed. At that point, the pueblos had simply had enough of Spanish domination. Having conceived a mortal hatred for Christianity and all Spaniards, they launched a unified offensive against the Spaniards on August 11, 1680. Caught off guard, many Spaniards were killed. Those who survived the first attacks fled to Santa Fe or to Isleta, one of the few pueblos that did not revolt. About fifteen hundred survivors at Isleta Pueblo then moved south toward El Paso. Meanwhile, about two thousand Pueblo Indians surrounded Santa Fe. Of about a thousand Spaniards in the village, only a hundred were men capable of bearing arms, but they managed to fight off the Indians.

The Spaniards used heavy matchlock muskets (harquebuses) first brought to New Spain early in the sixteenth century. For a hundred years these had been the prescribed arms of the Spanish military. This ten-gauge musket, which weighed fifteen to twenty pounds, was loaded with more than an ounce of gunpowder and a loosely fitting ball weighing about a twelfth of a pound. The weapon consisted of a tube of iron mounted on a wooden stock. The lower half of the mechanism had a trigger, and the upper half had a clamp or tube called the cock, which could hold a fuse made of twisted cord. When a man wanted to fire his musket, he would light the fuse with a much longer piece of twisted cord, which was often soaked in a saltpeter solution. In battle, this longer piece of cord was always lighted and burning at the rate of four or five inches an hour. The man would hold the butt against his shoulder and then pull the trigger, permitting the upper arm with lit fuse to fall and ignite the powder located in a hole on the top of the lower part of the mechanism.[2]

It is possible that a few Spaniards used wheel-lock muskets invented after the matchlock came into use. The wheel-lock mechanism used a steel wheel attached to a spring that revolved striking pyrites which emitted sparks when the trigger was pulled.

On September 21, 1680, more than a month after the revolt began, there was a lull in the fighting. The Pueblo Indian warriors permitted the Spaniards and several hundred Pueblo Indians who had converted to Christianity to leave Santa Fe and retreat about three hundred miles south to El Paso, where a fort (presidio) was built to protect the Spaniards who remained there. Many Pueblo Indians had died in the revolt, and more than 400 of the 2,500 Spaniards in New Mexico had been killed. The Pueblo Indians had sacked every building constructed by the Spanish and even destroyed crops in their fields.

Thirteen years later, in 1693, the Spanish reoccupied Santa Fe without force. The governors' palace was still standing, but the Indians had transformed the structure into a typical pueblo. They had placed adobe blocks in the small Spanish windows and doors, closing off all access at ground level, and entered the building from the roof using ladders. On top of the one-story structure they added two, perhaps three, floors, and they converted one of the towers into a kiva. For many years thereafter, the returning Spaniards used the tower as a place of worship. The Spaniards built a fort at Santa Fe to help protect the colonists and the Franciscans, who came back to save souls. Pueblo Indians openly submitted to Spanish authority, but other Indians did not. Comanches, having acquired horses, moved west from the plains and began to drive their Apache enemies out of northeastern New Mexico and into the province's western and southern regions. By the 1740s hostile bands of Apaches and Comanches mounted on swift horses were raiding Spanish settlements and missions, but they did not hesitate to attend summer fairs at Taos and Pecos Pueblos, where they traded buffalo meat, skins, tallow, and horses for manufactured goods.

By the early 1700s, the annual supply caravans no longer came the 1,500 miles from Mexico City; they originated at Chihuahua, about 350 miles south of Santa Fe, which had grown up around a Franciscan mission established in 1697 on the banks of the little Rio Chihuahua, a trib-

The North Pueblo of Taos as it appeared in the mid-nineteenth century. This illus-
tration appeared in El Gringo; or, New Mexico and Her People, *by William H.*
Davis, published in 1857. (Author's Collection)

utary of the Conchos. Juan de Oñate and his colonists had camped
nearby about a century earlier while heading north to New Mexico. Chihuahua (La Villa de San Felipe el Real de Chihuahua), located in a valley surrounded by mountains on all sides except the north, grew rapidly
after silver and later gold and copper were discovered in the nearby
mountains. Merchants and farmers then arrived to mine the miners, in a
town that grew around an oblong square flanked by a church, a royal
treasury office, a municipal office, and a number of mercantile stores.
On the southern edge was a convent and hospital built and run by Jesuits
until 1767, when Franciscans took them over after the Jesuits were
ordered to leave New Spain. The "Black Robes," as the Jesuits were called,
were arrested, dispossessed, taken to Veracruz, and transported to prison
in Spain.[3] The task of converting Indians to Christianity in New Spain was
thus left to the Franciscans. Within ten years the conflict between the sec-
ular and religious authorities in New Mexico subsided for good, when
the governor was given power to appoint, transfer, or remove Franciscans
from their posts.

By the mid-1700s, merchants from Chihuahua had gained control of the caravans supplying the missions and were making annual trips north to Santa Fe and beyond. While wagons were occasionally used to carry goods from Chihuahua, the standard mode of transport was mule trains, which were less expensive. Initially it took about sixteen weeks to travel the 350 miles from Chihuahua to Santa Fe, but eventually travel time was reduced to about six weeks. Chihuahua merchants with their agents in El Paso, Albuquerque, Santa Fe, and Santa Cruz soon gained a monopoly on the commerce of New Mexico. New Mexicans were almost continually in debt because their production of crops and handmade items rarely covered the purchase of manufactured goods and luxury items brought north by Chihuahua merchants. Complaints to Spanish authorities about the unscrupulous practices of Chihuahua's merchants and their agents were ignored.

Because little real money was in circulation in New Mexico, it was not uncommon for the greedy merchants from Chihuahua to earn 1,000 percent or more on their investment. The monetary unit then in use in New Spain was the large, mill-edged silver coin called the *peso duro,* which was minted in Spain and known in English as the "hard dollar," the word "dollar" coming from the old German *Daler* or *Taler,* first struck in 1519. In 1792, when Congress passed the first coinage act to establish both gold and silver dollars, the dollar became the official U.S. monetary unit. The gold dollar contained 24.75 grains of pure gold, and the silver dollar, nearly 372 grains of silver. At this ratio, gold coins were undervalued at the mint versus their value as bullion, while U.S. silver dollars had less silver in them than the slightly heavier peso, or "Spanish dollar." Eventually many American silver dollars were withdrawn from circulation because they were being exported to the West Indies and exchanged at face value for Spanish dollars, which were then melted down into bullion. The Spanish silver was then sold to the U.S. mint at a profit.

In New Mexico, however, silver pesos were almost nonexistent. Traders substituted three imaginary coins in their bookkeeping: the *peso a precios de proyecto* (pesos based on expected production), worth six reales; the *peso a precios antiguos* (pesos according to old prices), worth four reales; and the *peso de la tierra* (pesos in local products), worth two reales. This system was confusing to Spaniards and Indians alike in New Mexico, and worked to the advantage and profit of the Chihuahua merchants.

One account describes how a merchant could purchase a thirty-two-yard bolt of wool cloth for six silver pesos in Chihuahua and transport it to New Mexico, where there was no currency to exchange. There the merchant might trade the cloth for thirty-two bottles of New Mexican brandy, paying one peso (really a *peso de la tierra*) for each bottle, and later resell the brandy in Chihuahua for one silver peso per bottle, thereby making a profit of six reales on each. Or the merchant might trade thirty-two bottles of brandy for fifty-one bushels of corn using *pesos de precios antiguos,* each being the equivalent of four reales in real money. When resold in Chihuahua, the corn would bring ten reales per bushel, or a total of eighty-four pesos in silver from an original investment of six silver pesos for a bolt of cloth—a profit of seventy-eight silver pesos.[4]

In isolated New Mexico, trade was the primary economic activity, and the annual fair held in late summer at Taos Pueblo, and attended by Indians and Spanish settlers alike, was a major event. Taos was easily reached through valleys in all directions, and it was away from the eyes of Spanish officials. Even hostile Indians from the plains attended the fair, bringing hides, captives, and stolen livestock to trade for horses, knives, and manufactured goods. Most of the trade goods obtained from Indians were later traded to Chihuahua merchants when they arrived on their annual visits. Spanish officials in Santa Fe undoubtedly knew Taos existed, but chose to look the other way, even though all commerce in New Spain was supposed to be controlled by the Crown, which wanted to maintain its monopoly, fearing the effects of trade with outsiders, especially the French. As early as 1695, Apaches reported that the French had given arms to Indians on the plains. The Spaniards worried that hostile Indians in New Mexico would gain arms and enable France to break Spain's absolute control over economic policies. Occasional parties of Spaniards ventured onto the plains to look for the French, but found none.

Unlike the Spanish, however, the French did not seek to colonize. What settlements they established were used primarily to expand their influence through trade. In 1712, Étienne Veniard de Bourgmont, a young French officer, went up the Missouri River and lived for a few years with Indians. Between 1712 and 1717, he made at least two trips farther up the Missouri. He heard Indian stories about their trading with Spaniards from New Mexico. Although details are lacking, it is known that Bourgmont attempted to reach Santa Fe but failed.

Although he had traveled far out on the plains, his reports only inspired more French efforts to reach Santa Fe during the 1720s. But, like the Spaniards, the French did not fully grasp the geography of North America.[5]

As early as June 1720, Spaniards heard rumors that French settlements had been established among Pawnee Indians in what is now

The village of Don Fernando de Taos as it appeared in the mid-nineteenth century.
This illustration appeared in El Gringo; or, New Mexico and Her People
(1857), by William H. Davis. (Author's Collection)

Nebraska. Pedro de Villasur and a small but well-equipped force left
Santa Fe to investigate, reaching the Platte River several weeks later. The
Spaniards camped across a stream from a Pawnee village and tried to
learn from the Indians where the French had gone, but the Indians
refused to say, and at sunrise the following day they attacked the
Spaniards' camp. Villasur and about two-thirds of his force were massa-
cred; the Spaniards who survived fled and made their way back to New
Mexico.

The Spanish never did find the Frenchmen, who had been traveling
up the Missouri River and crisscrossing the plains, trading with Indians
in what is now Kansas and Nebraska. Contact with Frenchmen came
nineteen years later, in 1739, after two brothers, Paul and Pierre Mallet,
set out from an encampment just north of present-day St. Louis for
New Mexico, with a party of seven men identified as Louis Maria
Moreau, Emanuel Gailen, Jean David (known as "Petit-Jean"), Philippe
Robitaille, Joseph Bellecourt, Michel Beleau (often called "La Rose"),
and Jean-Baptiste Alarie. All were French Canadians except Jean David,
who had been born in France. They actually believed they could reach
New Mexico by ascending the Missouri River. At a point near where

Omaha, Nebraska, stands today, they realized that the Missouri did not cross the center of the continent and that they had traveled too far north. They then left the river and moved overland in a southwesterly course. When the party came upon the Platte River, they turned and followed it west.

We know some details of their journey because the Mallet brothers kept a journal. Although the original document has since been lost, a copy of an English translation exists, and it describes how on June 20, 1739, the Mallets and their party lost seven packhorses carrying their trading goods as they tried to cross the Smoky Hill River north of where Great Bend, Kansas, stands today. Ten days later they reached the banks of another stream, probably the Cimarron River in southern Kansas, where they found stones with Spanish inscriptions. Following the river upstream, they crossed what is now the panhandle of Oklahoma and then followed the Beaver River into what is now northeastern New Mexico. On July 5 they reached a Comanche village and the following day hired an Arikara Indian, who was a captive among the Comanches, to lead them to the Spanish settlements.

On July 22, the Mallet party arrived in Santa Fe, where they were pleasantly received by the Spaniards. The lieutenant-governor of New Mexico, Juan Paez Hurtado, welcomed them in his home. The Mallets sought permission to establish trade between Missouri country and Santa Fe, but since this was a decision for the Crown, they had to wait for word from the viceroy in Mexico City. When word was finally received early in 1740, the Mallets apparently were told that the Spanish would welcome the trade if the Mallets would bring passports and an official French decree permitting them to trade with the Spanish. The news was good, and when spring arrived, seven of the Mallet party decided to return east, leaving two behind. Louis Maria Moreau was already engaged to a Spanish woman, Juana Muñoz, whom he married about five months later. Jean-Baptiste Alarie also chose to make his home in New Mexico.

The Mallet brothers and five other men left Santa Fe on May 1, 1740, and headed east to find their way back to the Mississippi River and down to New Orleans. Ten days later they reached what was later called the Canadian River (probably for the French Canadian brothers) and followed it downstream for three days, until they reached a point where an Indian trail led north. There, in what is now Oldham County, Texas, the party split up. Emanuel Galien, Jean David, and Joseph Bellecourt decided to follow the Indian trail north and then go east and return to French Illinois. The Mallet brothers, along with Michel Beleau and

Philippe Robitaille, followed the Canadian River through present-day Oklahoma until they reached the mouth of Little River in what is now Hughes County, Oklahoma.

By then their horses were giving out, and the timbered country they were entering made travel on horseback difficult. The Mallet party abandoned their horses, constructed two elm-bark canoes, and floated down the Canadian until it ran into the Arkansas. Soon they came upon a camp of French hunters who were salting meat to take downstream to sell. From there the Mallet party made their way to Arkansas Post, near where the Arkansas flows into the Mississippi, a settlement founded in 1720 by John Law and populated by German colonists. There, before continuing down the Mississippi, the Mallet party told stories of their adventures in Santa Fe. Early in 1741, they arrived in New Orleans, where the Mallets delivered a letter to French authorities from Juan Paez Hurtado, who confirmed in writing that the Mallets had reached Santa Fe. Hurtado hinted that he would welcome trade with the French.

The arrival of the Mallet brothers and their two companions in New Orleans caused much excitement. Within a few weeks, André Fabry de la Bruyère, a clerk in the French navy, volunteered to take an expedition back to Santa Fe following the route used in the Mallets' return to New Orleans. The Mallets and their two companions went with Fabry's expedition, which left New Orleans in September 1741. The expedition, however, experienced numerous problems, some of which were Fabry's own doing. An inexperienced frontiersman, he ignored advice from the Mallets and others. The expedition was not successful and returned to New Orleans the following year.

Meantime, England and Spain had gone to war in 1739 over the issue of the Austrian succession. France joined Spain in the war in 1744, two years after Fabry's expedition had returned to New Orleans. The French-Spanish alliance made conditions favorable for trade. Although details are sketchy, it is known that in 1748 thirty-three Frenchmen arrived in Taos to trade and thirty-one returned east, two having decided to remain in New Mexico. Others arrived in the spring of 1749, including three Frenchmen—Pierre Satren, Louis Febre, and Joseph Raballo—who, like others, had been encouraged to make the journey by Paul Mallet. The trio left Arkansas Post in the fall of 1748 and arrived at Santa Fe the following spring. They were given permission to remain as residents and practice their much-needed skills in carpentry, tailoring, and barbering. Another party that arrived in Santa Fe early in 1750 included a Spaniard named Felipe de Sandoval, who with a party of Frenchmen had also been encouraged by Paul Mallet to make the journey. Part of the route they followed took them over Raton Pass in what is now northeastern New Mexico and what would later become the mountain route of the Santa Fe Trail.

In the fall of 1749, Pierre Mallet again set out for Santa Fe, carrying with him letters of credit from New Orleans merchants. He and three other men, apparently Frenchmen, arrived in New Mexico in November 1750 and announced that they had come to trade. By then the arrival of many Frenchmen in Santa Fe had so alarmed the governor of New Mexico that he sent a message to the viceroy in Mexico City, suggesting that the Frenchmen should not be permitted to return to their homes to describe what they had seen. Before the viceroy's reply reached Santa Fe, the governor sent Mallet and some of the other Frenchmen to Mexico City, where they were questioned by authorities and jailed. What happened to the men remains a mystery; they may have died in a Mexico City jail or in one in Spain. Other Frenchmen who chose not to make their homes in New Mexico may have been jailed in Sonora. The last party of French traders to arrive in New Mexico in 1752 was led by Jean Chapuis and Luis Feuilli. Their trading goods were confiscated and sold at auction even though Chapuis carried a French license giving him permission to trade with the Spanish. The two men were sent to Mexico City and then transported to prison in Spain.[6]

No other Frenchmen are known to have entered New Mexico between 1752 and 1762, the year France ceded Louisiana Territory west of the Mississippi River to Spain. But that treaty was kept a secret until 1763 when, at the end of the Seven Years' War, France ceded to Great Britain all French territory east of the Mississippi except for New Orleans. That was thirteen years before delegates from the thirteen British American colonies gathered in Philadelphia to declare their right to be independent and free from England.

THREE

Trails to Santa Fe, 1762-1807

It is the dim haze of mystery
that adds enchantment to pursuit.

—*Antonine Rivarol*

SPANISH FEARS OF French intrusions into New Mexico disappeared when Spain acquired Louisiana Territory from France in 1762. Covering more than 800,000 square miles between the Rocky Mountains and the Mississippi River, Spain's new territory served as a buffer between New Mexico and British territory, which began on the east bank of the Mississippi River and stretched east to the Atlantic Ocean. Any further threats to New Mexico, the Spanish now believed, would come from the Anglo-Americans. To ward off such threats, Spain decided to establish three military posts along the eastern edge of Louisiana Territory. One was located on an island in the Red River at Natchitoches in what is now northwestern Louisiana, where the French had built a stockade and trading post in 1714. The second fort was at Arkansas Post on the Arkansas River, and the third small fort was erected by Spanish soldiers on the banks of the Missouri River, where the stream flows into the Mississippi north of what is now St. Louis.

About a year after Spain acquired Louisiana Territory, Pierre Liguest Laclede, a thirty-nine-year-old trader from the New Orleans firm of Laclede, Maxent and Co., popularly called the Louisiana Fur Company, arrived at St. Genevieve, the earliest settlement in what is now Missouri, located about forty-six miles south of present-day St. Louis. Laclede's party included hunters, trappers, carpenters, and other artisans. Intent upon establishing an Indian trading post, Laclede thought St. Genevieve was too far south from the mouth of the Missouri River. He and his stepson, René Auguste Chouteau, then a boy of almost fourteen years, began to explore the Mississippi closer to the mouth of the Missouri River. Early in 1764 they selected a site for their trading post on a limestone bluff on the west bank of the Mississippi. Below, the river's current was swift, making it a good spot for a port. The location was nicknamed "Pain Court" ("short of bread") because of the lack of good agricultural land nearby. Soon a small settlement grew up around the trading post, which was also called "Mound City" because of nearby ancient Indian mounds, although as the settlement grew the mounds were destroyed. Laclede soon named the settlement St. Louis in honor of both Louis IX, the current king's patron saint, and the indolent king himself, Louis XV of France, a man bored by affairs of state whose main occupation was the pursuit of the pleasures of his position. Laclede laid out one long street paralleling the river and named it Rue Royale (now Main Street), and

This large limestone bluff marked the spot where St. Louis was established in 1764. As the town grew, much of the bluff disappeared to make room for buildings. This illustration appeared in Switzler's Illustrated History of Missouri, *published in St. Louis in 1881.* (Author's Collection)

soon he mapped a town and assigned lots to individuals, including himself. On his lot he built a home for his wife, who was known as Madame Chouteau after her first husband, and her two boys, René Auguste and Pierre.[1]

About forty-five miles downstream from St. Louis and opposite St. Genevieve on the east bank of the Mississippi River, near where the Kaskaskia River flows into the Mississippi, was the settlement of Kaskaskia. The town had been founded in 1703 as a Jesuit mission in an Indian village. French Canadian fur traders soon settled there and watched as St. Louis was established and grew. After British officers arrived in 1765 to take charge of Kaskaskia and the vast region east of the Mississippi ceded by France to England two years earlier, many French Canadians moved across the Mississippi to St. Louis, preferring to be under the French flag but not knowing that France had already given Louisiana Territory to Spain. Even when they learned this, the French Canadians remained in St. Louis, believing the territory would soon be ceded back to France. This explains why most of the 400 white residents counted in the first census at St. Louis in 1772 were of French extraction. The census also counted 287 slaves, giving St. Louis a total population of nearly 700 people.

The Spanish did not object to the French settling at St. Louis. Spain wanted to colonize Louisiana Territory to further protect New Mexico, but an empty Spanish treasury limited what it could accomplish not only in Louisiana Territory but also to the south in Spanish Texas, which already served as a buffer between British territory and New Mexico. Acquiring Louisiana Territory simply created more problems for Spain. Communication, already poor in Texas, was almost nonexistent in Louisiana Territory. Then, too, the Spanish knew little of the geography of Louisiana Territory, or of the Indians who inhabited it. Since some Frenchmen knew more about the territory than the Spanish, Spain relied upon officials of French heritage who decided to switch to Spanish service. One of them was Pierre "Pedro" Vial, a native of Lyons, France, who was destined to blaze three new trails for the Spanish.

Little is known of Vial's early life. He may have traversed the Missouri River before moving southwest, where he lived and traded among the Comanches, Wichitas, Wacos, and Tawakonis during the late 1770s and early 1780s, and where he occasionally helped to resolve conflicts between the Spanish and Indians. Vial supposedly was a gunsmith who repaired arms acquired by the Indians. Probably because of his ability to get along with the Indians, the Spanish asked Vial to open a road between San Antonio de Bexar in Texas and Santa Fe to improve com-

Pierre Chouteau, whose stepfather,
Pierre Liguest Laclede, founded
St. Louis, Missouri, in 1764.
(Courtesy Kansas State Historical Society)

munication between the two isolated outposts. The Spanish knew a more direct route was across what is now West Texas, but hostile Indians had forced them to abandon travel there. The Spanish used a safe but long and roundabout route from San Antonio to Saltillo, west and north to Chihuahua and El Paso, and north to Santa Fe, a distance of seventeen hundred miles.

In October 1786, Vial left San Antonio with one companion, Cristóbal de los Santos, and a packhorse loaded with provisions; they traveled in a northerly direction. Vial's diary, preserved in the archives at Mexico City, relates how he soon lost his provisions, became ill and fell from his horse, and then traveled 150 miles to find an Indian medicine man to doctor him. It was two months before Vial was able to continue his journey. When he reached an Indian village on the Red River in what is now southern Oklahoma, Vial and his companion followed the river westward. They stopped when winter weather arrived and spent six weeks in camp somewhere near present-day Wichita Falls, Texas. They then resumed their journey westward, crossing what is today the Texas Panhandle before entering New Mexico and arriving in Santa Fe on May 26, 1787. Their journey of more than eleven hundred miles had taken nearly eight months, but they had opened a second road to Santa Fe, nearly two hundred years after the first, the Royal Road from Chihuahua.

The evidence suggests that Vial told the governor of New Mexico that an even more direct route probably existed because he had wandered about on his journey. Thus, a few weeks after Vial returned to Santa Fe, the governor sent José Mares, a retired corporal in the Spanish army, back to San Antonio with Cristóbal de los Santos and two other men, including an Indian interpreter. With orders to find a more direct route, the small party left Santa Fe on October 8, 1787, and rode into San Antonio ten weeks later. Mares's route reduced the number of miles between the two locations, but he realized he could do better, and on his return journey he cut the distance to 845 miles. He arrived back in Santa Fe in late April 1788.

Less than a month after Mares returned, Spanish authorities directed Vial to open a road between Santa Fe and Natchitoches and then on to San Antonio. Vial and four other men left Santa Fe on June 20, 1788, along with ten horses plus two pack mules carrying provisions, tobacco, and presents for the Indians they met. By the time Vial's party returned to Santa Fe fourteen months later, they had traveled 2,377 miles.

Around the time Mares returned to Santa Fe, Spanish authorities were becoming concerned about reports of Anglo-American thrusts toward Santa Fe from the east and at French machinations toward New Orleans and Mexico following the French Revolution. The Spanish changed their policy toward Indians, realizing that in order to keep away outsiders they needed their cooperation, especially that of the Comanches, who were superior fighters. The Spaniards cultivated an alliance with the Comanches, who had the habit of keeping agreements. At about this time, Pedro Vial was again called upon to open a road between Santa Fe and St. Louis and to establish good relations with the Indians he met. Spanish authorities hoped that by opening the road to St. Louis they could bring European goods to Santa Fe at a cost of at least 40 percent less than those brought over the Royal Road.

Vial and two other men, José Vicente Villanueva and Vicente Espinosa, left Santa Fe with horses and supplies on May 21, 1792, bound for St. Louis. As he had done earlier, Vial kept a diary, in which he recorded how his party entered what is now the Texas Panhandle and then turned northeast, crossing what is now the Oklahoma Panhandle and entering present-day southwest Kansas. They located the Arkansas River by late June. On June 29, Vial's party came across some dead buffalo that Vial thought had been killed by Osage Indians. About four o'clock that afternoon, the party found Indians in a camp on the north bank of the Arkansas River. At first, Vial thought they were Osage. What happened next is told in Vial's own words:

They approached us, and with the river between us, we fired some shots into the wind so that they would hear and see us. They immediately began to move, and came across to us. The first who met us, greeted us affectionately, shaking hands. I asked them what tribe they were, and they told me they were Kansas. At the same moment they took possession of our horses and equipment, cutting our clothes with knives, leaving us entirely naked. They wanted to kill us, at which one of them cried to the others telling them they should not do it with rifles or arrows but with hatchet-blows or lances, because they had us surrounded and they might cause some unfortunate accident to themselves. In this conflict, one of them took our part, begging and supplicating the others not to take our lives. At that time I was approached by another whom I had known among the Frenchmen, and, taking me by the hand, he made me mount his own horse with him. Then another one came from behind and hurled a spear at me, but my good friend guarded me, dismounting from the horse, leaving me on it, and grabbed the evil-intentioned one. When they saw that, many of them rushed up and tried to kill me from behind, but a brother of the one who had just protected me, seated himself on the croup of the horse with the same intention [of protecting me]. That had hardly happened when I was approached by another Indian who had been a servant in the village of St. Louis . . . who spoke very good French, and he, recognizing me, began to shout, "Don't kill him! Don't kill him." And, taking the reins of the horse, he took me to his lodge and said, "Friend, now your Excellency must hurry if you want to save your life, because among us it is the custom and the law that, after having eaten, no one can be killed."[2]

As they ate inside the lodge, some of the chiefs asked Vial where he came from. He told them Santa Fe, and that he had been sent by the great chief, their Spanish father, to open a road to St. Louis. The chiefs then left Vial alone, and the next day he was reunited with his two companions. As Vial wrote in his diary, "Vicente Villanueba came out with his head cut and a dagger thrust in the belly that would have been fatal if, at the moment of receiving it, he had not pulled away." Vial noted that the Kansas Indians kept them naked for more than two weeks. Then he and his party were taken to a Kansas village located on the banks of the Kansas River just east of where Manhattan, Kansas, now stands. They remained there until the September 11 arrival of a French trader with two employees in a pirogue loaded with trading goods. The trader gave Vial and his companions clothing to dress themselves, a pound of vermilion, tobacco, four blankets, some cloth, two pounds of powder, four pounds of balls, and a musket.

Freed by the Kansas Indians, Vial and his companions left the village on September 16 with the trader and his companions. In their pirogue they traveled for eight days down the Kansas River to where it joins the Missouri River near present-day Kansas City, Missouri. Stopping frequently to hunt deer and bears, which abounded on the shores, the men continued down the Missouri to St. Louis, arriving early in October. There Vial and his two companions remained until the following June, delayed nearly a year because Spanish authorities in St. Louis had declared war on the hostile Osage Indians and no traders were permitted to travel on the Missouri River.[3]

The ban on travel was lifted the following spring, whereupon Vial and his companions, well equipped for their return journey to Santa Fe, left St. Louis on June 14, 1793. They traveled in a pirogue with four men up the Missouri River to St. Charles, then a new settlement with about a hundred residents. The next day Vial and his party set out with five traders in a pirogue up the Missouri. Travel was slow against the river's current. Instead of moving westward when they reached the spot where the Kansas River flows into the Missouri River, the party continued up the Missouri River to where the Little Nemaha River flows into it in what is now the southeastern corner of Nebraska. The party apparently was trying to avoid contact with the hostile Osage Indians. As Vial noted in his diary on August 24, the men with whom they were traveling were going to trade with the Pawnee Indians. They set up camp on the Little Nemaha, a general gathering point for trade with the Pawnees. Vial sent two men to find the Pawnees and to tell them the party needed guides.

When the guides arrived about two weeks later, they led Vial and his two companions over a trail that headed southwest across the prairie. After several days they reached a Pawnee village on the Platte River and were welcomed and entertained. In his diary, Vial described the Pawnees as being of good character, and mentioned that "they like the Spaniards a great deal." In council with the chief, Vial explained that he had come to open a road to Santa Fe. To this news the chief replied, "Oh, let the road be opened, that I may see a Spaniard coming from those of the west! Now they can go and come when they please."[4]

Vial and his companions remained in the Pawnee village for several days, buying ten horses from the Indians for their journey. On October 4, Vial and his party and seven Pawnees set out for Santa Fe, heading southwest across what is now central Kansas and into Oklahoma. Just before midnight on October 19, while camped beside a river (probably the North Canadian near present-day Dombey, Oklahoma), a band of Pawnees mistook Vial and his companions for Comanches and attacked. No one was killed, and peace prevailed after the attacking Pawnees realized their mistake. The following morning Vial and his party continued toward Santa Fe, arriving there about a month later, on the evening of November 15, 1793. Vial handed the governor a letter from the commandant of the Spanish troops at St. Louis.

When Vial later gave the governor his formal report on the journey, he asserted that if he had not been captured by the Kansas Indians on his initial trip, he could have reached St. Louis in twenty-five days. This statement made Spanish authorities suddenly realize that Santa Fe was not as far from the United States as they had thought or wished, and they became uneasy because the growing fur trade on the Missouri River was already attracting an increasing number of Americans. Then, too, with the American Revolution, Americans had won the reputation of being vigorous and uninhibited, and the Spanish knew they were moving westward toward the setting sun.

Across the world the same year Vial returned to Santa Fe from St. Louis, the French Bourbon king was executed during the French Revolution. Vial and other Frenchmen in New Spain got caught up in international politics after Spain joined other European powers in declaring war against the revolutionary French government. Early in 1794, the Spanish Crown renewed its repressive policy against the French, ordering the arrest and imprisonment of all Frenchmen anywhere in Spanish territory. The Crown feared that the French might be trying to spread revolutionary ideas in New Spain. Though two Frenchmen in New Mexico were arrested, Pedro Vial was not; he left Santa Fe and went to live with the Comanche Indians, perhaps on the advice of Spanish friends. Five years later, in 1799, Vial was living at Portage des Sioux, just north of St. Louis. By then Spain again looked favorably on France, which had reversed its course and formed an alliance with Spain against Britain, but British naval supremacy had cut off Spain from its colonies, causing serious economic problems in New Spain. After Napoleon gained control of France, he soon dominated Spain, and Louisiana Territory was ceded back to France in 1800. Three years later, Louisiana Territory was sold to the United States for fifteen million dollars. This was a blow to the Spanish, especially in New Mexico, who realized that the vast territory that had served as a buffer for thirty-seven years now belonged to the nation whose people they hoped to keep out.

. . .

ALTHOUGH PEDRO VIAL had opened routes to San Antonio, Natchitoches, and St. Louis, the Spanish did not use them for trade during the last quarter of the eighteenth century, perhaps because of pressure from wealthy merchants in Chihuahua. For the residents of Santa Fe and New Mexico, the Royal Road south to Chihuahua remained the only reliable link to the outside world. The merchants of Chihuahua extended their monopoly on trade in 1776 when Spanish authorities gave them the business of supplying troops in the northern garrisons.

About eleven years later, early in 1787, Francisco de Guizarnotegui, a Chihuahua merchant, was awarded a five-year contract to supply all of the provisions purchased by four military field companies in Nueva Vizcaya and the garrison at Santa Fe. Each military garrison placed its order at the beginning of each year and provided Guizarnotegui with a voucher on the royal treasury at Chihuahua to cover the cost of what it ordered. The merchant agreed to buy goods in Mexico City at certified wholesale prices and sell them at a profit of only 4 percent. If goods such as sugar, shoes, mules, and horses had to be purchased at Michoacán, Mexico, Guizarnotegui could add an additional 2.5 percent profit. All duties and costs of transportation were paid by the military garrisons. To defray the cost of freighting the supplies, Guizarnotegui was to receive two pesos for each twenty-five pounds carried from Mexico City to Chihuahua and an additional half peso for each mule load of about three hundred pounds from Chihuahua to the individual military garrisons.

During his first year Guizarnotegui received eighty thousand pesos, but he did not enjoy this huge volume of business for long. Spanish authorities, receiving many complaints about him, investigated, and in 1790 his contract was canceled. A new contract was awarded to twelve merchants in Chihuahua, but their sharp practices continued to drain the treasury and oppress the military, colonists, and Indians in New Mexico into the early nineteenth century.

While residents of New Mexico continued to complain about the high prices and limited selection of goods brought north by merchants during the 1790s, New Mexicans did enjoy relative tranquillity, because Pedro Vial had made peace with the Comanches for the Spanish. Both Spanish and Indian leaders seemed to realize they had more to gain from peace than from war. The Spanish presented more gifts to the Indians, including the Apaches, and both sides came to realize that while individual Spaniards and Indians would occasionally steal, raid, or murder, peace could continue while those who perpetrated the crimes were punished. The Indians came to accept Spanish punishment for such acts, but leaders on both sides worked to stop crimes before they occurred. Travel became safer in New Mexico as economic interests and mutual security seemed to unite Spaniards and Indians. Captain José de Zúñiga was able to open a pack-train route through Apache Country and across the mountains between Tucson and Santa Fe in 1795, something that would have been impossible a decade earlier. But even with the peaceful conditions, New Mexicans did not experience economic growth because of the monopoly on trade held by Chihuahua merchants. Spanish officials in New Mexico, however, still looked the other way when Indians and traders congregated at Taos and Pecos during annual fairs in July and August. Comanches, Arapahos, Pawnees, Navajos, Utes, and others brought buffalo hides, deerskins, blankets, and sometimes even captives to be sold or exchanged as slaves. Chihuahua merchants even attended the fairs to barter imported goods and join French, Spanish, and American trappers who carried pelts and trinkets. Still, the Chihuahua merchants usually made most of the profit. To the east, however, Americans were beginning to put the wheels in motion that would eventually eliminate the monopoly enjoyed by the merchants of Chihuahua.

FOR THE NEARLY fifty years before Thomas Jefferson became president early in 1801, he had been fascinated with the West. In 1792, Jefferson proposed that the Philadelphia-based American Philosophical Society

Thomas Jefferson (1743–1826) as he appeared as president in 1803, when he doubled the area of the United States by purchasing Louisiana Territory from France without specific constitutional authority to do so.
(Author's Collection)

engage an explorer to lead an overland expedition to the Pacific, but the idea was only discussed. After becoming president, Jefferson appointed Captain Meriwether Lewis his private secretary, and the two men often talked of the West and the need to explore it. Jefferson knew that Spain, which controlled the Louisiana Territory, including New Orleans, was growing weaker, so there was no urgency to the matter until Jefferson learned in the spring of 1801 that Spain had given Louisiana Territory back to revolutionary France. This alarmed him; he opposed French control of New Orleans, through which much American produce had to pass. When news came that the British were looking to settle along the northwest coast of the North American continent, Jefferson decided to send an expedition westward. At some point in the late summer or early fall of 1802, Jefferson directed Lewis to lead the expedition, ostensibly to locate the source of the Missouri River. Lewis began to determine how much such an expedition would cost and to make plans.

Aware that the Spanish had not yet turned over control of Louisiana Territory to the French, Jefferson unofficially asked the Spanish minister in November 1802 if Spain would object to the United States sending a small expedition to explore the course of the Missouri River. Word came back that the Spanish saw no problem with this plan. Then, with figures provided by Lewis, Jefferson sent a confidential message to Congress early in 1803 calling for funds to establish Indian trading houses on the western frontier in order to extend the nation's external commerce. Jefferson masked his real intent—to explore west to the Pacific—by seeking funds to promote commerce, something the Constitution gave Congress the power to do. Congress approved and voted a sum of $2,500.[5]

Careful planning now went forward in earnest. Jefferson began to draft his instructions to Lewis. They were lengthy, since there were so many things Jefferson wanted to know about the West. Meantime, Lewis set the objectives for the expedition and calculated how many men were needed to keep it a self-contained unit, how they would travel, what supplies were required, what gifts would be needed for the Indians they met, and many other things. About this time Lewis asked Jefferson if William Clark, a boyhood friend in Virginia who had since retired from the army as a captain, could be coleader of the expedition. Jefferson agreed, and in June Lewis sent a letter to Clark inviting him to do so. When Clark's positive reply was received in late July 1803, Lewis had already left Washington and was gathering supplies and other items for the expedition.

Meanwhile, Jefferson sent James Monroe to Paris as a special minister to aid the American minister to France, Robert R. Livingston, in trying to solve the New Orleans problem. The Spanish, who still administered Louisiana Territory, had denied U.S. merchants the right of depositing duty-free goods at New Orleans pending transshipment. Since Louisiana Territory was now owned by France, Jefferson wanted any one of four things: the purchase of eastern and western Florida and New Orleans; the purchase of New Orleans alone; the purchase of land along the eastern bank of the Mississippi River to build an American port; or the acquisition of perpetual rights of navigation and deposit on the Mississippi. On April 11, 1803, the French foreign minister surprised Monroe and Livingston by offering them a choice: either the American purchase of all of Louisiana or no deal at all. Although such a deal was beyond their authority, the Americans agreed, and in early May three documents antedated to April 30 were signed ceding Louisiana Territory to the United States. The cost was fifteen million dollars. As it turned out, Napoleon had decided to sell Louisiana because France's international situation had worsened. On December 4, 1803, the *National Intelligencer* in Washington, D.C., reported that Napoleon had sold Louisiana Territory to the United States. With Louisiana now in the hands of the Americans, the Lewis and Clark expedition took on new importance.

Timing was key. Initially, Lewis thought the expedition might go some distance up the Missouri River before winter set in. But, moving westward to meet Clark, who had been living in Indiana Territory, Lewis wrote Jefferson from Cincinnati on August 21, 1803, with different plans: after setting up winter camp in St. Louis, he intended to go up the Kansas River toward Santa Fe while letting Clark take a different route. Concerned about Lewis moving into Spanish territory, with its reported gold and silver mines, Jefferson wrote back that he should not go toward Santa Fe, that his mission was to follow the Missouri River to its source and beyond. Jefferson added that Spanish soldiers in the region would make a trek to Santa Fe more dangerous.

By the time Lewis received Jefferson's letter, however, he already had given up any thought of heading for Santa Fe. In general, it was true, Santa Fe continued to exert a magnetic attraction for Americans, because, though it had only three thousand inhabitants, it was the center of commercial activities for some forty thousand New Mexicans. But for now, Santa Fe would have to wait.

Lewis was in Pittsburgh on July 4, 1803, when he learned that the United States had purchased Louisiana Territory. He headed west the following day to join Clark and to give him the news. The two explorers left St. Louis on November 20, 1803, and established a camp near the mouth of the Missouri River, where they formed their expedition and spent the winter preparing for their journey. They were in the camp on December 20, 1803, when the southern portion of Louisiana was officially turned over to the United States in ceremonies at New Orleans. Less than three months later, on March 9, 1804, upper Louisiana was officially transferred to the United States from France in more ceremonies at St. Louis, which then had a population of about twelve hundred. The settlement had one bakery, two taverns, three blacksmiths, two mills, and one doctor. The following day Captain Amos Stoddard, an army officer representing the United States, proclaimed the establishment of American authority in this vast expanse. Several days later in Washington, D.C., Congress divided the Louisiana Purchase into the Territory of Orleans (which later became the state of Louisiana) and the District of Louisiana (everything else), which in the fall was placed under the jurisdiction of the Territory of Indiana.[6]

By then, Spain knew not only that the United States now owned the region bordering on New Spain, but the stated purpose of the expedition led by Lewis and Clark, a group also known as Jefferson's "Corps of Discovery." Still, the Spanish feared that the Americans were really seeking to discover their gold and silver mines. Soon after Lewis and Clark's expedition of forty-five men broke camp near St. Louis at six o'clock on the morning of May 22, to begin their ascent of the Missouri River in a 55-foot keelboat and two pirogues—boats hewn from tree trunks, slender, swift, and easy to handle—the governor of New Mexico received orders to send troops to intercept them and either force them to return or make them prisoners. During the next two years at least four parties of troops from Santa Fe searched for the expedition without success. Even the Indians met by the Spaniards had not heard of the expedition. Here again, the Spanish misconceptions about the geography of Louisiana Territory were evident. They did not realize that the headwaters of the Missouri River were far to the north and not close to New Mexico. But then Lewis and Clark didn't yet know where the mighty Missouri originated either.

In 1804, when the Corps of Discovery started out on its journey, St. Louis had become a major trading center for the growing fur trade. Most of the traders lived in St. Louis, and all trappers purchased their guns, powder, bullets, flints, axes, knives, awls, cotton and woolen stuffs, liquor, tobacco, and Indian trading goods there before going up the Missouri River to trap fur-bearing animals or to trade with Indians for buffalo hides, tongues, and tallow; bear tallow; and other products that were brought back to St. Louis and sold. St. Louis almost rivaled New York as a center for the fur trade, and companies maintained large offices in St.

This illustration by Frederic Remington is titled "Lewis and Clark" and appeared in Collier's Weekly, May 12, 1906. *Remington destroyed the original painting in 1908.* (Author's Collection)

Louis to encourage the handling and transportation of pelts and skins. It became common practice to put furs in hundred-pound packs. For instance, 10 buffalo robes constituted a pack; 14 bear, 60 otter, 8 beaver, 80 raccoon, 120 fox, and 600 muskrat skins were each considered a pack.

Stories about Santa Fe as a potential trading center were already well known in St. Louis. Even before Pedro Vial had blazed his trail from Santa Fe to St. Louis in 1792, other men such as the Mallet brothers had found their way across the plains to Santa Fe, adding to the growing number of legends told and retold along the Mississippi and Missouri Rivers about this mysterious town. To Americans today, all of this may seem absurd, but in a time when travel and communications were slow, when great distances had to be traversed, when accurate maps did not exist, Santa Fe was clouded in mystery for those who had not been there.

During the summer of 1804, the trading potential of Santa Fe caught

This nineteenth-century artist's drawing shows what is described as the first iron works in St. Louis. The illustration appeared in Switzler's Illustrated History of Missouri, *published in 1881 in St. Louis.* (Author's Collection)

the fancy of William Morrison, a merchant at Kaskaskia, Illinois Territory. He sent Baptiste LaLande, a French Creole, to Santa Fe with a supply of trading merchandise. LaLande was accompanied by a group of Pawnee Indians and was guided by José Gervais, who had taken a group of Pawnees to New Mexico in 1803. LaLande went up the Missouri River to a Pawnee Indian village located on the Platte River in what is now Nebraska and then followed the Platte to near its headwaters. The party then turned south toward Santa Fe. It appears that LaLande sent Gervais ahead to Santa Fe to see whether trade would be allowed. Some Spaniards came out to meet LaLande and escorted the party into Santa Fe in the late summer or early fall of 1804. The goods found a ready market, but LaLande did not return to Kaskaskia with Morrison's profits. Instead, he appropriated the profits for himself and made his home in Santa Fe, having found the New Mexicans agreeable, especially a group of female admirers. So far as is known, LaLande was the first to take trading goods overland from an American settlement to Santa Fe.

Less than a year after LaLande arrived in Santa Fe, James Purcell, a native of Bardstown, Kentucky, found his way to New Mexico. Purcell and two companions had left St. Louis in 1802 to hunt among the Osage Indians. Turning to follow the Arkansas River to the Mississippi en route to New Orleans, they were robbed of the furs they had accumulated by a band of Kansas Indians. Purcell and his companions managed to recover their property and then headed for St. Louis, only to lose their furs in the Missouri River near the mouth of the Kansas River. Purcell then fell in with a trader on his way up the Missouri to the Mandan Indians, and eventually went to the southwest to trade with the Indians of the plains. By the spring of 1805, Purcell and his Indian companions found themselves not far from the Spanish settlements, and, continuing on, they arrived in Santa Fe in June 1805. Like LaLande, Purcell did not return east but made his home in New Mexico.

The year Purcell arrived in Santa Fe, a twenty-six-year-old American army lieutenant, Zebulon Montgomery Pike, was directed to find the headwaters of the Mississippi River, since the United States sought to explore other areas of its Louisiana Purchase. Pike took an expedition north and, during the winter of 1805 and '06, reached Red Cedar (now Cass) Lake and Leech Lake in what is now Minnesota, believing them to be the Mississippi's source. (Less than twenty years later, in 1832, Lake Itasca was confirmed as the true source.) When Pike returned from his journey, General James Wilkinson, governor of Louisiana, directed him to explore the headwaters of the Arkansas and Red Rivers and at the same time to make peace with the Indians he met. With a company of twenty-two men, including Lieutenant James B. Wilkinson, Dr. John H. Robinson, three noncoms, sixteen privates, an interpreter named Baronet Vásquez, and fifty-one Osage captives, Pike left St. Louis on August 9, 1806, traveling by boat up the Missouri River to return the Osages to their home. Pike and his party then continued on to the Osage River and began moving overland on September 1, entering what is now east-central Kansas. On August 22, Pike met a Pawnee hunter and learned that Spanish soldiers were looking for his party.

When Spanish authorities in Santa Fe heard the previous spring of Pike's impending expedition, they sent an imposing cavalry force—one hundred dragoons and five hundred militia with more than two thousand horses and mules equipped for six months—to intercept Pike and at the same time visit the Comanche, Pawnee, and Kansas Indians in northeast New Spain. They went as far north as what is now Webster

County in south-central Nebraska, visiting with the Indians they met. But, hearing nothing about Americans, they returned to Santa Fe in October 1806, not realizing that Pike had not crossed the plains as rapidly as they had expected.

Meantime, Pike continued westward and then moved northwest across what is now Kansas, until he met a large number of Pawnees. They escorted him and his party to a large village of theirs located in what is now Webster County, Nebraska. There, in a grand council on September 29, Pike demanded that the Spanish flag displayed over the chief's door be taken down and replaced by a U.S. flag. In his journal, Pike related what happened: "After a silence of some time, an old man rose, went to the door, and took down the Spanish flag, and brought it and laid it at my feet, and then received the American flag and elevated it on the staff."[7]

To conciliate the Pawnees, Pike returned the Spanish flag to their keeping. When he told the Pawnee chief that he planned to continue on to the headwaters of the Arkansas River, the chief was against the journey but would not give his reasons. Perhaps he knew that Spanish soldiers had been searching for Pike (although by this time, early October, they had already returned to Santa Fe). Pike purchased a few horses from the Pawnees and in a compact body passed the Pawnee village and followed the Spanish trail toward the Arkansas River. The Pawnees did not oppose Pike and his men. At about the time Pike left the Pawnee village, the Lewis and Clark expedition was coming down the Missouri River more than two hundred miles to the east, nearing the end of the two-year-and-four-month journey that had taken them to the Pacific. They arrived back in St. Louis on September 23, 1806.[8]

Pike followed the Arkansas River west into South Park, a chain of grassy plateaus running north and south and enclosed by snowcapped mountains, located south of what is now Leadville, Colorado. Pike sighted one large peak located on the front range of the Rocky Mountains. On Thanksgiving Day, 1806, wearing only cotton clothing, Pike and his men climbed the 14,110-foot mountain that came to be named Pike's Peak, but they never reached the top. Pike and his party then wandered about searching for the Red River. Whether he was lost is still debated, but his party soon crossed the Sangre de Cristo Mountains and reached the Rio Grande, which Pike believed to be the Red River. Early in February 1807, Pike's party built a stockade on the Conejos River, a tributary of the Rio Grande in what is now south-central Colorado. From there Dr. John H. Robinson headed for Santa Fe ostensibly to locate Bap-

This is how the artist Frederic Remington imagined Zebulon Pike's arrival in Santa Fe in 1807, escorted by Spanish soldiers. (Author's Collection)

tiste LaLande, the trader who had remained there a few years earlier with profits that belonged to William Morrison, the Kaskaskia merchant.

As Pike wrote: "When I was about to sail [up the Missouri River], Morrison, conceiving that it was possible that I might meet some Spanish factors on the Red river, intrusted [*sic*] me with the claim, in order, if they were acquainted with LaLande, I might negotiate the thing with some of them. When on the frontiers, the idea suggested itself to us of making this claim a pretext for Robinson to visit Santa Fe. We therefore gave it the proper appearance, and he marched for that place. Our views were to gain a knowledge of the country, the prospect of trade, force, &c. whilst, at the same time, our treaties with Spain guaranteed to him, as a citizen of the United States, the right of seeking the recovery of all just debts."[9]

Several days after Robinson started for Santa Fe, about a hundred Spanish soldiers appeared at Pike's stockade and informed him that he and his men were in Spanish territory. Pike and his men ended up in Santa Fe and then were escorted to Chihuahua. Later they were taken by a circuitous route to the U.S. border near Natchitoches, where they were released on June 30, 1807.

When Pike's poorly organized report of his journey was set in type by John Binns and published in 1810 at Philadelphia, it was the first account in English describing a possible route to Santa Fe. Pike's bleak description of the southern plains, however, seems to have overshadowed his observations about the trading possibilities with the Spanish, at least in the eyes of most readers. Nonetheless, government officials in Washington, D.C., paid close attention to Pike's account, since they wanted the United States to establish trade with New Spain. Before they could move to do so, however, America went to war against Great Britain in 1812 and had more pressing business to conduct.

FOUR

Destination Santa Fe, 1807-1822

*Life affords no higher pleasure than that of surmounting
difficulties, passing from one step of success to another,
forming new wishes and seeing them gratified.*

—*Samuel Johnson*

EVEN BEFORE ZEBULON PIKE returned east in 1807, another party
left St. Louis determined to open trade with Santa Fe. It was led by
Jacques Clamorgan, then about seventy-four years old. Much of Clamorgan's life remains a mystery, but it is known that he was born in the West
Indies of mixed blood about 1734, and that as a young man he engaged
in the slave trade. He arrived in St. Louis about 1780 and became a merchant, financier, land speculator, and fur trader. Clamorgan had a glib
tongue and was endowed with a tremendous imagination. Although he
never married, Clamorgan kept a well-stocked harem of West Indian
women and fathered four children. Because of his lifestyle, Clamorgan
was not accepted socially by the aristocratic French Creoles of St. Louis.
To get what he wanted, he submitted to the wishes of Spanish officials
and soon became known as a statesman, an explorer, and a promoter.

Within a few years Clamorgan became the leader of merchants in St.
Louis, and in 1794 he organized and became director of the Spanish
Commercial Exploration Co., often referred to as simply the Missouri
Company. It was formed to oust British traders from Spanish territory;
capture the Indian trade; find a route to the Pacific, to join the Missouri
Country with Mexico and California; defend the Spanish empire along

its undefended and unexplored northernmost frontier; and protect strategic and rich Santa Fe. Of course, Spanish authorities did not object to the company's stated goals since they were in line with Spain's. By organizing the company, Clamorgan hoped the Spanish would assist him financially and grant all of his requests. But they did not.

Clamorgan's luck changed when Juan Manuel de Salcedo became the last Spanish governor of Louisiana in 1801. Clamorgan called the governor's attention to the British monopoly of the Indian trade on the upper Mississippi and upper Missouri, and British influence on the Omaha Indians, who prevented Spaniards from ascending the Missouri. Clamorgan accused the British of subsidizing the Omaha Indians and of having met with them in council. As proof, Clamorgan claimed that he had seen a copy of a journal made at the council meeting that clearly revealed English intrigues. Clamorgan begged the Spanish governor for a hundred militiamen and the privilege of exclusive trade rights with the Kansas and Platte River Indians. He got both.

Clamorgan's fortunes waned when the United States purchased Louisiana Territory. In 1807, he joined forces with Manuel Lisa, a St. Louis fur trader born in 1772 of Spanish parents. The two men formed a company to establish trade with Santa Fe, but before Clamorgan could lead a party westward, James Wilkinson, acting governor of St. Louis, who had his own ambitions in that direction, learned of the plan. He sent word to Pike, who had just left on his western expedition, to "take all prudent and lawful means to blow it up." To avoid trouble with Wilkinson and the government, Lisa publicly disavowed his intentions to establish trade with Santa Fe. But privately, he kept his financial interest in the venture and quietly encouraged Clamorgan to obtain a license to trade with the Pawnee Indians, to make it appear that the expedition had decided not to head for Santa Fe.

When Clamorgan's expedition left St. Louis early in August 1807, it consisted of three other Frenchmen, a black slave, and four pack mules loaded with trading goods. Clamorgan and his party visited Pawnee villages located in either north-central Kansas or south-central Nebraska and headed west but then turned southwest and arrived in Santa Fe on December 12. Unlike other expeditions from St. Louis, the Clamorgan party was not arrested and jailed; they were welcomed by Spanish authorities, who apparently were aware of Clamorgan's earlier work for Spain before Louisiana Territory was purchased by the United States. Clamorgan and his party traveled to Chihuahua, where he was allowed to sell his goods for profit. In the spring of 1808, Clamorgan's party returned to St. Louis by way of Texas and Natchitoches in lower Louisiana Territory.[1]

Considering Clamorgan's age, his accomplishment deserved more attention than it received, but upon his return to St. Louis, word of his success spread rapidly among traders. Manuel Lisa, who meantime had become involved in the fur trade on the upper Missouri, was delighted with the prospect of establishing regular trade with Santa Fe. Pike had reported, and in all likelihood Clamorgan related the same news, that in Santa Fe a hundred pounds of flour sold for two dollars, a mule load of salt cost five dollars, and a yard of superfine cloth cost twenty-five dollars. The same goods cost far less in St. Louis. It was only natural that the news was encouraging to St. Louis merchants, especially Joseph McLanahan, James Patterson, and Reuben Smith, a retired lieutenant in the U.S. Army. These three men, along with Manuel Blanco, a guide, and three black slaves, left St. Genevieve south of St. Louis with trade goods on December 20, 1809, and started for Santa Fe.

The fact that they made the journey during the winter was unusual, but the weather was preternaturally mild as the party followed an almost direct western course through the Osage and Pawnee nations before turning southwest. Less than three months after leaving St. Louis, they arrived at Taos, located north of Santa Fe, in February 1810. McLanahan, Patterson, and Smith carried with them a letter of introduction written by Father James Maxwell of St. Genevieve, but it did not help them with Spanish authorities. The Americans were soon arrested and taken to Santa Fe. Believing the trading goods were only a blind to shield their real purpose as American spies, the Spanish placed the Americans in chains and took them south to Chihuahua. One account says that the three Americans were forced to work in the Spanish mines under conditions of extreme hardship for two years before being released. They then made their way east, arriving at Natchitoches in April 1812 and continuing north until they reached St. Louis.[2]

The same year the three men returned to St. Louis, Manuel Lisa sent Charles Sanguinet to locate Jean-Baptiste Champlain, one of Lisa's best trappers. Champlain had not returned from the Platte River, where Spaniards reportedly sent annual expeditions to trade with the Arapaho Indians. Sanguinet carried a letter from Lisa to the Spanish expressing a desire to open trade. Lisa hoped Sanguinet would meet Spaniards who would lead the party to Santa Fe. To show he was serious about trading, Lisa sent much merchandise with Sanguinet, but Sanguinet never met any Spaniards, nor did he attempt to reach Santa Fe. He soon returned to St. Louis with the news that Champlain had been killed by Blackfoot Indians on the upper Arkansas River and that hostile Indians blocked the trail to Santa Fe. Lisa, frustrated by the turn of events, gave up his dream of opening trade with Santa Fe and turned his full attention toward the fur trade on the upper Missouri and in the Rocky Mountains. Lisa would go on to establish the Missouri Fur Company and would become the prototype of the "mountain man."[3]

While Lisa was awaiting word of Champlain's fate in December 1812, still another American party, moved by rumors that mercantile restrictions had been lifted, left St. Louis for Santa Fe. One of the Americans was Robert McKnight, a twenty-two-year-old Virginian, who had arrived in St. Louis perhaps two years earlier. He often visited with James Baird, an older man of forty-five, who made a living by constructing and selling beaver traps in his St. Louis blacksmith shop. There Baird, McKnight, and others heard stories from trappers and traders about the money to be made trading at Santa Fe. Baird, McKnight, Benjamin Shreve, and Michael McDonogh formed a partnership and hired five men and an interpreter. In late April 1812, their party left St. Louis on horseback with several mules laden with ten thousand dollars in trading goods, including velvets, silks, linens, and sheer muslins chosen to catch the fancy of women in New Mexico. Several days after the group left St. Louis, William Becknell—on instructions from James and Jesse Morrison, merchants at St. Charles, Missouri, across the Missouri River northwest of St. Louis—delivered a horse and a gun to McKnight somewhere in what is now central Missouri. The event itself is not significant except for the involvement of Becknell, who would later become known as the "Father of the Santa Fe Trail." As for McKnight and his party, they followed a direct route west across what is now Missouri, Kansas, and part of Colorado, where they turned south through Raton Pass to Taos. There they were arrested on orders from the governor and taken to Santa Fe, where their goods were confiscated and sold at auction to pay for their room and board, eighteen cents a day per man. After a brief time in Santa Fe, the Americans were taken south to Chihuahua and held for a time in an old military hospital before they were separated and each given a job to perform, some in different mines around Chihuahua, at least one as a servant. After eight years as prisoners, they were released in May 1820 after the king of Spain issued a decree directing that all foreigners imprisoned in the viceroyalty of Mexico should be freed. Baird is believed to have traveled alone back to St. Louis.[4]

Meantime, while some men in Missouri Territory dreamed of trading with Santa Fe, others dreamed of trading with Indians in Spanish territory and of trapping beaver for their pelts. An adventurer who did more than dream was Joseph Philibert, who obtained a license to trade with the Arapaho Indians on the eastern slopes of the Rocky Mountains. He

"A Citadel of the Plains" is the title of this Frederic Remington illustration, which appeared in Henry Inman's The Old Santa Fe Trail *(1897).* (Author's Collection)

and eighteen Frenchmen left St. Louis in April 1813 and traveled westward. By September they had crossed the mountains into the San Luis Valley and established a hunting camp. During the days that followed, two of Philibert's men looking for beaver dams were captured by Spaniards catching wild horses and taken to Santa Fe for questioning. Soon more than two hundred Spanish soldiers arrived at Philibert's camp, arrested everyone, and took them to Santa Fe. Philibert and his men were held for fifty days and then released, but their furs and goods were confiscated to pay the expense of their captivity. They were permitted to remain in Taos until February 1815, when they headed east. When they reached St. Louis, the July 29, 1815, *Missouri Gazette* told of their return and of Philibert's "broken fortune" and "ruinous business." Philibert, however, quietly related to two St. Louis merchants, Auguste P. Chouteau and Julius De Mun, that much profit could be found in the southern Rocky Mountains.[5]

By early September 1815, Chouteau and De Mun had organized their own expedition and on September 10 left St. Louis bound for the mountains, ostensibly to trap beaver. Their expedition consisted of forty-six

men, and their trip was uneventful as they pushed westward to the headwaters of the Arkansas River. There they camped on the Huerfano River
south of the Arkansas in land claimed by Spain. As Chouteau and the
trappers set about to trap beaver, De Mun, who spoke Spanish, went to
Santa Fe to request permission from the Spanish governor to trap on the
Rio Grande. He was denied permission and returned to camp, where
Chouteau and others had trapped many beaver. While Chouteau and
the others remained behind to continue trapping, De Mun returned to
St. Louis to obtain more supplies. De Mun and Chouteau agreed to meet
a few months later at the mouth of the Kansas River, where Kansas City,
Missouri, stands today.

After De Mun reached St. Louis, Chouteau and the trappers started
down the Arkansas River with forty-four packs of furs. In what is now
western Kansas, the party was attacked by Pawnee Indians and took cover
on an island in the Arkansas River that afterward was called "Chouteau's
Island." There they piled their fur packs and other baggage to make a
fort before battling the Indians. Seven Pawnees were killed while one of
Chouteau's party was killed and three others wounded. After the
Pawnees departed, Chouteau and his party continued down the Arkansas River and then overland to the mouth of the Kansas River, where they
placed the packs of furs on barges bound for St. Louis. With a new supply of goods brought by De Mun, he, Chouteau, and the trappers followed the Arkansas River westward and set up camp in the Sangre de
Cristo Pass at the headwaters of the Huerfano River.

Late in 1816, De Mun headed for Santa Fe again to seek permission
to trap in Spanish territory. This time he received a stern warning from
the governor to stay out of Spanish territory. De Mun returned to Chouteau and the others and they moved their camp farther down the Huerfano to wait for winter to end. There friendly Spanish traders provided
the group with bread, flour, and other supplies every week or so. In con-
versations with the Spanish traders, Chouteau and De Mun were encouraged that they might now receive permission to trap in Spanish territory.
Thus, in March 1817, De Mun again set out for Santa Fe. He had gone as
far as Taos when he was arrested by two hundred Spanish soldiers investigating a report that he and Chouteau had built a fort housing twenty
thousand American soldiers on the Purgatoire River. The soldiers led De
Mun back to his camp. When they found no American soldiers, they confiscated the trappers' furs and goods and ordered them to return to St.
Louis. Chouteau and De Mun, fearful of meeting Pawnees and of losing
the profits of their spring trade, persuaded the soldiers to let them travel
north instead of east. The expedition left but soon returned and set up

camp. On May 24, 1817, Spanish soldiers raided the camp, arrested everyone, and took them to Santa Fe. Chouteau and De Mun were put in chains and thrown into jail. There they lingered for forty-four days before being tried. Both men were sentenced to be stripped of their property and forced to kneel and kiss the Spanish document that had deprived them of their two years' worth of labor. Each man was given one inferior horse and ordered to leave New Mexico. When they reached present-day Kansas, Chouteau remained but De Mun and Philibert continued east to St. Louis, arriving there early in September 1817. They claimed a loss of more than thirty thousand dollars in fur, trading goods, and other property. Neither man ever made another trading trip to the Rocky Mountains.[6]

The following year, 1818, another Missouri trader devised a scheme to engage in the Santa Fe trade without having to travel all the way to Santa Fe. The trader, whose name is not known, made arrangements with a Mexican trader to meet at the international boundary and exchange trade goods and thereby avoid being arrested by Mexican authorities. Jedediah Smith, a twenty-year-old from present-day Bainbridge, New York, learned of the trader's plan to travel west across the plains, asked to go along with at least one packhorse of trading merchandise, and was told he could. Smith had left home as a teenager and clerked on a ship on Lake Erie before going to St. Louis, where he met the trader. Smith and two other men joined the trader in his journey west with packhorses and mules in hopes of then accompanying the Mexican trader back to Santa Fe.

Crossing what is now Kansas, Jedediah Smith carried a rifle, but he also kept handy a long string bow and quiver of arrows. On their journey one man asked Smith why he also carried a bow, like an Indian, when he had a good rifle and knew how to use it. Smith, the story goes, replied that he could use the bow with certainty, and that it had almost the range of his rifle and could kill any ordinary game. Smith said he believed that a man with a good horse, armed with a bow, could kill more buffalo out of a herd than a man armed with a rifle. Pointing to a hawk about seventy-five yards away, the man asked Smith if he could hit it. Smith replied by raising his bow and piercing the hawk. Later, when the party reached a herd of buffalo, Smith killed two with his bow and arrows.

When the caravan reached a spot near where Dodge City, Kansas, stands today, the Missouri trader, Smith, and the others waited for the Mexican trader. He did not come. After several days the American trader gave up and readied himself to start back toward Missouri and trade with the Indians. Smith told the trader that he would go on to Santa Fe with

The artist Frederic Remington titled this illustration "A Pack Train to Santa Fe, 1820." It appeared in Henry Inman's The Old Santa Fe Trail *(1897).* (Author's Collection)

the few trading goods his packhorse carried. The trader strongly advised him against the trip since Smith was inexperienced in plains and mountain travel, but Smith said he had made up his mind to go. The two other men traveling with the caravan said they would join Smith, and the following day they left the Missouri trader and crossed the Arkansas River into Mexican territory.

That night they camped in a small grove of trees on a creek in what is now Meade County, Kansas. The following day the three men saw a cloud of dust. They approached it with care and soon observed a party of Mexicans. Smith and his companions joined the Mexicans and learned that one of them was the trader who had planned to meet the American along the Arkansas River. When Smith told them that the American trader had given up and left, the Mexicans decided to return to Santa Fe. They let the three Americans accompany them, but before reaching Santa Fe a small band of Comanche Indians attacked the party. Thanks to the Americans and their rifles, they fought off the Indians.

What happened next is unclear, but Smith apparently disposed of his small stock of trading merchandise at Santa Fe without any interference from Mexican authorities. He then traveled north to Taos and turned west, later seeing the Great Salt Lake before crossing back over the Rocky Mountains and returning east following the Platte River. There he fell in with some trappers returning to St. Louis.[7]

THE NEW SPIRIT of freedom that motivated post-Revolutionary Americans had already resulted in a restless stream of humanity moving westward at the time of the U.S. Louisiana Purchase. Americans arrived in St. Louis even before upper Louisiana was officially turned over to the United States early in 1804. They continued to follow the earlier pattern of settling along the major waterways, which offered the best means of transportation, and beyond St. Louis new settlements began appearing along the Missouri River. Between 1804 and 1810, the population of what became Missouri doubled. By 1817, perhaps sixty thousand people had settled in St. Louis and westward along the Missouri River; the first and largest settlement west of St. Louis was the town of Franklin, on the Missouri about two hundred miles upriver from St. Louis.

The seeds of the town were planted about 1808, when Colonel Benjamin Cooper of Kentucky settled on some bottomland on the Missouri's north bank. By 1810, a colony of about 150 families, mostly from Kentucky, had joined him on what had become known as Cooper's Bottom. In 1816, Cooper's Bottom became part of the newly organized Howard County, named in honor of General Benjamin Howard, a Kentucky congressman. As counties go, it was huge, including all of that part of present-day Missouri north of the Osage River and west of Cedar Creek and the dividing ridge between the Mississippi and Missouri rivers. Its territory was later divided into thirty-one counties, nineteen north and twelve south of the Missouri River, besides parts of nine others.

Franklin was established in 1817, after settlers in Cooper's Bottom donated fifty acres for a town named after Benjamin Franklin. The new town, which became the seat of Howard County, had a public square two acres in size, and its principal streets were eighty-seven feet wide. Franklin grew rapidly, and before its first year ended, the town had 120 log houses, several two-story frame houses, two brick buildings, thirteen stores, four taverns, two blacksmith shops, two large steam mills, two billiard halls, a courthouse, a log jail, a post office, and the small newspaper office where the weekly *Missouri Intelligencer and Boon's Lick Advertiser,* started in 1817, was published. "Boon's (or Boone's) Lick"—which was dropped from the newspaper's masthead in late November 1819—was the name given to an immense tract of land lying on both sides of the Missouri River north and west of where the Osage River flows into the Missouri east of modern Jefferson City, Missouri, on to the western and northern territorial borders of Missouri. Franklin was located toward the eastern part of Boone's Lick, and in the minds of most settlers was its capital. The name came from Boone's Lick Springs, a place about eight miles from Franklin, where the upward seepage of chemical brines produced salt. Daniel Boone's sons, Nathan and Daniel Morgan Boone, began to gather the salt about 1807 and ship it down the river to St. Louis. This vast ill-defined region was described as having "rich agricultural land—alluvial, prairie, and rolling—and a fair proportion of timber."[8]

The rapid influx of immigrants into Boone's Lick Country was noted by the *Missouri Intelligencer and Boon's Lick Advertiser* on November 19, 1819:

> The emigration to this territory and particularly to this country, during the present season, almost exceeds belief. Those who have arrived in this quarter are principally from Kentucky, Tennessee, etc. Immense numbers of wagons, carriages, carts, etc., with families have for some time past been daily arriving. During the month of October it is stated that no less than 271 wagons and four-wheeled carriages and carts passed near St. Charles, bound principally for Boon's [*sic*] Lick. It is calculated that the number of persons accompanying these wagons could not be less than 3,000.

From the arrival of the first settlers west of St. Louis, farming was the chief occupation, but profits were limited because there was no system for selling and shipping produce to other markets. Transportation was a major problem. Until 1819, the most reliable means of reaching St. Louis from Franklin was over a trail that became known as the Boone's Lick Road. The poor economic conditions west of St. Louis produced a constant shortage of money and reinforced the barter system, but money was necessary to purchase new lands. Missourians seeking money turned to other businesses to supplement their meager agricultural incomes. Some became hunters and trappers. Others entered the fur trade, a business that annually totaled thousands of dollars. Still others opened general stores and other businesses to serve the settlers.

Life in and around Franklin was simple. In fact, people were reared in simplicity, lived in simplicity, and were happy in simplicity. Ruffles, fine laces, kid gloves, false curls, rings, combs, and jewels were nearly unknown. Wild meat was plentiful. Many settlers had small patches of corn, which during the early days was beaten in a mortar. The meal was made into a coarse but wholesome bread, though it contained much grit. Johnnycake and pones were served at the midday meal, and mush and milk was the favorite dish for supper. Many kinds of greens, such as dock and poke, were eaten. In season, the settlers enjoyed roasting ears of corn, pumpkins, beans, squash, and potatoes. Coffee and tea were used sparingly because they were scarce, and the hardy pioneer thought them fit only for children since they would not "stick to the ribs." Maple sugar was used, as was honey, which was only five cents a pound. Butter was the same price, while eggs cost only three cents a dozen. Women made nearly all the clothing needed by a family, and every house contained a carding loom and spinning wheel, which were considered as necessary for women as a rifle was for men.

Life gradually changed with the arrival of the steamboat. The first steamboat to moor at the St. Louis landing was the *General Pike,* commanded by Captain Jacob Reed, on August 2, 1817. But it never went up the Missouri River, nor did the *Constitution,* St. Louis's second steamboat, which arrived in October 1817. The Missouri River was shallower than the Mississippi. The first steamboat to prove the Missouri navigable was the *Independence* out of Louisville, Kentucky, in 1819. Constructed at Pittsburgh for use on shallow rivers, the *Independence* pushed up the Missouri River to Franklin. When the steamboat reached Franklin seven years after the settlement was founded, the *Missouri Intelligencer and Boon's Lick Advertiser,* May 28, 1819, reported:

> With no ordinary sense of pleasure we announce the arrival this morning, at this place, of the elegant STEAMBOAT Independence. Captain Nelson, in seven *sailing* days (but thirteen from the time of his departure) from St. Louis with passengers, and a cargo of flour, whisky, sugar, iron castings, etc., being the First *Steamboat that ever attempted the ascending of the Missouri.* She was joyfully met by the inhabitants of Franklin and saluted by the firing of cannon, which was returned by the Independence. The grand *desideratum,* the important fact is now ascertained, that Steamboats can safely navigate the Missouri River.

It only took the *Independence* three days to return to St. Louis from Franklin.[9]

This is an artist's depiction of the steamboat Western Engineer *as it appeared in 1819.* (Courtesy Kansas State Historical Society)

Less than three months later, the townspeople of Franklin turned out to see another steamboat approaching. It was the *Western Engineer,* built by the U.S. government at Pittsburgh for use on the Missouri River. The boat was seventy-five feet in length and thirteen feet wide, and drew nineteen inches of water. Aboard were Major Stephen H. Long—who had convinced President James Monroe that the upper Missouri should be explored with a steamboat—and a group of scientists including Thomas Say and Titian Ramsay Peale. To mystify and impress Indians along the river, the bow of the *Western Engineer* was shaped like the neck and head of a strange aquatic monster from whose open mouth rolled clouds of smoke. The steam engine and other equipment were hidden from view by a superstructure, as was the paddle wheel at the stern, which violently agitated the water as if it were the tail of the "monster."[10]

As the *Western Engineer* passed Franklin, located on the north bank of the Missouri, Long noted in his journal that on the south bank was another settlement consisting of eight houses on much higher ground. He was describing what would become Boonville, Missouri. Five miles upriver, across the La Mine River, stood another settlement called La Mine, and about ten miles to the northwest stood Arrow Rock. From these villages settlers came to the riverbanks to watch the *Western Engineer* as it slowly made its way up the Missouri. Many days later, after passing the spot where Kansas City, Missouri, now stands, and where the Missouri River turns north, the steamboat continued on to what is now Council Bluffs, Iowa. There the expedition spent the winter. Many men died of scurvy, and by spring the expedition was abandoned. It had been a disaster. Long was then directed to explore the vast plains stretching westward to the Rocky Mountains, which he did. When Long returned east, Dr. Edwin James, a physician who had accompanied him, prepared the official report of the expedition. Whereas Zebulon Pike, fourteen years earlier, had referred to the vast expanse of open country crossed by Long as the Great Sandy Desert and compared it to the Sahara, Long's report described it as the Great American Desert, a term that soon found its way onto maps and remained fixed in the American mind until after the Civil War.[11]

As more steamboats plied the Missouri River, to the south Spanish Texas was invaded by several armed bands of Americans bent on fomenting insurrection. It is easy to understand why Spanish officials patrolled thousands of miles of New Spain's mostly undefined border with Louisiana Territory trying to keep Americans out, especially traders who might attempt to invade New Mexico. At the same time the winds of revolution were blowing across New Spain. Colonists objected to Spain's attempt to strengthen its political control while limiting the power of the Catholic church. Then, too, New Spain was influenced by the Enlightenment, an intellectual movement that had started in Europe before the French Revolution and challenged many political and social institutions, such as the monarchy, class distinctions, and religion. Many colonists in New Spain had read the works of Jean-Jacques Rousseau and others, and began to question the legitimacy of New Spain's colonial relationship with Spain. The colonists were also influenced by the political examples of the American and French revolutions, both of which overthrew a monarchy and established a republican form of government.

In the fall of 1810, Father Miguel Hidalgo y Costilla, who was familiar with the ideas of the Enlightenment, launched a revolt to free New Spain from Spanish rule. The attempt failed, and he was captured and executed. But others kept the movement alive. Meantime, after years of failing to agree upon a definite boundary between the United States and New Spain, the two countries signed a treaty on February 22, 1819, setting the Arkansas River as the boundary. Spain also ceded Florida and its claim to Oregon to the United States. The following year a revolution in Spain established a liberal Spanish constitution that emphasized repre-

sentative government and individual liberty for all citizens. The elite in
New Spain did not like the change and, combining forces with colonists
they had previously opposed, declared independence from Spain in
1821, calling their new nation Mexico, a name derived from the Mexica
people who centuries earlier had founded the Aztec empire. In the
meantime in Missouri Territory, residents were pushing for statehood,
trying to survive the economic problems caused by the national panic of
1819, and eagerly following news of what was occurring in New Spain. It
was a time of change.

William Becknell, like so many other Missourians, faced economic
ruin because of the panic. Becknell, born in Virginia about 1787, moved
to St. Charles in 1810, two years before Missouri Territory was carved out
of Louisiana Territory. He found work gathering salt at Boone's Lick
Spring near Franklin and, as already noted, delivered a horse and a gun
to Robert McKnight in 1812. The following year, Becknell joined a company of U.S. Mounted Rangers commanded by Daniel Morgan Boone,
son of Daniel Boone, to fight in the War of 1812. As first sergeant he
helped to construct forts to protect Missouri Territory against Indians
and the British. In 1814, promoted to ensign, Becknell was in a unit
commanded by Major Zachary Taylor that was beaten by Indians in a battle where the city of Davenport now stands in eastern Iowa. When the
war ended in 1815, Becknell returned to Missouri Territory and
resumed gathering salt at Boone's Lick. Two years later, Becknell married, his first wife having died earlier. He borrowed money, purchased
two lots in Franklin, and operated a ferry on the Missouri River near
Arrow Rock, northwest of Franklin. But another two years later, the
panic of 1819 threatened him with financial ruin. He faced lawsuits
from creditors and was arrested, but a friend paid the bond.

Becknell believed he could salvage his financial affairs through trading in Santa Fe. By then he had heard that Mexico had proclaimed its
independence from Spain about five months earlier, although whether
Spain had given Mexico its freedom was not known. Desperate to solve
his financial problems, Becknell inserted a lengthy notice in the *Missouri
Intelligencer* on June 25, 1821. He advised readers that a company of men
would be organized to go westward "for the purpose of trading Horses &
Mules, and catching Wild Animals of every description." Becknell then
outlined in detail what would be expected of each man in the company:

> Every man will fit himself for the trip, with a horse, a good rifle, and as
> much ammunition as the company may think necessary for a tour or
> 3 months trip, and sufficient clothing to keep him warm and comfort-

able. Every man will furnish an equal part of the fitting out for trade, and receive an equal part of the product. If the company consists of 30 or more men, 10 dollars a man will answer to purchase the quantity of merchandise required to trade on.

No man shall receive more than another for his services, unless he furnishes more, and is pointedly agreed on by the company before we start. . . . There will be no dividend until we return to the north side of the Missouri river, where all persons concerned shall have timely notice to attend and receive their share of profits. It is requisite that every 8 men shall have a pack horse, an ax, and a tent to secure them from the inclemency of bad weather.

I think it necessary for the good order and regulation of the company that every man shall be bound by a [*sic*] oath to submit to such orders and rules as the company when assembled shall think proper to enforce.

Becknell added that he would be responsible for applying to the governor of Missouri Territory for permission to make the trip. He said that anyone interested, up to seventy in number, should sign up by August 4 and then meet at the farm of Ezekiel Williams, about five miles from Franklin, to "procure a pilot and appoint officers to the company."

Although Becknell's notice made no reference to the company's destination, there is little question that he had his eyes on Santa Fe from the beginning. No one in Missouri knew whether Mexican independence had become a reality, and if the revolution had failed, Becknell did not want to inform Spanish diplomats in the United States of his plan because they, in turn, could have warned Spaniards in New Mexico of his coming. Reference to trading merchandise hinted at the company's real purpose, which is what was discussed in early August, when Becknell and the seventeen men who had signed up gathered at Williams's farm to organize the company. Williams was the only man present with considerable experience on the plains. He undoubtedly related stories about the region the company would be crossing and about men he had known who had gone to Santa Fe only to be taken prisoner by the Spanish— stories that must have whetted the appetites of the Missourians in the company.[12]

Becknell received permission for the expedition from the governor of Missouri Territory at about the same time that Missouri was admitted to the Union as the twenty-fourth state, on August 10, 1821. Exactly how many men showed up on September 1, 1821, is not clear. One account says only four men appeared, but others suggest that there were twenty-one men when Becknell's party on horseback, with several packhorses containing trading goods, crossed the Missouri River at Arrow Rock and headed west. When they arrived at Fort Osage, about eleven miles east of present-day Kansas City, Missouri, George C. Sibley, the government factor, shared his knowledge about New Mexico with Becknell. Sibley had boarded in the eastern home of Dr. John H. Robinson, the member of Zebulon Pike's expedition of 1806 who had mapped the route, and was

Fort Osage, Missouri, as it appears today. This early trading post on the Santa Fe Trail, located on a high bank close to the Missouri River, has been restored and is now a tourist attraction. Passing the spot in 1804, the explorers Lewis and Clark thought it was a good place to build a fort. Four years later construction began. (Courtesy Missouri Department of Tourism)

later visited by Robinson at Fort Osage. From him Becknell probably gained valuable information about what route to follow and about conditions in New Mexico.

From Fort Osage, Becknell and his company moved westward, crossing the Osage River on September 20. Illness and rain slowed travel, but by the time they reached the sandy banks of the Arkansas River in what is now Kansas on September 24, they had seen buffalo and antelope in large numbers. On the plains they used buffalo chips to fuel their cooking fires, since trees were scarce except along the banks of streams.

Later, in putting his recollections on paper, Becknell recalled:

> The next day we crossed the Arkansas at a place where it is not more than eighteen inches deep, and encamped on the south bank. We left our encampment early the next morning, and about noon came to a large settlement or town of prairie dogs, which appeared to cover a surface of ten acres. They burrow in the earth, are of a dark brown color, about the size of a pup five or six weeks old, which they nearly resemble in every respect except the ears, which are more like those of a possum. Having a desire to taste its flesh, I killed one, a small part of which I roasted, but found it strong and unpalatable. Their sense of hearing is acute, and their apprehension of danger so great that the least noise of approach frightens them to their holes, from which they make continual and vehement barking until a person approaches within fifty or sixty yards of them, they then take to their holes with their heads elevated above the ground and continue barking until the approach is very near, when they disappear instantaneously. They often sit erect, with their fore legs hanging down like a bear. We found here a ludicrous looking animal [probably a badger], perfectly unknown to any one of our company; it was about the size of a raccoon, of a light gray color, had uncommonly fine fur, small eyes, and was almost covered with long shaggy hair; its toe nails were from one and a half to two inches in length; its meat was tender and delicious. We also killed one of the rabbit species as large as a common fox; it was of a gray color, but its ears and tail were black. It exhibited an agility in running a short distance after it was shot which exceeded anything of the kind we had ever witnessed.[13]

As Becknell and his party followed the Arkansas River, they saw more buffalo, killing one for food, and later they saw five wild horses. Becknell described the water in the river as clear, "although the current is much more rapid than where we first struck it. Its bed has gradually become narrower, and its channel consequently deeper. The grass in the low lands is still verdant, but in the high prairie it is so short that a rattlesnake, of which there are vast numbers here, may be seen at the distance of fifty yards; they inhabit holes in the ground."[14]

The party continued following the Arkansas River until near where Las Animas, southeastern Colorado, stands today. They turned southwestward and followed the Purgatoire River, which flows into the

Arkansas River. On November 1, 1821, light snow began falling and there was a strong northwest wind. Becknell recalled: "Having been now traveling about fifty days, our diet being altogether different from what we had been accustomed to; and expected hardships and obstacles occurring almost daily, our company is much discouraged; but the prospect of a near termination of our journey excites hope and redoubled exertion, although our horses are so reduced that we only travel from eight to fifteen miles per day. We found game scarce near the mountains, and one night encamped without wood or water."[15]

On Tuesday morning, November 13, 1821, about ten weeks after leaving Arrow Rock, Becknell and his party met a group of Spanish soldiers in what is now eastern New Mexico. The Spaniards were very friendly but spoke no English, and no one in Becknell's party spoke Spanish. The two groups camped together for the night, and the following morning the soldiers took the Americans to the village of San Miguel del Bado on the Pecos River. Its inhabitants, Becknell recalled, "gave us grateful evidence of civility and welcome." He met a Frenchman in the village who could speak Spanish. Becknell possessed enough French to communicate with the man, so he was hired as an interpreter. It was probably from him that Becknell learned the Mexican Revolution had been successful, although he may have guessed as much from the warm reception he and his men received. Soon after arriving in Santa Fe, Becknell met with Governor Facundo Melgares, who expressed his desire that Americans should come to Santa Fe. "If any wished to emigrate," Bucknell recorded the governor as saying, "it would give him pleasure to afford them every facility." After the revolution succeeded, Governor Melgares in New Mexico had been advised by a circular from the new government in Mexico City that, among other things, stated, "With respect to foreign nations, we shall maintain harmony with all, commercial relations, and whatever else may be appropriate."

Becknell and his company turned a handsome profit trading, and Becknell had time to observe the people. He later wrote that they

> lived in a state of extreme indolence and ignorance. Their mechanical improvements are very limited, and they appear to know little of the benefit of industry, or the advantage of the arts. Corn, rice and wheat are their principal productions; they have very few garden vegetables, except the onion, which grows large and abundantly; the seeds are planted nearly a foot apart, and produce onions from four to six inches in diameter. Their atmosphere is remarkably dry, and rain is uncommon, except in the months of July and August. To rem-

edy this inconvenience, they substitute, with tolerable advantage, the numerous streams which descend from the mountains, by damming them up, and conveying the water over their farms in ditches. Their domestic animals consist chiefly of sheep, goats, mules and asses. None but the wealthy have horses and hogs. Like the French, they live in villages; the rich keeping the poor in dependence and subjection. Laborers are hired for about three dollars per month; their general employment is that of herdsmen, and to guard their flocks from a nation of Indians called Navohoes [*sic*], who sometimes murder the guards and drive away their mules and sheep. The circumstance of their farms being wholly unfenced, obliges them to keep their stock some distance from home.[16]

About two weeks later, another party of Americans, led by John Mc-Knight and Thomas James, arrived in Santa Fe. Becknell and company's brief monopoly on American trade in New Mexico ended. Meantime, Becknell's company gathered to talk. What they discussed is not known, but Becknell later recalled that all but one member of the company decided to remain in New Mexico, perhaps to consolidate or expand their mercantile connections while Becknell returned to Missouri for more trading goods. After saying their good-byes, Becknell and a man named M'Laughlin left New Mexico on December 13, 1821, and headed back to Missouri with Spanish blankets, specie, mules, and burros acquired by trading. These mules and burros were probably the first to cross the plains between New Mexico and Missouri. According to Becknell's account, he took "a different course from that pursued on our way out, which considerably shortened the route." Becknell and M'Laughlin reached Fort Osage and continued on to Franklin. They arrived there on January 30, 1822, forty-eight days after leaving Santa Fe. Years later, H. H. Harris, whose father lived near the Becknell home in Franklin, recalled: "My father saw them unload when they returned, and when their rawhide packages of silver dollars were dumped on the sidewalk one of the men cut the thongs and the money spilled out and clinking on the stone pavement rolled into the gutter. Everyone was excited and the next spring another expedition was sent out."[17]

William Becknell had gambled and won. The dream of profit from trading in Santa Fe had been realized. The smell of success was in the air. Becknell spent time with his family but soon began planning for a second expedition to Santa Fe in the spring.

FIVE

The Santa Fe Trail, 1822-1825

Perseverance is more prevailing than violence; and many things which cannot be overcome when they are together yield themselves up when taken little by little.

—Plutarch

THE ST. LOUIS MERCHANT John McKnight, the trader Thomas James, his brother John, and six other men might very well have been the first Americans to open trade with Santa Fe had they followed a direct overland route westward from Missouri. They did not. On September 1, 1821, a few weeks before William Becknell and his party left Franklin, Missouri, overland for Santa Fe, the McKnight-James party loaded their twelve thousand dollars in trade goods on a keelboat at St. Louis and descended the Mississippi River to its junction with the Arkansas River, north of present-day Arkansas City, Arkansas. There they turned their keelboat west up the Arkansas River. Travel against the current was slow. Their vessel, perhaps sixty-five feet long and fifteen feet wide, had a keel running from bow to stern that gave the boat its name. Rising from the deck some four or five feet was the cargo box, cut off at each end, making it shorter than the boat. The boat was moved upstream by men onshore who pulled a rope or *cordelle* fastened to the top of the craft's mast. The rope passed through a ring fastened by a short line to the boat, thereby helping to guide it. Where the men could not pull the rope from the river's bank, poles were used to propel the boat. Planting their poles on the river bottom, pointing downstream, the men would push steadily against them and at the same time walk toward the stern on each side of the boat. On a good day a keelboat might cover fifteen miles.

About twenty-five miles beyond the mouth of the Cimarron River west of present-day Hominy, Oklahoma, they stopped because of low water in the Arkansas River. Leaving two men to guard the remaining trade goods, McKnight, Thomas and John James, and the others took some of their goods and followed a trail east to an Osage Indian village located near what is now Claremore, Oklahoma. There they traded for twenty-three horses from the Indians and then returned to the Arkansas River, where they rejoined the two men left to watch the trade goods that were loaded on the horses. They then set out overland, crossing what is now western Oklahoma and the Texas Panhandle into New Mexico. Years later, Thomas James claimed that his party reached Santa Fe on December 1, 1821, two weeks after William Becknell is known to have arrived, but neither man mentions the other in his recollections. It is difficult to imagine that they would not have met if in Santa Fe at the same time. James' memory may have been faulty.[1]

McKnight, James, and the rest of the party received a warm welcome in Santa Fe. While the James brothers and the others began trading, McKnight borrowed some money from Thomas James and headed south into Mexico to find his brother Robert, who had been a prisoner in New Mexico since his ill-fated trading expedition of 1812. John McKnight traveled about sixteen hundred miles south to Durango, where he located his brother, who had been released from prison. Together they started for Santa Fe, reaching it in April 1822.

Meantime, money became scarce in Santa Fe, and the James group could not sell all of the trading goods. Thomas James obtained permission to take goods to Sonora, where money supposedly was more plentiful, but he and his brother decided against making the journey and sold their goods to a Spaniard for a thousand dollars and an equal sum in horses and mules. Early in June 1822, the McKnight-James party left Santa Fe for Taos. Hugh Glenn, who had come west with Jacob Fowler to trade and trap, joined the party as it traveled toward Taos, about sixty miles to the northeast. There, Jacob Fowler, a seasoned plainsman in his late fifties, also joined the party as it turned east toward Missouri with 140 horses and mules. Eighty-three of the animals belonged to the McKnight-James party. Following the Arkansas River, the Missouri-bound traders met on June 13 a west-bound trading party consisting of Benjamin Cooper, the captain, his nephews Braxton and Stephen Cooper, Joel Walker, and ten other men from Franklin, Missouri. The Cooper party's pack animals carried four to five thousand dollars in trading goods. The two parties exchanged news and then continued their journeys.[2]

The James-McKnight party followed the Osage Trail to the Neosho River, where Osage Indians succeeded in stealing thirty-eight of their animals. McKnight, James, and several others then traveled by canoe and pirogue down the Osage and Missouri Rivers to St. Louis, arriving in mid-July. The other men in their party went overland, herding the remaining horses and mules.

The Glenn-Fowler party followed a circuitous route overland to avoid Indians. Somewhere in what is today Franklin County, Kansas, they made an unbelievable discovery. Fowler reined in his horse, dismounted, and squatted on the ground to look at the signs in the earth. Glenn and other men in the party also dismounted, inspected the signs, and shook their heads in amazement. None of them had ever seen such a sight on the plains. It was June 28, 1822, as Fowler later wrote in his diary. He and the other men were about fifty miles west of the Missouri border. Clearly visible in the ground before them were wagon tracks. Wagons were unheard of west of Missouri, except in New Mexico. Fowler and the others followed the tracks for about two days before losing them. Whether they realized their significance is not known. The tracks had been made by the first wagons to cross the plains from the east, wagons used in William Becknell's second expedition to Santa Fe.[3]

Becknell, after returning to Missouri from his first successful trading venture in Santa Fe, spent much of the winter of 1822 preparing to take a larger group back to Santa Fe. At one point he apparently met Jedediah Smith, who had returned to Missouri from Ohio after visiting his brother. Having traveled to Santa Fe over the dry route from the Arkansas River to the Cimarron, Smith convinced Becknell that he could use wagons to carry merchandise. Smith agreed to guide Becknell and his wagons to Santa Fe and probably either took some trade goods along or invested in Becknell's second trading venture.[4]

Becknell formed a company of twenty-one men, who purchased three thousand dollars' worth of trade goods. They loaded the merchandise onto three farm wagons, and on May 22, 1822, crossed the Arrow Rock ferry. By early June the company had entered what is now Kansas. As Becknell later recalled:

No obstacle obstructed our progress until we arrived at the Arkansas [near present-day Great Bend], which river we crossed with some difficulty, and encamped on the south side. About midnight our horses were frightened by buffalo, and all strayed—20 were missing. Eight of us, after appointing a place of rendezvous, went in pursuit of them in different directions, and found eighteen. Two of the company discovered some Indians, and being suspicious of their intentions, thought to avoid them by returning to camp; but they were overtaken, stripped, barbarously whipped, and robbed of their horses, guns and clothes. They came in about midnight, and the circumstance occasioned considerable alarm. We had a strong desire to punish the rascally Osages, who commit outrages on those very citizens from whom they receive regular annuities. One other man was taken by the same party to their camp, and probably would have shared like treatment, had not the presence of Mr. Choteau restrained their savage disposition.[5]

"Mr. Choteau" was none other than Auguste P. Chouteau, the St. Louis trader. He sent word to Becknell that he had recovered the horses and guns which had been taken from the men and requested that Becknell come to the Indian camp the following morning to get them. But the next morning, when Becknell and his men arrived, the camp was deserted. He found a note written on bark instructing him to follow Chouteau up a nearby river, but Becknell, suspecting treachery, refused, and he and his men returned to their own camp.

Becknell and his men were soon joined in their camp by another company of traders headed by John Heath. Together both parties continued westward up the south bank of the Arkansas River for eight days, and near where Dodge City, Kansas, stands today they struck southwest across the sand hills, entering what became known as the Cimarron Desert. Remembering the difficulties his party had experienced the year before, when they had traversed the 7,834-foot-high Raton Pass leading only packhorses laden with trade goods, Becknell knew his three wagons would not make it over the mountains. He chose to follow a level route to New Mexico.

The Cimarron Desert is not a true desert, but a sixty-square-mile piece of arid land with scant vegetation, much alkaline dust, and little water. But Becknell, Heath, and their men probably considered the area a true desert after their water supply was exhausted. The party might have died of thirst had they not come upon a stray buffalo that had drunk deep in the Cimarron River farther to the southwest. The groggy buffalo was killed and cut open, and the men drank the water in its stomach. They were thus able to reach the Cimarron itself, where they quenched their thirst and filled their water containers. After resting and regaining their strength, they continued southwest across what is now the Oklahoma and Texas Panhandles until they reached the Canadian River in present-day northeastern New Mexico. The country was rockier near the Canadian River, but they made good time with their wagons as they neared the site of what is now Watrous, New Mexico. There Becknell found familiar ground, ground over which he had traveled a year earlier after crossing Raton Pass to the north. He had no difficulty in leading Heath and the others to San Miguel. The journey from the Arkansas River to San Miguel had taken twenty-two days.

As Becknell's party neared San Miguel, he later recalled: "We saluted the inhabitants with 3 rounds from our rifles, with which they appeared much pleased. With pleasure I here state, that the utmost harmony existed among our company on the whole route, and acknowledge the cheerfulness with which assistance was always rendered to each other. We separated at St. Michael (San Miguel) for the purpose of trading more advantageously. Some of the company, among whom was Mr. Heath, remained there, and others I did not see again until my return."[6]

Becknell's company soon turned a reported profit of 2,000 percent on an investment of $3,000 in trade goods, which probably included broadcloth, muslin, drills, prints, some taffeta, calico, linen, velveteen, and perhaps other textiles. The company probably also sold clothing, buttons, buckles, handkerchiefs, razors, razor strops, writing paper, thread, needles, knitting pins, scissors, pots, pans, coffee mills, knives, shovels, hoes, axes, and other tools. They may even have transported a few cases of sherry and claret to Santa Fe. A great quantity of smaller items could be carried in the company's three wagons, and finally the wagons were sold. Becknell's wagon had cost him about $150 in Missouri. He sold it for $750, as did also the owners of the other two wagons.

Later, Becknell advised traders heading to Santa Fe "to take goods of excellent quality and unfaded colors. An idea prevails among the people there, which is certainly a very just one, that the goods hitherto imported into their country, were the remains of old stock, and sometimes damaged. A great advance is obtained on goods, and the trade is very profitable; money and mules are plentiful, and they do not hesitate to pay the price demanded for an article if it suits their purpose, or their fancy."[7]

Though Becknell provided few details on the land crossed, others later told how the country west of the Missouri border was rich, beautiful, and well watered, and had sufficient timber for firewood. The hard timber along the Neosho River bottoms provided the last wood of any consequence that would be found until travelers approached the moun-

MILEAGE AND STOPS ON THE SANTA FE TRAIL
CIMARRON (DRY ROUTE) BRANCH

Independence to:	MILES	TOTAL
Round Grove	35	
Narrows (*Wakarusa Point*)	30	65
110 Mile Creek	30	95
Bridge Creek	8	103
Big John Spring	40	143
Council Grove	2	145
Diamond Spring	15	160
Lost Spring	15	175
Cottonwood Creek	12	187
Turkey Creek	25	212
Little Arkansas	17	229
Cow Creek	20	249
Arkansas River (*Big Bend*)	16	265
Walnut Creek (*up Arkansas*)	8	273
Ash Creek	19	292
Pawnee Fork	6	298
Coon Creek	33	331
Caches	36	367
Ford of the Arkansas	20	387
Sand Creek (*leave Arkansas River*)	50	437
Cimarron River (*Lower Spring*)	8	445
Middle Spring of the Cimarron	36	481
Willow Bar	26	507
Upper Spring	18	525
Cold Spring (*leave Cimarron River*)	5	530
McNees Creek	25	555
Rabbit Ear Creek	20	575
Round Mound	8	583
Rock Creek	8	591
Point of Rocks	19	610
Rio Colorado (*Canadian River*)	20	630
Ocate	6	636
Santa Clara Spring	21	657
Rio Mora	22	679
Rio Gallinas (*Las Vegas*)	20	699
Ojo De Bernal	17	716
San Miguel	6	722
Pecos Village	23	745
Santa Fe	25	770

This chart lists the mileage and stops on the Cimarron or dry-route branch of the Santa Fe Trail between Independence and Santa Fe. It appears in Josiah Gregg's Commerce of the Prairies, *published in two volumes in New York in 1844.* (Author's Collection) tains near Santa Fe. The country beyond the Neosho was more barren. As a traveler moved west, the change was gradual, but to many the treeless prairie and plains were forbidding. During the spring and summer months, drought, heat, flash floods, and high winds were not uncommon, and during the winter months extreme cold, sudden storms, and blizzards made the region seem almost unbearable.

In addition to Becknell's second trip to Santa Fe in 1822, two other groups sought to duplicate Becknell's original success. Benjamin Cooper's expedition was one. Cooper, his nephews Braxton and Stephen

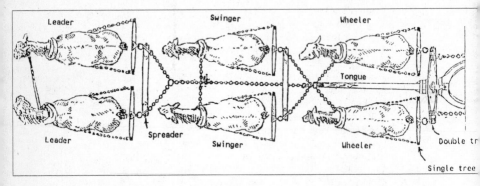

This drawing shows one way mules or horses were harnessed to provide the pulling force necessary to move freight wagons. The animals were controlled by means of a single rein called the jerk line (not shown) running back from the leader's halter and collar to where a driver either walked beside the wagon on the left side or rode in a saddle mounted on the last animal (the left wheeler). This illustration, with modifications, first appeared in George Shumway and Howard C. Frey's Conestoga Wagon 1750–1850 *(1964).* (Courtesy National Frontier Trails Center, Independence, Missouri)

Cooper, and twelve other men left Franklin, Missouri, early in May with pack animals reportedly carrying goods worth four to five thousand dollars. After it met the eastbound McKnight-James and Glenn-Fowler parties on June 13, 1822, Cooper's company followed the Arkansas River westward to the mountains and then turned south to Taos and Santa Fe. They returned to Missouri the following October and reported their expedition had been profitable.

A caravan of mule-drawn wagons, drawn by B. Kroupa, appeared in his An Artist's Tour, *published in London in 1890.* (Author's Collection)

The third expedition to leave Missouri for Santa Fe in 1822 was that of James Baird and Samuel Chambers. Both men had previously traveled to Santa Fe, in 1812, only to be arrested and jailed until 1820, when they returned to Missouri. By the summer of 1822, and after learning of Becknell's success, they formed a partnership with two other Missourians and left for Santa Fe to reenter the Santa Fe trade. They didn't start out until August, very late in the year to begin such a trip. The *St. Louis Enquirer* reported their late departure on September 2, 1822, and noted that there were nineteen men and sixty packhorses and mules loaded with goods in the party. When Baird and Chambers reached the Arkansas River, early snows forced them to make winter camp. Many of their horses and mules died of cold and hunger, leaving Baird and his men no choice but to cache their trading goods. They dug pits on high ground along the north bank of the Arkansas River and buried their trade goods. When spring 1823 arrived, the party traveled to Taos, bought pack animals, and returned east to where they had buried their

Some early trappers who turned to Santa Fe trading may have dressed like this man in Frederic Remington's "A Trapper and His Pony." (Author's Collection)

goods in the "Caches," as they became known, located a few miles west of present-day Dodge City, Kansas. Traces of the pits could still be seen in the early 1970s, although they have since vanished.

Only one trading party set out from Missouri for Santa Fe in 1823. It was led by Stephen Cooper and Joel P. Walker. They left Missouri in May, with each member of the party leading one or two packhorses and carrying an average of two hundred dollars in trade goods. When the party reached the Little Arkansas River in present-day Rice County, Kansas, Indians stampeded all but six of the traders' horses. Cooper and five other men returned to Missouri, bought more horses, and returned to where the original group waited. Continuing their journey, the party reached the Arkansas River and encountered the Baird-Chambers party, which included Joseph R. Walker, Joel Walker's brother. The party had already returned to the "Caches" and started for Santa Fe. The combined parties totaled fifty-five men and two hundred animals. Following the desert route, they suffered from thirst, and had to kill buffalo and drink the animals' blood to survive. By the time they reached Santa Fe, Mexican officials were obstructing trade between Missourians and Indians. The Baird-Chambers party did not have much success in trading, and on September 1, 1823, the company was dissolved at Taos.

Perhaps because of this trading failure, James Baird cut all ties with Missouri, remained in New Mexico, and applied for Mexican citizenship in October 1824. During the next two winters he trapped beaver in the mountains. By the early fall of 1826, Baird was in El Paso del Norte preparing to spend another winter in the mountains. In late October, he hired a few trappers and set out, only to become ill. He returned to El Paso. On a borrowed mattress, sheet, and pillow, James Baird, age fifty-nine, died on the morning of November 3, 1826, surrounded by a handful of American friends.[8]

As for the Cooper-Walker party of 1823, they succeeded in disposing of their trade goods and returned to Missouri in December with reportedly "400 Jacks and Jennets and mules, a quantity of beaver and a considerable sum in species."[9] The jacks (male donkeys) and jennies (hybrids born of a male horse and female donkey), and mules (hybrid offspring of jacks) brought back to Missouri from New Mexico by the Cooper-Walker party were a new variety. Since colonial times mules had been used in the East, but the Spanish mules were smaller in stature, standing eleven to thirteen hands high, and rarely weighed more than seven or eight hundred pounds. Their color varied from shades of grayish white or yellow to browns, blues, and dusty black. Missourians soon learned that the Spanish mules had incredible strength and endurance and fared better than horses where forage was poor and water scarce. Their flinty hoofs withstood well the shock and abrasion of rocky terrain. As one authority wrote, they "possessed native canniness—a combination of instinct, stubborn caution, and intelligence—which made them wary of precarious trails and impossible tasks."[10]

The Spanish mules brought back from New Mexico found a waiting market in Missouri, and they came to play a major role as pack animals on the Santa Fe Trail. Missouri soon became preeminent as a mule state, after farmers learned to breed them. The first European jack to enter Missouri was imported about 1838 by David Workman, who went to New Orleans and selected the animal from several brought to America from Malta by Jacob Baker aboard the ship *William Tell*. Workman brought the brown Maltese jack back to Missouri for E. Hayden of New Franklin, who used the animal in breeding. Later, the Kentucky mammoth jack was introduced in Missouri and crossed with the native product. Only after the beginning of the Santa Fe trade does one find mention of mules in Missouri newspaper advertisements for farm sales or notices of lost stock.[11]

BY THE MID-1820S, the growing importance of the Santa Fe trade attracted the attention of merchants in Missouri, who began to compete for the business of supplying traders. This is evident from the appearance of advertisements in Missouri newspapers by merchants seeking to sell trading goods, the first of which may have appeared in the *Missouri Intelligencer* at Franklin on January 25, 1825. A merchant advertised that he had for sale "mules suitable for the Santa Fe trade." On March 15 of that year, the same newspaper carried an advertisement from a St. Louis merchant calling attention to his firm's splendid assortment of goods "well adapted to the Santa Fe trade." A merchant in Franklin responded to the newspaper ad in the April 12, 1825, issue of the Franklin paper, noting that he had a large assortment of goods, purchased in New York and Philadelphia, "expressly for the Santa Fe market." The Franklin merchant told readers they could be supplied in Franklin on terms as good as in any other part of the western country.

Though the *Intelligencer* at Franklin began publishing advertisements in 1825, the columns of that same paper only occasionally mentioned the Santa Fe trade. When the *St. Louis Advocate* criticized the Franklin paper for overlooking the trade, the owner, Nathaniel Pattern, noted the criticism in the June 18, 1825, issue and thereafter made more mention of the trade, even though local news was not then a staple of weekly papers in Missouri.

Because of the problems from marauding Indians in 1822 and 1823, traders bound for Santa Fe in 1824 put together a large caravan in Missouri. Led by Stephen Cooper, it left for Santa Fe on May 16, 1824, and consisted of about eighty-three men including two servants, thirty thousand dollars in merchandise, two hundred horses and mules, two wagons, twenty Dearborn carriages, two carts, and one small cannon. The wagons probably had seen use on Missouri farms, while the Dearborn carriages were short, straight-sided wagons with three upright standards that supported a canvas roof and side and end curtains that could be rolled down during inclement weather. Because Dearborns were fairly top-heavy, they gained the reputation of frequently turning over. Traveling in the expedition led by Cooper were Augustus Storrs, who a year later would become U.S. consul at Santa Fe, and Meredith M. Marmaduke, later governor of Missouri. Alexander Le Grand, about twenty-four years old, was elected captain of the party a few days after leaving Franklin. Le Grand had come west a few years earlier from his native Maryland and had traveled to Santa Fe the previous year.

Marmaduke kept a journal on the trip, one of the earliest such records kept by anyone following the Santa Fe Trail. Excerpts from his journal tell us something of what the trip was like. For example, when Marmaduke's party struck the Arkansas River in what is now western Kansas, he wrote in his journal:

JUNE 8. Traveled 14 miles, and encamped on one of the branches of the Little Arkansas; killed 3 buffalo and 1 antelope. An alarm was this evening given by our hunters that several hundred Indians were approaching; a party went out to reconnoiter, and found them to be buffalo.

JUNE 9. Encamped on the Little Arkansas river, near the sand hills; killed 9 buffaloes. Saw this day at least five thousand buffalo, chiefly bulls.

JUNE 10. Pass the Sand Hills—saw this day at least ten thousand buffalo, the prairies were literally covered with them for many miles. Killed 9 buffalo today—we this evening arrived at the G. Arkansas river, and encamped on it; this river is at this place about 200 yards wide, but quite shallow as our hunters forded it, and killed several buffalo on the south side. At this place there is not the smallest appearance of any kind of tree or shrubbery of any kind; the whole country being entirely prairie. . . .

JUNE 11. Traveled about 8 miles on the Arkansas, and encamped on the bank at noon, at which time a great number of buffalo came running by the camp, and frightened the horses so that many of them broke off from the encampment at full speed, and joined in with the buffalo in the race, and with great difficulty were checked. I believe I must have seen this day at least ten or fifteen thousand buffaloes.

JUNE 12. In consequence of the horses which ran off yesterday, we remained at the same encampment, and unfortunately for many of us, at 1 o'clock in the morning a number of buffalo crossed the river at the encampment and passed through it, which frightened off about two-thirds of the horses of the party, many of which, however, were found in the course of the day and brought in.

Because the party had wagons and other four-wheel vehicles, they left the Arkansas River and turned southwest to follow the flat and dry Cimarron route. Marmaduke then wrote the following in his journal:

JUNE 29. Traveled 30 miles, left our encampment at 4 o'clock a.m., and traveled without making any halt until about 4 o'clock, p.m., without a drop of water for our horses or mules, by which time many of them were nearly exhausted, as well as a number of the men; a dog which had traveled with us during our journey, this day fell down and expired, such was the extreme heat and suffering. Fortunately for us all about 4 o'clock a small ravine was discovered and pursued for a few miles, and after digging in the sand at the bottom of it, water was procured in sufficient quantity to satisfy both man and horses, but not till after five or six wells were sunk; and such was the extreme suffering of the animals that it was with the utmost difficulty [that they] could be kept out of the holes until buckets could be filled for them. I never in my life experienced a time when such general alarm and consternation pervaded every person on account of the want of water.

Although the expedition experienced many hardships, it arrived safely in Santa Fe about dusk on July 31, seventy-six days after leaving Franklin, Missouri. Marmaduke described Santa Fe as "quite a populous place, but [it] is built entirely of mud houses; some parts of the city are tolerably regularly built, others very irregularly. The inhabitants appear to be friendly, and some of them are very wealthy; but by far the greater part are the most miserable, wretched, poor creatures that I have ever

Thomas Hart Benton (1782–1858) encouraged trade over the Santa Fe Trail soon after he was elected to the U.S. Senate from Missouri in 1821. Serving as a senator until 1851, Benton promoted the western explorations of his son-in-law John C. Frémont.
(Author's Collection)

seen; yet they appear to be quite happy and contented in their miserable priest-ridden situation. The city is well supplied with good water; provisions very scarce; a great many beggars to be seen walking the streets."[12]

At first, the party found it difficult to sell their goods because money was scarce and the goods brought from Missouri were not of the best quality. Still, when they left New Mexico in September for Missouri, one account suggests that the party carried $180,000 in gold and silver and furs valued at $10,000. Marmaduke, however, did not return with the main group; he spent about ten months in Santa Fe. During that time he observed the people and the place, and before leaving for Missouri on May 31, 1825, he recorded his observations. He was "astonished at the blind zeal and enthusiasm of the people, all professing the Catholic religion, which I found to be the only religion tolerated in the country, and which I do verily believe is the best that could possibly be established among them, as they appear to live more happy under their religious yoke than any other profession I have ever known, and I believe die as happily as any people in the world."

Regarding the manners and customs of New Mexicans, Marmaduke wrote: "I am reluctantly constrained to say, that I do not believe there is a people on the globe so entirely destitute of correct moral principles as the inhabitants of New Mexico. I scarcely know a single vice that is not indulged in by them to the very great excess, excepting that of intoxication, and the absence of this is owing to the scarcity of ardent spirits. In fact every vice resides among this people to the greatest extent that their poor, miserable situation will admit. In justice, however, I can not forbear to remark, that there does exist among them one solitary virtue, and that is hospitality to strangers; for when I consider the scarcity there of human diet, I believe no people would more willingly divide their morsel with the stranger than they, and that too without any demand or expectation of compensation; but if you offer to return them the value, or ten times as much, it will at all times be received."[13]

While Marmaduke does not describe in detail the food shared by the Mexicans, he undoubtedly found pinto beans—*frijoles*—usually seasoned with hot peppers, and the ever present *chili con carne*—chili with lean pork cut into one-inch squares and boiled until tender with sage, crushed garlic, and salt. When tender, the pork was removed from the liquid and fried in pure lard with the addition of just enough chili powder plus a couple tablespoons of browned flour. The meat-and-flour mixture in the frying pan was then returned to the liquid and allowed to boil down to the consistency of a medium-thick soup, which was served by itself or with rice and beans on the side. *Chili con carne* formed the center for the *tamale,* which was made by rolling a small quantity of cornmeal dough around the *chili con carne* and then encasing the whole in corn husks and steaming until cooked. It was nothing like what is sold in cans in grocery stores today. Marmuduke also would have found *tortillas* made of hand-ground blue cornmeal and fashioned into round, thin bread that looked something like pancakes. *Tortillas* served as pushers to scoop up the *frijoles,* which were then eaten, *tortilla* and all. They also served as the base for hot *tacos* and *enchiladas. Tacos* were made of fine *tortillas* half folded, filled with meat, and fried in deep fat. Removed from the fat, the *taco* was then stuffed from the side with green chili pepper sauce, chopped onions, grated cheese, and shredded greens. *Enchiladas* consisted simply of *tortillas* dipped in chili sauce and stacked one on top of another, like pancakes, with chopped onions and grated cheese sprinkled between the layers, the whole stack crowned with a fried egg.[14]

Marmaduke, apparently traveling with a Missouri-bound trading party, started east in early June 1825, about the time a small company left Missouri for New Mexico. The leader was Sylvester Pattie, a native of Kentucky and a hero of the War of 1812. With him was his son James O. Pattie and three other men. They crossed the Missouri River about sixty miles above St. Louis with ten horses packed with traps, trapping utensils, guns, ammunition, knives, tomahawks, provisions, blankets, and some trading goods. Sylvester Pattie had moved to Missouri with his family several years earlier and established a gristmill and a sawmill on the roaring Gasconade River. He had nine children including James Ohio, but in 1824 his wife died of tuberculosis. Dejected and unhappy in his desolate home, Sylvester decided on a trading venture. When his son James, then about twenty years old, begged to go along, the father consented. He organized the small party and they headed west.

Their route led them along the north bank of the Missouri River until the stream turned north where Kansas City, Missouri, stands today. Then they followed the east bank of the river north until they reached the point opposite where the Platte River flows into the Missouri. Crossing the river they came upon a trading post operated by Bernard Pratte and Company. Nearby, camped on the Platte River, were some horses, 300 mules, and 112 men preparing to head for New Mexico. Sylvester Pratte, the twenty-six-year-old son of Bernard Pratte, headed the expedition, which the Pattie party joined. The large group followed the Platte to a Pawnee Indian village of six hundred lodges, where they remained for five days. During that time Sylvester Pratte bought six hundred buffalo skins and some horses from the Indians, and Sylvester Pattie ransomed a captive Indian child. The expedition left the Pawnee village on August 11, 1825, and headed southwest toward New Mexico.

The expedition had two battles with Indians, encountered large herds of buffalo and wild horses, attacked a Crow Indian camp after finding the arrow-riddled bodies of two white men, and arrived at the ridge dividing the Republican and Smoky Hill River valleys in early September. A few days later, some of the men encountered a grizzly bear, which fatally injured one trader. By late September the expedition reached the Arkansas River in what is now eastern Colorado. About a month later, it reached Taos and continued on to Santa Fe. Although Sylvester and James Pattie traveled as traders, there is little evidence to suggest they engaged in that occupation. Once in New Mexico, they turned to trapping and joined a party that descended the Gila River; but their furs were stolen. Back in New Mexico, Sylvester gave up trapping to manage a copper mine, while James continued trapping. In 1828, Sylvester returned to trapping with James and they joined another party of trappers that followed the Gila to the Colorado River and then across the desert to California in search of furs. They were arrested by Mexican authorities in San Diego because they had no trapping license. Sylvester, who had collapsed while crossing the desert, died in May 1828 while in jail. James was later released. He took a ship to San Blas and traveled overland to Mexico City, where he was unable to gain recompense for his California losses. Traveling to Veracruz, he took another ship to New Orleans, where he arrived in August 1830. He then proceeded up the Mississippi and Ohio Rivers to Cincinnati, where about two months later he visited the office of the *Western Monthly Review,* met the editor Timothy Flint, and told him of his adventures. Fascinated by Pattie's story, Flint put it on paper, and the following year it was printed and published in Cincinnati by John H. Wood, titled *The Personal Narrative of James O. Pattie, of Kentucky.* It has since become a classic of western Americana.[15]

DURING THE EARLY years of the Santa Fe trade, 1821 to 1823, Missouri was struggling to survive a depression that started after the Napoleonic Wars. Economic troubles reached Missouri in 1819 when the Bank of St. Louis, founded two years earlier, failed. The Bank of Missouri, also founded in 1817, failed in 1821, the year Missouri became a state, leaving Missourians suspicious not only of banks but of all currency issued by banks. In June 1821, the Missouri legislature announced a moratorium on land debt, but it gave only partial relief because of the condition of the currency. In an effort to save the state from a barter system, its legislature established loan offices empowered to issue paper money based on the credit of the state. Still, most officials and merchants in Missouri refused to accept this money. But the Santa Fe trade, beginning with William Becknell's first successful trip in 1821, provided both specie and an important new source of income, as did the emerging fur trade centered in St. Louis. By 1824, Missouri's interests lay outside its boundaries, and Missouri governor Alexander McNair promoted Santa Fe trade nationally in *Niles Register,* on June 19, 1824, listing benefits such as spreading democracy, making friends with the Indians, expanding hunting and trapping, earning trade profits, and enhancing friendship between the United States and Mexico. By then another Missouri politician with energy and eloquence began to champion the West and especially the Santa Fe Trail.

Thomas Hart Benton, who had been elected a U.S. senator from Missouri in 1821, realized that his state's future lay in its strategic geographic position as gateway to the West. Benton, then in his forties, knew of William Ashley's fur-trading company's success on the upper Missouri. He was also aware that Thomas Fitzpatrick and Jedediah Smith had just discovered South Pass in present-day Wyoming, opening a trail to Oregon. Benton realized that these developments, along with the emerging Santa Fe trade, presaged a bright future for Missouri. Visiting his constituents during the summer of 1824, Benton was impressed with the fact that people in Missouri talked of almost nothing but trade with New Mexico. They told him the trade would increase if the government could mark a road to Santa Fe and arrange with the Indians to let travelers pass safely through the lands traversed by the trail. Before leaving for Washington, Benton promised to sponsor legislation for such a road, but he needed Missourians to send a petition to Washington explaining why a road was necessary. To obtain firsthand information, Benton asked Augustus Storrs, who had traveled to Santa Fe in 1823, to answer twenty-two questions. Benton knew he would have to have facts for his colleagues in Congress.[16]

From his home at Franklin, Missouri, Storrs, age thirty-four, a native of New England, penned answers to Benton's twenty-two questions, which covered the history of commerce between New Mexico and Missouri, the route followed, other possible routes, travel time, type of goods transported, duties, resources, and Indian relations. One question asked, "What protection, or facilities, can the United States grant, to promote the successful prosecution of this commerce in time to come?" Storrs replied:

A road, traced out from some point near Fort Osage, to the Arkansas, would be beneficial. It should be marked with mounds of earth, at proper distances, so as to be pursued without difficulty. Care should be taken to have it intersect all the creeks at the best fords that can be found within a convenient range; and a few laborers should accompany the reviewers, or commissioners, for the purpose of leveling the banks, and throwing up the mounds. The advantage of bridges would not compensate the trouble and expense of erecting them, because, in two or three years, they would all be either swept away, or out of repair. The circumstances of packers having always passed without difficulty, and of twenty-three wagons having performed the route without much detention, shows that this measure [bridges] is not absolutely necessary to the successful prosecution of this trade. . . . A garrison on the Arkansas would have a strong tendency to prevent the depredations of the Indians; but there are objections to the adoption of such a measure. It would have very little influence over the Indians most to be dreaded, unless established near the point where we leave that river. . . . Another objection is, that the buffalo will entirely leave a country traversed by white people, which they will not for the Indians. This fact might reasonably be doubted, were it not satisfactorily proved by experience. Several tribes of Indians that roam over the country, have not the least knowledge of cultivation. The buffalo are their means of support and commerce, and they would, doubtless, look with hostile feelings upon an establishment [fort].[17]

Storr's detailed answers were published early in 1825 as a congressional document, as were a petition and a descriptive letter to a Missouri congressman from Alphonso Wetmore, age thirty-two, a native of Connecticut. Wetmore had lost his right arm during the War of 1812. As captain and later major, he was a paymaster stationed at Franklin, Missouri, when he wrote a letter to the Missouri congressman John Scott observing that the "route pursued by the first adventurers was more circuitous than that at present traveled; and the distance, which was originally believed to present a serious obstacle to this trade, has been so much reduced by a better knowledge of the country, as to form no considerable objection to a profitable prosecution of this novel and interesting commerce. . . . The most acceptable service that could be rendered those engaged in this inland trade, would be to mark a road, so as to enable them to pursue their operations without loss of time or distance. This might be effected by erecting, at suitable intervals, stone pillars, or marks, to designate the track. The country abounds in stone suitable for this purpose."[18]

Wetmore also drafted a petition addressed to the Senate and House of Representatives calling for protection of the Santa Fe traders. He wrote, in part: "The protection which the trade demands chiefly refers itself to the Indians inhabiting or roaming over the intermediate country between Missouri and the Internal Provinces [of Mexico]. A right of passing is needed through their country, and security against the robberies and murders which all savages are prone to commit on the traveler and merchant. . . . The principal article carried out to the Internal Provinces, is cotton goods, the growth and manufacture of the United States. In opening a new, increasing, and permanent market for the consumption of this article, the people of Missouri mingle their interest, and divide their advantages, with the inhabitants of most sections of the union."[19]

The material provided by Storrs and Wetmore was read into the congressional record and printed as government documents. They aided Senator Benton when he introduced a bill to survey the Santa Fe Trail. To gain support from southerners and northerners alike, Benton applied the argument that cotton grown in the South and made into material in the North would be a large part of the commerce. The bill passed and was signed into law by President James Monroe on March 3, 1825, just before John Quincy Adams assumed the presidency. The law authorized the president to appoint commissioners to mark a road from the western frontier of Missouri "to the boundary line of the United States [the Arkansas River] in the direction of Santa Fe." The commissioners were charged with making treaties with the intervening Indian tribes for the marking of the road and for its unmolested use. It also authorized the president to negotiate with the Mexican government for permission to continue the road into New Mexico. The amount of ten thousand dollars was appropriated to pay the cost of marking the road, and twenty thousand dollars more for the expenses in making peace with the Indians. President John Quincy Adams appointed three commissioners to oversee the marking of what Missouri senator Benton called "a highway between nations."[20]

SIX

Surveying the Road to Santa Fe, 1825-1827

The road commences a mile or two south of Fort Osage. . . . It follows the neighborhood road until it crosses the Little Blue Creek; it then enters upon those extensive prairies which reach, without intermission, to the Mountains of New Mexico.

—*Archibald Gamble*

MISSOURIANS WERE NOT surprised when Benjamin H. Reeves was appointed one of the three commissioners to mark the road to Santa Fe. After all, he was the most influential citizen in Howard County, the center of Santa Fe trade in Missouri. Reeves arrived in Missouri from Kentucky in 1819; was a member of the first constitutional convention; and was elected state auditor, state senator, and in 1824 lieutenant governor, a position he resigned when appointed commissioner.

There also was no surprise among Missourians over the appointment of Colonel Pierre Menard, who became a merchant and trader in 1791 at Kaskaskia, Illinois. Menard was also a partner in the St. Louis Fur Company, and later in the Missouri Fur Company, headquartered at St. Louis. But soon after his appointment as commissioner, he resigned because of pressing business affairs. Thomas Mather, another well-known merchant at Kaskaskia, was soon named to take Menard's place. Mather had the social advantage of being a lineal descendant of Cotton Mather, the Puritan patriarch and theologian.

The appointment of the third commissioner, George C. Sibley, age forty-three, came as a surprise even to him. Sibley was the first factor, or Indian trader, at Fort Osage soon after it was constructed in 1808 by William Clark. There Sibley stayed until the fort was abandoned at the start of the War of 1812. When it was reopened in 1816, he returned as factor and remained in that position until 1822, when Congress abolished the system of federal factors. Sibley knew the Kansas and Osage Indians, and he was a good writer and reporter already familiar with the Santa Fe trade. In fact, he had a desire to enter the trade, but he put those thoughts aside when he accepted the position of commissioner, which he considered the greatest honor of his life.[1]

Before Thomas Mather was appointed to replace Menard, Sibley and Reeves met in St. Louis and decided to move ahead with preparations. It was agreed that Sibley would remain in St. Louis to obtain supplies, wagons, and men to drive them, and hire six expert riflemen as hunters. Reeves would move west into Missouri to purchase horses and mules and to hire a pilot, a surveyor, chainmen, hunters, and guards. He selected Joseph Cromwell Brown, age forty-one, as surveyor. A native of Virginia of Scotch-Irish stock, Brown came to Missouri on horseback during the summer of 1815 as a trained surveyor and helped to determine the baseline of the Fifth Principal Meridian. The following year he traveled from Fort Osage to the Arkansas River in what is now Kansas surveying the Osage Indian line. By 1825, Brown was the most experienced surveyor in Missouri. Archibald Gamble, who had assisted Brown in his survey work in 1816, was selected as the commissioners' secretary. Like Brown, the thirty-one-year-old Gamble was a Virginian and Scotch-Irish. To pilot the survey party, Reeves hired Stephen Cooper, who had traveled to Santa Fe several times.[2]

Meantime, more than a hundred men applied for jobs with the survey commission. A rather typical letter of application came from a man named James Logan:

Dear Col.
After my Particular Respects to you and a Desire for the welfare of your family me and mine is well I would be verry [sic] glad to see you and of all things to accompany you on your Route to St. afee [sic] if there is time and your company not made up write me. Stating In what way I shall go and with what Equipage and I will Come on with out fail if nothing happens more than I know of the woods is my Home and the forrest [sic] my own. Give my Respects to my friend Collo [sic] Burkhardt and Receive them your Self.

James Logan[3]

Logan was not hired. Reeves did hire William Sherley "Old Bill" Williams, thirty-eight, a lean six-footer who was born in North Carolina and grew up in Missouri, as Indian interpreter. Unlike Logan and many other applicants, Williams knew the country to be crossed. He was destined to become a well-known mountain man and guide and would later have streams, a mountain peak, and Williams, Arizona, named for him. Another experienced plainsman hired by Reeves, as a hunter and chainman, was Joseph Reddeford Walker, age twenty-seven, a native of Tennessee. Like Williams, Walker would become a well-known mountain man and is remembered as the "Capt. Walker" in Washington Irving's *Adventures of Captain Bonneville* (1837), which is ostensibly an autobiographical account of the western adventures of Benjamin L. E. de Bonneville, a Frenchman.[4]

Reeves hired men to be work hands—as distinguished from skilled workers and officers—who had to agree to adhere to camp regulations drawn up by Sibley. Original letters now in the files of the Missouri Historical Society describe the "hands" as all "gentlemen" coffee-drinkers able to saddle a horse and cook their victuals. Each had to furnish his own groceries and be an expert rifleman and hunter. The work hands agreed to have a mess separate from the commissioners and officials, including the surveyor Joseph C. Brown and secretary Archibald Gamble. They also agreed not to raid the commissioners' stores or tent and to maintain camp order and discipline. The contract, which most of the work hands signed, read:

> We the undersigned having engaged ourselves to the Commissioners appointed to mark out a road from the western frontier of Missouri to the confines of New Mexico, Do each of us promise and hereby bind ourselves to serve the said Commissioners faithfully and diligently and to the best of our skill and abilities. We will do and perform all such services as may from time to time be required of us by the Commissioners either as Chain Carriers, Axemen, Hunters, Waggoners, Hostlers, Packers, Labourers, or in such other capacities as the nature of the service may require. We will observe strictly such rules and regulations as may be established by the Commissioners for the proper government of the party, and in all things pertaining to the service obey their orders promptly and truly. And we engage to serve the Commissioners as above for and during the term of their Commission unless sooner discharged.[5]

While Reeves was buying nearly sixty horses and hiring men for the party, Sibley remained in St. Louis, where he located and purchased three used wagons and contracted a wagon-maker to build four more. When Sibley learned that representatives of the Osage and Kansa Indians were in St. Louis, he visited with them and told of plans to mark the Santa Fe Trail. The Indians did not object to the road and agreed to meet the commissioners once they arrived in their country to the west. Sibley also hired seven good men to drive the wagons. After several delays the wagons were ready, each painted light blue. The wagons were then loaded with the party's supplies, including large amounts of rice, flour, cornmeal, salt, and bacon; probably one or two kegs of whiskey; a keg of sundries (probably gifts for Indians); candles; a trunk of medicine and powder; axes; spades; a knife; tents; baggage; and a compass, chain, and other survey tools. The wagons were then driven westward across Missouri to Fort Osage, where the party gathered to organize.

On July 17, 1825, thirty-three men on horseback and seven other men, each driving a horse-drawn baggage wagon, left Fort Osage "running a line" to measure distance as the group set out for Santa Fe. Periodically, they marked the trail by erecting earth mounds at or near where the party camped each night. Sibley delayed joining the party for several days because of pressing private business that he wanted to finish. His absence, however, did not delay the work that had to be done. Joseph Brown, the surveyor, began measuring the distance traveled and keeping careful records of the course followed. Using his sextant, Brown first determined the latitude and longitude at Fort Osage, and another reading was made at the western border of Missouri, where the trail entered what is now Kansas. The party then continued on until August 1, when it camped next to Elk Creek, a branch of the Marais de Cygne River, about 142 miles from Fort Osage. There they rested and recovered from the heat and the pesky flies that seemed to be everywhere. Gamble left the party to locate Osage Indians and to invite them to meet the commissioners farther to the west.

On the morning of Wednesday, August 3, Sibley caught up with the survey party still camped next to Elk Creek. That day, hunters killed some elk for food. The following morning, August 4, the party broke camp, traveled seven miles, and then halted to graze their horses and eat breakfast in a grove of hickory trees. Late in the afternoon the party traveled another six miles and camped on the bank of what became known as Rock Creek. Sibley wrote in his journal, "The flies are now nearly all past." Sibley's day-by-day journal was later sent to Washington, D.C., with the commissioners' report, but it was lost among government records until 1938, more than a hundred years later. It was first published in 1952.[6]

Breaking camp on Friday morning, August 5, the survey party traveled six miles before stopping to eat breakfast in a grove of trees on the bank of the Neosho River. It was there that the town of Council Grove, Kansas, would later be established. Sibley wrote: "Here we find most excellent pasturage, and a large and beautiful grove of fine timber; and we determine to wait here for the Osages, who are expected in two or three days. Our Camp is arranged with the view of receiving our expected visitors in a suitable manner. Very few flies here." Sibley wrote he had traveled at night from Fort Osage to avoid the flies. He found that the greater part of the country traveled was prairie that was "tolerably level and smooth, affording good road, and with two exceptions, plenty of water at convenient intervals."

Archibald Gamble, the commissioners' secretary, and "Old Bill" Williams, the party's interpreter, arrived at the camp three days later, on the evening of Monday, August 8, with Pa-hu-sha (White Hair), chief Great Osages, Ca-he-ga-shinga (Foolish Chief), little chief of Great Osages, Shin-gawassa (Handsome Bird), chief Great Osages, Ca-he-ge-wa-tonega (also called Foolish Chief), head chief of Little Osages, and other Osage headmen and warriors. The fifty or so Indians camped nearby, and the following morning the commissioners held council with them.[7]

Sibley wrote in his journal: "The Commissioners explained to them fully and clearly what they desire respecting the road; and proposed to give them $800 as compensation for the privilege of marking it through their land, and the free use of it forever. After a few minutes conversation among themselves, the chiefs declared their assent to the proposition and expressed their readiness to execute a treaty to that effect. And they were told that the Commissioners would meet them again tomorrow, prepared to conclude and sign the treaty as now agreed on." The next day, Wednesday, August 10, the commissioners again met with the Indians. After the treaty was read and carefully explained to the Osages by "Old Bill" Williams, it was signed by the respective parties. A duplicate copy was given to the principal Osage chief. The commissioners then paid the Indians with goods valued at three hundred dollars and gave them an order through Auguste P. Chouteau, a trader then visiting their village, for five hundred dollars in ammunition, knives, and other goods.

As soon as the Osage Indians broke camp and left Council Grove, as Sibley named the place, "Old Bill" Williams left on horseback for the Kansas Indian village about forty-five miles away. His mission was to bring the Kansas chiefs to council with the commissioners. The survey party then broke camp, got their wagons across the Neosho River, and climbed out of the valley onto the prairie. "The prairie is very high and is generally strewed over with small flakes of limestone and flint. The grass is very short and wiry, except in the low places, where it is rich and good," wrote Sibley.

The survey party continued to "run the chain" and measure the distance it covered. At one point the party startled a group of elk, three or four of which were killed after a hard chase by the hunters. Two deer were also killed. The meat was a welcome addition to the party's diet. Three days later, on Sunday, August 14, the group camped on the bank of a small creek after measuring nineteen miles and sixty-three chains, each chain-length totaling sixty-six feet. About dark, "Old Bill" Williams rode into camp with two Kansas Indians. He said he had left fifty more Kansas about six miles back on the trail who would come into camp the following day. After discussion with the commissioners, Williams sent the two Kansas back to tell the others they would wait for them on the first creek the party came to with any timber. After the Indians left, the commissioners sat down for a supper of coffee, fried bacon, and biscuits cooked over buffalo dung, since there was no wood for fuel.

The following day, Monday, August 15, the party got up early, breakfasted, and began running the chain. Sibley rode ahead of the survey team looking for timber and found a small grove of trees on what is today Dry Turkey Creek, about seventy-eight miles west of Council Grove and about five miles south of present-day McPherson, Kansas. By afternoon the survey party arrived and camped under a very large, spreading oak tree. The Kansas, including Shone-gee-ne-gare, their great chief, soon appeared, and the commissioners explained why they were there and proposed the same terms that had been agreed on with the Osages. The Kansas accepted the terms without any hesitation and returned the next morning to sign the treaty. The survey party then broke camp and resumed its job of measuring and marking the trail to Santa Fe.[8]

It may have been at this meeting with the Kansas that Commissioner Reeves learned the Indian cure for the bite of a rattlesnake. Reeves later wrote that they "take the inner part of a turkey buzzard's maw. Dry it into powder—apply it to the wound."[9]

The following excerpts from George Sibley's journal capture something of the party's trail life during the days that followed:

MONDAY, 22D AUGUST. A very pleasant morning. The grass being very good here, we staid [sic] in camp all day for the benefit of the horses; and it is necessary also to unload and examine the stores and provisions, issue some blankets and clothing to the men, and shoe some of the horses. . . . Some sand hills still in sight. . . . Mr. Brown says the current of the Arkansas [River] is here about 2¼ miles per hour.

TUESDAY, 23D AUGUST. The morning fair and cool. Mercury 66 at 8 o'clock in the shade. At half an hour past eight we started again. The wagons continued up the river in the bottom. I rode out from the river upon the hills to view the country. . . . I had a fine view of the immense level plain through which the Arkansas runs . . . numerous buffalo grazing in every direction. . . . I turned in towards the river and got there at 12, where I found the company encamped on the bank, having drove today 9 miles.

WEDNESDAY, 24TH AUGUST. The morning cool and hazy. Wind from the south. Mercury 70 at 7. River falling. We left camp at 25 minutes past 8. Kept up in the river bottom about 2 miles, and passed a large island thickly timbered with cottonwood [trees], called Pit Grove. We passed a few scattered trees below this; and above, the river is distinctly marked by those trees as far as we can see. . . . We continued onward, and at 12, got to the Walnut Creek, called 6 miles above the Pit Grove. We crossed the Creek at a good ford, not far from the mouth, and camped on the bank in a bend, among some scattering walnuts and elms, where we found very excellent pasturage and plenty of fuel. The Creek is about 20 yards wide. Water clear and good, and plenty. Distance traveled today 8 miles and 25 chains—the road very good all the way.

THURSDAY, 25TH AUGUST. The morning fair and pleasant. Busy all day writing and gathering seeds. Buffalo passing all day near camp—several fat ones killed. At a short distance from camp, the men get great quantities of very fine plums. Horses doing very well here. We intended to stay several days. The day generally cloudy and warm. John Walker lost his horse, saddle and blankets. He ran off with a gang of buffalo.

FRIDAY, 26TH AUGUST. Morning hazy and cloudy. Cleared off at 9, and proved a fine day tho' very warm. Busy writing all day. Many of the men out killing buffalo.

SATURDAY, 27TH AUGUST. Very fine morning. After early breakfast Mr. Brown, Mr. Gamble and myself set out on an excursion northward, over the ridge, to ascertain the relative position of the Kansas and Arkansas rivers which are laid down on the maps as coming close together at this point. We rode north about 3 miles, and ascended the ridge—then over the ridge about 1½ miles same course, and descended into an extensive low flat prairie [Cheyenne Bottoms northeast of present-day Great Bend, Kansas] through which we continued about 4 miles passing through a marsh half a mile across, and came to a small creek running southeast, towards a large lake which is seen about 2 miles off in that direction. We continued on the same course, after crossing the creek, for about a mile, and came to a large pond, then we turned more westward, and in a short distance came to the same creek [Deception Creek] again at a bend. . . . It is very much inferior however to the river laid down on the maps as the Smoky Hill Fork. I am inclined to believe that there is still another and a larger stream a few miles farther north beyond a high ridge. . . . We staid [*sic*] in the shade about 2 hours, and then set out on our return to camp . . . arrived just at sunset having traveled nearly 30 miles. . . . A Mr. [Nathaniel Miguel] Pryor arrived at our camp today, with three other men, on their way to New Mexico on a trapping expedition. They came up the Arkansas from Cantonment [Fort] Gibson [Indian Territory].

SUNDAY, 28TH AUGUST. There fell a very heavy rain last night accompanied with high wind. We got everything wet in the tents. The morning fair but very warm—Mercury 74 at 9. After getting our baggage dried, which was not effected till 12 o'clock, we struck our camp at 1 p.m. and moved forward. Traveled over a rough and uneven bottom, near the river 6 miles and 78 chains, and halted on the bank [of the Arkansas River near modern Great Bend, Kansas] for the night. . . .

MONDAY, 29TH AUGUST. The morning very clear and warm. . . . After breakfast, we started at 45 minutes past 8. Traveled over very rough and uneven ground, through the bottom, very much cut up with wet slashes. The grass is rough and coarse and very much overrun with weeds. . . . Buffalo very plentiful.

TUESDAY, 30TH AUGUST. The morning clear cool and pleasant, a fine air stirring. After breakfast at 30 minutes past 8, we all started. The wagons and most of the party kept up the river bottom. Mr. Gamble and myself rode out upon the high prairie. We first rode nearly north about a mile to a remarkable rocky point [Pawnee Rock] which projects into the bottom from a high ridge; these rocks are very large and of a glossy black color; towards the river, the face is nearly perpendicular. We rode upon the top which is probably 50 feet above the plains below, and from whence there is a charming view of the country in every direction. . . . We saw a great many buffalo today, several [wild] horses, and a variety of other smaller game.

WEDNESDAY, 31ST AUGUST. The morning cool and cloudy and windy. The principle [*sic*] timber of this and the Walnut Creek . . . is ash, elm, box elder and cotton[wood]. The Creek having run down so that the wagons can cross, we set off again after breakfast at half past 8. Our way was over rather broken prairie, and at a greater distance from the river than we usually travel. At half past 10 we reached the Pawnee fork, and camped on the bank, a little below the fording place, at some large elm trees, having measured from the last camp 6 miles and 56 chains. A heavy rain fell while we were on the road. The Creek appears to be too full now to venture to cross it with the wagons; besides the banks required some digging at the ford. Here we have a beautiful camping place, and very fine range for the horses.

THURSDAY, 1ST SEPTEMBER. The morning cloudy and cool. Mercury 68 at 8 o'clock. The Pawnee River is here about 40 yards wide, banks pretty high, bottom sandy, water at present muddy. Timber Elm, Ash, Elder, Cotton[wood] Tree, Willow, and Grape Vines. Yesterday I turned off from the direct course and struck the Arkansas at the mouth of this River, and then coursed it up about a mile to the fording place near which we are now encamped, which is just at the foot of a high rocky hill. The path leading up from the mouth to the ford passes between the Pawnee and some cliffs of soft rock, upon the smooth faces of which are cut the names of many persons, who have at different times passed this way to and from New Mexico. Some Indian marks are also to be seen on these rocks. This ford of Pawnee River is 31 miles from Walnut Creek, and 330 from Fort Osage.[10]

During the days that followed, the survey party continued to move on a parallel course to the Arkansas River, passing the future site of Dodge City, Kansas. Keeping to the north side of the river, the party camped on Saturday, September 10, 1825, just below a high bluff about three miles beyond where Samuel Chambers and James Baird were forced to cache their trade goods during the winter of 1822–23. On Sunday, September 11, Sibley wrote in his journal: "We have now arrived at the point where by Mr. Brown's measurement, and observations, he supposes the 100th degree of West Longitude will strike the Arkansas—and from which upward, the Arkansas River is the boundary line between the United States and Mexico."

There Sibley and the others waited for several days expecting a messenger from Missouri with authorization for the party to continue marking the road through Mexican Territory to Santa Fe. Nathaniel Pryor and a party of trappers, who had been traveling with Sibley's party for many days, decided to move on to New Mexico. Sibley wrote a letter to Paul Baillo, a friend in Taos, and enclosed a letter he had been given in St. Louis. Addressed to Augustus Storrs in Santa Fe, that letter made Storrs U.S. consul in New Mexico. Sibley asked Pryor to deliver the letter to Baillo, who was instructed to give the enclosure to Storrs. Sibley also asked Pryor to deliver a stack of Missouri newspapers that he had carried west from Missouri. Pryor agreed and with his men left the survey party's camp and started toward Santa Fe.

On Tuesday, September 20, fearing the arrival of winter and disturbed that no messenger had arrived from the east with instructions for the survey party, the commissioners decided that Sibley should proceed to Santa Fe with the surveyor, interpreter, and nine men, plus two wagons and supplies; commissioners Mather and Reeves and the rest of the party would return to Missouri. Two days later the survey party split up. Sibley and his group traveled fifteen miles that day before camping on the bank of the Arkansas River. The next day, Friday, September 23, Sibley and his party continued their journey and, late in the day, while looking for a campsite, met a caravan of eighty traders heading east for Missouri. Sibley wrote in his journal that he bought a horse for thirty dollars from a man in the caravan, which had left Santa Fe twenty-three days earlier. Two days later, Sibley and his party crossed the Arkansas River near present-day Garden City, Kansas, and entered Mexican territory for the first time.

That day the surveyor Joseph Brown calculated that the group was 427 miles from Fort Osage and about 320 miles from Taos. Of the river crossing, Brown wrote: "At this place there are no banks on either side to hinder wagons. The crossing is very oblique, landing on the south side a quarter of a mile above the entrance on this side. The river is here very shallow, not more than knee deep in a low stage of the water. The bed of the river is altogether sand, and it is unsafe to stand long on one place with a wagon, or it may sink into the sand. After passing a few wet places just beyond the river, the road is again very good up to Chouteau's Island."

Sibley, Brown, and the others followed the south bank of the river until they reached a point opposite Chouteau's Island, where ten years earlier a party of traders led by Auguste P. Chouteau fought a battle with Pawnee Indians. Brown noted: "Many things unite to mark this place so strongly that the traveler will not mistake it. It is the largest island of timber on the river, and on the south side of the river at the lower end of the island is a thicket of willows with some cottonwood trees. On the north side of the river the hills approach tolerably high and on [one] of them is a sort of mound, conspicuous at some miles distance, and a little eastward of it in a bottom is some timber, perhaps a quarter of a mile from the river."[11]

From near Chouteau's Island, Sibley's party turned south, crossing the north fork of the Cimarron, until they reached the main river in what is now far southwest Kansas. There they passed below a rock bluff at the point of a hill called "Point of Rocks," one of three such landmarks so named along the Santa Fe Trail. They continued to follow the Cimarron River through what is now a tip of far southeastern Colorado and the western panhandle of Oklahoma, and Sibley noted in his journal that his party's horses suffered from want of grass and water. But they found some the following day, Friday, September 30, when they entered a large valley. Sibley wrote that they had to dig about eighteen inches in the sand to locate good water because that on the surface was sulfurous, brackish, and strongly seasoned with buffalo urine.

The party soon entered what is now northeastern New Mexico. On Thursday, October 6, Sibley wrote: "Ground covered with snow this morning, the air chilly but not cold. Mercury 38 at 7. Wind from the northwest. It continued to snow a little at intervals 'till 12. Mercury 42. At 1 it cleared off, and at 4 was entirely gone. Altho' this snow moistened the fuel [buffalo dung] we have been obliged to use for the last 10 days and made it unfit for use, we did not suffer for fire, for we were so very fortunate as to find at nearly a mile distant a log of drift wood, which amply supplied us."[12]

Three days later the temperature was near freezing as Sibley's party climbed to the top of a high ridge, where they saw in the distance a mountain and a butte lying close together that resembled a pair of rabbit ears. The location is about seven miles northeast of present-day Clayton, New Mexico. Although white men may have named the landmark the "Rabbit Ears," there is a story that it was named for a Cheyenne chief named Rabbit Ears, who had been killed by Spaniards in the area years earlier. Regardless, Sibley wrote: "The 'Rabbit Ears' is the first great land mark, and to it, we now shape our course." With the landmark to guide them, the party pushed ahead, averaging about eight miles a day. On October 19, they saw the entrance to what was called "Taos Gap," the trail to Taos. That night they camped on the bank of the North Canadian River. By then Sibley had decided to go to Taos instead of Santa Fe. As he explained in his journal: "If I had attempted to reach Santa Fe, by way of San Miguel, my horses must nearly all have failed, and many of them been lost. If I attempt to haul the wagons over the mountains loaded as they are, the horses must necessarily fail. If I leave the wagons and pack the horses, still the horses must fail, and probably the wagons be lost entirely. If I hire mules to pack my baggage, etc. over to Taos, I believe I shall be able to get the empty wagons over the mountains, and thus at a small expense save all my horses and wagons, and prove the existence of a wagon route over the mountains into the Valley of Taos."[13]

That night Sibley wrote another letter to Paul Baillo at San Fernando, the principal village in Taos, asking him to send ten good pack mules and two packers to take the party's baggage and supplies over the mountains to Taos. The following morning Sibley sent two men to deliver the letter with instructions to meet again at the foot of a mountain. Sibley and his party resumed their travel and five days later, as planned, met his two men along with Baillo and the packers and mules he had requested. Baillo brought along an old Comanche Indian to lead Sibley's two wagons through a pass south of the route followed by the mules carrying the baggage and provisions that had been in the wagons.

A few days later, on Sunday, October 30, 1825, Sibley's party arrived at Taos about noon. He wrote in his journal: "Our poor horses seemed to pluck up fresh spirits, on sight of fields and houses; they entered the village merrily at a good trot as if they meant to enjoy their full share of the honour of being the first wagons over the mountains into the Valley of Taos. . . . The distance from Fort Osage to Taos is 740 miles. I think it probable that we shall be able to straighten the road in several places as we return, and that it will be thus shortened about forty or fifty miles."[14]

In Taos, Sibley found a small party of traders who had arrived the day before from Franklin, Missouri. They carried a letter from Commissioners Reeves and Mather, which contained a letter from the War Department advising that the office had asked the Mexican government for permission to mark the trail. If such consent was received, the letter continued, Sibley would be told so by authorities in New Mexico. Sibley went on to Santa Fe and met with the Mexican governor, who was friendly and cooperative, but he did not have the authority to grant Sibley permission to mark the road between the U.S. boundary on the Arkansas River and Santa Fe. It was not until the following June that Sibley learned he could examine the western part of the road in Mexican Territory over which he had already traveled, but the Mexican government prohibited him from "marking or cutting it out, or establishing any works of any kind whatever."[15]

Discouraged, Sibley returned to his home at Fort Osage, Missouri, late in the summer of 1826. When the two other commissioners, already in Missouri, declined to join Sibley the following spring to travel across what is now Kansas—to correct part of their earlier survey, shorten the road distance, and name landmarks—Sibley and a party of twelve men left Fort Osage in May 1927, did the job, and returned two months later. Sibley then auctioned the horses, a wagon, and other public property used in the resurvey and completed a written report that was signed by the two other commissioners. The report was sent to Washington, D.C., on October 27, 1827. For their services, each commissioner was paid eight dollars a day. Sibley received more than Reeves or Mather because he had worked more days.

Newspaper stories reporting on the survey generated more interest in the Santa Fe Trail, but history shows that the survey itself was pretty much a wasted effort. Sibley's journal and Joseph Brown's field notes were not published by the government. If they had been, traders head-

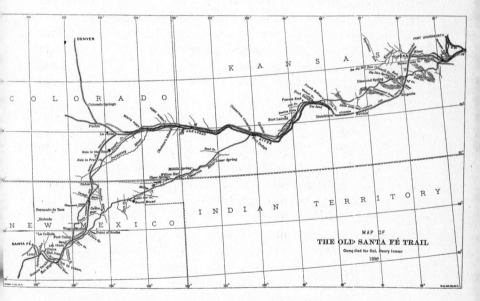

This late-nineteenth-century map of the Santa Fe Trail, produced more than seventy years after the government survey of the 1820s, appeared in Henry Inman's The Old Santa Fe Trail, *published in 1897 in New York. This map includes the route of the Atchison, Topeka and Santa Fe Railroad. After the arrival of the railroad at Santa Fe in 1880, there was no need to freight merchandise across the prairie and plains in wagon caravans over the Santa Fe Trail.* (Author's Collection)

ing for Santa Fe during the years that followed might have had easier journeys; the lives of some traders might have been saved. But the journal and field notes were filed away in Washington, D.C., and not discovered for decades, too late to do any good. Even the commissioners' marking of the trail with at least thirty-seven mounds of earth was likewise of little value because within a few years the earthen mounds were eroded by rain, snow, and wind.

During the years that followed, the Santa Fe Trail never became a true road. Although the remains of deep wagon ruts that can still be seen today in various places suggest it was an actual road, the trading caravans never did create a real one. The shifting eastern terminals during the trail's early years, the dry or mountain routes that stretched beyond the great bend of the Arkansas River, and numerous other variations plus the search for fresh grass caused caravans to move away from the ruts left by previous caravans. In wet weather, wagons followed the high ground to avoid the muddy ruts left by earlier wagons so as not to get bogged down. In dry weather, they followed river bottoms and draws, and in open country it was not uncommon for wagons to travel two or four abreast. The campsites along the trail were used by most caravans, but as the historian Max L. Moorhead observed, the Santa Fe Trail "was not a road, nor even a trace, but a series of tracks meandering over the plains in only the most general single course."[16]

SEVEN

---◆◆◆---

The Business of Trade, 1821-1829

*The successful business man sometimes makes his money
by ability and experience, but he generally makes it by mistake.*

—*Gilbert K. Chesterton*

ETWEEN 1821 AND 1824, perhaps ninety men annually invested
in the Santa Fe trade. Anyone could buy merchandise in Franklin
at prices 20 to 30 percent above those in Philadelphia, load it on a
wagon, and go to Santa Fe and sell it for a profit of 40 to 100 percent on
their investment. But by 1824, American goods glutted the market in
Santa Fe and northern Mexico, and traders had to go to the customhouse in Santa Fe, where Mexican officials placed a value on the merchandise without regard to the invoice prices. The value set by officials
might be 10 percent or 100 percent or even 130 percent above the actual
cost paid by the traders in Missouri. The tax paid by the traders was then
computed on the arbitrary value set by Mexican officials. Thus, in 1825
the character of the trade began to change. Large investors came on the
scene. Missouri merchants sought to capture their business through
newspaper advertisements, and the small number of investors organizing
caravans at Franklin hired more men to drive the wagons and to provide
protection on the trail.[1]

Franklin remained the center for trade between 1822 and 1826, but
the nearby town of Fayette had become in 1823 the county seat and
political center of Howard County. That was three years after the size of
Howard County had been reduced to its present boundaries, and new

counties made out of the remainder because of rapid settlement in the region. Much of the influx of settlers can be traced directly to the growth of the Santa Fe trade, which established Missouri as a supply base for the beef, pork, flour, and other foodstuffs raised by farmers, who found waiting markets where they could sell their produce and livestock.

The *Missouri Intelligencer,* which had been established at Franklin in 1819 by Benjamin Holliday, went through several changes in ownership. After Nathaniel Patten purchased the newspaper in 1826 and the Missouri River flooded much of Franklin, he moved the paper to nearby Fayette. When the river again flooded Franklin in 1828, residents moved the town about two miles north to higher ground and called the place New Franklin. Another flood soon washed away what was still left of Old Franklin, including the foundations of buildings that had been moved to high ground and the main street that once led from the river to the town's public square, where caravans bound for Santa Fe had formed their line of march. Only Old Franklin's cemetery, located on higher ground, escaped the eddies and whirlpools of the mighty Missouri. New Franklin survived, but by then other towns had been established in the new counties to the west and northwest. One of the new towns was Independence, founded in 1827, just east of what is now Kansas City, Missouri, which soon replaced New Franklin as eastern terminus of the Santa Fe Trail.[2]

Independence, whose name may have been inspired by the independent nature of President Andrew Jackson, was located about two miles south of the Missouri River and only twelve miles from the western border of Missouri. It was closer to Santa Fe than New Franklin; as the crow flies, Independence was about ninety miles west of New Franklin, and two miles from Independence was its own steamboat wharf. One early visitor described Independence as a "scattered town" consisting of "five or six rough log-huts, two or three clap-board houses, two or three so-called hotels, alias grogshops, a few stores, a bank, printing office, and barn-looking church."[3]

The year Independence was settled, James Aull, who operated a retail and commission business at Lexington, Missouri, which was on the Missouri River about thirty-three miles east of Independence, opened a branch store at Independence. Samuel C. Owens, who came to Missouri from Kentucky as a young man, was hired to run Aull's Independence store, which became a rendezvous for traders, hunters, trappers, and others heading west. Aull soon made Owens a partner in the Independence store, and he also formed a partnership with his brother Robert Aull and established other branch stores at Liberty and Richmond, Missouri. Because wholesaling was in its infant stages in the West and greater profits could be made by eliminating the middlemen, James Aull went east once a year to purchase supplies. He would leave Missouri in early January and return in March or April. Much of this time was consumed by horseback or wagon travel to St. Louis, where he took a stage to Louisville, Kentucky, and then to Pittsburgh and overland to Philadelphia. Travel in the winter was often slow due to storms and cold weather.

Once in Philadelphia, Aull would visit various firms and buy items needed for his trade, ranging from coarse wool and cotton cloth to more refined articles such as green gauze veils, head ornaments, and black silk gloves. He also purchased books and medical supplies for doctors back in Missouri as well as a plentiful supply of home remedies, including Epsom salts, castor oil, camphor, turpentine, quinine, Peruvian bark, snakeroot, rhubarb root, opium, paregoric, and pomade, an ointment made from apples. Aull also bought playing cards, bow strings, violin strings, Jew's harps, chessmen, and music boxes plus finer liquors, wines, and brandies. The heavier goods were boxed by Siter, Price, and Company, his Philadelphia representative, and usually sent by sailing ships down the Atlantic coast and around Florida to New Orleans and then by steamboat up the Mississippi River to St. Louis. The lighter items were moved overland by wagon to Pittsburgh, shipped down the Ohio River to St. Louis, and either taken overland or by steamboat up the Missouri River to Lexington.

On his return trip to Missouri, Aull would usually stop at Pittsburgh and purchase stoves, axes, plows, and hoes. During years when the corn crop in western Missouri was small and the production of corn whiskey dropped, Aull would buy as many as twenty barrels of rye whiskey from the firm of Anthony Beelen in Pittsburgh. As Aull traveled farther west, he might stop at Wheeling, Virginia (now West Virginia; residents of western Virginia loyal to the Union did not form a separate state until 1863). There he would purchase dry goods, paper, tableware, and saddles, especially for ladies. Women in Missouri insisted on saddles with blue plush seats that Aull could find only at Wheeling. From there he would continue west to Cincinnati, where he found peach brandy popular in Missouri, and all kinds of feathers. All of these purchases were sent to St. Louis by way of the Ohio River, and then on to Aull's store at Lexington, Missouri, from which he distributed the goods to his other stores. Much of Aull's business was conducted on credit. Eastern firms generally extended credit for six to twelve months before charging interest, but because it sometimes took longer than twelve months to collect on goods sold in Santa Fe, the business required much capital to avoid paying interest to eastern firms. The capital came from other business interests. Robert and James Aull fulfilled government contracts for the military, operated a sawmill, owned interest in three steamboats, and in 1834 constructed a mill near Independence to grind their own flour.[4]

Aull, like many other Missourians who profited from the Santa Fe trade, believed that the earlier survey and marking of the Santa Fe Trail plus the appointment of a U.S. consul at Santa Fe were evidence that the federal government was establishing a policy that would protect their interests. As they soon learned, however, that was not the case. When traffic to Santa Fe doubled between 1824 and 1825, traders returning to Missouri in the fall of 1825 complained that the Mexican government had again imposed heavy taxes upon their goods. Many Missourians thought the problem could be solved if the United States and Mexico signed a treaty. Some suggested that St. Louis be made a port of entry and delivery, with Mexican and U.S. customs officers who would know the actual cost of goods; late in 1825, St. Louis merchants asked Congress for this designation for their city. Missouri senator Thomas Hart Benton presented the merchants' appeal to the Senate, where it was referred to the Committee on Commerce. When the committee introduced a bill in March 1826, it also proposed ports of entry at Cincinnati and Louisville. But the bill died because opponents said it would require too many new revenue officers appointed by the president and would thereby increase executive patronage.

Indians along the Santa Fe Trail were another concern of traders. The treaties made by the survey commissioners had reduced difficulties with the Osage and Kansas Indians, but the Pawnees and especially the Comanches remained troublesome. The Comanches lived beyond the Arkansas River in Mexican Territory—outside the jurisdiction of the United States. Senator Benton proposed in 1826 that a military post be established on the Arkansas River to protect the traders, but General Jacob Brown, ranking officer of the army, said that supplying such a post would be difficult, and it was not approved. But Brown offered a substitute proposal to establish a cantonment with two companies of mounted infantry. However, the decision-makers in Washington favored a camp on the Missouri River instead of on the Arkansas, and Cantonment Leavenworth was established in the spring of 1827 by Colonel Henry Leavenworth, commander of the Third U.S. Infantry, atop a 150-foot bluff on the Missouri's west bank in what is now northeast Kansas. Troops were sent up the Missouri from Jefferson Barracks, a military post just south of St. Louis.[5]

While huts of logs and bark were being constructed at Cantonment Leavenworth, traders continued to traverse the Santa Fe Trail. In late

May 1826, a caravan of nearly a hundred men with wagons and carriages of almost every description left Franklin carrying a considerable amount of trading merchandise. The editor of the weekly *Missouri Intelligencer* at Fayette wrote on June 9, 1826: "It has the air of romance to see splendid pleasure carriages, with elegant horses journeying to the Republic of Mexico, yet it is sober reality. In fact the obstacles exist rather in the imagination than in reality. Nature has made a fine road the whole distance."

In May 1827, the largest trading caravan yet to travel the Santa Fe Trail from Missouri was captained by Ezekiel Williams and consisted of 105 men with fifty-three wagons and carriages. Augustus Storrs, newly appointed U.S. consul at Santa Fe, traveled in the mile-long caravan. Storrs observed that it was a sight "extremely beautiful to the eye of the spectator." The caravan arrived in Santa Fe without difficulty.[6]

Because traders experienced no serious Indian problems in 1827, there was a great expansion in traffic over the Santa Fe Trail in 1828. Exactly how many caravans headed for Santa Fe is not known, because no one kept track. Newspapers provided only scattered accounts. One party consisting of 150 men and many wagons loaded with about $150,000 in merchandise left Missouri in early May. A smaller caravan of about 50 men with goods valued at $41,000 left Missouri in late May. When these and other traders reached Santa Fe, they found to their chagrin that the Mexican government had introduced a new tariff raising the duties on many articles and also prohibiting the import of many things regularly carried by the traders. The result was lower profits.

As traffic over the trail increased, Indian problems also returned. When a caravan of about seventy traders with twelve hundred head of stock left Santa Fe in mid-August 1828 for Missouri, two men traveling ahead of the main caravan were shot by Indians in what is now Union County, New Mexico. One of the men, Samuel McNees, died near a small stream that the traders named McNees' Crossing. The bodies of McNees and the other man, Daniel Monroe, were carried forty miles to the Upper Cimarron Springs, where they were buried. A little later the surviving traders fired on and killed most of a small party of Pawnee Indians who approached their caravan. The Pawnees then went to war against the whites, and when the caravan reached the Great Bend of the Arkansas River, they attacked the traders and stampeded about seven hundred horses and mules. Apparently none of the traders or Indians were killed.[7]

A few weeks later, on September 1, 1828, a smaller caravan led by John Means left Santa Fe to return to Missouri. There were about twenty men in the party, including Milton Bryan, a twenty-one-year-old man whose mother lived in Boone County, Missouri. Bryan's personal recollections, after those of William Becknell, are the earliest we have from a Santa Fe trader. Bryan and the others in the caravan carried several thousand dollars in Mexican silver, their trading profit, and herded about 150 horses and mules loosely behind their four horse-drawn wagons. For a few days, the trip was uneventful, but when the caravan reached Upper Cimarron Springs, where they intended to make camp for the night, they went over a rise and found themselves entering a large camp of Comanche Indians. Bryan later wrote: "We could neither turn back nor turn to either side, on account of the mountainous condition of the country. We realized too late that we were in a trap from which it would require both Herculean and heroic efforts to escape."

There was only one road open to the traders: right through the Indian camp. With guns in readiness, the traders started through the encampment. An Indian chief met them with smiles of welcome and in Spanish invited the traders to spent the night. The chief added that his people had plenty of buffalo meat and that the young Indians would guard the traders' stock. Captain Means, in charge of the caravan, turned down the chief's invitation and gave the signal for the party to hurry on through. Means, a trader named Thomas Ellison, and Bryan were on horseback behind the wagons and horses when some Indians seized the bridle reins on the traders' horses and immediately began firing upon the white men.

Ellison and Bryan spurred their horses and got away, but Captain Means was hit and fell dead to the ground. As Bryan and the others raced away from the camp, many Indians jumped on their ponies and gave chase. "We succeeded in fighting them off until we got about a half-mile from their camp. Since darkness was setting in, we decided to go into camp for the night. We tied our old gray bell mare to a stake, and whenever any of us could do so, we would go and jingle the bell, thereby keeping our horses from stampeding. We corralled our wagons for better protection and were kept busy all night resisting onslaughts from the Indians," wrote Bryan.

At daybreak the traders moved out on the trail, only to be attacked again by the Comanches. Throughout the day Indians on ponies charged the caravan time and again. "We made but five miles of progress. It was a continuous fight, and we were harassed so greatly, it was very difficult for some of us to keep from falling into their hands," Bryan wrote.

Under normal conditions, the train could travel fifteen or more miles a day, but for four days it was slowed by frequent attacks. On the fifth day, as the traders moved onto the broad plains, there was no sign of the Indians. Some of the men felt that their pursuers had turned back, but about noon, the largest body of Indians yet seen swept down on the caravan, yelling loudly. Before Bryan and the others realized what was happening, the Indians stampeded all the 150 loose horses and mules. Almost by instinct, the Missourian William Y. Hitt galloped after the animals. He was about to turn a few head back toward the wagons when several Indians tried to capture him. He fought for his freedom from horseback and moments later escaped, but not unscathed. Bryan wrote that Hitt was "wounded in sixteen places. He was shot, tomahawked and speared."

Soon the ball from one of the traders' rifles found its mark, and an Indian toppled from his pony. Seeing one of their own hit, the rest of the Indians rode away. The lull gave the traders time to regroup, corral their four wagons, and build a breastwork with harnesses and saddles. They had barely finished the job when the Indians returned and made charge after charge at the small, makeshift fort on the plains. Fortunately the traders had a good supply of powder and bullets in their wagons. The Indians continued their attacks into the night, but when the moon went down about two hours after dark, they withdrew. There was a strange quiet in the darkness. For a minute or two not a man spoke. Quietly, they began to talk and soon realized they had to decide what to do next. Bryan later wrote:

> It was apparent to everyone that but two alternatives were before us. Should we resolve to die where we were or endeavor to escape in the gloom that surrounded us? It was a desperate situation, but our little band looked the matter square in the face, and after a council of war had been held, we resolved to save ourselves, if possible. In order to do so, it was necessary to leave our wagons, together with a large amount of silver coin in them, as we were unable to carry all of the latter in our flight. We packed up as much of it as we could carry, and bidding our wagons and hard-earned wealth a reluctant farewell, we stepped out into the darkness like specters, and hurried away from the scene of death. We knew that five hundred miles lay between us and the first settlement; but we were young, life was sweet, and we knew that there were loved ones at home who would look for our return with anxious hearts.

Just where their makeshift camp was located or how much silver was left behind is not known. What seems likely is that the Indians overran the camp the following morning and carried off the silver and other things. If not, perhaps some of the silver remains today buried along the

Santa Fe Trail. Regardless, the traders on that dark night in 1828 knew the Indians would discover they were gone and probably head east thinking the white men would take the most direct route toward Missouri. So the traders moved north as rapidly as they could walk in the darkness. Stopping only for brief rests, they walked all night and the next day and part of the next night until they reached the Arkansas River. By then they were growing weak. They had eaten nothing but some prickly pear cactus found along their route.

On the bank of the Arkansas River the traders slept. At daybreak, gambling that they were out of hearing of the Indians, they shot a buffalo and an antelope. "We ate without salt or bread, but no meal ever did or ever has tasted better to me than that one. Oh! but it was a feast for us all," Bryan wrote.

Bryan and the others then decided to lighten their loads by burying most of the silver coins they carried. Each man, however, would keep some. Reconnoitering a nearby island in the middle of the Arkansas River, they chose two cottonwood trees to bury their silver between. Bryan wrote that the silver amounted to more than ten thousand dollars. Another account, however, said it was closer to six thousand dollars. Regardless, and unknown to Bryan, they buried their silver on what was known as Chouteau's Island.

In an effort to avoid well-established trails closely watched by Indians, the traders continued north for three or four days until they reached a small stream, probably what is now called Pawnee River. They followed the stream eastward for ten days until they came upon the Santa Fe Trail somewhere near present-day Larned, Kansas. They then followed the nearby Arkansas River until they reached what is now called Cow Creek, north of modern Hutchinson, Kansas. Missouri was still two hundred miles to the east. Completely exhausted, the men made camp. The five strongest men agreed to go ahead to get help, leaving the remaining traders to get along as best they could. Bryan recalled what happened next:

I was one of the five selected to go ahead. I shall never forget the terrible suffering we endured. We had no blankets to sleep under, and it was getting late in the fall. Some of us were barefoot, and our feet were so sore we left stains of blood in every footstep. Deafness seized upon us so greatly, occasioned by our weak condition, we could not hear the report of a gun a few feet distant. Two of our men laid down their guns, saying they could carry them no farther, and would die if

Milton Bryan as he appeared several years after his adventures as a trader on the Santa Fe Trail. (Courtesy Kansas State Historical Society)

they did not get some water. We left them, and went in search of some. After following a dry branch several miles, we found a puddle of muddy water, from which we got half a bucket full. Although muddy, it was life for us, and we guarded it with jealous eyes. We returned to our comrades about daylight, and the water so refreshed them, they were able to resume the journey.

Bryan and the four other men resumed their weary march to the east, averaging about twenty miles a day. For eleven days they lived on what wild game they could kill—one turkey, one coon, one crow—some elm bark, and occasional wild grapes. After crossing the border into Missouri, they sighted a cabin near the Big Blue River about fifteen miles from Independence.

"The occupants of the cabin," recalled Bryan, "were women, seemingly very poor, but they offered to share with us a pot of pumpkin they were boiling. . . . They jumped on the bed while we greedily devoured the pumpkin, having to refuse some salt meat, as our teeth were so sore from long abstinence from salt. . . . We had not tasted bread or salt for thirty-two days. . . . In a short time two men came to the house, and took three of our party home with them."

The well and storm shelter visible in this photo did not exist when Milton Bryan and his party paused at Cow Creek Crossing in 1828. This photo, taken during the late 1860s, shows a caravan of wagons camped next to the crossing. (Courtesy Museum of New Mexico, negative no. 8285)

The next morning the settlers took Bryan and his four companions to Independence, where they told their story and how they had left their comrades behind. Without delay, seven men with fifteen horses rode out to the southwest to rescue the others, and within several days had found them and brought them back to Independence. By this time, Bryan had regained his strength. He bought a horse and started for his mother's home in Boone County, taking with him two hundred dollars in Mexican silver and a bank draft for five hundred dollars. That was all of his trading profit that he had been able to carry. When he reached Franklin, Bryan informed Captain Means's family of the man's death. It was a painful task for Bryan, who then proceeded to his mother's home, where he spent the winter recuperating.

The story of this trading party might end here, but it does not. By the spring of 1829, Bryan was determined to return to Santa Fe and, in the process, recover the silver buried on the island in the Arkansas River. He joined a new trading caravan of nearly forty wagons and about seventy men led by Charles Bent. Bent, who was born in 1799 in what is now Charleston, West Virginia, grew up in St. Louis, the son of a prominent judge. At age twenty-three, he was attracted to the western fur trade, but after a few years on the upper Missouri and in the Rocky Mountains, he turned to the more lucrative Santa Fe trade and was soon joined by his younger brother William.

Bent's 1829 Santa Fe–bound caravan was the first to be escorted by U.S. soldiers. In response to demands by Santa Fe traders for protection, President Andrew Jackson, who took office March 4, 1829, directed that four companies of soldiers escort the spring caravan as far west as the Arkansas River, the boundary between Mexico and the United States. Nearly two hundred soldiers of the Sixth Infantry under the command of Brevet Major Bennett Riley left their camp across the Missouri River from Cantonment Leavenworth and marched south along the western border of Missouri. In 1829, the U.S. Army had no mounted troops, but with Riley's soldiers were twenty heavily laden wagons and four carts carrying supplies, all pulled by oxen, plus a mule-drawn carriage carrying a six-pound cannon. Riley believed oxen could survive on the long journey by eating the grass along the trail. When he and his men reached the point where Kansas City, Missouri, stands today, they crossed the Missouri River and went a few miles to Round Grove, a camping spot in a beautiful grove of trees. There Riley and his men met the trading caravan captained by Charles Bent and began their journey down the Santa Fe Trail.

Bryan wrote that the soldiers and the traders "soon were out on the lonesome plains, seeing nothing alive but vast herds of buffalo and wild horses. Many of the soldiers had never seen any buffalo before, and took delight in slaughtering them. At Walnut Creek we halted to secure a cannon which had been thrown in there two years before, and succeeded in fishing it out. With a seine made of brush and grapevine, we caught more fine fish than we could dispose of; and one day a great deal of excitement was produced by a band of Indians running an enormous herd of buffalo onto us. The soldiers fired at them [the buffalo] by platoons, killing scores of them. We always traveled in two lines, and formed a hollow square at night, in which we all slept, except those on guard. Frequently some one would discover a rattlesnake or a horned frog in bed with him, and it did not take him long to get up."

Bent's caravan with its foot-soldier escort reached the Arkansas River near Chouteau's Island on July 10, 1829. There, on the international border, Brevet Major Riley established a camp, and the following day, Bryan and companions from the journey the year before went out with a squad of soldiers to recover the buried silver. "It was a few miles further up the Arkansas River, and when we came to the memorable spot, we found the money safe on the island, where we had left it. The water had

This painting by Oscar E. Beringhaus depicts an Indian raid on a caravan of traders being escorted by U.S. Army Infantry about 1828. The artist, born in St. Louis in 1874, traveled across the plains late in the nineteenth century to Taos, New Mexico, where he later made his home. He died there in 1952. Beringhaus's art was straightforward, simple, and clear. (Author's Collection)

washed the earth away, and the silver was exposed to the view of any one who might have passed along. We placed the money in sacks, and left it with Major Riley," wrote Bryan, who with his companions rejoined Bent's caravan and started for Santa Fe.

"We had not traveled far when our advance guard met some Indians. They turned, and when in two hundred yards of us, one man, Samuel Lamme, was killed, his body being completely filled with arrows. His head was cut off, and all his clothes stripped from his body. We had a cannon, but the Spaniards who drove it had it tied up in such a manner that it could not be utilized for some time; but when it was turned upon them, the Indians fled in dismay. The soldiers, hearing the firing, came to our assistance. The next morning the hills were covered with fully two thousand Indians, who had evidently gathered there for the purpose of annihilating us. The coming of the soldiers was indeed fortunate, for when the cowards saw them, they disappeared. Captain Riley accompanied us for a few days, and seeing no more Indians, he returned to his camp."

The remainder of the trip to Santa Fe was not uneventful. About a week after leaving Captain Riley, Bryan wrote, the caravan met

a hundred Spaniards, who were hunting buffalo. They had killed a great many, and were busy drying the meat. We waited for them to get ready, and all started for Santa Fe together. At Rabbit Ear Mountain, the Indians had built breast works in the brush, intending to fight us. The Spaniards went ahead, and had one of their number killed before dispersing the enemy. We passed Point of Rocks, and camped where the river runs through the Rocky Mountains. A Spaniard went out and killed a large panther, and next morning asked a comrade to go and help skin it. They saw Indians in the brush, and the first named Spaniard said, "Now for the mountains," but the other retreated, and was killed almost in reach of assistance. We concluded to change our destination, and to go to Taos instead of Santa Fe, but the Governor of the latter place sent soldiers to stop us, as Taos was not a port of entry. The soldiers guarded us for a week, until we reached Santa Fe. There we disposed of our goods, and soon began to think of the journey that would take us again to the loved ones at home.

When Bryan and the others in Bent's caravan left Santa Fe and started for Major Riley's camp on the Arkansas River, Bryan recalled that

seven priests and a number of wealthy families, comfortably fixed in wagons . . . accompanied us. The Mexican government sent General Bescario [Colonel Viscarra, inspector general of the Mexican Army], with five companies of soldiers and twenty-six friendly Indians, to guard us to the camp of Captain Riley. We had no trouble until we reached the Cimarron River, about sunset, when, just as we were getting ready to go into camp, the sentinels saw a hundred Indians approaching. They fired, and ran to camp. Knowing they were discovered, the Indians came and made friendly overtures. The friendly Indians with Bescario wanted to fight them, as they said the fellows meant mischief. We would not agree to stay all night with them, unless they would agree to give up their arms. They pretended they were going to do so when one of them placed his gun to the breast of our Indian interpreter, and fired. All at once a bloody scene ensued. Several of Bescario's men were killed, together with a number of

This aerial view shows "Point of Rocks" on the Santa Fe Trail in present-day Morton County, Kansas. There were four landmarks on the trail called "Point of Rocks" (see the glossary). (Courtesy Kansas State Historical Society)

mules. Finally the Indians were beaten, and tried to get away, but we followed them for some distance, and killed thirty-five of the treacherous rascals. Our friendly Indians were delighted, and proceeded to scalp the dead Indians, hanging their trophies on the handles of their spears. That night they indulged in a war-dance, which lasted until near morning.[8]

What Bryan did not relate was the savage cruelty displayed by the traders against the Indians. Philip St. George Cooke, who at the time was a junior officer under Major Riley, later wrote that the traders "took the skin from some of the bodies [of Indians] and stretched it on their wagons" before continuing their journey toward the Arkansas River. Even the Mexicans were shocked at the actions of the traders. Whether Bryan himself took part in this activity is not known.[9]

At the time, Bryan was unaware that back on the Arkansas River opposite Chouteau's Island, Major Riley had lost four soldiers to Indian harassment. The Indians also ran off seventy-five head of horses and oxen used to pull the troops' military supply vehicles. "Think what our feelings must have been," wrote Major Riley in his report, "to see them going off with our cattle and horses, when, if we had been mounted, we could have beaten them to pieces; but we were obliged to content ourselves with whipping them from our camp."[10]

For Bryan and others in the caravan returning to Major Riley's camp, the trip was uneventful, and once they arrived, the Mexican and American soldiers met. Major Riley hosted Colonel Viscarra, other Mexican officers, and guests in a feast on Chouteau's Island. Squatting on a large green blanket, Major Riley provided bread, buffalo meat, and salt pork, then considered a delicacy on the plains. Colonel Viscarra offered a large raw onion, and the feast was topped off with whiskey served in tin cups. Later, Colonel Viscarra feasted Major Riley and his officers in his large tent. Sixteen officers sat around a table with real silver and ate fried ham and cakes and drank chocolate and Mexican wines.

Lieutenant Philip St. George Cooke wrote that the next day

we had time to look about us, and admire the strangest collection of men and animals that had perhaps ever met on a frontier of the United States. There were a few Creoles, polished gentlemen, magnificently clothed in Spanish costume; a larger number of grave Spaniards, exiled from Mexico, on their way to the United States, with much property in stock and gold, their whole equipage Spanish; there was a company of Mexican Regulars, as they were called, in uniform, mere apologies for soldiers, or even men; several tribes of Indians, or Mexicans, much more formidable as warriors, were grouped about with their horses, and spears planted in the ground; Frenchmen were there of course; and our hardy veterans in rags, but well armed and equipped for any service; four or five languages were spoken; but to complete the picture, must be mentioned the 2000 horses, mules, jacks, which kept up an incessant braying. . . . In the dusk of evening, a large group of Mexican Indians came into camp, bearing aloft on spears the scalps which they had lately taken, and singing Indian songs; dark figures, with matted hair streaming over their shoulders, uttering the wild notes of their deep-toned choruses, they resembled demons rather than men. Suddenly one would enter the circle, and indulge in an extravagant display of grief, beating his forehead and breast, and howling like a famished wolf; and then dashing the scalps to the ground, stamp on them and fire his gun at them. After this propitiatory lament to the manes of the departed friend, or relation, he would burst forth, with the others, into the wildest and most unearthly song of triumph and exultation. The

Indian who had lost, and avenged his brother . . . made us speeches, unintelligible of course; but expanding his bare chest, and striking it forcibly with his palm, he would end them by exclaiming, 'Me die for the Americans.'[11]

Bryan makes no reference to these events in his narrative, but he may already have picked up his share of the recovered silver entrusted to Major Riley and started back for Missouri. There, Bryan retired as a Santa Fe trader.

EIGHT

The Growth of Trade, 1830-1835

*New Mexico possesses but few of those natural
advantages, which are necessary to anything like
a rapid progress in civilization.*

—*Josiah Gregg*

WHEN WORD REACHED the East that U.S. soldiers had safely
escorted William Bent's caravan back to Missouri, *Niles Weekly Register,* published in Baltimore, reported: "President Jackson has saved it
[the Santa Fe trade] this year by doing all that he could—granting an
escort of infantry; let Congress at the ensuing session perform its part by
granting an appropriation for mounting and properly equipping that
escort." Congress did talk about it but never made such escorts a government policy.

By the spring of 1830, Missouri traders knew the federal government
would not provide military escorts that year for the Santa Fe–bound caravans. With the Indian attacks of 1829 still fresh in their minds, the
traders preparing for the spring journey to Santa Fe realized they would
have to protect themselves. From experience they knew that if they traveled in one compact, well-armed body and corralled their wagons at
night, they could protect themselves from Indians. Though their organization was almost military, it was very democratic. Each man had a vote,
and the officers of the caravan were chosen by open balloting. First, the
men elected a captain of the caravan, nearly always someone experienced in trail travel, often a wealthy trader who knew the ways of the

Indians. Next, the men elected a lieutenant for each division of the caravan, the number of divisions depending on the caravan's size. Each lieutenant's duties were to ride in advance of his group of wagons and inspect the road and the crossings and warn the teamsters driving the wagons of rough spots on the trail. Each lieutenant also supervised the corralling of wagons when the caravan camped each evening. One authority observed that the first wagon to reach a campsite would park at an angle. The second wagon would then pull up at the same angle, next to the first wagon, stopping with its near hind wheel against the front wheel of the first wagon. This process was continued until the enclosure was completed. "It was sometimes in the form of a square—one division to each side if the caravan was composed of four divisions. But it was as often in a circle or an oval. The wheels were frequently chained and locked solidly together. Thus was constructed a sort of temporary fort or stockade. In case of attack it afforded a defense, and the animals were sometimes driven into it. The encampment was made where wood and water were to be had, if possible, and where the grass was sufficient for the animals of the caravan. Guards were always set at night, and every man was expected to take his turn at guard-duty."[1]

In addition to the election of a lieutenant for each division, a clerk, three judges to try offenses, an officer of the guard, and even a chaplain were elected along with someone to guide the caravan. Ceran St. Vrain may have been elected captain of the 1830 caravan that included Charles Bent. The caravan had about 130 men and 60 or 70 wagons pulled by oxen instead of mules or horses.[2]

Bent probably recommended the use of oxen since he had seen how successful they had been the previous year pulling Major Riley's military supply wagons on the trail. Bent had reported that oxen had performed almost as well as mules and that Indians were less likely to attempt to run off oxen. Bent also observed that as supplies were consumed by the soldiers and the weight of the military wagons reduced, unneeded oxen could be killed to feed the soldiers. When the military escort stopped at the Arkansas River the previous summer, Bent got Riley to loan him a yoke of oxen so he could test them as draft animals for the remainder of his caravan's journey to Santa Fe. Thus, when Bent set out from near Independence, Missouri, in May 1830, he knew oxen could perform well as draft animals. However, he soon learned that the animals' hooves became smooth and tender from so much walking over the grass-covered country. He thought the problem could be solved by shoeing the oxen with iron while on the trail, but few men knew how to do the job, and the oxen objected to the process. The problem was later partly solved by fitting oxen with moccasins made of raw buffalo hide. The moccasins worked well in dry weather but wore through when wet.

Oxen were harnessed to wagons with huge wooden ox yokes, a curved beam set on the animals' necks, just behind the horns. Curved wooden ox bows went down around their necks and attached to the yoke by being poked through holes and held in place by wooden pins or metal keys. The yoke had an iron ring hanging from the center, to which was attached the tongue of the wagon or the draw chain. The Spaniards and Mexicans, unlike the Americans, lashed the yoke to the horns of the oxen with a broad rawhide strap, perhaps a dozen feet long. Americans did not like this method because it tended to lift the animal's head and prevent a full thrust of its weight.

The traders also learned that oxen could pull heavier loads than the same number of mules, especially through muddy or sandy terrain. The cloven hoof of the oxen was firmer than the small hoof of the mule, but the strength of oxen dropped in areas where the prairie grass became drier and shorter. Although the original cost of a team of mules was much greater than a yoke of oxen, one trader later wrote that the loss ultimately sustained by them was less than with oxen, "to say nothing of the comfort of being able to travel faster and more at ease."[3]

Bent's caravan reached Santa Fe on August 4, 1830, without incident, and by the end of October was back in Missouri—but with less profit than hoped for because of high Mexican tariffs. When the annual trading caravan began to take shape in the spring of 1831, half of the two hundred wagons were drawn by oxen, the rest by mules. The traders took their wagons to Council Grove, 150 miles southwest of Independence. The early arrivals awaited the coming of the others. The time was spent resting and grazing the animals; making last-minute repairs to wagons, wagon tires, harnesses, and yokes; and repacking wagons. Since there was little timber to be found west of Council Grove, the traders usually cut and prepared timbers to be used should there be a breakdown on the trail. These things were done in the shade of the large elm, oak, ash, walnut, hickory, and cottonwood trees that marked Council Grove on the banks of the Neosho River. By 1831, Council Grove was becoming the rendezvous point where traders gathered to agree on rules for travel and to elect caravan officers. Elisha Stanley was elected captain of the caravan, and on May 27, 1831, the two hundred people in the caravan, including a few Spanish women, set out for Santa Fe carrying two small cannons and $200,000 in merchandise.

One young man traveling in the caravan was Josiah Gregg, age twenty-four, whose doctor had recommended a trip across the prairies for a change of air and habits to improve his health. Thirteen years later, Gregg would write *Commerce of the Prairies,* a classic work detailing the first two decades of the Santa Fe trade. Of his 1831 visit to Council Grove with Bent's wagon train, Gregg wrote: "The heterogeneous appearance of our company, consisting of men from every class and grade of society, with a little sprinkling of the softer sex, would have formed an excellent

A caravan on the Santa Fe Trail, as drawn by Frederic Remington. This illustration appeared in Collier's Weekly, *March 12, 1904. For some unknown reason, Remington destroyed the original illustration in 1908.* (Author's Collection)

subject for an artist's pencil. It may appear, perhaps a little extraordinary that females should have ventured across the Prairies under such forlorn auspices. Those who accompanied us, however, were members of a Spanish family who had been banished in 1829, in pursuance of a decree of the Mexican congress, and were now returning to their homes in consequence of a suspension of the decree. Other females, however, have crossed the prairies to Santa Fe at different times, among whom I have known two respectable French ladies, who now [1844] reside in Chihuahua."[4]

The caravan pushed westward, crossed the Arkansas River on June 11, and camped just west of where Dodge City, Kansas, stands today, near the celebrated "Caches." Following the desert route, the caravan soon came upon perhaps three thousand Indian warriors and their families, who camped near the traders. There was no trouble, and the caravan continued toward Santa Fe, reaching there in late July or early August. After disposing of the merchandise, Bent's caravan returned to Missouri.

The men with this corralled wagon train are preparing to resume their journey over the Santa Fe Trail. Their wagons were pulled by mules, who have more staying power than horses. Oxen were also used extensively to pull freight wagons over the trail where adequate grass could be found for feed. This drawing by Thomas Willing appeared in Henry Inman's 1897 book The Old Santa Fe Trail. *(Author's Collection)*

A smaller caravan also left Independence in the spring of 1831 bound for Santa Fe. Whether it left too late to join the annual caravan, or its traders chose not to travel with the others, is not known, but the small group set out on May 4 with twenty-two mule-drawn wagons, perhaps eighty men, and a six-pound cannon owned by the three veteran fur traders leading the company—William L. Sublette, David E. Jackson, and Jedediah Smith. Jackson and Sublette owned ten wagons, while

Smith owned eleven, and he was assisted by two of his younger brothers traveling with the caravan.

This was the same Jedediah Smith, now twenty-five, who supposedly first traveled to Santa Fe in 1818, then traded with Indians in what is now Kansas and eastern Colorado, and then joined General William Ashley in the fur trade on the upper Missouri River. At the same time the Kentuckian Sublette, then twenty-four, and Jackson, perhaps in his early thirties, had also joined Ashley. The three men and others in Ashley's party traversed the plains and Rocky Mountains trapping beaver. In 1826, they purchased Ashley's interest and proceeded to open great areas of the West to the fur trade, with Smith as the explorer, Jackson the field manager, and Sublette taking the year's catch of furs back to Missouri, selling them, and returning with supplies for another year. But in 1830, Smith, Jackson, and Sublette in turn sold the fur company. Smith was persuaded to enter the Santa Fe trade and convinced Jackson and Sublette to join him as partners.[5]

The first fifteen days of Smith's 1831 trading venture were uneventful, but on May 19, E. S. Minter, a clerk, was killed by Indians while hunting antelope. A few days later the caravan forded the Arkansas River and began the sixty-mile journey across the Cimarron Desert, what was known as the "dry route." The year was particularly arid and the caravan's water supply had dwindled. Smith, familiar with the route, turned directly south from the Arkansas River toward the upper pools of Crooked Creek, in what is now Meade County, Kansas. The watering hole was about fifteen to twenty miles south of the Arkansas River. Traveling through the sand hills, against a hot wind blowing sand and alkali dust, the caravan reached the pools late in the afternoon, only to find them dry. The following day, May 27, Smith left camp with Thomas Fitzpatrick to find water. Soon Smith sent Fitzpatrick back to get the rest of the party. Fitzpatrick, with his eyeglass, saw Smith traveling to the southwest. It was the last time Fitzpatrick saw him. When Fitzpatrick led the party with its wagons over the trail blazed by Jedediah Smith, they found no trace of him. Fearing the worst, the caravan continued southwest and reached Santa Fe on July 4, 1831.

The disappearance of Jedediah Smith remained a mystery until Smith's brother Austin purchased his brother's gun and pistols from some Mexicans in Santa Fe. They had obtained the weapons while bartering with some Comanche Indians. The Indians told the Mexicans they had taken the weapons from a white man they had killed on the plains in what is now southwest Kansas. Austin Smith described what he had learned in a letter sent to his father in September 1831; in 1912, Ezra Delos Smith wrote that his granduncle, Jedediah Smith, had

reached the Cimarron River at what was later known as Fargo Springs, in what is now Seward County Kansas. While his horse was drinking he dismounted, quenched his own thirst, and then remounted. Twenty Comanches, who were in hiding, waiting for buffalo to come to the water, came out, and Smith tried to get them to accompany him back to the wagons to trade, or to wait till the wagons came and trade there at the water. Their chief, a medicine man who believed that his great medicine rendered him invulnerable, tried to approach, but was warned back. The Indians succeeded in frightening Smith's horse, and as soon as it turned they shot at him with their arrows, one of which wounded him in the left arm. He instantly turned and shot the chief dead, and, drawing his pistols, killed an Indian with each. Then, grasping his ax, he dashed in among them, dealing death at every blow. Slashed with knife cuts and pierced with a lance thrust, he sank down from loss of blood. The Indians approached to scalp him, when he suddenly rose and stabbed three with his knife, and dropped dead. But he was not alone; there were thirteen of his enemies stretched dead on the ground. The Comanches concluded that he had been more than mortal, and that it would be better to propitiate his spirit; so they did not mutilate his body, but later gave it the same funeral rites they gave their chief.[6]

Before Sublette and Jackson returned to Missouri with Jedediah Smith's brothers, still another trading caravan, this one led by Charles Bent, left Independence, Missouri, on September 10, 1831. Oxen were used to pull the group's ten wagons. Bound for Taos, the majority of the party were Mexicans employed by Bent, who along with Albert Pike and a few other whites made up a party of thirty or forty men on horseback and in wagons. Pike was a young, unemployed schoolteacher from Massachusetts who had come west in search of opportunities. But, as he later wrote: "I thought that I was finally educated and that, therefore, my opportunities would be greatly improved. When I got out West I found my education did not amount to much. It was not practical and what a man needed out there more than a school education was practical, common sense."[7]

When Charles Bent's caravan came in sight of the Sangre de Cristo Mountains, Pike and a few other men rode ahead to Taos. Pike remained

Independence, Missouri, grew as it became the eastern terminal of the Santa Fe Trail during the 1830s. This illustration shows a busy street scene at Independence. It appeared in Santa Fe National Historic Trail, Comprehensive Management and Use Plan, *published in 1990 by the National Park Service, U.S. Department of the Interior. The artist is not identified.* (Author's Collection)

there about a week before going south to Santa Fe, a town he did not like. The food was different, and he was offended by the fandango, in which well-dressed women, including harlots, along with priests, thieves, and "half-breed Indians" all danced the waltz together. Pike described the governor's palace as nothing more "than a mud building, fifteen feet high, with a mud-covered portico, supported by rough pine pillars. The gardens, and fountains, and grand stair-cases, &c., are, of course, wanting. The Governor may raise some red pepper in his garden, but he gets his water from the public spring."[8]

Pike would later become a prominent journalist and lawyer in Arkansas, and still later a Confederate general during the Civil War. In 1861, he wrote what is often described as the finest version of the song "Dixie." Even later he became grand commander of the Supreme Council of the Scottish Rite, Southern Jurisdiction of the United States, a Masonic order with headquarters in Washington, D.C. Pike is perhaps best remembered as the first writer of significant prose about the South-

This nineteenth-century illustration by Thomas Willing, from Henry Inman's The Old Santa Fe Trail *(1897), shows the Pueblo de Taos north of Santa Fe.* (Author's Collection)

The Santa Fe traveler Albert Pike was offended when he watched a fandango in Santa Fe. (Author's Collection)

west. It appeared in *Prose Sketches and Poems, Written in the Western Country*, a book published in Boston in 1834.

IN NEW MEXICO, the mercantile system was slow to develop. Spain's long neglect of New Mexico and the numerous duties imposed upon goods sent there from the interior had hampered the development of trade. After the Mexican Revolution and the opening of trade with the United States, New Mexican merchants did not have the capital needed to engage in any large business deals with Americans, but the new governor of the province recognized that the increased trade with Missouri would be of benefit. Thus, in 1825 the governor commissioned Manuel Simón Escudero, a member of the Chihuahua legislature, to visit the United States and negotiate for American protection from Indians of caravans traveling over the Santa Fe Trail. Escudero joined a caravan returning to Missouri. Traveling with him were two Mexican merchants: one from Sonora, the other from Chihuahua, who led a pack train of five hundred horses and mules. Escudero traveled to St. Louis and then to Washington, D.C., where he met with the Mexican minister before returning to Franklin, Missouri, where the merchants disposed of their goods and purchased new ones, along with six or seven new wagons. Escudero and the merchants then returned to New Mexico. The merchants are the first Mexicans known to trade in the United States by way of the Santa Fe Trail. Five years later, in 1830, José Ignacio Ortiz, the alcalde of Santa Fe, traveled from Santa Fe to Independence and then east to Philadelphia to purchase merchandise, but it was not until the late 1830s that New Mexican merchants began making a concerted effort to obtain foreign goods directly instead of from their traditional Mexican suppliers.[9]

Americans dominated the trade through much of the 1830s, and Mexican dollars became the principal circulating medium in Missouri, but the merchandise carried to New Mexico became so plentiful, and money so scarce, that traders were forced to sell their goods for what they could get and then return home to Missouri. Steamboats carried goods from St. Louis up the Missouri River to Independence and other settlements, including Cantonment Leavenworth, which became Fort Leavenworth in 1833 when the War Department ordered that all cantonments be called forts. The change came just before Missourians became alarmed by the Black Hawk War of 1832. The war was the result of hostilities occurring the previous year, when Chief Black Hawk, leader of the Algonquian nation, which included the Sauk and Fox tribes, saw

This drawing by George Gray shows Fort Leavenworth in 1838. Steamboats delivered supplies to the port, located on the west bank of the Missouri River north of present-day Kansas City, Missouri. Supplies were then transported by wagons from a wharf up the road (lower right) to the post, which was established in 1827 to protect travelers on the Santa Fe Trail. The trail itself was located several miles to the south. (Courtesy Kansas State Historical Society)

whites plowing Algonquian ancestral burial grounds in Illinois. Black Hawk and his warriors began raiding outlying farms belonging to whites who thought that a treaty signed in 1824 had ceded all Indian lands east of the Mississippi to the government, paving the way for settlement in Wisconsin and western Illinois. Brigadier General Henry Atkinson moved against the Indians with a large detachment of regular troops from Jefferson Barracks south of St. Louis. In addition, several companies of militia from Illinois and Missouri were raised to assist the regulars. General Atkinson and his troops drove Black Hawk and his warriors from Illinois across the Mississippi River into Missouri. Black Hawk, however, returned to Illinois, where Atkinson demanded that the Indians go back across the Mississippi. When Black Hawk refused, Atkinson and his forces, who included a young militia captain named Abraham Lincoln, chased the Indians north into Wisconsin, where many were killed. Black Hawk was later captured and taken east to meet President Andrew Jackson. He was then forced to sign another treaty ceding more land in Wisconsin, and a portion of Iowa, to white settlement.[10]

The Black Hawk War had little effect on the Santa Fe trade, but during the summer of 1832 cholera broke out among soldiers at Jefferson Barracks near St. Louis, which then had a population of 6,918. Many residents fled; during the first two weeks of the outbreak, twenty to thirty people died each day. Although there was much concern in central and western Missouri that cholera might spread westward, it did not. By then, however, the annual spring caravan of traders bound for Santa Fe had already left Independence. In all, 110 employees and 40 traders with 70 wagons carrying goods valued at $140,000 made the journey.[11]

Independence suffered from the flooding Missouri River in 1833, though not as severely as Franklin had five years earlier. The steamboat landing at Independence was washed away by high water during the summer, and steamboat pilots had to go farther upstream to find another location to tie up and unload freight. Some stopped at Blue Mills or at Wayne City, several miles below Independence, but most tied up at Chouteau's Landing, where Francis Chouteau, son of Pierre, had in 1826 built a trading post and warehouse so that his American Fur Company could cater to French trappers and voyageurs. Chouteau's Landing was a few miles upstream from Independence. But when the steamboat *John Hancock*, a side-wheeler, came up the Missouri in 1832, it passed Chouteau's Landing and tied up on the south bank about two miles farther upstream, near the mouth of the Kansas River. The steamboat carried a stock of merchandise for John Calvin McCoy and docked at the point nearest McCoy's store, which was located four miles south in a new settlement called Westport. McCoy's general store catered to traders and trappers returning east. The spot where the *John Hancock* tied up became known as Westport Landing.

A few miles west of Westport in what is now Kansas, Moses R. Grinter, a twenty-one-year-old Kentuckian, was appointed by the government to operate a ferry across the Kansas River at what became known as Delaware Crossing, about four miles upstream from where the Kansas flows into the Missouri River. While the ferry made north-south travel easier, especially for military troops moving south from Fort Leavenworth, it was of little value to Santa Fe traders since it was located north of the trail.

Settlers, traders, and others found the country beyond the western border of Missouri very attractive. One writer observed:

> Except for its lack of mountain and sea, a more beautiful and attractive landscape can scarcely be found anywhere, than that near the

confluence of the Missouri and Kaw Rivers. In the late spring or early summer, it is especially charming, when the grass on the prairie is fresh and sprinkled profusely with flowers of many hues; when crabapple thickets, many acres in extent, are covered with pink blossoms, surpassing in depth of color and delicacy of fragrance the bloom of our orchards; when the mignonette-like perfume of the wild grape and the subtle sweetness of the sensitive brief, a species of mimosa, with its flowers like purple globes, sprinkled with gold-dust, entrance the senses. . . . The oppressive monotony of the wide prairie is broken by gentle slopes and deep ravines, well wooded with groves of stately oaks and walnuts, which form promontories of woodland, jutting out into the open-prairie sea; and graceful elms, tall cottonwoods and stately sycamores adorn the margins of the streams. Pleasant brooks wander through the valleys, and plenteous springs entice the wayfarer by the sparkle and murmur of their cool, sweet waters. The Mormons, who occupied for a time about 1833, a district of like character in the adjacent counties of Missouri, styled it the Land of Promise—the Garden of the Lord—and well they might.[12]

From the western border of Missouri to Council Grove, a distance of about 150 miles, caravans had little difficulty with Indians or in locating water. The rolling country, dotted with stands of trees, provided more than sufficient fuel for cooking fires. But beyond Council Grove there were fewer trees, often only buffalo chips could be found for fuel, and in dry years water was scarce. Then, too, there were unfriendly Indians. On January 1, 1833, a party of twelve traders apparently led by J. H. Carr was returning to Missouri with a mule pack train and more than ten thousand dollars in gold and silver. When they reached a point about 200 miles northeast of Santa Fe in what is now the Texas Panhandle, a band of Indians, probably Kiowas, attacked the traders as they traveled near the Canadian River. The *Missouri Republican,* March 3, 1833, reported that when the attack began a man named Pratte was killed while trying to catch a mule some distance from camp. Soon a man named Mitchell was killed, and several traders were wounded. The traders tied their mules to a small tree and dug trenches as quickly as possible. About midnight the party tried to get away, but they were driven back. The battle continued all of the next day until the traders ran out of ammunition. The whites were about to give up when they were hailed by the Indians, who told them in Spanish that they might go. The Indians may have given up hope of overrunning the traders' camp. By then all of the traders' mules had been killed. They abandoned their property, including their gold and silver, and the ten surviving traders started to walk east toward Missouri. Five of them soon left the river and followed a direct route, eventually reaching Missouri. The others apparently continued down the Canadian. Three of them made it to a Creek Indian settlement forty-two days later, but what happened to the other two is not known. They were never heard from again.[13]

As word of the Indian attack on Carr's mule train spread across Missouri and east to Washington, D.C., Congress in early March approved the establishment of a regiment of dragoons or U.S. Mounted Rangers. Colonel Henry Dodge was put in charge. On orders from the president, Dodge directed Captain William N. Wickliffe and more than 100 mounted rangers to escort the spring caravan to Santa Fe. Along with the mounted rangers were 25 infantry soldiers, six wagons to carry supplies, and a cannon. From Fort Leavenworth, the escort traveled to Round Prairie, a campsite on the Santa Fe Trail near the western border of Missouri. There Captain Wickliffe learned that the traders had been delayed at Independence because of heavy rains and the resulting muddy roads, and that the rendezvous had been changed to Council Grove to the southwest. The military escort took three weeks to reach Council Grove, where it arrived on June 13. After the trading caravan of perhaps 184 men and more than a hundred wagons and carriages carrying more than $100,000 in goods arrived, the large party set out for Santa Fe about June 19, 1833.

As the wagons and carriages left the Arkansas River and followed the dry route, there were almost continuous rains. Because of the moisture in the normally arid region, the traders couldn't help but leave behind a trail in the softened turf, something of a permanent trail for later groups to follow. One traveler in the caravan who may have especially appreciated the rains and the resulting plentiful drinking water was the twenty-five-year-old Mary Donoho. Accompanied by her husband, William, and their nine-month-old daughter, she was the first Anglo-American woman to go over the Santa Fe Trail. William Donoho was taking a large quantity of merchandise to trade.

Charles Bent had been elected captain of the caravan before it left Diamond Spring, fifteen miles west of Council Grove. At the Arkansas River, the military escort and the caravan parted company, and aside from the rain encountered by the traders beyond the Arkansas River, the journey to Santa Fe was uneventful. Details of the caravan's return journey to Missouri are sketchy, but after it joined the waiting military escort at the Arkansas River and moved toward Missouri, Indians attacked. Though no one in the caravan or escort was reported killed or wounded, the Indians supposedly hemmed in the group. For want of food, fourteen of the escort's horses had to be slaughtered.[14]

Three persons who had traveled to Santa Fe did not return with the caravan to Missouri: William and Mary Donoho and their daughter. After disposing of his merchandise, William entered the hotel business and operated the La Fonda Hotel on the Plaza. There, during the next few years, Mary Donoho gave birth to another girl and a boy. In 1837, however, when citizens rose up against the Mexican governor Albino Pérez and several leading men of Santa Fe were killed, William Donoho decided that Santa Fe was not a fit place to live and to raise his children. In the fall of that year, the Donohos joined a trading caravan returning to Missouri and took with them three Texas white women William had rescued from Comanche Indians. The women had been taken captive in Texas, brought to New Mexico by the Comanches, and now they returned to their homes in Texas. Less than two years later the Donohos left Missouri and moved to Clarksville, located in northeast Texas.[15]

INDIAN COMMISSIONERS proposed in early 1834 that a military garrison be established near the Santa Fe Trail on the Arkansas River above the Little Arkansas River, but General Henry Leavenworth, the new commander of the southwestern frontier, opposed the plan. When he arrived to take command at Fort Gibson in what is now eastern Oklahoma, he asked to be furnished with some of the newly organized dragoons. Leavenworth sent word to Missouri that the annual spring caravan would receive an escort and that dragoons would meet the traders on the Santa Fe Trail. When the caravan left Independence in May 1834, it was captained by Josiah Gregg and consisted of about 160 men and eighty wagons. Fifty of the men were traders, including Ira G. Smith, brother of the late Jedediah Smith. The caravan carried $150,000 in merchandise, including a small Ramage printing press with an iron bed and platen that would a year later print New Mexico's first newspaper—*El crepúsculo de la libertad* (The dawn of liberty)—published at Taos by Padre Antonio Martínez. About the same time the caravan left Independence, Captain Clifton Wharton left Fort Gibson with fifty men of the new First U.S. Dragoons with pack animals, one wagon, and several head of cattle to feed the soldiers. Reaching the Santa Fe Trail in modern Neosho County, Kansas, the dragoons followed the trail to near present-day Durham, Marion County, Kansas. There the soldiers waited until the trading caravan arrived on June 8, and the next day accepted Captain Wharton's offer to escort their caravan west.

The journey was uneventful until about June 26, when a party of about a hundred Comanches began following the caravan and the dragoons and camping about a mile away from them each night. When the traders and dragoons reached the Arkansas River, Captain Wharton wanted to arrange a meeting to invite the Indians to meet Colonel Henry Dodge, who was planning an expedition onto the prairies, but Josiah Gregg and four other traders, without Wharton's knowledge, crossed the river and warned the Indians to keep away. Hard feelings developed between Wharton and Gregg, and when Gregg asked Wharton to escort the caravan as far as the Canadian River in Mexican Territory, Wharton refused. Gregg resigned as captain of the caravan, and Ira G. Smith was elected in his place. That night the Comanches broke camp and moved eastward. The next day, Captain Wharton and the dragoons left the caravan and started back to Fort Gibson as the caravan continued its journey toward Santa Fe without difficulty.

After a summer of trading, the traders organized their homeward-bound caravan and moved out of Santa Fe in early September. By the time the traders left the Canadian River, there were 140 men and forty wagons heading for Missouri, which they reached in early October without difficulty. The *Missouri Republican* in St. Louis reported on October 24, 1834, that the traders "brought in, as near as can be ascertained, $40,000 in gold, $140,000 in specie, $15,000 worth of beaver, 50 packs of buffalo robes, 12,000 pounds of wool, and 300 head of mules, valued at $10,000."

By the time the traders had returned to Missouri, word was spreading across the plains and prairies that Charles Bent had built a fort on the Arkansas River east of the Rocky Mountains for the purpose of trading with the Indians. Four years earlier, Bent had met Ceran St. Vrain, another Missourian, who had been a clerk for Bernard Pratte and Company, a prominent St. Louis mercantile firm. Bent and St. Vrain entered the Santa Fe trade during the late 1820s. By 1830, they became partners and concluded that if they had an office in Santa Fe where they could store their merchandise until demand increased in the fall, they could make a better profit. Under this plan Charles Bent made the buying trips to Missouri while St. Vrain remained in Santa Fe to sell the goods. It worked well, and soon they opened a store on the south side of the main plaza opposite the Palace of the Governors. Then they opened another in Taos. Their business prospered, first as the firm of Bent and St. Vrain and later, after Bent's brother William entered the partnership, as Bent, St. Vrain and Company. The company expanded its operations onto the southern plains, a move that would make it the largest and strongest

William Bent (1809–1869) became a partner in the firm of his older brother Charles and Ceran St. Vrain. After Charles Bent was killed in 1847, and St. Vrain retired in 1849, William Bent became sole owner of the firm. That year, disgusted at the low price the government had offered him for Bent's Fort, he blew it up and built a new post to the east along the Arkansas River. (Courtesy Kansas State Historical Society)

merchandising and fur-trading firm in the Southwest during the middle nineteenth century.

Charles Bent's young brother William played a significant role in helping the firm capture some of the Indian trade. About 1830, he was operating a trading camp somewhere between present-day Canon City and Pueblo, Colorado. A party of Cheyenne warriors stopped at the camp one day and inspected the trade goods, and then most of them left. But two Cheyennes lingered and were still in the camp when William Bent saw a party of Comanches approaching. The Cheyennes and Comanches were enemies, and Bent quickly hid his two visitors before the Comanches arrived. The Comanches, however, saw the Cheyenne moccasin prints in the earth and demanded to know where their enemies were. Bent lied and said all of the Cheyennes had left his camp. The Comanches departed, apparently to look for the Cheyennes. Bent's action in thus saving the lives of two Cheyenne warriors led to the establishment of a close relationship between the Bents and the Cheyennes. It became even closer a few years later after William Bent married Owl Woman, daughter of a Cheyenne medicine man named Gray Thunder.[16]

By 1831, William Bent had convinced his brother Charles and Ceran St. Vrain that there was much money to be made in the Indian trade along the Arkansas River, the international boundary between the

This is the reconstructed Bent's Old Fort, a National Historic Site, as it looks today. Located on the mountain route of the Santa Fe Trail, it is eight miles northeast of La Junta, Colorado. (Author's Collection)

United States and Mexico. Under William's supervision, they built a trading post on the U.S. side of the river in a large grove of tall cottonwood trees known as the Big Timbers, about twenty-five miles east of where the Purgatoire River flows into the Arkansas. The site was west of present-day Lamar, Colorado. The post soon attracted much Indian trade. But then John Gantt and Jefferson Blackwell built another trading post called Fort Cass on the Arkansas River closer to the Rocky Mountains. It was located on the site of present-day Pueblo, Colorado, about ninety miles west of the Bent post. To meet the competition, the Bents and St. Vrain moved toward the Rockies and built another post, called Fort William, about three miles east of Fort Cass. In an apparent effort to show up the rather crude trading post constructed by the Bents and St. Vrain, Gantt and Blackwell hired some Mexicans in the spring of 1833 to build a larger and more impressive post of adobe about six miles below the mouth of Fountain Creek on the Arkansas River east of Fort Cass.

Competition between the two groups became intense as each sought to control the Indian trade. Not to be outdone, the Bents and St. Vrain took a bold act and moved their business east on the Arkansas River to a spot that may have been suggested by an old Cheyenne Indian. Near the location of present-day La Junta, Colorado, they began construction in

1832 of a large, castlelike trading post of adobe on the north bank of the Arkansas River. William Bent brought crews of men from New Mexico to make the adobe, using raw wool as a binder. However, smallpox swept through the Mexican workers and delayed construction of Fort William, as the post was first called; it later came to be known as Bent's Old Fort. Soon after the epidemic subsided, the Bents and St. Vrain sent a wagon train out of Santa Fe toward Missouri, but because the train carried supplies for Fort William, the wagons followed a different route, going north from Santa Fe to Taos, then over Raton Pass to the Arkansas River, and then east to Fort William. Their journey opened to wagons what became known as the mountain branch of the Santa Fe Trail. Although longer than the Cimarron or dry route, it had more water and was therefore safer. The eleven wagons in the caravan dropped off supplies at Fort William and then, loading whatever pelts and buffalo robes had been taken in trade with the Indians, continued east to Missouri.

A view of the open yard inside the reconstructed Bent's Old Fort near La Junta, Colorado. (Author's Collection)

A view of the trade room in the reconstructed Bent's Old Fort. Items for sale included everything from rifles to candles. (Author's Collection)

A view of the trade-room shelves in the reconstructed Bent's Old Fort containing items that would have been for sale to teamsters and travelers who followed the mountain route of the Santa Fe Trail during the late 1830s and early 1840s. Even blocks of Chinese tea were available. (Author's Collection)

Bent's Fort, as most people came to call Fort William, probably was completed late in 1834. It was indeed impressive and put to shame Gantt and Blackwell's post many miles to the west. The location of Bent's Fort on the open plains gave it a massive appearance, although it probably was only about 180 by 135 feet, with outside walls constructed of thick adobe blocks. There were two bastions, one located at the southeast corner, the other at the northwest corner of the structure. Inside each bastion at the second-floor level hung sabers; heavy lances with long, sharp blades; pistols; and flintlock muskets. These were to be used should attackers attempt to take the fort by using ladders on the outside walls. Over the main gate on the east side was a watchtower room, on top of which was a belfry and a flagpole that flew the American flag. The belfry contained a large bell, which was used to sound alarms and to signal the hours of meals. The watchtower was a single room containing a chair and a bed. Windows were on all four sides, and on a pivot in the center was a long telescope. If the man on duty in the watchtower noticed anything unusual outside, he would give the alarm and signal the herder

The blacksmith shop in the reconstructed Bent's Old Fort as it looks today. (Author's Collection)

outside the post to bring in the horses, which were never turned loose to graze unguarded. Inside the post's adobe walls at ground level were the stores, warehouses, and living quarters. They ranged around the walls and opened into a large patio. On the west side of the post, opposite the main entrance, was another gate; this opened into a corral that was actually outside the main walls. The corral, however, had adobe walls of its own that were eight feet high, and the corral gate leading to the outside was made of metal plate.

On the west side of the post's second level a large room contained a billiard table that had been transported from Missouri with the other necessary game supplies. A bar was built along one end of the room. About two hundred yards southwest of the post, near the Arkansas River, stood an icehouse, also built of adobe. In the winter when the river was frozen, the building was filled with large squares of ice chopped from the stream. When summer arrived, fresh meat was kept cool in the icehouse, which also provided an ample supply of ice for cold drinks.[17]

During the years that followed, the Bents and St. Vrain accumulated much wealth as traders. Just how much is not known, but Captain Lemuel Ford, who visited Bent's Fort soon after it was constructed, observed that they would buy a buffalo robe for about twenty-five cents' worth of trade goods and later sell the robe in St. Louis for five or six dollars. They followed the age-old practice of buying low and selling high. In addition to their Indian trade from Bent's Fort, the firm also had income from trading in Santa Fe, Taos, Chihuahua, and to the north on the South Platte River.

NINE

Over the Trail, 1835-1840

There are two times in a man's life when he should not speculate: when he can't afford it, and when he can.

—*Mark Twain*

BY 1835, the process of freighting merchandise from Missouri to Santa Fe had become rather routine. Traders reported few problems with Indians, perhaps because of the presence of soldiers. Then too, a year earlier Congress had passed legislation regulating trade with Indian tribes and establishing the Department of Indian Affairs within the War Department. Some tribes in what is now eastern Kansas were receiving annual annuity payments from the government in 1835. In Missouri, merchants seeking to capture more of the trade continued to advertise in local newspapers, but editors pretty much limited their news coverage of the trade to the departure of the annual caravan, its size, the value of the merchandise being carried west, and accounts of the traders' return and how they had fared in business. When copies of the Missouri newspapers reached the East, stories about the Santa Fe trade were reprinted and widely read. In Baltimore, *Niles Weekly Register,* July 18, 1835, reported that the annual spring caravan had left Independence in May with about 140 men, 40 of them traders, and about seventy-five wagons loaded with merchandise valued at $130,000. When the caravan returned to Missouri in October, the earliest published account appeared in the *Missouri Intelligencer* at Columbia on October 24, reporting that the caravan had returned with about three hundred mules, some horses, furs, and other items, plus $200,000 in specie. The report was reprinted in eastern newspapers.

The following year, 1836, the annual spring trading caravan left Independence in May. A few days later it was overtaken by Charles Bent's seven-wagon train loaded with supplies and goods to sell or trade at Bent's Fort. He undoubtedly purchased luxury items for trappers, including hogsheads of black New Orleans molasses, candies, blue jars of Chinese ginger, and tins of Bent water crackers manufactured in Massachusetts by a distant cousin. As David Lavender wrote in his classic *Bent's Fort* (1954), Bent "thought he would impress mountain men with the thought that the big lodge on the Arkansas had its own private brand of biscuit." Bent joined the larger train for protection. Had he traveled alone, his small caravan probably would have been attacked by Indians. There is some dispute concerning the size of the 1836 caravan. One account recorded late in the nineteenth century indicates there were 150 men and fifty-seven wagons. But Josiah Gregg, in his classic *Commerce of the Prairies* (1844), noted that there were 135 men, 35 of them traders, and seventy-five wagons. Gregg, who is probably correct, noted that the annual caravan carried merchandise valued at $130,000.[1]

Traveling with Bent was Robert "Doc" Newell, a twenty-nine-year-old veteran mountain man, who had come west from his native Ohio to St. Louis. There he learned the saddler's trade before joining a trapping party in 1829 and spending six years in the Rocky Mountains. After going east in 1835 to visit relatives in Ohio, Newell returned west in 1836 and joined Bent's caravan. After it arrived at the fort, Newell returned to the mountains and trapping.

Also with Bent's caravan was Richens Lacy "Uncle Dick" Wootton, who had been hired in Independence as a mule driver. Wootton, not quite nineteen years old, had been born in Virginia. He moved with his family to Kentucky and then lived with a relative on a Mississippi cotton plantation before going to Missouri, where he found a job driving a team of mules for one of Bent's wagons. Later, Wootton remembered:

> I learned then, what I did not know before, that all the movements of a big wagon train had to be made with military precision. When we went into camp at night all the wagons were pulled up close together so as to form a sort of circle. Then the mules were unhitched and driven to water, after which they were "picketed," that is, hitched by long ropes to stakes driven in the ground, outside of the line of wagons, so that they could graze during the night. So many men were detailed every night to stand guard, and they were stationed far

enough away from the wagons so that they could see all the stock and prevent any of the mules or horses from being stolen. The mules were pretty good guards themselves by the way. If they slept any at all they were very light sleepers, because whenever anything, whether it was a wild animal or an Indian, came near the camp, the mules would commence snorting in a way which would at once attract the attention of the guard to the object of suspicion. While the guards were on the lookout for unwelcome visitors of any kind, the men who were not on duty wrapped themselves in their blankets and lay down on the ground inside the circle of wagons to sleep as soundly as though there was no such thing as danger to be thought of. They slept however with their rifles by their sides, and the crack of a sentinel's gun would bring them to their feet full armed in a moment's time.[2]

When the caravan reached Little Cow Creek and camped for the night, Wootton was assigned to stand guard for the first time on the journey. He recalled:

My instructions were to shoot anything that I saw moving outside of the line of mules farthest out from the wagons. Nothing had happened so far on our trip, to occasion any alarm or anxiety about our safety, and I didn't expect anything was going to happen that night. Still I didn't feel at all inclined to go to sleep, and kept a sharp lookout. About one or two 'clock at night I heard a slight noise, and could see something moving about, sixty or seventy-five yards from where I was lying on the ground. I wasn't a coward, if I was a boy, and my hair didn't stand on end, although it may have raised up a little. Of course, the first thing I thought of was Indians, and the more I looked at the dark object creeping along toward the camp, the more it looked to me like a blood-thirsty savage. I didn't get excited, although they tried to make me believe I was afterward, but thought the matter over and made up my mind that whatever the thing was, it had no business being there. So I blazed away at it and down it dropped. The shot roused everybody in camp, and they all came running out with their guns in their hands to see what was up.

I told them I had seen what I supposed was an Indian trying to slip into camp and I had killed him. Very cautiously several of the men crept down to where the supposed Indian was lying. I stood at my post and listened to their report, and by and by I heard one of the men say, "I'll be cussed if he haint killed Old Jack." "Old Jack" was one of our lead mules. He had gotten loose and strayed outside the lines, and

Richens Lacy "Uncle Dick" Wootton (1816–1893) left Virginia and came west in 1836. He joined the firm of Bent and St. Vrain at Independence, Missouri; traveled to Bent's Fort; and was sent to trade with the Sioux Indians. He trapped and traded in the Rocky Mountains and scouted for the U.S. military during the Mexican War before engaging in a variety of pioneering activities at Taos and Denver. In 1865, he built a toll road over Raton Pass on the mountain branch of the Santa Fe Trail. (Courtesy Kansas State Historical Society)

the result was that he met his death. I felt sorry about it, but the mule had disobeyed orders you know, and I wasn't to blame for killing him.[3]

The large caravan did run into Indians at Pawnee Fork. More than 250 Comanches charged the caravan's camp three or four times on a bright moonlit evening, trying to stampede the traders' mules. Before the battle ended, three Comanches were killed. The Indians withdrew and did not return. A few days later the caravan reached the Cimarron crossing of the Arkansas River. There the annual caravan turned southwest and followed the dry route to Santa Fe while Bent's seven wagons headed west following the Arkansas River toward Bent's Fort. A few days later Bent's group met Ceran St. Vrain, who with a party of mounted men had come east to escort them to the fort.

As THE PROCESS of trading fell into something of a pattern, so did the journey over the trail. Whether bound for Santa Fe or going to Missouri,

This drawing by William Henry Jackson titled Grub Pile! *shows teamsters preparing a meal on the trail. Below the Dutch oven (lower center) is a supply of dried buffalo chips used to fuel the fire.* (Courtesy National Park Service, United States Department of the Interior)

most caravans came to follow a daily routine from one day to the next. Travel was slow, between twelve and fifteen miles a day. There were regular campsites along the route. Once a caravan arrived at a campsite the wagons were corralled, the oxen freed from the yokes or mules unhitched and driven off to the best grass available. Night herders watched the animals until morning and slept in the moving wagons during the day. Within the corral of wagons, fires were built, and the mess cooks prepared a simple meal of bread, baked earlier in the day, and coffee. Before dawn the animals were driven into the corral. Oxen were yoked up, or mules hitched to wagons. Blankets were rolled, tied, and thrown into the wagons, and before the sun appeared on the eastern horizon, the wagons were moving.

Caravans usually halted for noon—this was called "nooning"—about ten or eleven o'clock in the morning. The time often depended upon the weather and how far the wagon master wanted to take the train that day. If the day was hot and the wagons had made good time during the morning, the noon halt might last until the middle of the afternoon. Again the wagons were corralled and the animals turned out. The men had a light meal, which was called "breakfast," and then rested in the shade of the wagons or trees, if any were to be found at the campsite. Sometimes the men carried out chores and repaired their gear. Just before the breaking of camp in the afternoon, the principal meal of the day was served. This was called "dinner," and it usually included cooked meat and fresh-baked pan or skillet bread. The cooks usually made enough bread to supply the men in the evening and early the following day.

Meat was supplied by at least two hunters. Each morning they set out ahead of the wagon train to hunt for game. They might kill a buffalo or an antelope, skin and butcher the animal where it fell, and then carry the meat on a packhorse or mule to where the caravan planned to stop at noon. Sometimes, however, they were unable to find game, and then everyone had to eat the dried meat carried by most caravans. At each meal the men were organized into messes. The traders usually messed together. The teamsters, bullwhackers, and most other employees formed one or more separate messes. If Indians—usually Delawares and Shawnees—were employed as hunters for the caravan, they formed a mess of their own. Each man had his own quart cup and tin plate and carried his own hunting knife in a sheath. No one had forks or spoons. Each man marked his cup and plate, usually by scratching his initials or mark on them. The men of each mess chose a cook from among their own number, and after each meal every man washed his own cup and plate. The food, though simple, was wholesome and abundant. Meat was the staple, but they also had bread and plenty of coffee, and occasionally boiled dried apples and rice. Usually there was brown sugar, though sometimes they had to depend on the old-fashioned "long sweetening, simply New Orleans molasses."[4]

. . .

THE MISSOURI constitution of 1820 gave the state's general assembly the power to restrict and regulate the incorporation of banks. Only one bank could be in operation at any one time, though it could have five branches, provided not more than one branch was established during any one legislative session. The capital of a bank incorporated by the state was never to exceed five million dollars, of which the state might furnish half. At the time, only the Bank of Missouri was in operation, having been chartered in 1817, but it failed in 1822. For fifteen years the state legislature consistently refused to incorporate another bank, leaving Missouri the only state in the Union without a bank. This prevented the issuance of paper currency in Missouri. Although some paper money from other states began flowing into the state, businesses relied heavily on the flow of Mexican silver specie, which poured in from the Santa Fe trade. Each Mexican silver dollar contained 374 grains of fine silver, while the American silver dollar contained 371¼ grains, and both were accepted. But in 1836, wildcat banks in surrounding states began flooding Missouri with their issue and driving out the Mexican silver. When Missourians demanded the establishment of a bank, the Missouri State Bank was established in 1837 to aid the circulation of specie but not paper money.

One Missouri newspaper editor wrote:

It is well known that Col. [Senator] Benton is uncompromisingly opposed to the whole paper money system, as bad in principle, and worse, if possible, in practice. To Banks of Discount and Deposite [sic] and of Exchange, he is as friendly as he is unfriendly to a Bank of Circulation—to a Bank which can make money. Our Bank is not of the latter class. The Bank Directors have unanimously resolved that no bills for less than $20 shall be issued, and no more bills shall be issued than can be redeemed in specie, if all the bills were to be presented on the same day—thus making it one of irresistible strength, a bank not to be broken, a *specie paying* bank *in fact*, as well as in promise. . . . The people of the State of Missouri are opposed to *all Banks*. So are we. But let us not be misunderstood. . . . We mean that we are opposed to national or local Banks as constituted in this country. The Bank of the State of Missouri is different from all others. . . . Of course, when we express our opposition to Banks, we refer not to ours, but to the miserable paper manufacturers scattered over the country.[5]

When the Bank of Missouri opened its doors during the summer of

1837, the nation was entering another depression, the first since 1819. It was caused by wild speculation in land and an overextension of credit. But the Bank of Missouri survived as a specie-paying bank and was soon recognized as one of the soundest financial institutions in the nation. In fact, within a month of its opening, it became a bank of deposit for the U.S. government and served as a place of deposit for traders returning from Santa Fe.

The annual caravan of traders in 1837 left Independence in May with 160 men and about eighty wagons. Josiah Gregg was among the 35 traders who made the trip, which was without problems, but soon after they began disposing of their merchandise in New Mexico, the northern Pueblo Indians revolted. The events leading up to the revolt began about two years earlier, when Texas declared its independence from Mexico and claimed a large chunk of New Mexico, including Santa Fe and Taos, a wide strip of territory stretching northward from the present-day Texas Panhandle into what is now southwest Kansas, and a portion of Colorado and Wyoming. At the same time, the Mexican government was reorganized and began collecting taxes directly from people. The government also imposed higher duties on the American traders arriving with their heavily loaded freight wagons in Santa Fe. The New Mexican governor, Manuel Armijo, was ousted, and Albino Pérez was sent north to replace him, but he was an outsider. Until his arrival the Mexican government had let New Mexicans administer their own affairs, and they resented the changes. Josiah Gregg later wrote that Manuel Armijo and Padre Antonio Martínez of Taos, a champion of the people, plotted the revolt, but this is still debated. The violence began after relatives of the alcalde refused to pay a debt of a hundred pesos. They appealed, only to see the alcalde imprisoned. A mob gathered, and soon large groups of Pueblo Indians marched on Santa Fe from the north. Governor Pérez gathered a small force of about 150 militia. What happened next is told in Gregg's words:

> With this inadequate force, the Governor made an attempt to march from the capital, but was soon surprised by the insurgents who lay in ambush . . . when his own men fled to the enemy, leaving him and about twenty-five trusty friends to make their escape in the best way they could. Knowing that they would not be safe in Santa Fe, the refugees pursued their flight southward, but were soon overtaken by the exasperated Pueblos; when the Governor was chased back to the suburbs of the city, and savagely put to death. His body was then stripped and shockingly mangled: his head was carried as a trophy to

the camp of the insurgents, who made a foot-ball of it among themselves. I had left the city the day before this sad catastrophe took
place, and beheld the Indians scouring the fields in pursuit of their
victims, though I was yet ignorant of their barbarous designs.[6]

About two thousand Pueblo Indians made camp in the suburbs of
Santa Fe as though preparing to plunder the city. American traders
feared the worst, but the Indians only seized the property of their victims, which afterward was distributed among the victors. One of the Indians' boldest leaders, José González of Taos, was elected governor. The
families of the unfortunate victims were left destitute, and the American
traders who had given credit to them had no way to recover their losses.
They appealed to the American minister in Mexico City. Meantime,
Manuel Armijo raised an army and hurried to Santa Fe early in January
1838 as three hundred Mexican soldiers arrived from Chihuahua. This
combined force defeated the rebels who had gathered north of Santa
Fe. González was shot without a trial, and an uneasy peace settled over
Santa Fe.

On April 4, a party of twenty-two Americans, including Josiah Gregg,
left Santa Fe for Missouri along with twelve Mexican servants, seven wagons, one smaller Dearborn wagon, and two small cannons. The trip was
uneventful except in the Cimarron Valley, where Pawnee Indians attempted but failed to stampede the Americans' stock. Thirty-eight days
after leaving Santa Fe, the party arrived at Independence. Gregg and the
other traders, including two identified only as "Messrs. Ryder and
Payne," brought with them about $150,000 in specie and bullion.
Whether Gregg and others returned to Santa Fe that summer with new
merchandise is not clear, but overland trade from Missouri languished
during 1838 because of the Pueblo revolt and the higher duties imposed
by the Mexican government the previous year. One account suggests
that only seven wagons journeyed from Missouri to Santa Fe in the
spring of 1838 (possibly Gregg's party returning), yet another indicates
that a hundred men, twenty of them traders, took fifty wagons with
goods valued at $90,000. It may be that the bulk of the trade that year
was conducted by Mexican traders. A temporary military post called
Camp Holmes had been established in early June 1835 about five miles
northeast of present-day Purcell, in what is now central Oklahoma, to
host a meeting of representatives of several Indian tribes to sign a peace
treaty with the United States. The treaty was signed in August 1835. Following this, Auguste P. Chouteau established a small fortified post on the
site of the camp to trade with the Comanches, Kiowas, Wichitas, and

other western tribes. He operated the trading post until December 1838, when he died at Fort Gibson in present-day eastern Oklahoma, where he had gone for the winter. Chouteau was fifty-two years old.

Back in Missouri, lawmakers had been pushing Congress to make Independence a port of entry. Pointing out that goods conveyed by sea were entitled to a return of duties, they proposed that merchandise be taken to Santa Fe in its original packaging, along with paperwork certifying that duty had been paid at the Independence port of entry, and that the traders owning the goods would receive a rebate. But Congress took no action in 1835 or 1836, the year Arkansas was admitted as the twenty-fifth state. Two banks were chartered in Arkansas that year, but both failed during the national depression of 1837. With a debt of $3 million and no banks, the state's early years were marked by hard times. Thus, in 1839, the Arkansas legislature approved the incorporation of the Chihuahua Trading Company with a capital of $200,000. The company's organization was noted in the *St. Louis Republican,* March 23, 1838, along with its stated purpose of opening trade between Arkansas and Chihuahua. Arkansas lawmakers also made demands on Congress similar to those made earlier by Missourians to benefit traders, but eastern congressmen still opposed the measures because their constituent merchants feared new competition from the West.

Early in 1839, Josiah Gregg learned the French were blockading the Mexican ports through which Chihuahua was supplied. Believing that there was a waiting market for merchandise in Chihuahua, Gregg decided to take a caravan there as early in the spring as possible. He decided not to set out from Independence but to shift his operations south to Van Buren, a settlement on the western border of Arkansas. Not only would the route be shorter, but the grasses would green up earlier than on the established route from Missouri, thereby providing food for his oxen. Whether Gregg was somehow linked to the Chihuahua Trading Company formed the previous year is not known, but along with another trader, George C. Pickett, he fitted out a caravan consisting of thirty-four men and fourteen road wagons carrying about $25,000 in goods. In addition, the caravan had a carriage, a Jersey wagon, and two swivel cannons. Half the wagons were drawn by eight oxen each, the rest by mules. They set out on April 21 following a route on the north side of the Canadian River to Santa Fe, where they would turn south to Chihuahua.

Chihuahua had been visited by a few Americans even before the Mexican Revolution in 1821. Most were taken there as prisoners after having been arrested in New Mexico for illegal trading. A few years after the Mexican Revolution, when Missouri traders were welcomed in New Mexico and the Santa Fe market became glutted with foreign goods, Missouri traders got permission to travel south to Chihuahua to sell their goods. A trader named Stephenson (or Stevenson) led a party of traders, including Henry Connelly from Boone County, Missouri, from Santa Fe south along the Camino Real to Chihuahua, a route that had changed little in more than two hundred years. The traders experienced many problems with Indians and suffered greatly from hunger and thirst before reaching their destination.

During the years that followed, other American traders visited Chihuahua, including Josiah Gregg, who had traveled there in 1835 with three other men and two empty wagons to purchase Mexican fabrics. For traders taking goods to Chihuahua, it soon became the custom to rent space for a store on the main plaza and to offer their merchandise at both wholesale and retail prices. As soon as they sold their goods, most would return to Missouri and purchase a new consignment, but some Americans made their homes in Chihuahua and arranged to receive new consignments of goods from Missouri each year.

About three weeks after Gregg's little caravan left Van Buren on April 28, 1839, the *Arkansas Gazette,* published at Little Rock, predicted in its May 15, 1839, issue that good effects would likely come to western Arkansas when the traders returned with Mexican gold. Meantime, Gregg's caravan had crossed the Arkansas River a few miles above the mouth of the Canadian Fork. What happened next is told by Gregg:

We had only proceeded a short distance beyond, when a Cherokee shop-keeper came up to us with an attachment for debt against a free mulatto, whom we had engaged as teamster. The poor fellow had no alternative but to return with the importunate creditor, who committed him at once to the care of "Judge Lynch" for trial. We ascertained afterwards that he had been sentenced to "take the benefit of the bankrupt law" after the manner of the Cherokees of that neighborhood. This is done by stripping and tying the victim to a tree; [then] each creditor with a good cowhide or hickory switch in his hand, scores the amount of the bill due upon his bare back. One stripe for every dollar due is the usual process of "whitewashing"; and as the application of the last is accompanied by all sorts of quaint remarks, the exhibition affords no small merriment to those present with the exception, no doubt, of the delinquent himself. After the ordeal is over, the creditors declare themselves perfectly satisfied; nor could they, as is said, ever be persuaded thereafter to receive one red cent of the amount due, even if it were offered to them. As the poor mulatto was also in our debt, and was perhaps apprehensive that we might exact payment in the same currency, he never showed himself again.[7]

An officer and forty First U.S. Dragoons had been ordered to meet Gregg's caravan and escort it to the Arkansas River, but while they were traveling toward Santa Fe a messenger arrived and informed Gregg that the dragoons had been sent to quell fresh troubles among the Cherokees and probably would not join the caravan. To Gregg's surprise, however, the dragoons were waiting at Camp Holmes, near present-day Purcell, Oklahoma. Together the traders and dragoons moved westward. When they came upon buffalo a few days later, Gregg wrote: "Very few of our party had ever seen a buffalo before in its wild state; therefore at the first sight of these noble animals the excitement surpassed anything I had ever witnessed before. Some of our dragoons, in their eagerness for sport, had managed to frighten away a small herd that were quietly feeding at some distance." But the next day he noticed three men on foot some distance away chasing a herd of buffalo. Two of the men were Gregg's cooks, the third a Creek Indian traveling with the caravan. The men in the caravan moving westward lost sight of the hunters, and Gregg had almost given them up for lost when one of the cooks returned. He related how he had chased buffalo all day but failed to kill one. Then he told how he came upon a wounded buffalo calf, which he attacked. Although the calf tried to butt the cook, he finally succeeded in killing the animal. As Gregg wrote, "One thing seemed pretty certain, that they were all cured of the 'buffalo fever.' "[8]

The traders and dragoons made their way across what is now western Oklahoma. After reaching Mexican Territory, the dragoons apparently bid the traders farewell and returned east. Gregg and the others reached Santa Fe in late June, spent several days there, and then headed south along the Rio Grande on the Royal Road, a fairly well-defined road running between the mountains and the river. During dry weather, caravans hugged the riverbed, but during rains they moved to high ground. Traders traveled through a pass called La Jornade del Muerto ("The Day's Journey of a Dead Man") and then, beyond El Paso on the broad plains, blazed their own trails between established campsites. The distance between Santa Fe and Chihuahua was about six hundred miles, less than the distance from Santa Fe to Independence, Missouri.

Gregg's caravan reached Chihuahua on October 1, 1839, forty days after leaving Santa Fe. By the end of the month, he had sold his goods to a couple of English merchants, saving him from having to rent a store. Gregg enjoyed Chihuahua:

> When compared with Santa Fe and all the towns of the North, Chihuahua might indeed be pronounced a magnificent place.... The ground-plan is much more regular than that of Santa Fe while a much greater degree of elegance and classic taste has been exhibited in the style of the architecture of many buildings; for though the bodies be of *adobe,* all the best houses are cornered with hewn stone, and the doors and windows are framed in the same. The streets, however, remain nearly in the same state as Nature formed them, with the exception of a few roughly-paved side-walks.... Chihuahua is surrounded on every side by detached ridges of mountains, but none of them of any great magnitude.... The most splendid edifice in Chihuahua is the principal church, which is said to equal in architectural grandeur anything of the sort in the republic.... A little below the *Plaza Mayor* stands the ruins of San Francisco—the mere skeleton of another great church of hewn-stone, which was commenced by the Jesuits previous to their expulsion in 1767, but never finished.... The dilapidated building has since been converted into a sort of state prison, particularly for the incarceration of distinguished prisoners.[9]

Gregg and his caravan left Chihuahua after selling out and arrived back in Santa Fe in early December. The party remained there until late February, when they returned to Van Buren, Arkansas, traveling much of the way on the south side of the Canadian River. The company returned with some Mexican gold, which may have briefly offered a boom to the economy around Van Buren, but the town never replaced Independence as the eastern terminus of the trail. In fact, the route west from Van Buren never replaced the earlier trail from Missouri across present-day Kansas.

Perhaps a month after Gregg left Van Buren, in April 1839, the annual spring caravan of traders departed from Independence for Santa Fe. One account noted that the group consisted of fifty-three wagons and ninety-three men, although another report observed that there were only forty "immense waggons" and nearly four hundred mules. Whatever the case, Dr. David Waldo and Manuel Alvarez led the caravan. Alvarez the previous winter had purchased merchandise in New York City and Philadelphia valued at more than $9,000 to take to New Mexico. Eight to ten of the caravan's wagons were owned by him and were estimated to have a total value of $2,500 before he left Independence.

When the caravan corralled for the night on the east bank of Pawnee Fork near present-day Larned, Kansas, a party of nineteen mounted men from Peoria, Illinois, led by Thomas J. Farnham, came into the traders' camp with their pack mules. They remained with the trading caravan for protection until it reached the Arkansas River. There the traders turned southwest toward Santa Fe, and Farnham's party headed west for Bent's Fort and their final destination of Oregon.[10]

Back in Missouri, a small caravan of eighteen traders with a few wagons left Independence on the first day of July bound for Santa Fe. There were several Mexican citizens in the party, including Don Antonio José Luna and José de Jesús Branch, whose homes were in Taos. There also were a handful of Americans, including Matthew "Matt" C. Field, a twenty-nine-year-old actor who had given up the theater and joined a caravan heading for Santa Fe. We know more about his caravan than the larger annual trading party because Field kept a journal. Although his journal was mostly in verse, Field later wrote of his adventures in a series of articles published in the *New Orleans Picayune*. The small caravan in which he traveled passed near Pawnee Rock in late July. Of the landmark, Field wrote: "Pawnee Rock springs like a huge wart from the carpeted green of the prairie. It is about thirty feet high, and perhaps a hundred around the base. One tall, rugged portion of it is rifted from the main mass of rock, and stands totally inaccessible and alone. Some twenty names are cut in the stone, and dates are marked as far as ten years back."[11]

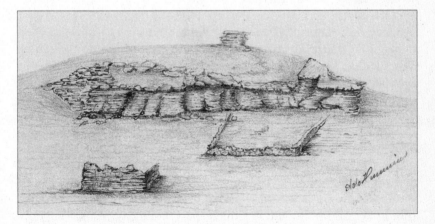

Pawnee Rock, which was on the Santa Fe Trail east of present-day Larned, Kansas, as it appeared in 1867. (Courtesy Kansas State Historical Society)

Field's caravan reached Bent's Fort in mid-August and soon continued west to follow the mountain route through Raton Pass. Of that journey, Field wrote:

Not the most beautiful, but certainly the wildest and most romantic scenery which we saw in our whole travel, was while making our way through a range of hills which formed, as it were, a young growth of the high mountains we saw beyond. In performing this part of our journey, we were obliged to follow the wandering of a clear, pebble-paved stream, called the Ratone, and sometimes, where cliff and precipice utterly barred our way, the wagons were obliged to be drawn along in the bed of the creek. At one place, so difficult was our progress, that we advanced but a mile and a half in a day. Overhanging branches and projecting roots were obliged to be cut away, and heavy rocks removed, for the creek was barely wide enough to admit the wagons between the rugged banks. . . . One unfortunate wagon was upset three times, and once right into the creek. A shelving ascent had been prepared with sticks and stones to enable the wagons to leave the water, at a place where no further progress in it could be made, when the body of this unlucky vehicle turned directly over, leaving twenty-five hundred weight of merchandise in the water, while the relieved mules dashed up the bank with its wheels. A surly and dissatisfied driver had charge of this wagon, and it was strongly suspected that he occasioned the mischief by design. The place was truly most awkward and dangerous, but still, while he met three disasters in one day, the other wagons all came through safe.[12]

Once over Raton Pass, the small caravan traveled to Taos and then to Santa Fe. There Field was introduced to Señora Toulous, whom he described as "the supreme queen of refinement and fashion" in Santa Fe. She was known as Doña María Gertrudiz Barcelo, Lona Barcelona, and Madam Barcelo, but she was most often called simply La Tules. Tradition has it that she was born in Spain, lost her mother in New York, came west and lived briefly in Taos, and then moved to Santa Fe. Field described La Tules as having a neat figure but not handsome, shrewdly intelligent, with manners that were free but not ungraceful. He wrote that she could waltz with elegant ease, adding that "she had become wealthy by dealing *monte,* and her bank was open almost every evening (not in her own house but in another part of the city), herself superintending while an assistant dealt the cards. We found the Alcalde on several occasions acting the part of dealer, his passion for the game leading

This illustration by Frederic Remington may have been based on wagon-train travel over Raton Pass. Titled An Ox Train in the Mountains, *it appeared in* Harper's Weekly, *May 26, 1888.* (Author's Collection)

him still to finger the cards although he had been three times stripped of accumulated property by unfortunate luck. Monte and the fandango are the only amusements of the place, and the people spend the evening in strolling from one to the other. Traders often lose the profits of a whole season in an hour's play, and when the last dollar is gone they walk off to a fandango, choose a partner and dance away care, never dreaming of curing misfortune by suicide."[13]

Field remained in Santa Fe until late September and then joined a small eastbound caravan of five wagons owned by Mexican merchants, including Don José Chávez, bound for Independence. They reportedly carried sixty thousand dollars in specie as they followed the Cimarron route east. They were accompanied as far as the Arkansas crossing by a Mexican military escort of twenty-five soldiers riding mules and headed by Lieutenant José Hernández. The traders also carried with them a brass cannon for added protection.

When Field and the small caravan left their camp on Rabbit Ear Creek, they met a Santa Fe–bound caravan of thirty-six wagons from Missouri, but otherwise the return journey was uneventful. Upon reaching Council Grove, Field and six others rode ahead to Independence, arriving there on October 30, 1839.

THE MEXICAN MERCHANTS whom Matt Field accompanied up the Santa Fe Trail in 1839 were not the only Mexican traders who traveled to the United States that year. José Cordero and José Olivares, merchants at Chihuahua, also made the journey to Santa Fe and then went east to establish commercial relations with American commission merchants and suppliers. What Cordero purchased is not known, but records kept at the New Mexican customhouse suggest that he returned with 42,000 yards of cotton textiles, and Olivares with a small amount of unknown merchandise.

The trips of Chávez, Cordero, and Olivares marked a change in the pattern of trade over the Santa Fe Trail as a result of an increased demand for foreign goods in Mexico. Merchants in New Mexico and Mexico resented paying substantial markups on goods brought from the United States and, beginning in 1839, an increased number of them made annual trips up the Santa Fe Trail to purchase goods. Most left Santa Fe in April or early May and traveled to Independence before going east by steamboat to Pittsburgh and then overland to Baltimore, Philadelphia, and possibly New York City to purchase goods.[14]

The number of steamboats plying the Missouri, Mississippi, and Ohio Rivers continued to increase. The *St. Louis Republican,* May 16, 1839, told readers that until April 20 of that year, 378 steamboats had been constructed to the east. "Of these there were built at Pittsburgh and its immediate vicinity, 130; at Wheeling, 22; at Cincinnati, 83; the residue at different points along the Ohio." The newspaper calculated that the average cost of a steamboat was $25,000, and the total amount of money spent on them had been $9,480,000. The newspaper then complained that eastern manufacturers were draining money from Missouri and elsewhere in the West.

This destructive drain is kept up not only in the purchases and building of steamboats, but for a thousand other articles. Look at the immense sums sent annually to the Ohio for castings, nails, wrought iron in various articles, such as shovels, forks, chains, knives, &c. &c.; for cotton yarns and cotton cloths, paper, glass, furniture, woolen fabrics, in a word, almost every description of articles. Is there a natural or artificial obstacle to the manufacture of either of these articles here? Has any attempt been made that has not proved successful? No, no. Is not the raw material in every thing as abundant here as there? Nay, is not a large portion of the materials then manufactured taken from here? Yes. Then, why will not our citizens take the subject in hand?

Gradually more goods were manufactured in St. Louis, but it was over a decade before there was a notable change in the pattern of traders going east from Missouri to purchase merchandise. But the year 1839 did mark change for Missouri traders. When they reached Santa Fe that summer, the New Mexico governor Manuel Armijo imposed an arbitrary import duty of five hundred dollars per wagon, regardless of its size or

The Conestoga wagon became a popular freight wagon on the Santa Fe Trail. This late-nineteenth-century photo shows a Conestoga being pulled by six horses in Pennsylvania, but on the Santa Fe Trail mules or oxen were used to pull the large wagons, which were capable of carrying more than a ton of freight. (Courtesy Smithsonian Institution, Washington, D.C.)

the value of its contents. Some traders stopped their caravans before reaching Santa Fe and emptied as many wagons as they could, reloading merchandise onto the others until they were bulging. The empty wagons were abandoned or burned. Merchants also began to consider using larger wagons. Some Missouri traders were already using Conestoga wagons, which originated in the Pennsylvania Dutch area of southeastern Pennsylvania sometime between 1720 and 1750. The wagon was heavily built with a bed that was higher at both ends than in the middle, and it was topped with a dull-white cloth cover that rested on several hoops stapled to the sideboards. The curve of the canopy was even more pronounced than the curve in the bed. Not only could the Conestoga carry a larger load than the smaller farm or road wagon, but its shape was such that the contents would not spill out the ends when it was going up- or downhill. From a distance the Conestoga assumed a boatlike outline that inspired the nickname "prairie schooner." Some people referred to it as the "Pitt schooner," since by the late 1830s most of them were manufactured in Pittsburgh and shipped west by steamboat to Missouri.[15]

Traders used the Conestoga until wagon-makers in Missouri created even larger options. One wagon-maker about whom much has been written is Joseph Murphy, whose mother sent him to America from Ireland in 1818, when he was thirteen years old, to live with three uncles on a farm near St. Louis. Upon arrival, Joseph learned that his uncles had disappeared after their farm failed and they lost the property. Joseph soon apprenticed with Daniel Caster, a St. Louis wagon-maker, to learn the trade. A year later he was given a bench next to Sammy Mount, a veteran wagon-maker, who taught him how to judge the quality of lumber by merely feeling the grain, and how to build quality into a wagon. In 1825, Murphy went into business for himself, and two years later he built his first wagon for the Santa Fe trade. It was a small vehicle, and he sold it to Jacob Jarrett for twenty-seven dollars. The money so pleased Murphy that he set about building another wagon, and then more.

After Governor Armijo imposed the five-hundred-dollar tax on each wagon arriving in New Mexico, Murphy began to produce larger wagons to carry the traders' goods. He hired German-born workmen, who brought the same care to the wagons they made in St. Louis that the Pennsylvania Dutch brought to the Conestoga wagons. Murphy continued to select seasoned timber for his wagons and used only young saplings for the spokes. He made the axles of wood, since iron cracked under the torment of travel on the Santa Fe Trail. When each wagon was finished, it was loaded onto a riverboat at St. Louis and transported by steamboat up the Missouri River to Independence, where it was rolled ashore and put into service.

The exact size of the Murphy wagon is still debated. His son Anseim recalled that "wheels were seven feet high, the height of the bed was such that a man standing inside would barely disclose the top of his head. The wagon was moved by four pair of oxen. The rims of the wheels were eight inches wide . . . and the tongue was fifty feet long. The wheels were not bound with iron, which could not be obtained."[16]

Another source, the historian Henry P. Walker, also believed these large Murphy wagons had a longer wheelbase and higher sides than the Conestoga. Walker said the bed was sixteen feet in length and six feet in height. He wrote that all of the holes in a Murphy wagon were made with a hot iron rather than with an auger. Certainly an auger was faster, but Walker claimed the holes were drilled one size smaller than the bolt they were to take. He noted that the burning with a hot iron prevented cracking or rotting around the bolt, and that the small size of the holes assured a tight fit.[17]

Still another source, William F. "Buffalo Bill" Cody, who never traveled the trail to Santa Fe but later accompanied two freight caravans using Murphy wagons on the Oregon Trail, wrote forty years later that each Murphy wagon was capable of carrying seven thousand pounds of freight. Cody added, "The wagon-boxes were very commodious being as large as the rooms of an ordinary house, and were covered with two heavy canvas sheets to protect the merchandise from the rain."[18]

TEN

Years of Change, 1840-1845

*All business proceeds on beliefs
or judgments of probabilities,
and not on certainties.*

—*Charles Eliot*

FROM ABOUT 1824 UNTIL 1840, trading caravans traversing the Santa Fe Trail dominated Anglo-American activity on the prairie and plains between Missouri and the Rocky Mountains. Next in numbers were the fur traders carrying supplies to the annual mountain men rendezvous in the Rockies and the traders licensed to trade with Indians. This pattern began changing in the 1840s when trading forts were built in the vast region lying north of the trail to capture Indian business and the fur trade. This shift came as a declining market for beaver pelts brought an end to the era of the mountain man. In fact, the last annual rendezvous was held during the summer of 1840 on the Green River near present-day Daniel, Wyoming. After that most of the mountain men left the fur trade. Some of them, including Joel Walker, settled in Oregon Country, where Father Pierre-Jean De Smet, S.J., the missionary and explorer, had traveled from Westport, now part of present-day Kansas City, Missouri, in 1840. Four years earlier, Protestant missionaries, including Marcus Whitman, had settled in Oregon Country, the vast region that included much of today's Pacific Northwest and was then claimed by both Great Britain and the United States.

South of the Santa Fe Trail, Texians, as the early settlers of Texas called themselves, had declared their independence from Mexico in March 1836 and formed the Republic of Texas. By 1840, the second president of Texas, Mirabeau B. Lamar, was securing diplomatic recognition from France, England, Belgium, the Netherlands, and several German states, but these nations refused to loan money to Texas so that the republic could expand westward to the Pacific. Lamar's efforts angered Mexico, as did his order to expel all Indians from Texas, which started a lasting war with the Comanches.

For traders in Missouri, the year 1840 saw a decline in the Santa Fe trade. Josiah Gregg estimated that no more than $50,000 in goods were taken by Missourians to New Mexico that year. Not since 1824 had the value of merchandise transported to Santa Fe been so low. The decline was largely blamed on New Mexican governor Armijo's new $500 duty. At the same time, the increased number of Mexican traders seems to have affected their Missouri counterparts. In fact, the annual spring caravan that left Independence for Santa Fe in 1840 was composed mostly of Mexican traders and was much smaller than usual. Eleven wagons were owned by the Mexican Don Juan Chávez y Castillo, who had spent the winter in the East purchasing merchandise. His wagons carried goods valued at $75,000, a figure not included in Gregg's estimate. A smaller group of wagons, along with thirty mules owned by Manuel Alvarez, was also in the caravan led by Darby H. Cantrell, an American. An even smaller party of three wagons was led by another, unidentified American. While the value of his merchandise is not known, records indicate that he paid $1,286 to customs officials when the caravan reached New Mexico.[1]

As it moved slowly toward Santa Fe, the caravan met two Boone County, Missouri, traders named Hicks and Marney, and a Mexican trader going east. The Independence-bound caravan consisted of twenty or thirty wagons and carried about $200,000 in specie and bullion, some of it apparently Hicks and Marney's profit from the previous year's trading. The balance, about $50,000 in bullion and $30,000 in specie, belonged to a Mexican trader from Chihuahua who was going east to buy new merchandise.[2]

Goods and profits carried by Mexican traders in 1840 were either missed or not known to Gregg, since they were not included in his estimate. Nor did he include the value of up to fifteen thousand buffalo robes plus thirty packs of beaver pelts, twelve sacks of buffalo tongues, and one pack of deerskins brought to Independence over the Santa Fe Trail from Bent's Fort on the upper Arkansas River. Charles Bent and Ceran St. Vrain's wagons arrived in late June at Independence, where the robes and furs were loaded aboard the steamboat *Euphrasie* and transported down the Missouri to St. Louis to be sold. If each buffalo robe sold for six dollars, the going rate, Bent and St. Vrain earned ninety thousand dollars.[3]

By 1840, Bent and St. Vrain were regularly shipping their previous winter's trade in robes and furs from Bent's Fort to Independence. In April 1841, Charles Bent left the fort for Independence with eighteen loaded wagons and pack mules. On the Santa Fe Trail in what is now central Kansas, Bent's party met the annual spring caravan from Missouri bound for Santa Fe. Both caravans stopped to exchange news and then resumed their journeys. Bent's caravan reached Independence on June 10, 1841, the same day the Santa Fe–bound spring caravan reached Cimarron Springs in present-day Grant County, Kansas. Now traveling with the Santa Fe–bound group were nine men from Indiana in three wagons. They had left Independence later than the spring caravan but caught up with it near the Arkansas River. One of the Indiana men, perhaps John McGuire, later wrote a letter home that was published in an Evansville, Indiana, newspaper. The author recalled:

> We overtook the caravan in sight of the Arkansas . . . and attached ourselves thereto for duty in crossing the river, which is much larger than at the mouth, and always muddy, and rolling her quicksand into bars almost every hour, so that fords or crossings are dangerous and uncertain. From the Arkansas river the scarcity of water commences, and even the little to be had is so deeply impregnated with salt, sulfur, &c, that stern necessity alone brings the traveler to the use of it. On the Simerone [Cimarron] river there are one or two good springs, at one of which we met of the Arapaho Indians five hundred warriors, who treated us with a proper friendship, elated with their success ten days before, when, in battle, they killed seventy-six Pawnees. We gratified them with encamping on the battle ground, where the unburied bodies were yet unbroken. The next day we visited their Lodge, six miles from the battle ground, where we had a full view of savage life in a perfect state of nature; amongst five hundred women and children, there were but few that had ever before seen the dress and equipage of the white man.

Making his first trip to Santa Fe, the letter-writer was impressed with western scenery. Eight to ten days after leaving the Indians, within sight of the Rocky Mountains, he wrote:

From day to day, as we approached them, the beauty of the scenery increased, and when within twenty miles, the reflection of the sun through the melting snow that eternally crowns their highest peaks, is splendid beyond description. Here the traveler beholds a chain of many hundred, nay, thousands of miles, piled up, as it were, until they reach to heaven, with stone, uncovered with verdure or shrubs of any kind; nothing but the white caps of snow, and the rough and terrific precipice, varied for the eye to behold, until you reach the crossings of Red River, at the foot of the mountain; and here the pine and cedar tree again, on the mountain side and in the valley, greets the eye once more; and here on this plain we had to encounter about three hundred Eutwa [Ute?] warriors, but, after repeated skirmishing, they were fain to retreat, without effecting any damage of consequence. From here to the good town of Bogas, we found water, wood, and good cheer. The caravan arrived in this city [Santa Fe] on the 2d July, all in good health, in less than two months, the quickest trip ever made over the desert.

Whether the caravan broke any record in traveling from Independence to Santa Fe is not known, but the Indiana letter-writer did provide an interesting description of Santa Fe in 1841:

It is situated in a valley ten miles long, and from two to five wide, surrounded by immense mountains covered with pine and cedar trees, and affords the most beautiful scene the eye can conceive or mind imagine. Santa Fe is the seat of Government of New Mexico, and is commanded by a Governor-General. It is also a military post, port of entry, and depository of all the ancient archives of the neighboring States. The houses are built of raw bricks, two feet long, six inches deep, and one foot wide, made with straw and mud, and dried in the sun, and such is the durability that many houses more than two hundred years old are standing and look well; they are only one story high, handsomely whitewashed inside, with dirt floors. Even the palace in which his Excellency resides has no other than a dirt floor, but they are generally covered with carpets: the houses are covered with stones and dirt, and are flat-roofed, perfectly weather proof. The city contains six churches, generally richly fitted out. The population is about eight thousand inhabitants, all rigid Roman Catholics. It is situated on a small branch of the Rio del Norte, and about fourteen miles from the main river, which is near the size of the river Wabash at

Vincennes. The ladies, certainly, are far more beautiful in this country than those of the same ranks in America, their jetty black hair, piercing black eyes, slender and delicate frame, with unusually small ankles and feet, together with their gay winning address, make you at once easy and happy in their company. Perhaps no people on earth love dress and attention more than the Spanish ladies, and it may be said of a truth, that their amorous flirtations with the men are matters to boast of among themselves. They did work but little, the Fandango and Siesta form the division of time. The Fandango is a lascivious dance, partaking in part of the waltz, cotillion, and many amorous movements, and is certainly handsome and amusing. It is the national dance. In this the Governor and most humble citizens move together, and in this consists all their republican boast. The men are honest—perhaps more so than those of the same class in the United States, proud and vain of their blood—the descendants of the ancient Spaniards and Pueblo Indians, the descendants of their great monarch, Montezuma. This has been the case since the year 1836. In that revolution fell the most honorable and beloved of all the native Spaniards in Mexico, and all his family were banished. In the city, there is but one office of justice, the Alcalde, and he has nothing to do.

The commerce of this place is certainly very considerable, and although there is but one gold mine worked here now, and one copper mine, yet the daily receipts afford about six or seven hundred dollars net. More than from one to two hundred and twenty hands are employed at work. The revolution has put every thing aback here in the mining departments, as they were generally held by natives of old Spain, and accounted forfeits to the General Government after the revolution. This thing will soon be settled, and then the Holy City will appear in all her gaudy plumage again.[4]

How many freight wagons comprised the annual spring caravan of 1841 is not known, but when it returned to Independence in early September, only one or two old traders were in the party along with the freighters and their wagons. Some Mexicans were also with this caravan, carrying perhaps eighty thousand dollars and a quantity of valuable furs. Several days later a small party of Americans with six or eight wagons and a large number of horses and mules also reached Independence. From what is known, they were stragglers from the earlier group, perhaps slowed by the presence of so many horses and mules.[5]

In early October 1841, three Mexican traders—Armijo, Chávez, and DeGordin, who must have decided not to spend the winter purchasing merchandise in the East—left Independence for Santa Fe with a large caravan of about thirty wagons loaded with seventy-two tons of merchandise (apparently purchased in Missouri) plus 350 mules. This was rather late in the season for them to leave, but travel over the Santa Fe Trail had become so routine that traders sometimes gambled on winter weather arriving late. Charles Bent also left St. Louis with a wagon train loaded with merchandise bound for Bent's Fort. En route the caravan met a messenger from the fort with news that an expedition of Texians was on its way to conquer New Mexico and to divert the trade from Missouri to Texas. Lamar, Texas's president, wanted to annex New Mexico. The Texas commissioner in Santa Fe, William Dryden, had written Lamar that two-thirds of all New Mexicans and all of the Pueblo Indians would welcome control by Texas, so Lamar had raised an expedition to conquer New Mexico.

The best firsthand account of that expedition is George Wilkins Kendall's two-volume *Narrative of the Texan Santa Fe Expedition,* published in 1844 by Harper Brothers in New York City. Kendall, the thirty-two-year-old editor and owner of the *New Orleans Picayune,* joined the expedition not as a Texian but as an American with a U.S. passport. Kendall must have reasoned that if the expedition failed, he could disassociate himself from the adventure, but he turned out to be wrong; news of the exploit spread to the States and to New Mexico. Disguised as a trading expedition bound for Santa Fe, the party of more than three hundred men, including Kendall and one brass howitzer, was under the command of General Hugh McLeod, who set out in June 1841 from Austin for Santa Fe, about six hundred miles away. But crossing the Staked Plains of present-day West Texas and eastern New Mexico, they got lost and for a time traveled in circles, suffering from hunger and thirst.

Meantime in Santa Fe, Governor Armijo had learned that the expedition was heading for New Mexico. He attempted to arouse the citizens to counter the threat but failed. After some delay he succeeded in obtaining a promise from the Mexican government for funds and soldiers to defend the province, and he sent scouts to its eastern and northern borders to watch for the invaders. When an advance party of three men from the expedition reached a small village east-southeast of Santa Fe, they were arrested, taken to Santa Fe, and jailed. They escaped, but one man was killed near Santa Fe and the other two were taken to San Miguel and again jailed. Another advance party of five men including Kendall was soon captured, marched to San Miguel, and jailed, but later taken to Santa Fe. Governor Armijo then had priests in Santa Fe and elsewhere tell the people that the Texians coming to New Mexico planned to steal, burn, and rape. This successfully aroused the citizens, many of whom became terrified of the Texians. Manuel Alvarez, acting U.S. consul at Santa Fe, demanded that Governor Armijo protect Americans and their property. The governor promised to do so but ordered all foreigners to remain in their homes. Armijo then marched soldiers eastward; they arrested and disarmed the rest of the Texians near the Pecos River. The captives were cruelly treated, taken to Santa Fe, and later marched on foot to Mexico City and imprisoned.[6]

Charles Bent learned of the Texian expedition on the Santa Fe Trail while he was returning to Bent's Fort. Soon after reaching the fort he left for Taos, where he was arrested and taken to Santa Fe. Governor Armijo claimed that the arrest was a mistake, that Taos officials had misunderstood their orders; he may have feared that, if word of the arrest reached Bent's Fort, Bent's men might come to his aid. A couple of days after Mexican soldiers started to march the Texians to Mexico City, a freed Charles Bent returned to Taos to attend to his business interests there. At about the same time, Alvarez and sixteen Americans set out from Santa Fe for Independence. It was mid-October—much too late in the season to start such a journey. The weather was cold, and a blizzard with deep and drifting snow caused the party much delay. It took them fifty days, but they reached Independence just before Christmas.[7]

When word reached Texas that its expedition had failed, Texians were infuriated. Meantime, Lamar lost his reelection bid to Sam Houston, who had preceded him as the republic's first president. Relations between Texas and Mexico were strained, and when Americans sought the release of Texians in prison, diplomatic problems increased between the United States and Mexico.

Conditions in Santa Fe were still unsettled in the spring of 1842, when the annual spring caravan set out from Missouri for New Mexico. The caravan was the largest in three years, consisting of 120 men with sixty-two wagons, all drawn by mules, carrying English and American merchandise valued at between $150,000 and $160,000. Of fifteen traders in the caravan, perhaps seven or eight were Mexican, the rest American. One of the traders was Manuel Alvarez, the acting U.S. consul at Santa Fe, who was returning to Santa Fe with new merchandise to stock his store. Several days after leaving Independence, the caravan may have met another one coming from Santa Fe with at least six Mexican traders planning to go east to Pittsburgh, Pennsylvania, to make contracts for wagons, harness, and merchandise to be sold in Mexico. One account suggests the six traders carried seventeen boxes of specie containing about $350,000 to make purchases in the United States. The westbound caravan may also have met Bent, St. Vrain and Company's spring wagon train heading for Independence. Charles Bent led the train, which arrived at Independence in early May bringing 283 packs of buffalo robes, 30 packs of beaver pelts, 12 sacks of buffalo tongues, and one pack of deerskins. Kit Carson was among those coming from Bent's Fort, and he brought with him his young half-Arapaho daughter to be cared for and educated in Missouri.[8]

Whether any of the caravans came upon a lone Mexican heading east is not known, but one such person—Martias Dias—arrived at Independence in May 1842. He related how he had dug out of a Santa Fe jail with tools supplied by friends and then made his way to Taos, stolen a horse and mule, and fled to Bent's Fort, where he obtained assistance, including supplies. Dias had subsequently traveled east over the Santa Fe Trail to Independence. George Kendall's *New Orleans Weekly Picayune,* June 13, 1842, noted: "If this story is correct he [Martias] is probably the first traveller who has ever 'gone it alone' across the immense prairies of the West." Published accounts of the Texian expedition do mention a man named "Matias" or "Martias."[9]

By 1842, the importance of Independence and nearby settlements as jumping-off points for places west of Missouri now attracted emigrants bound for Oregon in addition to Santa Fe traders, bullwhackers, merchants, and others. The first organized group of Oregon-bound emigrants headed west in 1841, and others followed during subsequent years. Lieutenant John C. Frémont of the U.S. Topographical Engineer also headed west from near Westport in early June 1842 on his first Rocky Mountains exploration, but he followed the trail to Oregon across present-day Kansas, not the Santa Fe Trail. Frémont chose Kit Carson as his guide after having met him on a steamboat between St. Louis and Chouteau's Landing on the Missouri. During the summer of 1842, twenty-six steamboats plied the Missouri River west of St. Louis, bringing people and goods. One of these steamboats, the *Lebanon,* was carrying merchandise belonging to several Santa Fe traders that was valued at about eighty thousand dollars, including about twenty thousand dollars' worth of goods belonging to New Mexico's governor, Armijo. The *Lebanon* sank in early August in five feet of water about fifty miles below Independence. Acting U.S. consul Manuel Alvarez said that when Armijo learned of the loss, he "became excited to a high degree against all the citizens of the United States." Later, Armijo admitted that his loss was insured.[10]

Another person to arrive at Independence early in 1842 was Charles Alexander Warfield, the son of a well-known New Orleans merchant.

Warfield had proposed to a friend of Sam Houston, again president of the Republic of Texas, that an expedition of volunteers be organized to overthrow the provincial governments of New Mexico and Chihuahua. Houston liked the idea, probably because Texas might acquire New Mexico, perhaps divert the Santa Fe trade to Texas, and retaliate against Mexico for holding members of the Texian expedition captive. Houston ordered that Warfield be commissioned a colonel in the Texas army and given the authority to commission junior officers. He also authorized him to invade New Mexico and Chihuahua under the flag of Texas.

Soon after Warfield reached Independence, he met John McDaniel, who claimed to have lived in Texas and served in its militia. While this was true, McDaniel neglected to mention that he had later turned to robbery and murder, something Warfield probably did not know when he commissioned McDaniel as a captain and ordered him to recruit other men in the service of Texas. Warfield headed west to the Rocky Mountains, where he hoped to raise a group of volunteers. From what is known, McDaniel recruited only fourteen men, and he and they were more interested in robbery than in serving Texas. On April 1, 1843, a few weeks before the annual spring caravan was to start west from Independence, McDaniel and his men left Westport intent on robbing Mexican traders along the Santa Fe Trail. Then, apparently, McDaniel and his men bragged about their plans, and some citizens of Independence wrote to the superintendent of Indian affairs for the West in St. Louis reporting what they had heard. About three days after McDaniel and his men rode out of Westport, the federal government sent sixty U.S. First Dragoons from Fort Leavenworth to pursue them, with instructions to arrest them because they had no passports. The soldiers, however, failed to find the men.

As McDaniel and his men pushed westward over the Santa Fe Trail, they came upon a Mexican on a mule who, he explained, was riding east toward Independence to get help for his employer, the Mexican trader Don Antonio José Chávez, stranded farther west along the trail. Chávez, a member of one of the wealthiest families in New Mexico and the son of the first governor in New Mexico following independence, had left Santa Fe for Missouri in February. His caravan consisted of only two wagons, fifty-five mules, and fifteen men, but while they were following the Cimarron route the weather had become bitterly cold because of a winter storm sweeping eastward out of the Rocky Mountains. During the days that followed, all but five of Chávez's mules died from exposure. Ten of his men deserted. Using only one of his wagons, Chávez and five men pushed ahead, but they finally were forced to stop and establish a winter camp on what later became known as Jarvis Creek. Stranded, Chávez then sent his employee and the best mule east for help.

Learning of Chávez's situation, McDaniel somehow got the Mexican to lead him to Chávez's camp. There, the McDaniel band took Chávez and his men captive, moved everyone several miles away and made a new camp, and then robbed their captives. But when McDaniel began talking of killing Chávez and his men, some of his own men objected; those opposed to the killings then talked of departing with their share of the spoils. That night their horses and captive mules stampeded, leaving everyone on foot. The next morning the men who were against the killings picked up their plunder and started walking toward Missouri.

Now unopposed, McDaniel was free to do what he wished. He apparently thought there was more plunder to be found and asked Chávez where it was. Chávez refused to answer. A little later McDaniel reportedly beat Chávez until he admitted he had more money but refused to disclose its location. McDaniel lost his temper and led Chávez to a nearby ravine. When Chávez still refused to talk, McDaniel shot him and then told Chávez's five Mexican employees to go back to New Mexico, probably hoping they would not survive the winter weather or unfriendly Indians as they traveled on foot (they were later rescued alive). McDaniel and his remaining men picked up their booty and started walking east to Missouri. Eventually McDaniel and the others were arrested and brought to trial. Court records indicate that McDaniel did find some money hidden in Chávez's clothing, but the fact that a great deal of gold and specie was never found gave rise to a legend that Chávez must have buried it near his first camp on Jarvis Creek before the plunderers arrived. As for McDaniel, he and one of his men were hanged in Missouri, and the others who had remained with him received prison sentences.[11]

Warfield, who had recruited McDaniel, was able to raise only about two dozen volunteers in Colorado, and he did lead them toward New Mexico. Near the present town of Mora, New Mexico, Warfield and his men attacked a troop of Mexican soldiers and killed five before retreating. While camped near Wagon Mound, Mexican soldiers in pursuit ran off Warfield's horses and forced the colonel and his men to walk two hundred miles north to Bent's Fort. There Warfield disbanded his little army and started for Texas, never succeeding in his plan to conquer New Mexico, let alone Chihuahua.

Also unsuccessful was Jacob Snively, another man who received a colonel's commission from the Republic of Texas along with orders to intercept Mexican traders on the Santa Fe Trail. He gathered nearly two hundred men and rode north from Texas to the Arkansas River during

This illustration by A. L. Dick of a trading caravan arriving at Santa Fe appeared in Josiah Gregg's Commerce of the Prairies *(1844).* (Author's Collection)

the spring of 1843 to wait for Mexican traders. The spring caravan from Santa Fe was made up mostly of Mexicans and left in April carrying between $250,000 and $300,000 in silver. Eleven of the Mexican traders planned to travel to New York City to purchase new merchandise. Since it had been rumored in Santa Fe that Texians would be waiting for them on the Arkansas River, the forty-two wagons, 180 men, and twelve hundred mules followed the Cimarron or dry route to avoid them, and the caravan safely reached Independence by mid-May. But back on the Santa Fe Trail, west of the cutoff for the Cimarron route, Snively's party of Texians still waited. And it was there that Charles Warfield, returning to Texas, came upon Snively's camp. When an Independence-bound wagon train from Bent's Fort led by Charles Bent passed Snively's camp, Warfield learned of Chávez's murder and McDaniel's involvement. Warfield and Snively also learned from Bent that New Mexico governor Armijo and six hundred soldiers were marching to meet the annual spring caravan from Independence at the international border.

Arrival of the Caravan at Santa Fe.

Thomson Willing's drawing of a trading caravan arriving in Santa Fe. It appeared in Henry Inman's The Old Santa Fe Trail *(1897).* (Author's Collection)

Soon after Bent's caravan continued east, Snively ordered Warfield to take a few men and delay the Mexican soldiers' advance. Warfield and the men had traveled only a few miles over the Cimarron route when they met an advance party of about a hundred Mexican soldiers. Warfield and his men killed or captured all but two of the soldiers, who fled and returned to the main party. When Governor Armijo learned what had happened, he returned to Santa Fe. Snively, Warfield, and the others waited for the spring caravan, but soon about seventy of Snively's men—including, apparently, Warfield—became restless and decided to return to Texas. But Snively still had about a hundred men, and they continued their wait, not knowing that as Charles Bent's caravan had traveled east, they had met Captain Philip St. George Cooke and a large party of dragoons camped at the Walnut Creek crossing. Cooke and his men were escorting the annual spring trading caravan from Missouri to the international boundary. More than half of the caravan's fifty wagons were owned by five Mexican traders who had joined ten American traders for the trip. Together the traders had 136 armed men, half American, half Mexican. It probably was Bent who told Cooke where the Texians were waiting for Mexican traders, and on the last day of June 1843, Captain Cooke and his dragoons came upon Snively and his men in camp on the Arkansas River about ten miles east of present-day Dodge

City, Kansas. Carrying two howitzers, Cooke's dragoons were a stronger force than the Texians. Snively and his men surrendered. The Texians were disarmed and permitted to march back to Texas, while the spring caravan of Mexican and American traders continued safely to Santa Fe.[12]

The Texian expedition, Warfield and Snively's adventures, and the murder of Chávez caused such great concern in Mexico that President Santa Anna on August 7, 1843, closed all customhouses in New Mexico and one in El Paso, and suspended all trade from the United States over the Santa Fe Trail. But after word reached New Mexico months later that Chávez's killers had been arrested and Captain Cooke had disposed of Snively's volunteer army, Santa Anna withdrew his order, and on March 31, 1844, reopened the border and trade. Santa Anna is quoted as saying that Cooke's action "was the first act of good faith ever shown by the United States toward Mexico."[13]

When word reached Missouri that the Mexican border was again open, it came too late for traders who already had canceled the 1844 spring caravan from Independence. This proved to be fortuitous because heavy rains fell beginning in March in what is now Kansas and Missouri. Travel was difficult, and on April 23, nearly a hundred men, three or four Mexican women, and some children traveling with fifty wagons heading for Missouri from Santa Fe were delayed at the Pawnee Fork crossing in present-day Pawnee County, Kansas. Charles and William Bent and Ceran St. Vrain were among the stranded, as was Rufus Sage, a Connecticut printer who had entered the fur trade in 1841. Sage later wrote, "bands of buffalo that thronged the vicinity abated somewhat the annoyance of delay." After about four weeks the travelers were able to resume their journeys east, but the wet weather moved with them. There was so much rain during May and into June 1844 in what is now eastern Kansas and Missouri that the Kansas and Missouri rivers flooded. Where the Missouri meets the Mississippi River north of St. Louis, on May 20, 1844, the Mississippi was within two feet of the record set during the great flood of 1826, and about a month later it was even higher, thirty-eight feet seven inches above the low-water mark, which was more than four feet higher than the level reached during the great flood of 1785. The rain wreaked havoc with the Santa Fe traders since it slowed their wagons, which often became mired in mud. At times the wagons could not cross the smaller creeks and streams, which had swollen in size and depth.[14]

The effect of the rains and flooding of 1844 came too late to be mentioned in Josiah Gregg's *Commerce of the Prairies*, which was published in the spring of that year. The *New Orleans Weekly Picayune* reviewer on September 23, 1844, noted that the two-volume work "should be in the possession of every one who feels any interest in the destinies of this country, as connected with the ultimate occupation and settlement of the prairies and the north-western portion of Mexico by the Anglo-Saxon race." Gregg's work would fix in the minds of readers, mostly in the East, the character of the people of New Mexico, who would soon become citizens of the United States, and it would help foster the notion of "manifest destiny," the growing nationalistic belief that Americans had a natural right to occupy all of the land between the Atlantic and the Pacific

Dr. Josiah Gregg (1806–1850), author of Commerce of the Prairies, *first published in New York in 1844. The two-volume classic details the history of the first two decades of the Santa Fe trade as seen through the eyes of Gregg, himself a trader.* (Author's Collection)

(although the phrase itself first appeared in print in an editorial of July 1845 in the *Democratic Review,* edited by John L. O'Sullivan).[15]

WITH WORD THAT Mexico's borders were again open, traders in Missouri began organizing a fall caravan for Santa Fe. One man who joined was James J. Webb, a twenty-six-year-old Connecticut native, who after working in business at St. Louis for a year and a half purchased on credit there about twelve hundred dollars of merchandise and had the goods freighted by steamboat to Independence, where Colonel Samuel C.

Owens furnished him with a wagon and four yoke of oxen, also on credit. The wagon was valued at one hundred dollars, and the cost of each yoke of oxen was twenty-eight dollars. Separately, Webb and the other traders took their loaded wagons and started down the Santa Fe Trail to Council Grove, where a caravan of forty men, twenty-three wagons with fifty yoke of oxen, and about 140 mules had convened. Colonel Owens, who had eight wagons, was elected captain, and he appointed four guards. Webb later wrote that the four guards "drew lots for choice of men; and the guard organized, leaving a cook for each mess free from guard duty. This being the last place where we could procure hard wood for repairs of wagons, one day was spent in cutting and slinging timber under the wagons and preparing for an early start the next morning."

Leaving Council Grove, the small caravan stopped at Diamond Spring and "partook of mint juleps and passed a vote of thanks to the public benefactors who some years before had transported and set out some mint roots at the spring which by this time had increased to a bountiful supply for all trains passing." The journey of the small caravan with which Webb traveled was uneventful except for sickness among some of the men, the sight of large herds of buffalo, and a few friendly Indians. For Webb, the journey of seventy days was exciting, and although it was not a financial success, it did whet his appetite for such a life and for other trading ventures to Santa Fe.[16]

About a month after Webb's caravan left for Santa Fe, three other caravans headed west. The first, a train of about twenty wagons led by Charles Bent and Ceran St. Vrain, was bound for Bent's Fort. About the middle of September a train of twenty-five wagons led by Albert Speyer left for Santa Fe with perhaps twenty wagons led by Dr. Henry Connelly and Edward J. Glasgow. On the Cimarron River, they were caught in a severe sleet- and rainstorm and lost so many mules that their wagons were stranded. Speyer and Connelly went ahead to New Mexico, purchased new mules, and returned. Their wagons apparently reached Santa Fe in late November. As late as two years afterward, traders heading for Santa Fe reported that the skulls and bones of about a hundred mules could be seen in the Willow Creek area near the Cimarron River.[17]

In spite of the rains and floods that hampered travel in the spring of 1844, the year turned out to be profitable for many traders. The *Journal*, a new weekly newspaper started at Independence, estimated that after the floodwaters subsided, $400,000 in specie and about $50,000 in buffalo robes and furs arrived in Missouri from New Mexico. The value of the merchandise taken to Santa Fe in August and September was about $200,000 by eastern standards.[18]

JOSIAH GREGG'S TABLE

YEARS	AMOUNT OF MERCHANDISE	NUMBER OF WAGONS	NUMBER OF MEN	PROPRIETORS	GOODS TAKEN TO CHIHUAHUA	REMARKS
1822	15,000		70	60		Pack-animals only used.
1823	12,000		50	30		Pack-animals only used.
1824	35,000	26	100	80	3,000	Pack-animals and wagons.
1825	65,000	37	130	90	5,000	Pack-animals and wagons.
1826	90,000	60	100	70	7,000	Wagons only henceforth.
1827	85,000	55	90	50	8,000	
1828	150,000	100	200	80	20,000	3 men killed, being the first.
1829	60,000	30	50	20	5,000	1st U.S. escort, 1 trader killed.
1830	120,00	70	140	60	20,000	First oxen used by traders.
1831	250,000	130	320	80	80,000	Two men killed.
1832	140,000	70	150	40	50,000	Party defeated on Canadian, 2 men killed, 3 perished.
1833	180,000	105	185	60	80,000	
1834	150,000	80	160	50	70,000	2nd U.S. escort.
1835	140,000	75	140	40	70,000	
1836	130,000	70	135	35	60,000	
1837	150,000	80	160	35	80,000	
1838	90,000	50	100	20	40,000	
1839	250,000	130	250	40	100,000	Arkansas Expedition.
1840	50,000	30	60	5	10,000	Chihuahua Expedition.
1841	150,000	60	100	12	80,000	Texas Santa Fe Expedition.
1842	160,000	70	120	15	90,000	
1843	450,000	230	350	30	300,000	3rd U.S. escort—Ports closed.

This table shows the estimated amount of merchandise, apparently in pounds, taken to Santa Fe from Missouri between 1822 and 1843, the number of wagons used to carry it (when known), the number of men (employees), the number of proprietors (traders who owned the merchandise), and that portion of the merchandise taken to Chihuahua (when known). It cost approximately ten to twelve cents per pound to transport goods from Missouri to Santa Fe, but only six to eight cents per pound to move it from Santa Fe to Chihuahua by pack mules or wagons. This table was compiled by Josiah Gregg and is copied from his Commerce of the Prairies, *published in 1844 in New York.* (Author's Collection)

Early in 1845, Santa Fe traders probably cheered when word reached Missouri that Congress on March 3 had passed and President John Tyler had signed into law a measure providing for rebates on imported merchandise upon which duties had been paid, when the goods were reexported through Missouri or Arkansas to Mexico. This was what residents of Missouri and Arkansas had lobbied for. The measure also provided for inspectors to be appointed at Independence, Missouri, and at Van Buren and Fulton, in southwest Arkansas, near the border with Texas.

The seventeenth of the same month, the *New Orleans Weekly Picayune* reported that seven traders had made "the tedious winter journey across the prairies," traveling first to Bent's Fort and then east to Missouri. Most traders preferred to travel during warmer weather because of the hazards of winter travel. Who these off-season traders were is not known, but by this time the more experienced traders who had traveled many times between New Mexico and Missouri took more chances in their travels.

When spring arrived, the normal rains did not come. By April, the Missouri River was very low. In fact, the floods of the previous summer had changed the course of the river in many places, creating snags, stumps, and sandbars that hampered navigation. Only a few steamboats were able to make it up the Missouri from St. Louis to Independence, where about April 16 a small caravan of traders arrived from Santa Fe. One of them was James J. Webb. The caravan had followed the route over Raton Pass to Bent's Fort before moving east to Missouri. Meantime, the day Webb's party arrived in Missouri, a caravan of about a hundred wagons left Santa Fe for Missouri. Even though relations between the United States and Mexico had been strained, the weekly *Western Expositor* published in Independence predicted that the year's overland trade would be considerable.[19]

Newspapers in Missouri and elsewhere also reported on the increase in emigrant companies leaving for Oregon from Independence, Westport, and the new settlement of St. Joseph, Missouri, located on the Missouri River about fifty miles north-northwest from present-day Kansas City, Missouri. In May 1845 alone, 223 wagons; 954 men, women, and children; and 9,425 cattle and 108 horses and mules set out from St. Joseph on the trail to Oregon. During the same month, about 2,000 or 3,000 people with 200 wagons left Independence for the same destination, following the Santa Fe Trail a few miles into what is now Kansas, where at a fork emigrants could turn northwest to follow one of several trails leading to the Platte River road to Oregon. On May 18, 1845, Colonel Stephen W. Kearny and 280 well-mounted and -equipped First U.S. Dragoons marched from Fort Leavenworth toward the Platte on an expedition to the Rocky Mountains. Their mission was to protect the emigrants and to impress the Indians with their presence and military reconnaissance. Kearney and his dragoons would travel more than two thousand miles in the longest undertaking of dragoons in the West until that time, and they would return east over the Santa Fe Trail in August. There, Kearny's homeward-bound soldiers met several caravans of traders heading for Taos, Santa Fe, and Chihuahua. One of those trains may have been that owned by Bent and St. Vrain, which consisted of eighteen wagons, each pulled by five yoke of oxen, carrying about five thousand pounds of merchandise hauled westward from Westport, Missouri, which by 1845 had several business houses and a population that was growing. A few years earlier, the Frenchman Pierre Roi had constructed a road from the town four miles north to Westport Landing, which had been established about 1837. Steamboats there could unload trading goods, merchandise, and supplies for the Santa Fe and Indian trade and for the Rocky Mountain fur trade. Bent and St. Vrain's train starting from Westport marked the beginning of the town's importance as an eastern terminus of the Santa Fe Trail.[20]

ELEVEN

The Mexican War and the Santa Fe Trade, 1846-1848

*How good bad music and bad reasons sound
when we march against an enemy.*

—*Nietzsche*

B Y THE EARLY 1840s the idea of bringing the Republic of Texas into
the Union became so popular in the East that when the Virginian
John Tyler succeeded to the presidency following the death of William
Henry Harrison in 1841, Tyler sponsored a treaty of annexation. But it
failed to pass the Senate because a presidential election was approaching
and the senators voted along party lines. After James K. Polk was elected
president in 1844, Tyler, still in office, succeeded in getting signed a joint
congressional resolution to annex Texas on March 1, 1845. Texians soon
agreed to join the Union, and on December 29, 1845, President Polk
signed the proclamation making Texas the twenty-eighth state. The Mexican minister in Washington, D.C., who had warned the government that
Mexico would consider annexation an act of war, asked for his passport
and left. The Mexican government refused to recognize the independence of Texas or the Rio Grande as an international boundary and sev-
ered its ties with the United States.

Anticipating a possible invasion by Mexican forces in Texas, President
Polk ordered Brigadier General Zachary Taylor to take troops from
Louisiana to the Nueces River in south Texas. Meantime, Polk sent John
Slidell to Mexico City to try and settle the two nations' differences. When
Slidell's mission failed, General Taylor then moved his forces to the Rio

Grande, and there, on April 25, 1846, Mexican forces crossed the river and attacked the Americans. When word of the attack reached Washington, Congress declared war on Mexico (May 13, 1846), authorized the president to call up fifty thousand volunteers for twelve months' service, and voted ten million dollars for an invasion of Mexico. In addition, the regular army was increased from about seven thousand men to more than fifteen thousand. The general in chief of the army, Winfield Scott, proposed that two American armies be sent into Mexico, one to move from the Rio Grande south through Monterrey to capture Mexico City, the other to move west and seize New Mexico and California. American warships were sent to blockade the principal Mexican seaports.

Even before he learned that war had been declared, Taylor moved his troops across the Rio Grande, captured Monterrey by mid-September, and then declared an eight-week armistice. While reorganizing his forces from a new headquarters west of Saltillo, the Mexican general Antonio López de Santa Anna and fifteen thousand troops attacked Taylor and his forces at nearby Buena Vista. After a two-day battle, Santa Anna and his army retreated, and General Taylor's forces soon controlled the Mexican states of Coahuila, Nuevo León, and Tamaulipis.[1]

To the north, Brigadier General Stephen Watts Kearny prepared to take what was called the "Army of the West" over the Santa Fe Trail to New Mexico from Fort Leavenworth, the army's main supply depot for all the West. The post was stocked by steamboats coming up the Missouri River from St. Louis and points east. When national attention was focused on Fort Leavenworth, a St. Louis newspaper sent a reporter to inspect the post. In the July 10, 1846, issue of the *New Era*, the reporter described Fort Leavenworth and noted that some of its buildings were "situated about 400 yards from the steamboat landing, on the summit of the first swell of land which gradually rises from the river. The area of ground occupied by the buildings, lawns and streets, is but little short of 20 acres, in the form of a square. Besides the public buildings of the Fort, several small log and frame houses are to be seen on the northern and western suburbs occupied by the families of regular soldiers, and of persons laboring for the Government. The powder magazine is located near the centre of a beautiful lawn finely shaded by forest trees, and in the heart of the Fort. It is completely fire and bomb proof. West of the Fort, is the parade ground. It is a beautiful space, and admirably calculated for the purpose. Southwest, at a distance of half a mile, is the Government farm, about 1100 acres of which is now under cultivation."

When Kearny received reports of a grain shortage in New Mexico, he insisted that adequate provisions be sent along with his army. But nei-

ther the army nor commercial freighters had sufficient wagons and manpower to do the job. The military decided to do its own freighting, and quartermaster agents began buying wagons in Pittsburgh, St. Louis, and anywhere they could find them for sale. Orders were issued to dismantle the wagons and ship them by steamboat to Fort Leavenworth. Other agents had in the meantime crisscrossed Missouri buying oxen and

This view of Santa Fe from Fort Marcy appeared in Harper's New Monthly Magazine, *April 1880.* (Author's Collection)

mules to pull the wagons. Some were purchased at Independence, where Edwin Bryant, an emigrant heading for California, purchased three ox teams for his own journey. "The average price paid per yoke was $21.67, which was considered very cheap. The streets were filled with oxen offered for sale by neighboring farmers, but few of them were in good condition or well-trained," wrote Bryant, adding, "Young and medium-sized cattle should be selected for a journey over the plains and mountains, in preference to the heavy-bodied and old; the latter almost invariably become foot-sore, and give out after traveling a few hundred miles."[2]

Meantime, other government agents bought thousands of pounds of bacon at five cents per pound plus large quantities of other foodstuffs from merchants in St. Louis. These provisions were also loaded aboard steamboats and sent up the Missouri River to Fort Leavenworth, where the army began hiring teamsters at twenty-five to thirty dollars a month

This drawing from Harper's New Monthly Magazine, *July 1880, depicts Kearny's soldiers crossing the mountains to Santa Fe during the Mexican War.* (Author's Collection)

to drive the wagons. Their pay was better than what Kearny's soldiers were receiving.

Unfortunately, the provisions arrived at Fort Leavenworth before most of the wagons. Kearny and his army of about sixteen hundred men could not wait and had all available wagons loaded with supplies and sent with the first military units leaving for New Mexico in mid-June. As more wagons arrived by steamboat, they were assembled, loaded with provisions, and sent in small groups over the Santa Fe Trail toward New Mexico. The wagons, however, were carelessly loaded. Some of them carried nothing but food; others carried tents or cooking utensils or miscellaneous supplies. The army's inexperience in freighting stores across the plains soon became evident. Many of the teamsters hired to drive the wagons were new to the job, and few knew how to care for the oxen and mules. To make matters worse, when wagons reached Bent's Fort on the Arkansas River, many of the teamsters refused to continue the trip to Santa Fe, pointing out that they were contracted to drive only as far as Bent's Fort. There was much confusion and great expense, nearly fifteen cents for each pound of freight the army transported. Kearny's men,

Frederic Remington's Troops Going to Mexico, 1847, *as it appeared in Henry Inman's* The Old Santa Fe Trail *(1897).* (Author's Collection)

strung out along the trail, had either feast or famine, depending upon what supplies had been loaded in the freight wagons that accompanied them. The first soldiers to reach Santa Fe actually ran out of food about a day before arriving in mid-August. Given these difficulties, it is not surprising that about two years later, in 1848, the army opened its freighting in the West to private citizens with competitive bidding, which marked the true beginning of the freighting industry in the West.[3]

When Kearny's troops first approached Santa Fe, Governor Armijo, after first pretending to rally a defense force, abandoned the town and fled south into Mexico, thanks to the efforts of some American traders. Kearny and his troops entered Santa Fe the following day. Kearny proclaimed New Mexico a territory of the United States; established a civil government; appointed territorial officials, including Charles Bent as governor; and began constructing Fort Marcy on a hill overlooking the governor's palace. In his proclamation, Kearny absolved the people of New Mexico from all allegiance to their constituted authorities and by a stroke of the pen transformed them into citizens of the United States. (The Territory of New Mexico would not be created until 1850, however, under an agreement to ease the tension between the North and the South over the extension of slavery into new territories. The Compromise of 1850 divided the area east of California into the Territories of New Mexico and Utah, and both were opened to settlement by settlers against slavery and those holding slaves. What became New Mexico Territory included present-day Arizona.)

EVEN BEFORE the Mexican War began in 1846, relations between the United States and Mexico had caused a high state of tension along the Santa Fe Trail and among traders, who in 1845 reportedly succeeded in transporting merchandise to New Mexico valued at about $350,000. The following year, even as General Kearny and his army were heading for New Mexico in June, an increased number of trading caravans from Missouri were traveling toward Santa Fe. The traders appeared to sense that New Mexico would soon become a territory of the United States, thereby eliminating the duty Santa Anna had imposed on each wagon-load of goods. Some of the traders probably also realized that the American soldiers, many of them Missouri volunteers, would increase the market for merchandise.

One caravan of several traders and their wagons left Council Grove on June 21, 1846, with forty-five wagons. One of the traders was Samuel

Susan Shelby Magoffin as she appeared in 1845.
(Author's Collection)

Magoffin, whose older brother James had entered the Santa Fe trade during the late 1820s. James soon became a partner in Samuel's trade, and together they took many caravans to Santa Fe and Chihuahua. Usually the brothers traveled together on the trail, but on this trip James had gone ahead of everyone, including Kearny and his army, because he was on a secret mission for the government—to negotiate U.S. possession of New Mexico without bloodshed. James Magoffin's wife was a cousin of the New Mexico governor, Manuel Armijo. In a secret conference, James convinced Armijo that he should not resist, and he also secured an alliance with Armijo's second in command. Despite his success in Santa Fe, when James Magoffin attempted to play the same role in Chihuahua, he was arrested by the Mexican government and jailed for nine months.

Samuel Magoffin's eighteen-year-old wife, Susan Shelby Magoffin, a Kentucky native, accompanied him as he led the trading caravan to Santa Fe behind General Kearny and his forces. She kept a diary of the journey, the first such record of Santa Fe Trail travel known to have been kept by a woman. It is filled with circumstantial detail and her personal impressions. For instance, when Susan Magoffin and her husband reached Pawnee Fork on July 4, 1846, she wrote:

The traders are all stoped [*sic*] here by an order of Government, to wait the arrival of more troops than those already ahead of us, for our protection to Santa Fe. We are quite a respectable crowd now with some seventy-five or eighty wagons of merchandise, beside those of the soldiers. When all that are behind us come up we shall number some hundred and fifty. And it is quite probable we shall be detained here ten days or a week at the least. I shall go regularly to housekeeping. It is quite a nice place this, notwithstanding the number of wagons and cattle we have for our near neighbours. With the great Arkansas [River] on the South of us, the Pawnee creek to the S.W. and extensive woods in the same direction. From the west the buffalo are constantly coming in, in bands of from three or four to more than fifty. The sight of so many military coats is quite sufficient to frighten all the Indians entirely out of the country. So we have nothing to fear either on account of starvation, thirst or sudden murder.[4]

Several days later the large trading caravan and that of the soldiers continued west toward Bent's Fort. On Sunday, July 12, she wrote that the "Sabbath on the Plains is not altogether without reverence. Every thing is perfectly calm. The blustering, swearing teamsters remembering the duty they owe to their Maker, have thrown aside their abusive language, and are singing the hymns perhaps that were taught by a good pious Mother. The little birds are all quiet and reverential in their songs. And nothing seems disposed to mar that calm, serene silence prevailing over the land. We have not the ringing of church bells, or the privilege of attending public worship, it is true, but we have ample time, sufficient reason &c for thinking on the great wisdom of our Creator, for praising him within ourselves for his excellent greatness in placing before us and entirely at our command so many blessings; in giving us health, minds free from care, the means of knowing and learning his wise designs."[5]

Elsewhere along the Santa Fe Trail, all was not bliss on that Sunday. When troops under Lieutenant Colonel Charles F. Ruff arrived at Walnut Creek Crossing that day, where the Magoffins had camped about a week earlier, the soldiers met another trading caravan bound for Santa Fe. It was owned by Edmund Hoffman, a merchant from Baltimore. When one of Hoffman's traders sold eighteen-cent whiskey to the soldiers at the exorbitant price of a dollar per pint, the concession was shut down by the military, with the added threat that his goods would be confiscated.[6]

The Magoffin party reached Bent's Fort in late July. Susan wrote in her diary that from afar the fort was like an ancient castle.

It is built of adobes, unburnt brick, and Mexican style so far. The walls are very high and very thick with rounding corners. There is but one entrance, this is to the East. Inside is a large space some ninety or a hundred feet *square*, all around this and next [to] the wall are rooms, some twenty-five in number. They have dirt floors—which are sprinkled with water several times during the day to prevent dust. Standing in the center of some of them is a large wooden post as a firmer prop to the ceiling which is made of logs. Some of these rooms are occupied by boarders as bed chambers. One is a dining-room—another a kitchen—a little store, a blacksmith's shop, a barber's do an icehouse, which receives perhaps more customers than any other.

On the South side is an enclosure for stock in dangerous times and often at night. On one side of the top wall are rooms built in the same manner as below. We are occupying one of these. . . .

This drawing of Santa Fe, titled "Morning on the Plaza," includes American traders and military officers. The illustration appeared in Harper's New Monthly Magazine, *April 1880.* (Author's Collection)

They have a well inside, and fine water it is—especially with ice. At present they have quite a number of boarders. The traders and soldiers chiefly, with a few *loafers* from the States, come out because they can't live at home. There is no place on Earth I believe where man lives and gambling in some form or another is not carried on. Here in the Fort, and who could have supposed such a thing, they have a *regularly established billiard room!* They have a regular race track. And I hear the cackling of chickens at such a rate some times I shall not be surprised to hear of a cock-fight.[7]

After twelve days at Bent's Fort, the Magoffin party departed for Santa Fe and arrived there in late August, some days after General Kearny and his men had raised the American flag over the town. Samuel and Susan Magoffin moved into a small four-room house under the shadow of a church. Susan wrote in her diary that she had not been inside the church, but could "vouch for its being well supplied with bells, which are chiming, it seems to me, all the time both night and day."[8]

This may have been the church linked to Josiah Gregg in a tale still told in Santa Fe about a church whose vicar, or *vicario,* had traveled abroad and seen churches with large outside clocks that struck the hours. The vicar asked Gregg, who was quite mechanically oriented, if he could build such a clock for his church in Santa Fe. Gregg said he could and signed an agreement. The vicar agreed to pay Gregg a thousand dollars. On his next trip to Missouri, Gregg brought the intricate clock parts and soon built and installed the clock between the two towers of the church. Each hour, a small figure of a black man would come out from the clock and bow for each stroke. This pleased the people of Santa Fe, who considered the clock a wonder. The vicar, however, soon concluded that he had agreed to pay Gregg too much and only gave him seven hundred dollars. Not many days later the man in the clock failed to appear. The residents of Santa Fe, knowing the vicar had not fulfilled the terms of his contract, blamed the failure of the figure to appear on the vicar. The vicar sent a letter to Gregg, who had gone east, and asked him to bring the necessary materials to repair the clock when he returned. The vicar also promised to give Gregg the balance due. When Gregg returned to Santa Fe, he repaired the clock and was paid in full.[9]

On her journey to Santa Fe, Susan Magoffin took with her Josiah Gregg's two-volume *Commerce of the Prairies* as a guide and quoted it in her journal on several occasions. When she witnessed her first mirage, or "false-pond," she wrote: "It is so deceiving to the eye, that the thirsty traveler often breaks from his party with anxious eyes and heart to gain first the long wished for luxury, but ere he reaches the brink it vanishes from his sight. The philosophy of the false-ponds is scarcely as yet understood. To use the language of my predecessor, Mr. J. Gregg, from whom I have gained my information respecting them, 'It has usually been attributed to *refraction,* by which a portion of the bordering sky would appear below the horizon; but there can be no doubt that they are the effect of *refraction* upon a gas emanating from the sub-scorched earth and vegetable matter, or it may be that a surcharge of carbonic acid precipitated upon the flats and sinks of the plains, by the action of the sun, produces them.' "[10]

The exact number of traders who set out from Missouri with merchandise following Kearny's army to New Mexico is not known, but Josiah Gregg estimated the total value of goods taken to Santa Fe in 1846 at over a million dollars, which he observed was "more than treble that of any previous season." Even before the year ended, someone who kept figures on the annual exports from Missouri to New Mexico reported in Independence that thirty-nine firms had engaged in the trade up to September, using 351 wagons, 12 smaller kitchen wagons, and about 50 carriages. Between 750 and 800 men traveled in the caravans with "baled up" merchandise valued at about $950,000.[11]

"To die anywhere seems hard, but to heave the last breath on the burning, desolate prairie seems hard indeed," wrote Lewis Garrard in his book Wah-To-Yah and the Taos Trail *(1850). This illustration of a burial of a man who died while traveling to Santa Fe appeared in* Santa Fe National Historic Trail, Comprehensive Management and Use Plan, *published in 1990 by the National Park Service, U.S. Department of the Interior. The artist is not identified.* (Author's Collection)

Not included in the export figures reported in Independence were the goods carried by Norris Colburn's nineteen wagons, which left Missouri in early October. The *Western Expositor,* published in Independence, reported that Colburn was making his second trip of the year to New Mexico, "a thing unprecedented in the annals of prairie travel." A day or two later, A. P. Kean and Jacob Hall, merchants at Independence, left with perhaps nine wagons of provisions and goods, hopeful of finding a market among the American soldiers in Santa Fe. Still another caravan of twenty-eight wagons left the Missouri border bound for Santa Fe about October 12. It was owned by the Lexington, Missouri, mercantile firm of Bullard, Hooke and Company. The *Independence Expositor* reported that it was the latest time of year that a caravan had ever left Missouri for Santa Fe, implying that winter storms and severe cold might pose a threat. That is exactly what happened. While the caravan was camped south of the sand hills on the Cimarron River, a winter blizzard struck. Twenty head of oxen escaped in a stampede, and some mules died. The traders buried or cached their goods, returned to the Arkansas River, and went up the river to Bent's Fort for relief. In January, the traders took six wagons and

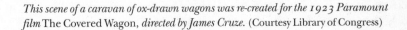

This scene of a caravan of ox-drawn wagons was re-created for the 1923 Paramount film The Covered Wagon, *directed by James Cruze.* (Courtesy Library of Congress)

retraced their steps to where they had buried their goods. Whether they continued on to Santa Fe is not known.[12]

In October 1846, Pawnees attacked still another caravan about twenty miles below the Arkansas crossing. With only a reported five guns among the traders, the Pawnees captured and robbed all nineteen wagons, took about fifty mules, and then allowed the traders to continue afoot. Teamsters later recalled how the Indians cut open three hundred sacks of flour and scattered it to the winds. The prairie for miles around was white, as if covered with snow. The Indians then took the sacks to make clothing.[13]

Several days later yet another caravan, this one consisting of twenty-four wagons carrying government supplies to New Mexico and captained by Daniel P. Mann, was attacked by as many as five hundred Pawnees about thirty miles below the Arkansas crossing. The forty teamsters, who had twenty-nine guns but only eighty cartridges, corralled all of their wagons except one carrying bacon, which the Indians burned. One teamster was killed and four were wounded in the fight, during which the Indians stampeded all but about a dozen horses and mules. At dark, Captain Mann and his men, taking the wounded, set out for the Arkansas River, and then went upstream many miles until they came upon another caravan camped along the river. There they found help.

Though many caravans bound for Santa Fe were attacked by Pawnees, one captained by Ceran St. Vrain met no hostile Indians. St. Vrain's caravan of twenty-three mule-drawn wagons loaded with merchandise left Westport, Missouri, about September 15, 1846, bound for Bent's Fort. Traveling with St. Vrain was the seventeen-year-old Hector Lewis Garrard of Cincinnati, Ohio, who for some reason later reversed his first two names. Fascinated by John C. Frémont's adventures in the West, Garrard convinced his parents to let him go west on a pleasure trip. Near what is today the Osage-Douglas County line in eastern Kansas, St. Vrain's caravan met a small party of men returning to Missouri. One man in the party was the twenty-three-year-old Francis Parkman, who was returning to Missouri from the eastern slopes of the Rocky Mountains. Parkman and Garrard probably greeted each other but of course did not know that both would become authors of classic narratives of the West, Parkman with *The California and Oregon Trail* (1849) and Garrard with his *Wah-To-Yah and the Taos Trail* (1850), both published in New York City. Garrard's work might have been simply another forgotten narrative by a nineteenth-century western traveler had it not been for the January 1847 Taos revolt against the American occupation of New Mexico, of which Garrard's book contains the best nonmilitary account.

With U.S. troops in control at Santa Fe, the door was opened for American traders, including Solomon Jacob Spiegelberg, who first came to Santa Fe in 1844. He worked in a general merchandise store, where he learned Spanish and the commercial needs of the people. In the fall of 1847, he reportedly quit his job, took $365 in savings, bought merchandise, and followed Colonel W. A. Doniphan and his soldiers as they marched south to Chihuahua. He made a good profit, returned to Santa Fe, and opened his own mercantile business late in 1848 on the south side of the Plaza. But when Kearny later established a military govern-

Solomon Jacob Spiegelberg arrived in Santa Fe in 1844 and later became a prominent merchant on the Plaza. (Courtesy Museum of New Mexico, negative no. 11023)

ment in Santa Fe, merchants, including Spiegelberg, had to pay an ad valorem tax on their imports. Naturally, they protested.

Meantime, not all New Mexicans liked Kearny's military rule and the appointment of Charles Bent as governor. The strong-willed Bent already had his enemies, including the powerful Martínez family of Taos and Indians living nearby who resented Bent's trading with their enemies. But the revolt, when it came, was based on resentment of the American conquerors and fears of land seizure. Bent, St. Vrain and Company had stores in Santa Fe and Taos and at Bent's Fort, and when Charles Bent heard of unrest around Taos, he went there in hopes of restoring order but became instead a symbol of what many people, especially the Indians, resented. Early in the morning a mob broke down the door of Bent's house in Taos, shot him, and scalped him. They also killed other Anglos. All of this is detailed in Garrard's book, including his joining William Bent and a party of trappers, who left Bent's Fort for Taos with an eye on revenge only to learn that Colonel Sterling Price and his troops had come from Santa Fe, put down the uprising, and had the ringleaders executed.

Several weeks after Kearny and his army arrived in Santa Fe, an Englishman, George F. Ruxton, arrived for a visit. He was on a journey from Mexico north through the Rocky Mountains. Ruxton had served as an officer in the British army in Canada, but he found military life oppressive. He sold his commission and spent a winter in the wilds of Ontario and northern New York State living with an Indian friend. He then traveled to England and Africa before going to Mexico and starting his trek northward to the Rocky Mountains. From what is known, Ruxton was not a typical traveler but was acting in the dual capacity of roving commercial attaché of the British diplomatic service and commercial agent of the Mexico government. His mission was to reestablish the Santa Fe trade that had been disrupted by the Mexican War. Arriving in Santa Fe after Kearny and his troops had taken control, Ruxton was not impressed with the town.

> The appearance of the town defies description, and I can compare it to nothing but a dilapidated brick-kiln or a prairie-dog town. The inhabitants are worthy of their city, and a more miserable, vicious-looking population it would be impossible to imagine. Neither was the town improved, at the time of my visit, by the addition to the population of some three thousand Americans, the dirtiest, rowdiest crew I have ever seen collected together. Crowds of drunken volunteers [American soldiers] filled the streets, brawling and boasting, but never fighting; Mexicans, wrapped in serapes, scowled upon them as they passed; donkey-loads of hoja—corn-shucks—were hawked about for sale; and Pueblo Indians and priests jostled the rude crowds of brawlers at every step. Under the portals were numerous monte-tables, surrounded by Mexicans and Americans. Every other house was a grocery, as they call a gin or whisky shop, continually disgorging reeling, drunken men, and everywhere filth and dirt reigned triumphant.[14]

Although Ruxton had planned to remain some time in Santa Fe, he became so disgusted with the town's filth and disorder that he left a few days after arriving and headed north through the valley of Taos to Bent's Fort. In New Mexico, Ruxton found a "bitter feeling and most determined hostility against Americans," which he believed was caused by their bullying and overbearing demeanor and their failure to conciliate the New Mexicans. This was just before the Taos uprising was put down.

After taking Santa Fe, Kearny continued west to California, where U.S. forces defeated the Mexican army at Los Angeles, and on March 1, 1847, he established civil government. A little more than a year later, in the village of Guadelupe Hidalgo a few miles north of Mexico City, the war ended when the United States and Mexico signed a treaty that was later approved in Washington. It gave the United States a vast region— Texas, New Mexico, and the area westward to the Pacific and northward to Oregon.

MANY OF THE Missouri traders, teamsters, and bullwhackers who traversed the Santa Fe Trail were Freemasons, then perhaps the largest and most widely established fraternal order in the world. The order was brought from England to America and established lodges during the 1730s in Boston and Philadelphia attempting to teach its members a moral philosophy of life. Many of the signers of the Declaration of Independence and George Washington, the first president, were Masons. The order grew and spread rapidly westward as the nation was settled. By the 1840s, it was not uncommon for Freemasons in Independence, Missouri, to commemorate the departure of their brother Masons leaving with trading caravans for Santa Fe, or those who were emigrants about to follow the trail to Oregon. Edwin Bryant witnessed such activities at Independence in May 1846 when he was preparing to travel to Oregon. He wrote:

> The lady-masons, that is, the wives of the members of the fraternity, walked in procession to and from the church. A large audience was collected to hear the address, and participate in the exercises. The address was delivered by Mr. Reese, the grand-master, or principal masonic officer in pathos. The orator, at the close of the discourse, consigned us all to the grave, or to perpetual exile. He was responded to in suitable and eloquent terms, on behalf of the Santa Fe traders and the emigrants to Oregon and California, by Col. Waul and Col. Russell. After the addresses, an original hymn, written for the occasion, as I understand, was sung with much feeling by the whole audience, to the tune of "Old Rosin the Bow." These farewell ceremonies

were concluded by an affecting prayer and benediction. The ladies of the auditory, I thought, were the most interested in and excited by these proceedings. Some of them wept, and manifested strong emotions.[15]

Even before the Mexican War ended, the importance of the Santa Fe Trail for commerce between Missouri and New Mexico became even greater. More and more caravans crisscrossed the plains carrying merchandise and supplies. It was only natural that some sought to make a living off the travelers. In April 1847, Albert G. Boone and James G. Hamilton, who owned the firm of Boone and Hamilton at Westport, Missouri, opened a store at Council Grove on the Santa Fe Trail. They sent Seth M. Hays, a native of Kentucky and a reported descendant of Daniel Boone, to operate the store with a license to trade with the Kansas Indians who lived in the area. When Hays arrived, the only other structure at Council Grove was a blacksmith's shop established by the government a year earlier to repair military wagons heading for Santa Fe. One Missouri volunteer heading to New Mexico, E. N. O. Clough, wrote that he visited with Hays, "who is making money hand over hand." Clough said Hays charged $2 for a gallon of molasses, 35 cents for a pound of cheese, and 75 cents for a plug of tobacco, "and rotten at that." A very coarse pair of brogans cost $3.50.[16]

A few months before Hays opened the store, construction was started, far to the west of Council Grove, on a small government stockade near the Arkansas River west of present-day Dodge City, Kansas, within sight of the "Caches." Forty civilian teamsters, headed by the wagon master Daniel P. Mann, began building what was first called Mann's Fort, later Fort Mann, in April 1847. Mann and his men had been sent by Captain W. M. D. McKissack, the army quartermaster at Santa Fe, who later wrote that because of the great number of abandoned wagons along that portion of the trail, the government decided to construct Fort Mann to provide a rest and repair station halfway between Fort Leavenworth and Fort Marcy at Santa Fe. Fort Mann consisted of only four log houses, each connected by framework with defensive holes for a cannon and small guns, and large gates, a foot thick, secured on hinges. Unofficially, Fort Mann was called many things by teamsters, bullwhackers, and soldiers—Fort Sod and Fort Sodom, among others. At one point the post reportedly had its own temperance society, but by 1851 the crudely constructed post had become so vermin-infested and unsanitary that it was closed and replaced by another log-and-sod set of buildings constructed nearby and called Fort Atkinson.

ONE OF THE MORE colorful figures on the Santa Fe Trail during the late 1840s was Francis X. Aubry, born near Maskinongé, Quebec, on December 3, 1824. He grew up on a farm there and then left to seek his fortune. Early in 1846, when war with Mexico appeared imminent, the twenty-two-year-old Aubry, a small man of perhaps a hundred pounds with black piercing eyes, was in St. Louis listening to traders talk of the expected expansion of the United States and new opportunities in New Mexico and Chihuahua.

Even before General Kearny and his army left Fort Leavenworth bound for New Mexico, Aubry decided to enter the Santa Fe trade. He

The trader Francis X. Aubry (1824–1854) made many trips over the Santa Fe Trail and broke speed records for covering the distance between Independence, Missouri, and Santa Fe. (Author's Collection)

obtained credit from the St. Louis firm of Lamoureux and Blanchard and purchased trade goods. On May 9, a few days before the United States declared war on Mexico, Aubry set out from Independence with James Webb and George Doan and other traders bound for Santa Fe. Aubry paid Webb and Doan $117 to carry his freight and $15 for board. The traders' caravan arrived in Santa Fe on June 23 without difficulty, to find American soldiers in control. Aubry disposed of his trade goods and returned to Missouri in August along with John McKnight, an American trader in Chihuahua. Together they carried $50,000 to $60,000 in specie. How much of that money was Aubry's is not known, but his profit

$100,000 WORTH OF NEW GOODS!!!

Of All Kinds Just From the U. States.
THE LARGEST AND BEST ASSORTMENT OF
DRY GOODS & GROCERIES, BOOTS, SHOES, HARDWARE &C.
That Was Ever Opened in the City of Santa Fe,
B. F. COONS
Wholesale & Retail Dealer in All Kinds of Merchandise

I WOULD inform the inhabitants of Santa Fe and the surrounding country, that I will arrive in Santa Fe within a few days, with the largest and best assortment of new and fashionible goods ever brought to this market, as I have the advantage of all other merchants in laying in my stock of goods> I am fully confident that I can sell lower than any person bringing out goods this season. My stock consists of the following articles,-

150 bales Manto,	75 Blue do,-
200 bales Leanso,	75 Black do,
100 bales Moun.,	800 Ps. Pt. Stuffs,
75 bales Contenia Blanco	600 Blue Satinett
25 bales Bed Ticking,	200 Black do,
100 bales Fancy Prints,	150 Casimere do,
100 Flannel do,	200 Prints, do,
29 White, do.	100 Black & Other Colors,
200 Ps. Black Muslin,	200 Barred Muslin, do,
200 Red, Green do,	100 Boxes Ribbon,
100 Black Velvet Cotton, do	100 Black Cloth do,
25 Silk do, do,	50 Blue do,
600 White Cambrick,	100 Red Cloth do,

TOGETHER WITH,

A proportionate lot of Cotton Hose, Silk Hdkfs., Blk. Cravats, Cotton & woolen socks, Cotton woolen and silk shawls, Cintos laces, Red flannel shirts, Linen and Cotton thread, Blankets, Silk Hose, Candle wicking, Elastic suspenders, Jeans vestings, Lawns, Gingham, Muslins and in fact every thing necessary for this or any other trade.

In connection with the above, I have the best, the largest and most superior lot of

GROCERIES

Ever Imported to this country, consisting of Rum, Gin, Peach and Apple Brandy, Irish Whiskey, Port, Maderia, Malaga, and Champaign Wines, Lemon Syrrup, white and brown Sugar, Raisins, Candles, Candies, Pepper, Spice, smoking and chewing Tobacco, Fine Cigars, Soap, Cinamon, Mackerel, Oysters and Sardines, American and Spanish Playing Cards, Indigo, Salaratus, Pipes, bar Lead, Powder, and many other articles too numerous to mention, with a large lot of

HARDWARE & QUEENSWARE

Of all kinds, Axes, Hose, Spades, Nails, brass and iron Tacks, Butts and Screws, cotton Cords, Coffee mills, Lock of all kinds, Saws, pen and pocket Knives, also butcher and table Knives, Dirks, Pistols, Guns, Rifles, Files, Chisels, Gimblets, Augers, Hatchets, Hammers, Rules, Manes, and everything else in this line. Also a large lot of

(Continued)

$100,000 WORTH OF NEW GOODS!!!

BOOTS AND SHOES, AND READY MADE CLOTHING,
Toys and Fancy Goods, Drugs, Paints, Oil, &c., Tin ware, Hats and Caps, Military cloths and Trimmings and all kinds of Stationary &c. &c.

I have taken the greatest pains possible in assorting the above stock of goods into different lots amounting to from 8 to 10 thousand dollars so to be able to sell to my old customers at whole sale. A fine and well assorted stock of goods, and at such prices as will suit the times. I would inform my old customers that I will sell as heretofore, on time if necessary.

I merely ask my old friends from the Rio Abajo, and Rio Arriba, that I am coming and want them to await my arrival before they purchase, for I do say I will not be undersold by any one. B. F. COONS

This advertisement was copied from the Santa Fe Republican, *July 6, 1848. B. Frank Coons, a St. Louis merchant taking merchandise to Santa Fe, apparently had someone rush to Santa Fe ahead of his wagon train to place the advertisement. Coons traveled over the trail several times. He made a trip in the spring of 1846 but did not start back to Missouri until January 1847 and had to travel through deep snow. After the mules pulling his wagons died, Coons and others walked the last two hundred miles to Missouri. He made another trip to Santa Fe that spring and met Francis X. Aubry returning to Missouri. After selling his merchandise in Santa Fe, Coons returned to Missouri in seventeen days, a record beaten only by Aubry. Coons made another trip to Santa Fe in 1848 carrying the merchandise listed in his advertisement.* (Author's Collection)

probably amounted to several thousand dollars, enabling him to repay Lamoureux and Blanchard in St. Louis.

Of importance to recorded history, Aubry kept a journal of his trip, and knowing that Missourians were starved for news from New Mexico, he shared it with the *Daily Missouri Republican,* which printed portions of his journal. Perhaps it was then that Aubry began to think of himself as a messenger who carried the news quickly. He found the Santa Fe trade not only profitable but very satisfying, and in 1847 he raised six thousand dollars to purchase wagons and supplies and left for Santa Fe in mid-April. Since the only mail service between Missouri and New Mexico was an occasional army express from Fort Leavenworth, Aubry publicly offered to carry the mail, which he paused to pick up before catching up with his wagons already on the trail. Unlike on his first trip to Santa Fe, Aubry encountered hostile Indians on his second journey. One of his men was killed and scalped, and at Fort Mann, Aubry and his teamsters rescued two men who had fought off Indians for two days after a handful of soldiers at the post had fled. The rest of the journey was uneventful, and Aubry and his wagons arrived at Santa Fe in early July, where he disposed of his trade goods within a week and prepared to start back to Missouri late in the month. One report suggests that Aubry sold his wagons and mules to another eastbound group for six thousand dollars.

Carrying mail to Missouri, Aubry joined a trader from Chihuahua, a company of Missouri volunteers returning home, and sixty-five government wagons that left Santa Fe on July 28. Near Pawnee Fork, Aubry left the caravan and raced ahead over the Santa Fe Trail, perhaps motivated by the desire to carry the news faster than anyone else. He arrived in Independence on August 31, having covered three hundred miles in four days, an unprecedented feat. He then went to St. Louis, where the editor of the *Daily Missouri Republican* interviewed him and learned that Aubry would make a second journey in early September to Santa Fe with more merchandise to sell. This was news, since the seasonal Santa Fe trade normally ended by September. Again offering to carry any mail destined for Santa Fe, Aubry bought new wagons and merchandise and left Missouri on September 25, 1847, for Santa Fe. There were no problems until Aubry and three of his men, all riding mules, left the caravan at the Red River crossing to race ahead. About fifty Indians on foot surprised and chased the four men, who made it safely into a village on the Moro River, later continuing their journey into Santa Fe. Aubry's wagons arrived the next day. Coming so late in the season with new merchandise gave Aubry an advantage, and he quickly disposed of his stock. He also delivered copies of the *Daily Missouri Republican* to the editor of the *Santa Fe El Republicano–Santa Fe Republican,* a newspaper printed in English and Spanish. The editor reprinted excerpts from the Missouri papers.

Not content to remain in Santa Fe for the winter, Aubry announced that he would return to Missouri in late December and offered to carry mail east for anyone. On December 22, Aubry, along with four of his men and a servant, a free black man named Pompey, rode out of Santa Fe. Aubry, as the Santa Fe newspaper reported, intended to make the trip to Missouri in eighteen days. He and his party made good time, but Mexican bandits stole ten mules, three mules died because of hard riding, Indians delayed the party for about seven hours, and they lost nearly ten hours when a snowstorm struck. In following the Santa Fe Trail across what is now Kansas, his men gradually tired and dropped back, and his servant gave up about sixty miles west of Council Grove. But Aubry endured and dashed ahead, averaging about a hundred miles a day during the last three days. He arrived in Independence on January

5, 1848, fourteen days after leaving Santa Fe. Aubry's ride broke the previous record, set by Norris Colburn in 1846, by ten and a half days. After resting for about a week in Independence, Aubry took a steamboat to St. Louis, where the *Daily Missouri Republican,* January 11, 1848, applauded his ride, adding: "Such a rate of travel is unprecedented in Prairie life, and speak[s] much in favor of Mr. A's indisputable courage and perseverance." The newspaper pointed out that Aubry had beaten the hazards of travel over the Santa Fe Trail where, during 1847, forty-seven Americans had been killed, 330 wagons destroyed, and 6,500 animals stolen.

Aubry spent the rest of January and February 1848 in Missouri but left for Santa Fe in mid-March with fifteen wagons and mail. Since the greening of the prairie and plains had not yet occurred, Aubry carried enough corn to feed his animals until they reached Fort Mann. From that point on, he believed the growing prairie grasses would be sufficient feed for his animals. The trip was uneventful, and Aubry arrived in Santa Fe on April 21, a few days ahead of his wagons. He rested a few weeks in Santa Fe and then departed with six other men for Missouri late in the day on May 19. He hoped to make the trip within ten days. Although he killed three horses and two mules by hard riding, escaped from Comanches who robbed him of his provisions and the mail, and walked forty miles to Fort Mann to buy a fresh mount, Aubry arrived at Independence early on the morning of May 28, only eight days and ten hours after leaving Santa Fe.

Not content with the new record, and determined to make three round-trips between Missouri and Santa Fe in one year, Aubry soon bought new merchandise at St. Louis, had it shipped by steamboat to western Missouri, and was on the trail with about thirty loaded wagons by the middle of July; he reached Santa Fe on August 5, 1848. For the return to Missouri, Aubry announced that he would try to break his own record. Santa Fe having been something of a gambling capital, tradition has it that Aubry, who stood only five feet two inches tall, was challenged to make the trip to Missouri in only six days. Aubry bet a thousand dollars that he could.

Early on the morning of September 12, 1848, Aubry's servant saddled a fast horse, had the saddlebags filled with food and a canteen of fresh water, and walked the animal to the Plaza. A few minutes later the little man with a black goatee and long black hair arrived and was greeted by a group of men. Some of them shook Aubry's hand and wished him good luck. Others may have patted him on the back and told him not to hurry. Others simply watched as Aubry swung into the saddle, waved good-bye, and rode out of Santa Fe at a fast gallop. Ahead of him he had fresh horses positioned along the route, and when he reached Las Vegas, New Mexico, he changed mounts. Riding one horse and leading two others, Aubry turned toward Point of Rocks. Riding all night, eating and sleeping in the saddle, he stopped only at relay points to change horses. By the dawn of the second day he had strapped himself to the saddle to prevent his falling off while dozing.

Aubry passed a wagon train bound for Santa Fe without stopping for the news, as was the custom. Nor did he stop hours later as he sped past a Mexican pack train. At his next relay point he waited only long enough for his man to stir the coals under a pot of coffee and to saddle a fresh mount, a yellow mare, a Spanish dun named Dolly. She was Aubry's favorite horse. The hours probably seemed like days as Aubry galloped toward Point of Rocks. Leaving the high country behind, Aubry did not spare Dolly, and she did not seem to mind. The autumn chill was in the air. Soon clouds hid the sun and it began to drizzle, but Aubry did not slow his pace. Pushing on, he began to look for his fresh horses and their keeper. Soon he saw the camp, but as he pulled up he found no horses, only a dead man who had been scalped by Indians. Aubry had no choice; he spurred Dolly on. During the next twenty-six hours Aubry covered nearly two hundred miles. The yellow mare set what undoubtedly was a record for one horse. But would she last? Aubry did not find out. When he met a wagon train, he got a fresh horse from the wagon master, who promised to take Dolly back to Santa Fe. Aubry rode on toward the Arkansas River, the halfway mark.

Above a ford on the Cimarron River southeast of present-day Ulysses, Kansas, Aubry found three fresh horses hidden for him by one of his men in a patch of timber. Mounting one horse and leading the others, he continued east. He did not spare horseflesh now, and after ten miles the first horse gave out. Another ten miles and the second horse wore down, and not quite another ten miles the third horse, exhausted, stumbled and fell dead. Aubry had driven the horses too hard. Hiding his saddle and blanket in some tall grass, Aubry, his silver-plated bridle in hand, set out on foot running and walking. The hours passed. Ten miles. Fifteen miles. After more than twenty miles he reached the crossing on the Arkansas River that was to become known as "Aubry's Crossing." He staggered across the river and fell to the ground exhausted.

After several minutes he caught his breath, got to his feet, and walked about a mile to Fort Mann. There he asked to see a friend, but he was told the friend was out hunting buffalo. Aubry said he would wait, and curled up in a corner and slept. When the friend returned two hours later, Aubry got up, conducted his business, borrowed a horse, and galloped off past Pawnee Rock and on to Council Grove, where new horses were waiting. Aubry paused long enough for coffee to boil, and then, tying himself on a fresh horse, rode east from Council Grove in a swinging gallop. Independence was still 150 miles away. It took Aubry twenty-four hours to travel that distance, during most of which it was raining.

At about ten o'clock on the night of September 17, 1848, down the street from the Merchants Hotel in Independence (it was then sometimes called the Noland House), a horse and rider, half running, half staggering, were seen approaching. As they reached the front of the brightly lit hotel, a man in the doorway yelled, "Aubry's here!" Men rushed out of the bar to lift the now-motionless rider from his blood-soaked saddle. Aubry was alive but weak. He had made the ride from Santa Fe in five days and sixteen hours and had won his bet with eight hours to spare. Inside the hotel Aubry could only whisper, but everyone listened as he ordered some ham, eggs, and coffee. Then he was helped to bed. Aubry told the proprietor to wake him in three hours. The proprietor waited six.

With only six hours' rest Aubry headed for St. Louis to make arrangements to send his third wagon train of the season to Santa Fe. He set out from Independence on October 8 with a large stock of merchandise, but on Cow Creek in present-day Rice County, Kansas, Apache Indians attacked, killed a stock herder, and ran off many of his animals. Aubry rode ahead to Santa Fe to obtain forage and new animals. He left there on December 15 with fifteen newly hired men to rejoin his caravan, but he had to return to hire more after six deserted. His wagons eventually arrived in Santa Fe after losing 150 mules, some to winter weather, others stolen by Indians. Aubry had kept his word. In one year he had succeeded in taking three trading caravans from Missouri to New Mexico.[17]

TWELVE

Forts, Emigrants, and Freighting, 1849-1852

Whatever necessity lays upon thee, endure:
Whatever she commands, do.

—*Johann Wolfgang von Goethe*

THE NEWS SPREAD RAPIDLY along the Pacific Coast following the discovery of gold in late January 1848 at the sawmill owned by John Augustus Sutter near Coloma, California. To the east, however, distance and poor communication slowed the pace of the news. As word trickled to Missouri, some people believed reports of gold in California were "make-believe" on the part of the U.S. government to get the newly acquired land "quickly populated." But late in the year evidence reached Missouri confirming that gold had indeed been discovered in California. It arrived at the Missouri River town of St. Joseph, about fifty miles north of Independence, on Wednesday, November 22, 1848, with a small party led by Jacob Wittmer, who had been sent east to escort Sutter's wife and daughter westward to California. Wittmer's party carried large quantities of "the Feather river gold dust," and a St. Joseph chemist assayed a portion of the dust and declared it "pure gold." As the news spread, the skeptics kept quiet.[1]

By March 1848, Missourians and other gold-seekers began to gather at Independence and other jumping-off points along the Missouri River, mixing with emigrants bound for California and Oregon. The first "forty-niner" caravan, made up of ten Missourians and many easterners, including a party from Ohio, left Independence on April 14, followed

St. Joseph, Missouri, as it appeared about 1850. The town is located on the Missouri River above Kansas City, Missouri. (Courtesy Kansas State Historical Society)

Independence, Missouri, during the early 1850s. This engraving appeared in United States Illustrated *(1854).* (Courtesy Kansas State Historical Society)

the Santa Fe Trail for a few miles west of the Missouri border, and then turned northwest on what was now being called the California-Oregon Trail. Three days later there were nearly 2,500 emigrants in Independence, another 100 in Westport, and about the same number in the settlement called Kansas, Missouri, preparing to leave for California.[2]

The town of Kansas, Missouri, four miles north of Westport, sat on a bluff above the Missouri River. Below, on a narrow levee, Westport Landing had been established in 1837 on fifteen acres of the town site. Fourteen men had organized the Kansas Town Company early in 1838 on a 257-acre estate fronting on the river, but their legal ownership was not settled until 1846, when lots were sold and the town, destined to become Kansas City, Missouri, began to grow. By 1848 the town had a population of a few hundred people, nearly ten stores, two or three warehouses, several blacksmith's shops, three rather crude hotels, a gunsmith, and a wagon-maker. There was talk of building a church. The town's life was on the wharf where steamboats tied up to unload supplies, merchandise, and new wagons manufactured in St. Louis bound for the Santa Fe Trail a few miles to the south.

Although most freight was taken over the Santa Fe Trail between spring and late fall, some travelers did not hesitate to attempt the journey during the winter. Oliver P. Hovey, editor of the *Santa Fe Republican*, undoubtedly knew the risks, but on February 10, 1849, he and six other men left Santa Fe bound for Missouri. Six of the men apparently rode mules, while the seventh drove the wagon. The weather was cold, but during the days the sun was warm. The journey was uneventful until the small party reached the Lower Cimarron Springs and camped. Early the next morning, Indians ran off all but two of their mules. Hovey and the others cached many belongings, abandoned the wagon, and packed fifteen days' worth of food, clothing, and bedding on the backs of the two remaining mules. They then set out walking, leading the mules. For three days and four nights it rained and sleeted almost continuously. After traveling sixty miles, they reached Fort Mann, which had been abandoned the year before. There they found a cache of salt pork left by some soldiers. After a few days' rest, Hovey and the others again started walking east with the two mules. A few days later they met the Santa Fe–bound express and obtained provisions and another mule, and then continued on to the Little Arkansas River, where they camped. There Hovey and two others left their provisions with the remaining four men and rode their mules east. They reached Council Grove in two days and arranged to send help to the other four men. Hovey's small party obtained fresh supplies and continued riding east, arriving at Independence on March 25.[3]

This lithograph shows Kansas City, Missouri, about 1852. The steamboat is moving down the Missouri River toward St. Louis. This view appeared in United States Illustrated *(1854). (Courtesy Kansas State Historical Society)*

An early view of Westport Landing, now part of Kansas City, Missouri. In the distance (left of center) is the town of Westport. The view looks west-southwest from the Missouri River (right). (Courtesy Kansas State Historical Society)

By the time Hovey's group arrived at Independence, the town was bustling with emigrants and gold-seekers preparing to follow the California-Oregon Trail. In fact, St. Joseph and other towns on the Missouri River were becoming crowded with emigrants and gold-seekers organized into a variety of companies with such names as St. Joseph Mining Co., Illinois Union Band, Mt. Pleasant Mining Co., Banner Company, and The Charlestown Mining Company. They followed the Santa Fe Trail several miles west of the Missouri border until they reached a point near present-day Gardner, Kansas. There the trail split. The Santa Fe Trail continued to the left, but the trail to the right was to California and Oregon. It followed a northwesterly course across what is now Kansas into present-day Nebraska, where it turned west and followed the Platte River toward the Rocky Mountains. It was this trail that the first caravan of "forty-niners" followed, an emigrant road from its beginning.

But between April and September 1849, about 2,500 emigrants from perhaps a dozen states chose to follow the Santa Fe Trail instead of the California-Oregon Trail. One of the first parties of gold-seekers to do so consisted of nine men and two boys from Greenville, Illinois. A great deal is known about their experiences because one member, H. M. T. Powell, a small English-born shopkeeper, kept a journal. The historian Howard R. Lamar described Powell as "a crochety, moralizing Victorian with such a keen sense of honor that he often quarreled with his friends and associates both on the trail and in California."

Although a participant in the journey, Powell had the knack of keeping his journal more as a keen observer with an eye on describing significant facts and details than a personal diary. Powell, his son Walter, and eight other men and one boy left Greenville on April 3, 1849, in several wagons. They paused in St. Louis to see the town and a performance of Dan Rice's Circus before crossing Missouri to near Independence, which Powell described as "a straggling kind of village, the chief part round a public square." Powell might have written more, but instead noted in his journal that Independence was "unworthy of my particular remarks."

After Powell and his party struck the Santa Fe Trail and crossed the western border of Missouri into what is now Kansas, they camped on the open prairie. In the middle of the night, one of the men, Isaac W. Carter, became ill. He died the next afternoon. "We all separated and walked apart to indulge our sad thoughts alone," wrote Powell, who then added that "about sunset we consigned him to his last home." Two men in the party cut an inscription on a board for the head of his grave. It read:

FLT
ISAAC W. CARTER
CONCORD, N.H.
DIED MAY 17TH 1849
AGED 35 YEARS

The next morning Powell and another man in the party put a bouquet of wildflowers at the head of the grave; a third man contributed wildflower seeds. The party then broke camp and followed the road west, which "seemed like a lengthened cemetery. The mounds of graves of the emigrants thrown up at intervals on either side of the road and the bones and remains of cattle and mules strewn in all directions was but a dismal sight," wrote Powell. When the party camped near Bull Creek close to other parties of emigrants, Powell met Captain Grove, a Virginian who had earlier traveled to Santa Fe and then westward to the Gila River in present-day Arizona. Grove told Powell that there was nothing to hinder his party if they followed the trail to Santa Fe and then westward over a wagon road blazed by Philip St. George Cooke and the Mormon Battalion during the Mexican War. Powell and his party followed the Santa Fe Trail.

Before the party reached Santa Fe, two other members died and were buried along the trail. On May 31, 1849, when the party reached Diamond Spring, Powell wrote:

Why it should be called "Diamond Springs," I cannot tell. There is very little that sparkles about it. It boils up about the size of my arm with some force, bringing with it a considerable quantity of heavy black sand. I dipped up a pail full, where it wells up, and there was at least a quart of sand settled at the bottom, and the water itself is turbid. We moved on from Diamond Springs and passed along a Prairie of entirely different character from any we have yet seen; flat, with a gradual ascent along the line of road, so that for the first time we could see a long distance ahead. The soil is still rich, but the roads are bad from recent rains. We supposed our Camp tonight on the Prairie to be about 9 or 10 Miles from Diamond Spring. When we arrived at Camp we found the Missouri Company had commenced a corral, ourselves and the Palmetto Company completed it.[4]

On June 11, Powell's party met a caravan from Bent's Fort with wagons loaded with buffalo robes. "Our Train stopped and they left a light mule waggon a short time with us to give us an opportunity to write home. Of course, I availed myself of the opportunity." Powell added that he talked with members of his party who were dissatisfied. He then noted in his journal: "I think it not improbable the whole Company will break up at Santa Fe." Three days later, the party reached Fort Mann, which Powell described as "a small fortification made of Cottonwood logs and turf, all falling to pieces." He added:

> In it and around it were great quantities of iron, broken waggons, etc., etc., etc. Uncle Sam is rich and good natured and can bear this waste without any complaint. A large band of Arapahoes had encamped in a grove opposite the fort and some of our party went over. Indians are around and among us now all the time, and "swap"—"swap" seems the favorite word. They have large droves of horses and mules feeding near their Camps. We continued on from Fort Mann, say 10 Miles, and corralled near the river opposite a grove of timber. Since the sand hill ceased on the other side there is scarcely any timber to mark the course of the river. The grove near which we are and those near Fort Mann and Jackson Grove are therefore prominent. It appears we have traveled more Miles per diem since leaving Pawnee Fork than I have got down. The road is so level and beautiful, that I am not surprised at making a mistake.[5]

Powell's party reached Santa Fe in mid-July. Powell had hoped to talk with Kit Carson about the route west of Santa Fe to California, but the latter had gone to Taos. Powell met a friend who had talked with Carson and was assured that the route west was practicable for ox teams. Of Santa Fe, Powell wrote: "It is unnecessary to describe: others have done it sufficiently. It is a miserable hole; gambling and drinking in all directions. The most memorable thing I did here was to go into a barber shop and have my mustache, which had grown very long and flourished finely, cut off and part of my whiskers."[6]

It took Powell eight months to reach San Diego, after which it was another four hundred miles up the coast to the gold diggings. Powell never did strike it rich and had to work at manual labor to survive. In 1852, he and his son boarded a ship for Panama and started home.

It is not known whether the California gold rush influenced Alexander Barclay's decision in 1849 to build a trading post at the junction of the Mora and Sapello Rivers near present-day Watrous, New Mexico. Barclay had spent four years as bookkeeper at Bent's Fort during the late 1830s. He then helped to start a settlement that is today Pueblo, Colorado, and made an unsuccessful attempt to raise buffalo calves for

The interior of a saloon in Santa Fe about the time H. M. T. Powell, an English-born shopkeeper, visited there in 1852. Powell described Santa Fe as "a miserable hole, gambling and drinking in all directions." (Author's Collection)

Keno, monte, and other games of chance were popular in early Santa Fe saloons and gambling halls. (Author's Collection)

profit before beginning to build the trading post with a partner, Joe Doyle, in the spring of 1849. This was about two years after the government had constructed Fort Mann. Barclay supervised the construction while Doyle went to St. Louis to buy merchandise to stock what became known as Fort Barclay. It was something of a miniature Bent's Fort, a two-story, sixty-five-foot-square structure with circular bastions at two opposite corners. Fort Barclay soon became a stopping point for traders, soldiers, and others traversing the Santa Fe Trail. If Barclay expected to sell the post to the government for a military fort, he probably was disappointed when, in 1851, the government began construction of Fort Union about seven miles away on land Barclay and Doyle owned. Fort Barclay was closed the same year.

Fort Union was essential to the military's plans. For 250 years Apaches and Navajos, their territory being slowly invaded, had terrorized the Rio Grande settlements, and to the east on the plains travelers courted death from Kiowas and Comanches who were under equal pressure. When the United States acquired New Mexico, the nation inherited from Mexico what the historian Robert M. Utley described as "an Indian problem of frightening magnitude." Initially, the government met the problem with about thirteen hundred American soldiers scattered among eleven outposts in settlements throughout the Territory of New Mexico. In Washington, D.C., however, Secretary of War C. M. Conrad was not pleased with the army's performance in New Mexico. It had been costly and showed little progress in solving problems with the Indians. Thus on April 1, 1851, Conrad directed Lieutenant Colonel Edwin V. Sumner of the First U.S. Dragoons to take command in New Mexico and revise the whole system of defense. Sumner moved the army's headquarters and principal supply depot from Santa Fe to Fort Union, and he soon replaced the scattered outposts in New Mexico with new posts closer to the Indians.[7]

Fort Union, strategically located near where the mountain and Cimarron branches of the Santa Fe Trail came together, became the principal supply and staging center for all military operations in the Southwest, and within a few years it became the hub of a great network of forts located in Texas, New Mexico, and parts of Arizona, Colorado, and Kansas. Fort Union's lifeline was the Santa Fe Trail, which linked the post to Fort Leavenworth. Fort Union's location, a hundred miles from Santa Fe, made it difficult for the soldiers to engage in gambling and other demoralizing temptations found in the town.

. . .

A drawing of Fort Union soon after the military post was established northeast of Santa Fe on the Santa Fe Trail. The illustration appeared in El Gringo; or, New Mexico and Her People, *by William H. Davis, published in 1857.* (Author's Collection)

DURING 1849, the news columns of Missouri newspapers were dominated by stories about the California gold rush and the thousands of emigrants and gold-seekers passing through their state. The *Missouri Republican* also paid attention to a new wagon road blazed from Fayetteville, Arkansas, across Cherokee land in what is now northeastern Oklahoma to the Santa Fe Trail at Turkey Creek in present-day McPherson County, Kansas. A California-bound caravan led by Captain Lewis Evans laid out the road, and where it met the Santa Fe Trail, a large stone was planted and inscribed:

TO FAYETTEVILLE, ARK. 300 MILES—CAPT. EVANS COM'Y. MAY 12, 1849.

The new wagon road became known as the Cherokee Trail.[8]

Though there was much activity in the Santa Fe trade during 1849, the previous year's trade had glutted the New Mexico market, and many traders who reached there early in the summer of 1849 found nearly every village overstocked with goods. Missouri newspapers did not report much on the poor conditions of the Santa Fe trade, but editors did pay attention to other news from along the trail. For instance, trading caravans returning to Independence in early July reported that both sides of the Arkansas River, from the big crossing to Fort Mann, were "literally lined" with Indian camps. One man said that very friendly Indians had gone so far as to help get a stalled wagon out of the Arkansas River and made no reference to the profits being carried back to Missouri.[9]

In mid-September 1849, Francis X. Aubry organized a large caravan in the town of Kansas, Missouri, and set out for Santa Fe. In addition to Aubry's own vehicles there were ten wagons belonging to another trading firm and thirteen wagons belonging to James M. White, who had opened commission and forwarding houses in El Paso and Santa Fe the previous year. White was taking his family and a few servants to Santa Fe. About October 23, following a snowstorm and very cold weather, and only about seven days out of Santa Fe, White decided to rush ahead with his family in two carriages. He left his wagons with Aubry and headed toward Santa Fe. About two days later, near Point of Rocks, nearly a hundred Jicarilla Apaches attacked the two carriages and killed six men in the party, including White. The Indians took captive Mrs. White, her daughter, and a black woman servant. Aubry and his caravan reached Santa Fe a day after news of the massacre arrived. He sent word to friends in Las Vegas, Taos, and other nearby villages to send out Pueblo Indians and Mexicans to negotiate the return of the captives, and a reward of more than a thousand dollars was offered for Mrs. White's safe return. Aubry and others contributed substantially to the reward. Numerous rescue parties tried unsuccessfully to locate the Apaches. Kit Carson reportedly rode with one party, but no trace of the missing woman was found until an army search party in November tracked and found the Apaches and Mrs. White. Before the soldiers could rescue the woman, the Apaches killed her in sight of the troops with an arrow through the heart. Then they fled. The black woman servant and White's daughter were nowhere to be found, but two years later a girl matching the description of the daughter was seen living with Comanches. There was much speculation that the girl had survived and been sold to the Comanches, but her fate was never determined.[10]

A caravan belonging to James Brown of Pettis County, Missouri, was more fortunate than James White's. Brown's twenty wagons filled with new merchandise left Independence for Santa Fe in September, and it had no difficulties until it reached a point about forty miles beyond the Arkansas River in mid-November. There a severe three-day snowstorm stranded the wagons thirty miles from any timber for firewood. The oxen died. Ten men were left in charge of the wagons while the others started walking back to Missouri to purchase new oxen. They got to Independence in January and began to organize a relief train with provisions and fresh oxen, which did not leave Missouri until early March but reached the stranded men before the month was over. They also found another stranded Santa Fe trader, Moses Goldstein of Independence, and seven of his men. The relief party learned that the stranded men had had to burn two wagons while waiting for help.[11]

During 1850, there was little change in trading conditions at Santa Fe, and as pressure on their lands mounted the Indians south of the Arkansas continued to be troublesome. One caravan belonging to a trader named Browne was attacked, and ten teamsters were killed. Indians also attacked and robbed other caravans south of the Arkansas River. They did not venture north of the river, where soldiers were stationed at what became known as Fort Atkinson in June 1851 and another military encampment on the upper Arkansas. In addition to the problems with Indians, traders were confronted with very dry conditions that year. The spring rains never came, and by summer the area was experiencing a drought. There was little vegetation, and the Arkansas River was lower than traders could remember. Many of their oxen died from "dry murrain," a fatal disease caused by bad drinking water. The *Missouri Republican* reported that nearly all wagon trains lost animals.[12]

UNTIL THE MEXICAN WAR, there was no U.S. postal service between Council Grove and New Mexico. From the international boundary of the Arkansas River to Santa Fe, the Mexican government had no postal service, and the semimonthly mail that operated between Santa Fe and Chihuahua, where American traders had business interests, was irregular because hostile Indians often attacked travelers. People relied on wagon caravans to carry the mail, and between Missouri and New Mexico the journey usually took about three months. When the Mexican War began, the military began carrying the U.S. mail to and from Santa Fe along with military dispatches by contract for each trip. After gold was discovered in California, the federal government came under increased pressure to improve mail service in the West.

On October 1, 1849, a U.S. Post Office was established in Santa Fe, and William S. McKnight was appointed postmaster to receive the U.S. mail carried from Fort Leavenworth. The post office may have been located on the west side of the Plaza in Santa Fe, where before the war the Mexican government had maintained an office for Chihuahua mail. It was not until July 1, 1850, that the first regular mail service went into effect between Independence, Missouri, and Santa Fe. David Waldo, a medical doctor at Independence who had become a Santa Fe trader, won a four-year contract in competition with eight other bidders. He agreed to deliver the mail once a month between Independence and Santa Fe and set up a schedule whereby at 8 a.m. on the first day of each month one six-mule mail carriage would depart Santa Fe and another of the same size would depart Independence. Both carriages would follow the Cimarron route. Each carriage was painted in an elegant style and had a watertight body, elliptical springs, and iron axles. Waldo agreed to deliver the mail within twenty-nine days. Although he was the contractor, the carriages belonged to Waldo, Hall and Company, which he owned with Jacob Hall and William McCoy, men experienced in the Santa Fe trade. Each carriage was guarded by eight men, each armed with a Colt rifle, a Colt revolver, and a hunting knife. The *Missouri Commonwealth* observed that if attacked, the guards could discharge "one hundred and thirty-six shots without stopping to load! This is equal to a small army armed as in the ancient times, and from the looks of this escort, ready as they are either for offensive or defensive warfare with the savages, we have no fears for the safety of the mails." The newspaper added that the contractor had established "a sort of base of refitting at Council Grove, a distance of 150 miles from this city [Independence], and have sent out a blacksmith, and a number of men to cut and cure hay, with a quantity of animals, grain, and provisions; and we understand they intend to make a sort of traveling station there, and to commence a farm. They also, we believe, intend to make a similar settlement at Walnut Creek next season."[13] The colorful mail carriages soon became a common sight on the Santa Fe Trail, often passing traders' slow-moving caravans going between Missouri and New Mexico and government caravans and troops going to and from Fort Leavenworth and New Mexico.

About two weeks before the regular mail service began, Aubry and two other traders were returning to Missouri with a caravan of ten wagons and two hundred mules. Below the Middle Spring of the Cimarron, as Aubry later wrote in his diary, his trading caravan met a military party heading for New Mexico. There were a hundred recruits walking on foot, with the officers on horseback and wagons carrying provisions and the families of commissioned officers. The party was under the command of Major Gouverneur Morris of the Third Infantry. Aubry mentions Major Morris in his diary but not Morris's wife, Anna Maria, who was in camp with her husband on the Cimarron River.[14]

Like Aubry, Anna Morris kept a diary, and in her entry for Saturday, June 22, she wrote: "Left Cimarrone [*sic*] Spring at 6 Ocl[ock] marched 20 miles & encamped on the bed of the Cimmarrone [*sic*] where we dug for water & attained some pretty good & very clear—Near sun down Mr.

Aubry's train arrived from Santa Fe & encamped near us—by it I sent my journal home." On her journey to Santa Fe, Anna Morris rode in a Third Infantry ambulance with her maid. As the wife of an officer, she never cooked a meal, and a laundress washed her clothes. It was a style she had been accustomed to before her marriage. Born in Morristown, New Jersey, in 1813, a community named for her wealthy family, Anna Morris was thirty-six years old as she headed for Santa Fe. Her husband, Gouverneur, was then about forty-six and also came from an aristocratic background. Her diary provides a woman's perspective of Santa Fe Trail travel in 1850. On Thursday, July 4, she wrote: "Left Ocati at 6 Ocl[ock] marched 20 miles & encamped at 2 Ocl[ock] at Wagon mount Santa Clara spring. delightful water plenty of grass. *no wood*—soon after our tents were pitched we had quite a severe hail storm. The doct[or] is the only one who has had a merry making in honor of the day he made egg nog for all of us—he has kept very quiet about those eggs he had been saving up for this occasion—It has cleared off delightfully and we shall encounter less dust tomorrow in consequence of the storm—At this place the Express mail men eleven in number were murdered about a month since—The Spring here is called Santa Clara, it is the best water we have had on the route, grass pretty good, no wood."[15]

When the military caravan reached San Miguel on Tuesday, July 9, it halted for an hour at the Pecos River and then traveled four miles to San José, where it camped. Anna Morris wrote in her diary:

the day being very warm and oppressive we . . . were glad to avail ourselves of the grateful shade of the Mexican adobe—the most uninteresting place from the out side I am sure—We entered a low door way and found ourselves in as cool a house as we were in before—lounges and beds all around the room, no chair, the mud floor was covered with buffalo robes & other skins—The walls hung with Images, pictures of Saints, Crosses, looking glasses and rosettes made of paper— the whole arrangement was neat & orderly—We were received by a good looking Mexican woman, who seated herself on the floor and busied herself making cigarettes & smoking them—She took little pieces of shucks from under the skins on the floor & filled them with tobacco from a paunch on her side her daughter a fine looking girl of fifteen always brought her fire to light her Cigarettes and altogether they were the most indolent looking set I have ever seen—I sent up to our tent for some sugar which I gave the woman and with "Muchos [*sic*] gracias" bade her good bye—I find the mountain air much more agreeable than that of the plains and the grateful shade of the pine & cedar trees makes our marches less warm tho' every one looks a little fagged & anxious to get thro'.[16]

When she reached Santa Fe, Anna Morris wrote in her diary that she was not at all disappointed in its appearance, but in the next breath she added: "It is the most miserable squalid looking place I ever beheld except the Plaza there is nothing decent about it. . . . The houses are mud, the fences are mud, the churches & courts are mud, in fact it is *all* mud." Anna Morris remained in Santa Fe until her husband was sent east in 1853.[17]

In the fall of 1851 Francis X. Aubry, who continued to make more than one trading journey between Missouri and Santa Fe each year, accomplished another goal. He left Las Vegas, New Mexico, in mid-September with a caravan of about thirty wagons and three hundred mules. Aubry, who had sought to find a better trail to the Arkansas River earlier in the year, tried again on this journey. At Cold Spring in what is now the Oklahoma Panhandle, Aubry traveled ten to forty degrees east of North and found "an excellent wagon road, supplied with water and grass, and avoiding the *Jornada* and Cimarone [Cimarron] trail altogether." This new trail became known as Aubry's Cutoff, and it saved about fifty-two miles. It also avoided many miles of desolate country. About the time the caravan reached Cottonwood Crossing, Aubry dashed ahead of his wagons and reached Missouri in forty-nine hours, covering a hundred miles a day. He was riding his favorite mare, Dolly, when he rode into Independence on October 11, 1851, completing his third round-trip of the year.[18]

In 1851, Independence, Missouri, had a population of about 2,500 people, and much of the Santa Fe trade was still being conducted there. The town, however, had gained more prominence as a jumping-off point for most of the emigrants following the California-Oregon Trail, who purchased the supplies they would need for their journey, including draft animals, and repaired their wagons at Independence. Only a few miles west of Independence, the town of Kansas now had several hundred residents, more businesses, three churches, and a new hotel. In August 1851, Paul Wilhelm, Duke of Württemberg, visited the town and wrote, "Kansastown is quite picturesquely situated on some hills along the Kansas river near its junction with the much bigger Missouri. The main street is about thirty feet above the water level. The houses are of both baked brick and boards, the latter called 'frame' houses. It is a lively little place. Here most travelers bound for the West purchase what they require for their long overland journey. Moreover, the neighboring hordes of semi-civilized Indians buy their supplies here."[19]

Early in 1851, the town of Kansas got its first newspaper, a weekly called the *Kansas Public Ledger,* which began reporting on the Santa Fe trade. On May 30 the paper noted: "Most of the following gentlemen have either started or will this week start trains of wagons from Kansas to Santa Fe and other places in New Mexico. This list does not include any of the large number of trains which left here previous to this week." The paper then listed forty-eight names, including that of Kit Carson, a list, the editor noted, that had been made up from the register of the Union Hotel. The hotel had been built a few months earlier by William Gilliss, an early pioneer in the area. It was constructed of brick and consisted of forty-six furnished rooms. Gilliss apparently rented the hotel to William G. Barclay, who operated it and may even have named it. Perhaps to drum up business while the traders were away, Barclay wrote a letter to the *St. Louis Republican* that was printed on June 3, 1851, in which he noted: "I write to you from a point which is getting to be more and more a favorite resort with those engaged in the Santa Fe trade.... The Traders seem well pleased with the treatment they receive here." Every room in the hotel was furnished. There was even a pump in the kitchen, and attached to the hotel was a large brick stable, a hundred feet long, with a large cattle yard adjacent. Whether Barclay failed to make a go of the hotel is not known, but the following year he gave up the business and entered the Missouri River steamboat trade, and Gilliss advertised that his hotel was for rent.[20]

The *Kansas Public Ledger,* May 30, 1851, also reported that "not less than 300 wagons have left Kansas [Missouri] this spring for the Plains, most of which have gone to Santa Fe. The trade between this point and N.M. is rapidly increasing. Already not less than 1,500,000 lbs. of freight for the country has been landed here and shipped for its destination, and there is much yet to arrive from St. Louis." By the time the 1851 trading season ended in the fall, about 120 traders had reached Santa Fe, taking 557 wagons. The value of the merchandise transported to Santa Fe from Missouri between May and October was not recorded, and none of the wagons carried government freight.[21]

From what is known, none of the traders experienced serious difficulties that year in reaching Santa Fe, but that was not the case when Colonel Edwin V. Sumner dispatched seventy-one wagons and 473 mules from New Mexico to Fort Leavenworth in November. He was sending the mules to be wintered at the fort, where the expense of caring for them would be much less than in New Mexico. When the military caravan reached a point about fifty miles west of Council Grove, it ran into a sleet- and rainstorm and about 275 mules died, a more costly loss for the military than if the mules had remained in New Mexico.[22]

Another small caravan heading east from Santa Fe also had problems. Although facts are few, tradition has it that the small caravan consisted of California gold-seekers returning east. They supposedly traveled the southern route across what is now Arizona and New Mexico to Santa Fe and then eastward over the Santa Fe Trail. They apparently experienced no problems until they reached the Arkansas River a few miles south of modern Offerle, Kansas. There they camped for the night on the south side of the Arkansas River on land that years later became part of the Lightner Ranch.

Early the following morning, as the travelers were breaking camp, someone in the group saw a party of Indians approaching from some distance. Fearing the worst, the party quickly forded the river and, once on the other side, prepared to defend itself. Meantime, two men in the party placed all of the gold the group carried in a Dutch oven and buried it under a small tree near the riverbank. Then the worst did happen. The Indians charged across the river and killed everybody but an eight-year-old girl, whom they took captive. Her fate is not known, but later events suggest that she may have survived: About 1918, sixty-seven years later, a woman arrived at Kinsley, Kansas, and hired Lee Smith, a driver, to take her to a place on the Arkansas River south of town. On the drive, Smith later recalled, the woman kept looking at maps and checking a notebook. She appeared to know exactly where she wanted to go, and they ended up at the old Santa Fe Trail crossing. Once there, she convinced Smith to drive to the other side, and he forded the low river in his auto.

Here the woman located several mounds of earth about seventy-five feet beyond the crossing. Pointing to the mounds, she told Smith that she believed that people from a wagon train, killed by Indians years before, were buried there. Still unaware of what the woman was looking for, Smith began to question her and learned that she lived in the East and was a relative of someone who had escaped the massacre. Although she spent some time looking over the ground and poked around with a stick under a large old tree, Smith said she found nothing. He drove her back to Kinsley and never saw her again. Whether the story of buried treasure is true is not known, and no contemporary accounts of a massacre of a party of gold-seekers have been located.[23]

Another tradition relates how silver bullion was buried on the Cimarron River south of present-day Richfield, Kansas. According to the tale, five men, including one named Alexander, all from Illinois, had taken three wagons loaded with dry goods to Santa Fe during the early 1850s. They sold their goods and started east but got only as far as the Cimarron River. There, one night in camp, Indians drove off their horses. The men buried their silver, piled their wagons on top of it, and burned them, and then started walking east to Missouri, where they arrived safely but in poor condition. Their silver may still be buried close to the Cimarron River in present-day Morton County, far southwest Kansas.[24]

BY 1852, several women had traveled the Santa Fe Trail. Probably the earliest were Mexican women traveling with traders from Chihuahua during the early 1840s. In 1846 came Susan Magoffin, whose diary of the journey brought her much attention. But her diary, while interesting, is not as impressive as the narrative of Marian Sloan Russell, who with her mother and her brother Will became passengers in a caravan led by Aubry that left Fort Leavenworth along with a government freight train during the summer of 1852. Marian Russell described how they paid for their transportation:

> Mother had planned that we were to take passage in Captain Aubry's train, for the Indians were bad along the Santa Fe Trail and she had great confidence in him. Captain Aubry's train was encamped at Fort Leavenworth waiting until more wagons arrived westward bound. The more wagons the greater safety from attack by the Indians. At last a big government train pulled in from the east and Captain Aubry made plans for an early departure.
>
> Passengers on the government train included three young men. Two were army officers enroute to Fort Union. The third was a graduate doctor from West Point. These young men offered mother, Will and me transportation as far as Fort Union if mother would prepare their meals enroute for them. Mother gladly agreed for transportation from Fort Leavenworth to Santa Fe, New Mexico, in 1852, was $250.00 and, of course, there was also half fare for the children. She saved $500 for cooking for the young men, besides which they furnished the provisions.

Her lengthy narrative, written years later, reflects the impressions of a seven-year-old crossing the prairie and plains for the first time. The following excerpts capture the sights and sounds and feelings she experienced:

> I remember so clearly the beauty of the earth, and how, as we bore westward, the deer and the antelope bounded away from us. There were miles and miles of buffalo grass, blue lagoons and blood-red sunsets and, once in a while, a little sod house on the lonely prairie—home of some hunter or trapper. . . .
>
> Sometimes we were alarmed by the Indians, threatened by storms, and always it seemed we suffered for want of water.
>
> Minute impressions flash before me; the sun-bonneted women, the woolen-trousered men, little mother in her flounced gingham, brother Will walking in long strides by our driver, voices of the lonely and homeless singing around blazing campfires. . . .
>
> Our wagon was packed with boxes and bales of merchandise for Fort Union. Only the high spring seat was left for mother, Will and me. Back of the freight and on top of the packed merchandise was our bedding and camp equipment. There was a place in back among the bedding where one might rest as the wagon rolled onward. I always got sleepy and climbed back for my nap in spite of the bumps and shakes of the wagon.
>
> Mules draw a wagon a bit more gently than horses, but oxen are best of all. 'Tis true that they walk slowly but there is a rhythm in their walking that sways the great wagons gently.
>
> Soon we were on the Cimarron Cut-off and were building our cooking fires with buffalo chips. My chore was to gather the buffalo chips. I would stand back and kick them, then reach down and gather them carefully, for under them lived big spiders and centipedes. Sometimes scorpions ran from beneath them. I would fill my long full dress skirt with the evening's fuel and take it back to mother.[25]

One evening after the caravan neared Fort Union, Aubry joined the Russells at their campfire and informed them that they were now in New Mexico Territory. Marian Russell wrote that Aubry then said: "This is the land, where only the brave or the criminal come. This is called, 'the Land without Law.' But it is a land that has brought healing to the hearts of many. Many an invalid I have had in my caravans, but before they reached Santa Fe they were eating buffalo meat raw and sleeping soundly under their blankets. There is something in the air of New Mexico that makes the blood red, the heart to beat high and the eyes to look upward. Folks don't come here to die—they come to live and they get what they come for."[26]

Soon after reaching Santa Fe, Aubry, then twenty-eight years old, returned to Missouri and organized another caravan. By mid-September, he was again heading for New Mexico carrying, among other goods, twenty-nine bales of clothing from Westport to Fort Union, for which he was paid $12.50 per hundred pounds. Aubry and his caravan unloaded their government cargo at Fort Union and then reached Santa Fe in mid-October. This was his last trip over the Santa Fe Trail. By then, he told friends, the region along the trail was no longer the frontier. Aubry decided to take ten wagons loaded with goods, a herd of 3,500 sheep, and more than a hundred surplus mules and horses to California. The following year he gathered 14,000 sheep and drove them from New Mexico to the booming California market. When he returned to Santa Fe in August 1854, he stopped at a cantina run by the Mercure brothers on the south side of the Plaza. A few minutes later Aubry was dead, knifed to death during an argument with Colonel Richard H. Weightman, a former newspaper editor in Albuquerque. Weightman was arrested and tried, but a jury acquitted him, saying he had acted in self-defense. Aubry was buried in Rosaria Cemetery in Santa Fe.[27]

THIRTEEN

New Tensions and Trade, 1853-1860

*Above the vague and receding horizons forever
broods a pathetic solemnity, born of distance,
silence and solitude.*

—John J. Ingalls

B Y THE TIME Francis Aubry was making his last trip over the Santa
Fe Trail in 1852, the army depot at Santa Fe had been moved to
Fort Union, and the military government in New Mexico had lifted the
ad valorem tax on imported goods, permitting free trade between Missouri and New Mexico for the first time since 1822. In the fall of 1852,
Bent's Fort was no more. After Fort Laramie on the Oregon Trail was
sold to the government in 1849, William Bent opened negotiations with
the War Department to sell Bent's Fort. But his price apparently was too
high and the government's actions at this remove seem unjust and
unfriendly, especially after many years of Bent's welcoming so many government explorers and military parties at his fort. He had, for example,
permitted his post to be used as a supply depot and hospital for the army
during and after the Mexican War. One morning in the fall of 1852,
William Bent had the fort's supplies and merchandise loaded onto
twenty wagons and moved five miles down the Arkansas River to Short
Timber Creek. There a camp was established. The following morning
Bent rode alone back to the fort. Those who remained with the wagons
in camp soon heard an explosion. William Bent had blown up the fort
rather than sell it to the government at what he considered an unfair

price. Bent returned to the camp and led his wagons and men to Big Timbers, a large stand of trees located on the Arkansas River nearly sixty miles to the east. There Bent and his men spent the winter trading with Indians and building what became known as Bent's New Fort.[1]

It was a time of change along the Santa Fe Trail. To the east at Fort Leavenworth on the Missouri River, the quartermaster general refused to approve repairs on buildings because he believed the post was not best suited for military operations. A group of army officers were ordered to select a site for a new post "at or near a point on the Kansas River where the Republican fork unites with it." They recommended a spot 130 miles southwest of Fort Leavenworth near where the Smoky Hill and Republican Rivers form the Kansas River. The new post was first called Camp Center, but after construction began in 1853 it was renamed Fort Riley, after General Bennett Riley, who had fought in the Mexican War and was the last territorial governor of California.[2]

Soon the military laid out a new wagon road from Fort Leavenworth southwest to near the site of present-day Topeka, Kansas, and then westward along the north side of the Kansas River to the new post. But one traveler over the route wrote in June 1853 that the road "was the roughest and most disagreeable one that ever was traveled by any man since the days of Moses." The traveler added that the road "was an incessant crossing of creeks, sloughs, quagmires, swampy bottoms and rocky hollows, the entire route."[3]

Government wagons began carrying freight over this route to Fort Riley in 1853, and government caravans bound for other forts along the Santa Fe Trail traveled from Fort Leavenworth to Fort Riley and then south to where they met the Santa Fe Trail. But one of those posts, Fort Atkinson, west of present-day Dodge City, Kansas, was abandoned in 1853, and its government property was transported to a new military camp located where Walnut Creek flows into the Arkansas River near what is now Great Bend, Kansas. En route to the new camp, soldiers came upon the bodies of three Mexicans. One of the soldiers, Percival G. Lowe, later recalled: "One [Mexican] was still breathing, and blood was trickling from the scalped heads. Lowe and the other soldiers concluded that the dead men belonged to a large Mexican train camped below along the Arkansas River some distance away. The Mexicans were hunting antelope in the hills above the river when killed. The Indians had taken the dead men's ponies and arms. The soldiers followed the Indians' trail a short distance, but it soon became obliterated by the tracks of thousands of buffalo."[4]

Emigrants continued to move westward in 1853, heading for California or Oregon from Independence, Westport, or other jumping-off points along the Missouri River. Exactly how many followed the Santa Fe Trail to Bent's New Fort is not known, but the number was considerable. One party of twelve gold-seekers left Westport in mid-May with a light-traveling pack train following the trail. One of the men, G. Harris Heap, wrote in his journal that east of Walnut Creek his party "had already overtaken and passed several large wagon and cattle trains from Texas and Arkansas, mostly bound to California. With them were many women and children." When the pack train reached Walnut Creek, Heap wrote: "This is the point at which emigrants to Oregon and California, from Texas and Arkansas, generally strike this road. They prefer the route

This is the escort wagon, the standard freight carrier of the U.S. Army, which was capable of carrying between three and five thousand pounds. This wagon was manufactured by the Kentucky Wagon Manufacturing Company at Louisville. (Courtesy Smithsonian Institution, Washington, D.C.)

which leads them through the South Pass—to the one on the Gila, or Crooke's route."[5]

Newspapers in Missouri paid greater attention to emigrants heading west and the arrival and departure of the U.S. mail to Santa Fe and Salt Lake City (the latter begun in 1850) than to the traders and merchants involved in the Santa Fe trade, aside from printing the advertisements of outfitters. Their travels had become so commonplace that editors did not see them as news. Even frequent skirmishes between trading caravans and Indians along the trail received little attention because they either were not reported or were weeks or months old when the news reached Missouri. Indian problems had increased over the western half of the trail because, in part, belligerent Texans had forced large groups of Kiowas and Comanches to leave their state following depredations against the increasing number of white settlers. Those Indians moved north and lived along the heavily traveled trail.

The recollections of old freighters and others attest to the increase in Indian attacks on caravans. One such adventure did not appear in print until twenty-seven years after it occurred. It began in April 1853 when James M. Fugate, a young man from Missouri, hired a teamster to take a wagonload of merchandise to Santa Fe. The wagon joined a large caravan of forty men and perhaps thirty-five wagons, each pulled by six yoke of oxen. Each man was armed, most with a rifle, a Colt navy revolver, and a bowie knife. Several days after the caravan struck the Santa Fe Trail, three other Santa Fe–bound wagons, with twelve men, joined the group Fugate was traveling with. By May 21 the caravan reached a point near what is today Hutchinson, Kansas, and there they made camp just before noon.

After the men had prepared their noon meal and had started eating, someone yelled "Indians!" Before the men could corral their oxen and wagons, the Indians on their ponies were charging around the wagons, "yelling and firing like demons." Fugate continued:

We were completely encircled by the savages, who proved to be Comanches, swinging upon the opposite side of their ponies exposing but little of themselves to our aim by firing under their horses' necks. Their deadly missiles were soon playing havoc among our cattle. The poor creatures were madly surging and bellowing around, endangering us to a death beneath their feet, worse to be feared within the enclosure than the foe without. This new danger soon drove us outside the enclosure of wagons in full view of the Indians.

We had now fairly got our hands in, and were tumbling their ponies at a rapid rate. Few Indians after their ponies fell escaped a rifle bullet. The Indians were narrowing their circle until twenty-five yards scarcely intervened between us. But the motion of the steeds unsteadied their aim until it was but random, while the closer they pressed us the more destructive became every shot we fired. Such fighting could not last long. After the first few rounds the savages mostly substituted the gun with the bow and arrows. Finding themselves getting most terribly worsted in the combat, they made a dash to ride down and tomahawk us all in one death struggle. I tell you, then, we had no child's play. Outnumbered four or five to one in a hand-to-hand fight to the death, is a serious thing. We were soon mingling together, but driven against the wagons, we could dodge or parry their blows with the tomahawk, while the rapid flashes from the celebrated "navy" in each man's hand, was not so easily avoided by the savage warriors. We made the ground too hot for them, and with yells of baffled rage, they broke and fled, carrying off all their killed and wounded but three, which they had to leave.

Now for the first time since the fight began we had time to take in our situation. One of the bravest and best of our comrades, young Gilbert, was shot through the heart. . . . He lay as he fell, with his hand clenched around the stock of his gun as though he would take the weapon with his departed spirit to the other world where he might avenge his death upon the savages who had paid such a dear penalty for their last work. Many others of our company were wounded, two of them severely. The dead and dying ponies were scattered about on the prairie with the arms and accouterments [sic] of their savage owners about them; while several of our cattle were also dead and dying from wounds made by missiles aimed for us. We spent the rest of the day burying the dead, caring for the wounded, and gathering up the spoils of the fight. We destroyed everything belonging to the Indians that we could not carry away, and at dusk moved about a mile to the river where we camped. The men talked about their chances of fighting their way to New Mexico with such a small force. The future seemed hopeless until J. W. Jones, the wagon master, swore he would reach Santa Fe, "or go to hell. We dare not show the white feather."

The group passed a peaceful night, but about dawn, as the men guarding the oxen turned them out to graze, about five hundred Cheyenne Indians, some mounted on horses but more on foot, tried to steal the cattle. "Those on foot," wrote Fugate, "engaged the guards, while those mounted tried to get between the cattle and the corral, thus cutting them off. The firing immediately roused the camp to arms; and in the face of the firing by the Indians we surrounded the cattle, and drove them back into the corral. Then the fighting began in good earnest. At first we proved too much for them, and they retreated into a low sag south of the corral; but quickly returned with more desperate energy than at first. Then forming solid lines, six or eight deep, made a forced charge on the wagons from the south, yelling like demons, and firing through under the wagons. It never seemed as if so few men could withstand such an assault. Our men were prepared for them, however, and, firing from behind and under the wagons, gave them a warm reception as they came up."

At the east end they broke through and came into the corral; but of those who came through it is a question if any ever returned. They were immediately shot and clubbed with the guns. I broke my own gun-stock over the head of one of the miscreants. There were nine of them left within the corral dead. The Indians, seeing the fate that had befallen their comrades who went through under the wagons, began a hasty retreat, and were quickly followed by the entire pack as fast as they could run. They took refuge in a low range of sand hills along the Arkansas river, some 60 or 80 rods to the south, from which they emerged occasionally during the morning to harass us. We followed them up toward the sand-hills, firing at them to the best possible advantage; but when we had got as far as the low sag, we were ordered to retreat to the wagons. Our wagon-master, after the dead Indians, outside and in, were all counted, reported 60 Indians killed. Our own loss was five killed and several wounded, some mortally. There was another camp of 35 men, sent out by Majors & Russell of Missouri, about half a mile west; and about 9 or 10 o'clock they formed a line and came down toward the Indians. Seeing this we formed [a] line and advanced to join them, and move together upon the Indians. They, upon the other hand, seeing our movement, beat a hasty retreat across the river.

We buried our dead on a point between two draws a little southwest of camp; and about 2 o'clock broke camp, and in company with Majors & Russell's outfit, started westward. About 5 or 6 miles west we had a slight brush with the Indians, but nothing serious until we arrived at Pawnee Rock, which we reached about 2 or 3 o'clock next day and camped about 200 yards to the south of the rock. Nothing unusual transpired during the night. About 8 o'clock next morning, just as we had brought our cattle up to the corral, and were yoking them up, a band of Cheyennes, to the number of about 300, suddenly made a dash from the north, part of the Indians coming in on each side of the rock, and immediately surrounded our corral of wagons, with a terrible war-whoop. The usual manner of making such a corral was to form a circle with the wagons, running them as close behind each other as possible, with the left hand or driver's side innermost. When the circle was complete, an opening the size of a wagon was left for a gate, which was closed by a single wagon just inside the circle, so placed that it could be run aside or back into the gap, or "gate." During the night, and times of danger, the cattle are kept within this enclosure or "corral," as it is called; at other times they were turned out to graze, in charge of several men. On the left-hand side of the wagon-bed, above the wheels, there was a small box about five feet long, prepared with a hinged cover that pitched so as to shed rain. This box contained, in a convenient position, the arms, ammunition, lunch, trinkets, etc., of the driver. Leaving our cattle just as they were, some yoked, some partly yoked, we instantly seized our weapons and pitched in vigorously to repulse the assault. The Indians opened a heavy fire from the start. They made strainers of our wagon-boxes by perforating them with bullets and arrow-heads. The Indians who were mounted fired high, and may possibly sometimes have hit some of their own men on the opposite side of the corral.

After firing in this way for a while, and finding they could gain nothing, they beat a hasty retreat to the south, taking with them their dead and wounded, who were in nearly all cases tied to their ponies, as was shown by the thongs that lay by some of the dead ponies, where the riders had cut loose and got away. In this fight we had one man wounded, and several cattle killed. From here on we had to fight the Indians every few days. We had engagements at Pawnee Fork, again near Dodge, again at Cimarron, here by the Apaches and Arapahos, again at Mount Aubrey, Kearney Co. At this place we arrived the next day after the slaughter of a party of Spaniards who were going east from Santa Fe, to purchase goods. We found ten dead Spaniards, and one wounded still living, with his scalp off, though he died the morning after. At the first peep of the day, the next morning after we arrived there the Indians—Apaches and Arapahoes—attacked us, first firing on the guards, and then coming up by slow, cautious movements, seeking every buffalo-wallow, or other slight protection to cover themselves. So stealthily and steadily did they advance that almost before we were aware of it we had eight men lying dead. All this time we kept up a vigorous and pointed fire, always aiming and firing with intent to kill. About 10 o'clock, finding they could not capture our train, they retreated the way they came, leaving their dead on the ground. These, amounting to between 50 and 80, we piled up on the plains, and left for the coyotes and buzzards.

We remained here four days, and buried our dead and the Spaniards—19 in all—in one trench. In the meantime—and this we tell in a whisper—we amused ourselves at target-shooting, using for a target the head of some luckless Indian, which would be placed in all conceivable positions to be shot at. We had some more fighting now and then until we reached Fort Bent, after which we were out of the hostile country; and reached Santa Fe in safety, with what we had left of men and animals. We lost no wagons, and carried our cargo entirely through.[6]

Fugate's narrative, written years later, is probably embellished by his memory and time, but it leaves little to the imagination about the dangers of travel over the Santa Fe Trail during the early 1850s.

While those involved in the Santa Fe trade undoubtedly kept business records, only bits and pieces of information can be found regarding their annual profits and losses. But scattered records have survived in the files of historical societies and on the pages of early newspapers that provide at least some sense of the numbers. For instance, in 1857, at least three hundred merchants and freighters were engaged in the trade, and 9,884 wagons loaded at the levee at what is now Kansas City, Missouri.[7]

The July 25, 1859, issue of the weekly *Kansas Press* published at Cottonwood Falls, Kansas Territory, about twenty miles south of Council Grove, computed the amount of money invested in 1858 for transportation in the Santa Fe trade as:

1,510 wagons at $200	$302,000.00
361 horses at $100	$36,100.00
3,707 mules at $100	$370,700.00
14,515 oxen at $37.50	$544,312.50

When one adds wages, provisions, and incidentals, the total cost for 1858 was $1.4 million. Profits were evidently being made, but details are lacking.

By the late 1850s, freight wagons had generally become standardized. Made of wood, they were light but strong in construction. The wagon bottoms were slightly curved to prevent loads from shifting while going

This drawing by William Henry Jackson is titled Yoking a Wild Bull. (Courtesy National Park Service, U.S. Department of the Interior)

up or down hills, and the front extended forward like the prow of a ship. The rear was square with an end-gate that was hinged at the bottom and opened outward. Sockets along the side of the body held hickory bows, over which was stretched a sheet or white osnaburg cover. When properly adjusted, stretched tight, and tied down, the cover was weatherproof. Each wagon was capable of holding as much as five thousand pounds, and experience had taught traders and freighters how to load them to carry the greatest amount of freight. Experience also taught wagon manufacturers how to build vehicles that would provide the best possible service on the trail. For instance, all of the wood used in building them was thoroughly seasoned. It was kept under cover for at least two years after it was cut. Special attention was given to the wood used to make the wheels, since a wagon rolling over the trail was no better than its wheels. The hubs, spokes, and felloes or fellies (each held two spokes) were usually made of white oak, although occasionally plain hedge wood, called Osage orange, was used. Iron tires became commonplace. Before each journey, teamsters carefully inspected, and if an iron tire seemed loose, it was taken off, heated, and reset. This was also done

An eastern artist's depiction of a corralled caravan of wagons early in the morning, with the men roping oxen to yoke them before the wagons could be moved onto the trail. (Courtesy Nebraska State Historical Society)

This is a replica of a "Santa Fe wagon" near the entrance to the reconstructed Bent's Old Fort near La Junta, Colorado. The "Santa Fe wagon" probably was a modification of the older Conestoga wagon with a straight bed and without the complex joinery of rails and uprights characteristic of the Conestoga body. The wagon could carry six thousand pounds and was produced by several wagon-makers in Missouri. (Author's Collection)

along the trail. While iron axles were experimented with during the late 1840s, they were abandoned because if one broke or bent while traveling, it was impossible to repair. Thus, wagon axles were made of strong white oak.[8]

One writer, Randolph B. Marcy, who was experienced in taking caravans of military wagons across the prairie and plains, wrote a handbook for overland travelers in which he provided advice on repairing broken wagons:

The accidents most liable to happen to wagons on the plains arise from the great dryness of the atmosphere, and the consequent shrinkage and contraction of wood-work in the wheels, the tires working loose, and the wheels, in passing over sidling ground, oftentimes falling down and breaking all the spokes where they enter the hub. It therefore becomes a matter of absolute necessity for the prairie traveler to devise some means of repairing such damages, or of guarding against them by the use of timely expedients.

The wheels should be frequently and closely examined, and whenever a tire becomes at all loose it should at once be tightened with pieces of hoop-iron or wooden wedges driven by twos simultaneously from opposite sides. Another remedy for the same thing is to take off the wheels after encamping, sink them in water, and allow them to remain over night. This swells the wood, but is only temporary, requiring frequent repetition; and, after a time, if the wheels have not been made of thoroughly seasoned timber, it becomes necessary to reset the tires in order to guard against their destruction by falling to pieces and breaking the spokes.

If the tires run off near a blacksmith's shop, or if there be a traveling forge with the train, they may be tied on with raw hide or ropes, and thus driven to the shop or camp. When a rear wheel breaks down upon a march, the best method I know of for taking the vehicle to a place where it can be repaired is to take off the damaged wheel, and place a stout pole of three or four inches in diameter under the end of the axle, outside the wagon-bed, and extending forward above the front wheel, where it is firmly lashed with ropes, while the other end of the pole runs six or eight feet to the rear, and drags upon the ground. The pole must be of such length and inclination that the axle shall be raised and retained in its proper horizontal position, when it can be driven to any distance that may be desired. The wagon should be relieved as much as practicable of its loading, as the pole dragging upon the ground will cause it to run heavily. When a front wheel breaks down, the expedient just mentioned can not be applied to the front axle, but the two rear wheels may be taken off and placed upon this axle (they will always fit), while the sound front wheel can be substituted upon one side of the rear axle, after which the pole may be applied as before described. This plan I have adopted upon several different occasions, and I can vouch for its efficacy.

The foregoing facts may appear very simple and unimportant in themselves, but blacksmiths and wheelwrights are not met with at every turn of the roads upon the prairies; and in the wilderness, where the traveler is dependent solely upon his own resources, this kind of information will be found highly useful.

When the spokes in a wheel shrink more than the felloes, they work loose in the hub, and can not be tightened by wedging. The only remedy in such cases is to cut the felloe with a saw on opposite sides, taking out two pieces of such dimensions that the reduced circumference will draw back the spokes into their proper places and make them snug. A thin wagon-bow, or barrel-hoops, may then be wrapped around the outside of the felloe, and secured with small nails or tacks. This increases the diameter of the wheel, so that when the tire has been heated, put on, and cooled, it forces back the spokes into their true places, and makes the wheel as sound and strong as it ever was. This simple process can be executed in about half an hour if there be fuel for heating, and obviates the necessity of cutting and welding the tire. I would recommend that the tires should be secured with bolts and nuts, which will prevent them from running off when they work loose, and, if they have been cut and reset, they should be well tried with a hammer where they are welded to make sure that the junction is sound.[9]

There is no question that in the 1850s most American and Mexican traders and merchants prospered by taking caravans of merchandise between Missouri and New Mexico, with some traveling between Chihuahua and Missouri. Some traders had engaged in the Santa Fe trade for years, but others were newcomers to the business, including John M. Kingsbury. In 1853, Kingsbury, age twenty-four, became a partner with James J. Webb, who first got involved in the trade in 1844. By 1854, they had opened a general dry-goods store in Santa Fe, which then had a population of about four thousand. Kingsbury ran the store while Webb, who lived in Connecticut, supplied the goods by wagon train from Missouri once a year. Kingsbury learned quickly what his customers wanted and described the merchandise needed in letters to Webb, which are preserved in the files of the Missouri Historical Society at St. Louis and the DeGolyer Library at Southern Methodist University in Dallas.[10]

The U.S. mail arrived in Santa Fe once a month provided the weather was good and Indians did not try to stop the mail carriages. Kingsbury's letters might take sixty days to reach Webb in Connecticut, and a reply that long again. The Massachusetts native William H. Davis was appointed U.S. attorney for the Territory of New Mexico in 1853 and traveled down the Santa Fe Trail to his new post. He later wrote of his experiences in a little book titled *El Gringo; or, New Mexico and Her People* published in New York in 1857. In its pages Davis recalled how people in Santa Fe, especially Americans, anxiously awaited the arrival of the monthly mail:

> Many a heart beat once more with renewed gladness when the mule-teams drove into the Plaza, and the conductor deposited the leathern bags of love and news down at the door of the post-office. None but those exiled a long distance from home and friends, and living among a strange people, can fully appreciate the arrival of the mail, and more especially when it arrives but once a month. How quickly a crowd assembles around the office door, waiting for the "open sesame," when they can enter and receive their letters! While standing there, anxious thoughts chase each other through the head and heart, and you are not wholly at ease until you should have read every line and syllable addressed to you. You cannot help imagining the intelligence you may receive; several weeks have elapsed since the last advises, and in that time sad changes may have taken place among the loved ones at home. Perhaps death has invaded the sacred circle of friends and taken away the one most prized, for the grim monster invariably seeks the dearest first.[11]

The following year, Americans in Santa Fe probably cheered when a new mail contractor promised to deliver the U.S. mail twice a month. Jacob Hall won the contract, taking it away from David Waldo, Hall's former partner, and five other bidders. When Hall won, the only established post offices were at Independence and Westport, Missouri, and at Fort Union, Las Vegas, and Santa Fe in New Mexico Territory. But Hall soon provided passenger, mail, and express service to several other places in what is now Kansas and New Mexico. Communications were improving.[12]

. . .

THE MISSOURI COMPROMISE of 1820 admitted Missouri as a slave state (that is, one permitting slavery within its borders) and Maine as a free state (one banning slavery), thereby maintaining an equal number of free and slave states in the Union. The compromise, however, prohibited slavery in the remaining area of the Louisiana Purchase north of the parallel marked by the southern boundary of Missouri. Until 1850, Congress managed to avoid a major showdown on the question of slavery, but then California sought statehood following the discovery of gold and an influx of Americans. Debate over slavery began anew. California was admitted as a free state on September 9, 1850, under a compromise that left open the issue of slavery in the territories of New Mexico and Utah. The controversy temporarily subsided until January 4, 1854, when Illinois senator Stephen A. Douglas reported out of the Senate Committee on Territories a bill that would organize a territory called Nebraska in a part of Louisiana Territory where slavery was prohibited by the Missouri Compromise.

Historians disagree about Douglas's complex motives for introducing the bill, but one reason certainly was his interest in removing Indians in the proposed territory from the region west of the Missouri River, and encouraging a continuous line of settlements extending to the Pacific Ocean. Some authorities believe that Douglas's underlying motivation was promoting a transcontinental railroad over a central or northern route. Regardless, his proposal clearly reflected the "Manifest Destiny" mystique shared by so many Americans in the 1840s—the belief that Americans should, and were naturally destined to, occupy the entire continent, and that it was God's wish that the soil be used intensively by agricultural settlers rather than nomadic Indians. Douglas's motives, however, became less important when the bill in its final form created two territories—Kansas and Nebraska—and declared the Missouri Compromise void, gaining Southern support for the bill. The Kansas-Nebraska Act passed both houses of Congress in late May 1854 and was approved by President Franklin Pierce on May 30. The measure permitted the new territories to decide the slavery question for themselves and provided for their admission into the Union as either free or slave states. The act continued to stir intense controversy. In the North, in particular, opposition to it inspired the formation of a new antislavery party, the Republicans, with the rallying cry of "Free Men and Free Land."

There were fewer than fifteen hundred white people in Kansas Territory on the day President Pierce created it with the stroke of his pen. Perhaps seven hundred of these were soldiers, many stationed at Fort Leavenworth. An equal number were civilians living at various Indian missions and trading posts and at several points along the Santa Fe Trail, but soon some Missourians began to settle in the new territory. Other Missourians sought to influence events in Kansas to ensure harmony along their state's western border, and during most of 1854 relations between the residents of Missouri and Kansas Territory were agreeable. This changed when New England abolitionists started to recruit emigrants for Kansas in a highly publicized campaign that verbally attacked those who supported slavery. The campaign attracted the attention of the nation's press and made Kansas Territory a symbol of the slavery issue, especially after abolitionists arrived to make their homes. Some Missourians, most of them favoring slavery, also settled, but more came to vote in the first territorial elections in 1855 and then returned to their homes in Missouri. A proslavery territorial legislature was elected, and violence and corruption followed in eastern areas of Kansas Territory, where most of the population was then centered.

The new frontier town of Lawrence, about forty miles west of what is now Kansas City, Missouri, became the stronghold of the free-state settlers. Missourians sacked the town in May 1858, and open warfare followed in what has since been called the "Border War." While these conflicts were occurring, the Santa Fe trade continued to prosper. Wagons owned by American and Mexican traders continued to traverse the trail, while others freighted government goods from Fort Leavenworth to Fort Riley, Fort Union, and other posts along the road and in New Mexico. Often there was more money to be made in freighting goods for the government than for merchants. One man, Alexander Majors, turned from taking merchandise to New Mexico for merchants to carrying government freight. With another partner, William H. Russell, he signed a contract to transport army supplies from Fort Leavenworth to Albuquerque during the summer of 1854 at a rate of $10.83 per hundred pounds. They operated a hundred wagons pulled by oxen. Some of their wagons also carried government freight to military posts along the Oregon Trail.

One of their employees on a New Mexico–bound caravan was James A. Little, an Indiana native making his first trip west. He later recalled that the caravan started out with more than five hundred oxen and forty large wagons. Ten of the wagons were old, but thirty were new ones being sent out by the government for use by the army. Little wrote: "Each wagon was as large as four ordinary wagons and carried a load averaging three tons." When the caravan started back to Fort Leavenworth, there was an outbreak of smallpox among the teamsters. Little left the group and traveled alone. At Council Grove, he joined a caravan owned by a

Mexican trader bound for Missouri. Little remembered that there were four passengers traveling with the Mexican train, "a single white lady, two young white men and a negro" and that the two young men were rivals for the woman; one of them later married her.[13]

During the spring of 1854, the *Western Dispatch* on May 19 reported: "We noticed several weeks since, the arrival of several wagons at Westport, loaded with wool from New Mexico. This is a new feature in the trade of that country, and we think if carried on properly, will be profitable." The newspaper observed that Westport merchants Charles E. Kearney and William R. Bernard, who had become partners in 1853, outfitted 600 wagons that year. In 1854, they outfitted 822 wagons, and in 1855, 1,217.[14]

By 1855, about a year after Kansas Territory was organized, the town of Kansas, Missouri, had replaced Independence as the eastern terminus of the Santa Fe Trail. In fact, the towns of Kansas (now Kansas City, Missouri) and Westport, Missouri, were beginning to grow together into one city. To the northwest, Fort Leavenworth had increased in importance as a shipping point for government stores for Indians and to military forces, not only in Kansas Territory and posts along the Santa Fe Trail, but for posts to the north along the Oregon Trail in Nebraska Territory and what became Wyoming.

The opening of Kansas Territory to settlement in 1854 saw the arrival of entrepreneurs seeking to capitalize on the needs of those traveling over the trail. At 110 Mile Creek, near present-day Overbrook, Kansas, Fry P. McGee opened a store to sell provisions to travelers. He also built a bridge over the creek and charged a toll of twenty-five cents for each wagon that crossed. McGee's bridge appears to have been the second toll bridge constructed on the trail, the first having been built in 1846 over what became know as Switzler's Creek, because John Switzler had built the bridge. To avoid the prohibition against whites settling in what was then Indian country, Switzler married an Indian woman and became a member of her tribe. The third toll bridge constructed on the trail was at 142 Mile Creek, about twenty miles east of Council Grove. The bridge was built by Charles Withington, who opened a combination store, saloon, mail station, and blacksmith shop while collecting a toll from travelers using his bridge. Still other toll bridges were constructed by 1860—one over the Neosho River at Council Grove, and one to the west, at the crossing over the Little Arkansas River. The Kansas territorial legislature set the toll rates at fifty cents for each wagon or vehicle, ten cents for each large animal, five cents for each small animal or person, and ten cents for each man and horse. About twenty-one miles southwest of the

Little Arkansas River crossing was the Cow Creek crossing, where Dr. Ashael Beach established a trading ranch in 1858. He obtained a charter to build a toll bridge, but before it could be built, William Edwards constructed a bridge nearby. Beach's son Abijah, who had come west to join his father, sued for an injunction against Edwards's bridge because it had been built within the geographical limits of their charter. The threatened legal action caused Edwards to back down and sell his bridge to Beach for fifty dollars. Beach's bridge and trading ranch were later owned and operated by William "Buffalo Bill" Mathewson.[15]

In 1860, three years after Chris H. Strieby, a wagon-maker, arrived in Council Grove, he and another man named Whitsett built this stone blacksmith shop located on the Santa Fe Trail. There Strieby shoed oxen, horses, and mules and mended wagons. The shop remained in operation until 1920. (Author's Collection)

Another entrepreneur was Malcolm Conn, age twenty-four, who arrived in 1855 at Westport seeking a business opportunity. The Maryland native found a job with the merchant Silas P. Keller, a Virginian, who ran a business on Main Street. Keller competed for the western trade with such firms as Kearney & Bernard, Bake & Street, A. G. Boone, Edward Price, and J. G. Hamilton. Within two years Conn moved to Council Grove, 150 miles southwest of Westport on the Santa Fe Trail. Conn may have been encouraged to move there by Keller, who was a

An unidentified artist made this drawing of a trading ranch at what became Lakin, Kansas Territory, on the Santa Fe Trail. The structure was a dugout made of sod cut from ground. (Author's Collection)

stockholder in the Council Grove Town Company, organized in 1857. Conn became a partner of Thomas C. Hill, the man who built the "Last Chance Store," a small one-story stone building on the west side of the little town within a few yards of the Santa Fe Trail. Conn, Hill, and their partner, Munkres, then built in 1858 the "Stone Store," as it came to be known. The following year, apparently, Conn bought out his partners and competed directly against Seth M. Hays & Co. By 1860, Conn was the wealthiest person in Council Grove. The census that year lists Conn as having a personal estate of $10,000. Seth Hays and his partner, G. M. Simcock, each had personal estates of $8,250.[16]

A traveler's impression of Council Grove appears in the diary of Heinrich Balduin Mollhausen, a German who traveled from Santa Fe to Fort Leavenworth during the summer of 1858. He and his party approached the town from the west, and in his diary he wrote:

> We reached the edge of the elevation from where we had a view of the wooded valley of the Neosho and the delightfully situated little town of Council Grove. We halted almost involuntarily in order to feast our

Malcolm Conn, a Maryland native who became a prominent merchant at Council Grove, Kansas Territory.
(Author's Collection)

eyes longer on the landscape which was lovely beyond all description. The dense, vigorous forest with its strange distinct contours hid the little river from our view. But I thought that I had never seen anything more beautiful and more charming than when I looked down on the tops of the oaks and hickories, the sycamores and cottonwoods which with their magnificent shades of color blended together as in one single carpet, and as I watched, the shadows of light feathery clouds glided along lazily and yet animatedly over the expanse of the woods and darkened the fresh green of the trees for a few minutes at a time. . . .

We rode down from the upland and when we entered its only and very broad street we noticed crudely painted signs on all the houses on both sides of the street; the houses numbered about thirty. By these signs we saw that the place was inhabited exclusively by merchants. There were also two inns and each stood out because they were painted white. We entered one of them which also had a store connected with the hotel.

We halted there only long enough to read an 8-day-old newspaper and to eat breakfast which was served us by an old negress and consisted chiefly of fresh, cool buttermilk and cornbread. We bought as much of the buttermilk as we could put in our bottles, and enriched in this way we left the town. After crossing the Neosho we rested for several hours in the shade of tall trees. While the mules were enjoying themselves in the rich grass, we refreshed ourselves by a bath in the little river and not until the sun had crossed the noon line did we leave the charming valley.[17]

Although Mollhausen made no reference to trading or freighting caravans in Council Grove, traffic over the trail and through that little town was tremendous during the late 1850s, especially after gold was discovered in far western Kansas Territory, in an area that is now part of Colorado. One of the first people to carry the news of the discovery of gold to eastern Kansas Territory was a husky Delaware Indian named Fall Leaf. He had gone west in summer 1857 as a military guide. As he was returning east, Fall Leaf met a group of Missourians who had found gold along the eastern slope of the Rocky Mountains. The Indian prospected and also found some gold before continuing his journey east. On a spring day in 1858 he rode his horse into Lawrence. His arrival probably would have gone unrecorded had he not stopped to show his gold freely. Fall Leaf even offered to guide anyone to where it could be found in the Rockies.

The Pioneer Store in Council Grove, Kansas Territory, operated by the firm of Van Camp, Keith and Tenney. This photo was made about 1858. (Author's Collection)

The Last Chance Store, built in 1857 by Thomas C. Hill on the west side of Council Grove, a few yards from the Santa Fe Trail. It was the last place in town where travelers could buy supplies before moving out onto the Trail and the prairie and plains. (Author's Collection)

Indians had found the precious metal in the mountain streams of present-day Colorado during the eighteenth century, if not earlier. Some Mexicans found gold in the Rockies during the 1840s, but their discovery was accompanied by little fanfare. About 1850 a band of educated Cherokee Indians from Georgia, bound for California's goldfields, discovered gold in the Rockies as they paused to camp along mountain streams. After the strike played out, they continued on to California, but when they returned to Georgia, William Green Russell, a white man who had married a Cherokee woman, heard the stories of gold in the Rocky Mountains. In the spring of 1858 he and a party of gold-seekers left Georgia to strike it rich in the Rockies not knowing that news of the gold discovery was already spreading east. Kansas Territory, like much of the nation, was beginning to feel the effects of the economic panic of 1857, which had resulted from the rapid expansion of the nation westward and the speculation that followed. Prices and wages had dropped sharply, and some businesses had failed. It was only natural that a dream of quick riches suddenly gave everyone hope. The gold fever not only struck many residents of eastern Kansas Territory, but as word reached Missouri and was flashed east by the telegraph, another gold rush began.[18]

When you add more gold-seekers to the emigrants already bound for California or Oregon plus the traders and merchants involved in the Santa Fe trade, the mass of humanity moving westward creates an almost unbelievable picture. Newton Ainsworth was at the Lone Elm Campground west of Westport in May 1858. He described what he had originally witnessed when he revisited the campground years later: "I saw [in 1858] wagon trains camped on this Lone Elm camping ground until they covered more than this entire quarter section. In their desire not to be detained, and to be on the road first in the morning, they commence at twelve o'clock at night to hitch up and pull for the trail, and the last teams did not pass where we are now standing until four o'clock in the afternoon. At one time, for three days in succession, the last teams going out of camp had not passed here before hundreds were going into camp. The rush to the Pike's Peak gold fields in 1858 was what made for the heavy emigration and the heavy loads of freight that year. All the roads north, east and south led to the Lone Elm campground."[19]

Gold-seekers bound for Colorado followed the Santa Fe Trail to Bent's New Fort and then continued west to the Rocky Mountains, many moving north to Cherry Creek, the site of present-day Denver, Colorado. One gold-seeking party left Lawrence, Kansas, on May 26, 1858, taking along provisions to last six months plus gold-digging implements. The party, including two women and a baby, followed the Santa Fe Trail to Bent's New Fort and turned north along the Rockies until it reached the base of Pike's Peak on July 6. There, James Henry Holmes and his wife, Julia Archibald Holmes, decided to climb the mountain instead of searching for gold. They reached the summit four days later, making Julia Archibald Holmes the first white woman to climb Pike's Peak.[20]

The following year, 1859, the residents of Westport were surprised to see a wagon, without mules or oxen but propelled by sails, bound for the Santa Fe Trail. A man named Thomas had created a "windwagon," as he called it. Aboard were Thomas and five other men bound for the goldfields. The vehicle was about twenty-five feet long and seven feet across. It was covered with canvas like an ordinary prairie schooner, but above the covering was a small deck on which the navigator operated the sails attached to a mast that towered twenty feet above the deck. Down the trail the "windwagon" traveled until it was out of sight. Though Thomas intended to reach the goldfields in six days, averaging a hundred miles a day, his "windwagon" only got as far as a point near Council Grove before turning over. The passengers did not reach the goldfields on this

This is an artist's idea of what the "windwagon" built by "Windwagon Thomas" probably looked like. From Missouri, it got as far as Council Grove, Kansas, in 1859 before turning over. (Author's Collection)

trip and made their way back to Westport using a different form of transport.[21]

As has been the case in countless gold rushes, it was merchants who reaped the greatest benefits. The immediate beneficiaries of the Kansas gold rush were the merchants in Missouri River towns from Westport north to Council Bluffs, Iowa, and their suppliers in St. Louis, New Orleans, and points east. The steamboat companies also did well since they carried increasing amounts of goods and gold-seekers to jumping-off points. Although figures have not been found, merchants at Council Grove undoubtedly benefited from the increased traffic over the Santa Fe Trail, as did Bent's New Fort, where the gold-seekers usually stopped before continuing west to the front range of the Rocky Mountains, where they turned north to the goldfields. To the south, Santa Fe was unaffected by the gold rush, but by then the Santa Fe trade was reaching new proportions.

By 1860, trade between Missouri and Mexico had reached such a magnitude that the *New York Herald* sent a reporter west to obtain the statistics. In his letters to the newspaper, he reported that 16,439,134 pounds had been transported to Mexico that year, employing 7,084 men, 6,147 mules, 27,920 yoke of oxen, and 3,033 wagons. The reporter noted that many wagons bound for Mexico carried a great deal of common whiskey, "for which there seems to be an unlimited demand for consumption, and a large profit on the sale. Beside whiskey, fancy groceries, cotton domestics, prints, notions and Indians goods were popular. In returning to Missouri, the wagons carried wool, buffalo robes, dried buffalo meat, Mexican dollars sewed up in rawhide sacks, gold dust, and occasionally a small quantity of silver ore."[22]

By 1860, the standard accessories for a freight wagon consisted of six or eight bows and a pair of wagon covers of osnaburg, a heavy, coarse linen cloth. Santa Fe traders had learned from experience that two sheets of osnaburg gave better protection for their cargo than a single thickness of canvas. In addition, each wagon usually carried a couple of water kegs, a tar bucket, and a long box that hung on the rear and served as a container for such fuel as wood or buffalo chips, and as a feed trough for the animals when in camp. Most also carried a gunnysack for collecting buffalo chips for fire fuel when wood was not available.

That year, 1860, the merchant Seth Hays in Council Grove kept track of the traffic passing through his growing town. He reported that between April 24 and October 1 there had been 3,519 men, 2,667 wagons, 478 horses, 5,819 mules, 22,738 oxen, 61 carriages, and 6,819 tons of freight going west through Council Grove, and these figures, he noted, did not include travelers, emigrants, or men engaged in private business.[23]

To control the threat of hostile Indians along the trail, more U.S. troops were needed. In fact, in a letter to the superintendent of Indian affairs at St. Louis, William Bent, agent for the Upper Arkansas Indians, appealed for two new permanent forts along the trail. Bent wrote: "I consider it essential to have two permanent stations for troops, one at the mouth of Pawnee Fork, and one at Big Timbers, both upon the Arkansas River. . . . To control them [Indians] it is essential to have among them the perpetual presence of a controlling military force."[24]

A. B. Greenwood, commissioner of Indian affairs, picked up on Bent's appeal in a report that described as critical the relations between

Seth M. Hays, the first permanent settler in Council Grove, Kansas, was a merchant. He later kept an inn and ran a saloon. (Author's Collection)

Indians and traffic over the trail. He noted that the discovery of gold in Colorado had increased travel over the route and that as a result the Indians were having immense difficulties trying to maintain their natural subsistence. Because of Bent's appeal, Greenwood's report, and the government's desire for official mail stations, construction of a new post began during the summer of 1859 on Pawnee Fork, west of present-day Larned, Kansas. Its location, about midway between Fort Leavenworth and Bent's Fort, was a favorite camping ground for Indians. It was first called "Camp on the Pawnee Fork" and in early February 1860 was renamed Camp Alert, but by the summer of 1860 it was moved three miles west to a place that had a natural defensive advantage. The post's new location was on the south side of Pawnee Fork, with a bend of the creek affording a natural barrier on two sides. There permanent sod buildings were soon constructed, and on May 29, 1860, the new post was named Fort Larned, in honor of Colonel Benjamin F. Larned, paymaster of the U.S. Army.

With the presence of more military troops along the trail, white travelers felt more at ease. In a letter to a friend written on June 28, 1860, from Peacock's trading ranch on Walnut Creek, east of present-day Great Bend, Kansas, the Westport trader Albert Boone reflected this feeling.

Here we are—15 days out—almost without an effort; found the road good beyond all expectation, was treated with marked kindness by every person on the road. Water was rather scarce for drinking and wells low, yet our little party was amply furnished and our water tanks filled from all the wells and springs. If the Northern route [across central Kansas Territory] surpass this, then I say go it who wants, but this is good enough for me, and this far I never have seen better. The whole face of the prairie has been covered with buffalo for the last two days. Our friend Geo. Peacock, the present occupant of this post, is the prince of good fellows—has everything a traveler wants, from an ear of corn to the greatest luxury. His store, as well as that of Hays & Co. of Council Grove, and M. Conn's are equal to any in Westport, and kindness shown us by all those gentlemen and the many good things presented to us, will not soon be forgotten, and is sufficient recommendation, if nothing else, to insure travelers to come this route. Our stock, down to chickens, all look as well, and better even than when we left. I met the Kaws on the Buffalo hunt at Owl Creek, where Jarvis [Chávez] was killed by the whites, and they supplied us liberally with buffalo meat. I am told that here we have near us, on our right and left, U.S. troops in one or two miles of us, but have not seen one. The road is clear of hostile Indians.[25]

Although the Indians appeared to be under control, and traders, freighters, and others had learned to overcome many of the natural obstacles and conditions, the decade to follow would bring new threats and renewed hostilities from Indians along the trail.

FOURTEEN

The Civil War, 1861-1865

It is well that war is so terrible—
else we should grow too fond of it.

—Robert E. Lee

THE PEOPLE OF Kansas Territory were taken by surprise when Kansas became a state on January 29, 1861. They had not had time to plan a state government. Although the Free State party had gained control of the territorial legislature in 1857 and drew up a constitution rejecting slavery in 1859 which Kansas voters supported, the U.S. Senate, which was controlled by proslavery elements, rejected it. Statehood did not seem possible—but then Jefferson Davis and other southern senators walked out of the Senate, giving that body a free-state majority. The bill to admit Kansas to the Union as a free state was reintroduced and passed. The bill had to go back to the House of Representatives, however, because of a Senate amendment concerning the judiciary. The House passed it, and the following day, January 29, 1861, Kansas became the thirty-fourth state in the Union. Less than three months later, on April 12, 1861, the Confederate general P. G. T. Beauregard opened fire on Fort Sumter in Charles Harbor, South Carolina, and the American Civil War began.

To the west, Union forces began to concentrate at Cairo, Illinois, in order to control steamboat traffic at the point where the Ohio River flows into the Mississippi. Steamboat travel was disrupted, and some boats coming down the Ohio carrying merchandise bound for Missouri and the Santa Fe trade were slowed. On May 10, 1861, a Union force captured a large band of men at St. Louis believed to be training for Confederate service. Their capture caused a riot on the streets of St. Louis in which thirty people were killed. Missouri was torn by what some described as its own war between Northern and Southern supporters, especially along the state's western border with Kansas, where the earlier struggle between free-state and slavery forces had set the stage for the Civil War now under way.[1]

Small bands of Missourians began raiding towns across the border in Kansas, including Gardner, located on the Santa Fe Trail, which was

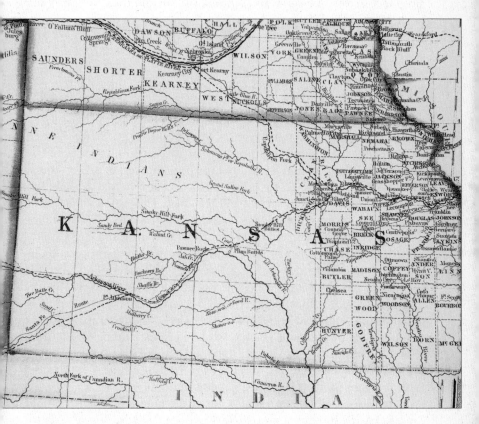

This 1861 map of Kansas shows the organized counties all located in the eastern part of the state. The route of the Santa Fe Trail from Fort Riley (above the second "A" in "KANSAS") to the southwest is marked by dashes. The trail split (under the first "A") with the mountain route following the Arkansas River west and the Cimarron or dry route turning southwest. (Author's Collection)

sacked and burned. In turn, bands of Kansans calling themselves *Jayhawkers* raided towns in Missouri. Men were killed and wounded on both sides, and the fear of more attacks and greater tension caused by the war slowed activity at the eastern end of the Santa Fe Trail; business in Kansas City and Westport declined. There was, however, no overall loss in commerce on the trail, because within weeks the trade shifted to Fort Leavenworth and the safety of U.S. Army protection. Steamboats bypassed Kansas City and unloaded their wagons at Fort Leavenworth, where freighters loaded their wagons and moved south through the hills of eastern Kansas until they hit the Kansas River at Moses Grinter's ferry. There they paused as each wagon was ferried across the river individually. Once across, the caravans continued south and then west, keeping to the west side of Turkey Creek, to a point near present-day Lenexa, Kansas, where the Fort Leavenworth road struck the Santa Fe Trail. Still other wagons traveled southwest of Fort Leavenworth toward Fort Riley, some going from Fort Leavenworth via Lawrence to Topeka and striking the Santa Fe Trail at a point between present-day Burlingame and Wilmington, Kansas, and then on to Council Grove. A great number of New Mexican traders also used these routes to avoid trouble at Kansas City and Westport even though business leaders through a newly formed local chamber of commerce promised that government troops would be stationed at Westport and a few other towns to the west to protect them. In New Mexico, however, the territorial legislature passed a resolution favoring Leavenworth as the eastern terminal. This action came about the time the government opened a new military road in 1862 from Fort Leavenworth to Topeka, Junction City, Salina, Ellsworth, and Fort Larned. This road was used chiefly by the government for the transportation of military stores and troops.

The war probably seemed a long way off for people in New Mexico, but at Fort Union, officers with Southern sympathies resigned their U.S. commissions and headed east soon after the hostilities began. One of them was Major Henry H. Sibley, who had been commander at Fort Union. Sibley hurried to Virginia and got Confederate president Jefferson Davis to open a theater of war in the West to invade New Mexico. With a commission of brigadier general and authority to organize an army of Texans, Sibley started west about the time Lieutenant Colonel John R. Baylor and 300 mounted Texans occupied Fort Bliss at El Paso, Texas, and then moved up the Rio Grande and seized Mesilla and nearby Fort Fillmore, soon capturing about 500 Union troops who had fled the post. In early August, Baylor established the Confederate Territory of Arizona, which included the present states of Arizona and New

Mexico. Meantime, Sibley had gone to San Antonio, Texas, organized about 2,500 men in three regiments, and moved to Fort Bliss.

To the north at Fort Union, officers organized a citizen army of New Mexico volunteers. East of Fort Union, the troops began constructing massive earthen parapets shaped like giant arrowheads extending out two hundred feet from each corner. In each angle was one of Fort Union's buildings. The parapets supported firing platforms and artillery emplacements. Geometrically resembling an eight-pointed star, the fortification became known as the star fort. The whole thing was designed to block the Santa Fe Trail to any Confederate advance from the south.

To the south, Sibley's troops moved north from Fort Bliss in January 1862 with the goal of capturing Albuquerque, Santa Fe, and Fort Union. Sibley's Confederate forces, armed with horse pistols, flintlock muskets, shotguns, squirrel rifles, and bowie knives, reached Santa Fe in early March 1862. The Union garrison of troops at Santa Fe withdrew to Fort Union, Sibley's next objective. But before he and his troops reached the

This photograph was made of the Elsberg-Amberg wagon train on the Plaza in Santa Fe about six months after the Civil War began. One of the wagons (left) was pulled by oxen, the others by mules. (Courtesy Museum of New Mexico, negative no. 11254)

post, the Colorado First Regiment of Volunteers, covering an average of forty miles a day, crossed snow-covered Raton Pass and arrived at Fort Union. Several days later the Confederate and Union forces battled at Glorieta Pass on the trail leading west to Santa Fe. The battle was a draw, and each side withdrew believing it had won, but a body of Union troops sent south around Glorieta Pass destroyed the Confederates' supplies. Without supplies, the Confederates were forced to leave New Mexico. That was the last Confederate attempt to capture New Mexico.[2]

At the eastern end of the Santa Fe Trail, Confederate guerrillas were continuing to make trouble. William Clarke Quantrill and his men attacked Aubrey, Kansas, close to the Missouri border, on March 7, 1862, killing three men. The Union Army then issued Special Orders No. 2, declaring that "guerrilla" bands like the one led by Quantrill were not Confederate soldiers but outlaws. Orders were given to kill them on the spot if captured. The order strengthened Quantrill's hand because Missourians with Southern sympathies did not like it. More of them joined Quantrill, and soon they controlled all movement in Kansas City, Missouri, just across the border from Kansas. Quantrill was sworn in as a Confederate captain in August 1862, and on September 2, he and about 150 men raided Olathe, Kansas, located on the Santa Fe Trail, northeast of Gardner. Every wagon in town was taken by members of Quantrill's force to carry their loot back to Missouri, and when they ran out of wagons in town, Quantrill ordered his men to steal more from nearby farms. Before fleeing back to Missouri, Quantrill's force killed six men. Soldiers from Fort Leavenworth gave chase and killed two members of Quantrill's band, but Quantrill and others escaped.

By early October 1862, Quantrill and some of his men returned to Kansas, this time killing fifteen Union soldiers guarding a wagon train on the Santa Fe Trail southwest of Kansas City. Quantrill and his men then surrounded what is today Shawnee, Kansas, killing, looting, and burning before fleeing south to winter with Confederate troops in Arkansas.[3]

In the spring of 1863, a group of Confederates under the command of Dick Yeager left Missouri and rode down the Santa Fe Trail in scattered groups of two or three so as not to attract attention. They met outside Council Grove on May 4 and set up a camp. The next day Yeager, suffering a toothache, rode into Council Grove to find a dentist and had a tooth pulled. While there he met the merchant Malcolm Conn, whom he had known before the war. Later Conn visited with Yeager in his camp, where he learned that Yeager planned to raid and burn Council Grove. Conn, however, reminded Yeager of their friendship and of the strong Southern sentiment held by many townspeople in Council Grove and convinced him not to burn the town. Yeager and his men left Council Grove alone but the next day raided a store on the Santa Fe Trail owned by Augustus Howell at Diamond Spring, west of Council Grove. Howell was shot and killed, and his wife was wounded. Yeager and his men then apparently turned east and rode back toward Missouri following the Santa Fe Trail. But at Rock Springs they killed a cavalry soldier on leave, and at Black Jack, they robbed everyone on a stagecoach bound for Santa Fe. When they reached Gardner, they took the express agent prisoner and stole a package containing two hundred dollars, took over a hotel, robbed the patrons, stole the best horses in the stable, and then fled across the border into Missouri.[4]

In Kansas City and Westport, some businesses failed because of poor wartime economic conditions. The prominent freighting firm of Russell, Majors, and Waddell failed in 1862, but not because of the war—poor business practices, including overextension of its resources, brought it down. Alexander Majors, one of the principals in the firm, was described by the late Texas writer J. Frank Dobie as "the lead steer of all freighters." Majors, who was born near Franklin, Kentucky, in 1814, became a farmer. In 1846, when he was thirty-two years old, he agreed to take a wagon loaded with Indian trade goods west to the Pottawatomie reserva-

Alexander Majors (1814–1900) became a Santa Fe trader in 1848. In 1854, he went into partnership with William H. Russell and William B. Waddell in the business of freighting military supplies in the West. (Courtesy Kansas State Historical Society)

View of a caravan of ox-drawn freight wagons crossing the plains during the late 1850s. (Author's Collection)

tion in what became Kansas. He was paid well for the journey, and in 1848 he entered the freighting business with six wagons taking goods from Independence, Missouri, to Santa Fe. Two years later, in 1850, he was given a contract to transport military supplies, and the following year he supervised a caravan of twenty-five wagons taking merchandise from Missouri to Santa Fe. He also made a second trip that year from Missouri to Fort Union, gaining a reputation as a reliable freighter.

When the army announced that it would award a two-year contract for freighting of stores from Fort Leavenworth, then the army's main supply depot in the West, he went into partnership with William H. Russell, a Vermont native who was in the mercantile business at Lexington, Missouri, and William B. Waddell, a former Virginian who had been Russell's business partner since 1852. They pooled their resources, won the government contract, and soon became the preeminent freighting organization in the West.

Majors, more than Russell or Waddell, was responsible for developing a workable pattern for the firm's freighting operations, and he issued rather specific instructions to his wagon masters printed in a little leaflet titled *Rules and Regulations for the Government of Outfits; Train Book.* Majors's instructions included the following:

> When about corraling, caution your men against exciting the cattle, by hallooning [*sic*] and cracking whips at them. They should be so careful that a long, deep-toned "whoa" would stop their teams in the exact spot required. . . .
>
> If water be near the camp, let the cattle feed to it instead of being driven there. But if necessary to drive them, let them linger some time about the water, so that they all may become cool and have a chance to satisfy their thirst. . . .
>
> In driving cattle to the corral, men enough must be employed to encircle them and drive them directly in, and when at a distance from the camp, drive them very slowly, as fast driving injures them greatly.
>
> No man should begin yoking before the cattle have had two or three minutes to become quieted in, then all should enter and yoke in a quiet gentle manner. First yoke the wheelers and chain them to

This illustration of a bullwhacker and a caravan of freight wagons on the Santa Fe Trail appeared in Santa Fe National Historic Trail, Comprehensive Management and Use Plan, *published in 1990 by the National Park Service, U.S. Department of the Interior. The artist is not identified.* (Author's Collection)

the front wheel outside corral, or hitch them to the tongue; secondly yoke the leaders and fasten them to the wagon, on the inside, and so on until the whole team is yoked, and hitched up, when they will be taken out of the corral and hitched to the wagon.

Once the wagons were on the trail, Majors's instructions were to drive the oxen one to two miles after the morning start, stop to allow the animals to breathe and urinate, and then drive seven to ten miles, or until about ten o'clock in the morning. During this stop, the oxen should be unyoked and allowed to graze for two hours, allowing the men time to prepare and eat breakfast. After two hours, the group should resume operations for a second seven to ten miles and then camp again for three to four hours, for supper and more grazing for the oxen. Then they were to carry on until dark. Majors expected the wagon master to travel fourteen to eighteen miles each day. If the wagons were empty, he expected two or three additional miles a day. Whether in camp or on the trail, another rule was that employees were not to swear, gamble, or drink whiskey. Majors expected old bullwhackers who had become victims of bad habits to abandon them when coming to work with his firm.

Majors recalled that rattlesnakes were a great annoyance during his

William F. "Billy" Shamleffer, an early merchant in Council Grove, Kansas, as he appeared late in life. (Courtesy Kansas State Historical Society)

early years on the trail, often "biting the mules and oxen when they were grazing. At first, mules were used altogether for traveling, but they would either die or become useless from the bite of a rattlesnake, and the men would sometimes be sent ahead of the caravan with whips to frighten the snakes out of the pathway, but later on, the ox-teamsters [bullwhackers], with their large whips, destroyed them so fast that they ceased to trouble them to any great extent."[5]

In April 1860, Majors joined Waddell and Russell in establishing the Pony Express, an express mail service from St. Joseph, Missouri, to California that lasted until October 1861, when the overland telegraph was completed. The added financial expansion plus an earlier overextension of their wagon-freighting business resulted in the collapse of their firm in 1862. Majors continued in the freighting business but never on the scale of earlier years, and never again to Santa Fe over the Santa Fe Trail.[6]

AFTER DICK YEAGER and his men left Council Grove in the spring of 1863, the town remained free of Confederate threats for the balance of the Civil War, and its businesses continued to prosper from the Santa Fe trade. Evidence of this is the amount of trail traffic through the town in 1863: 3,000 wagons, 618 horses, 20,218 oxen, 8,046 mules, 98 carriages, and 3,072 men passed through Council Grove transporting 15,000 tons of freight valued at $40 million. The Council Grove merchant William F. Shamleffer remembered that the Old Pioneer Store owned by T. S. Huffaker sold $400,000 in merchandise during one two-year period in the early 1860s. Of that total, $12,000 was in whiskey sales, but during the same period the store sold only $15.40 worth of Bibles. Shamleffer also remembered:

> It was the business of the local trader to keep an eye out for sore-footed oxen which usually pulled the great freight wagons, who would buy them for from $25 to $35 apiece, and keep them about thirty or sixty days, have them shod, and sell them back for from $100 to $125 each. He [the trader] had to deal in all kinds of lumber, from large pieces like saw logs, and also keep all kinds of lumber for sale. In his stock were found every known variety of goods for use on the frontier, from ox yokes and repairs to cambric needles, from small boxes of pills to barrels of whisky. There was always a large per cent to lose in shipping whisky "from the river [Missouri]," for the freight boys usually carried gimlets, and at convenient watering places on the road

William F. "Billy" Shamleffer's store in Council Grove, Kansas, during the early 1860s. The Santa Fe Trail ran in front of the store. Some of Shamleffer's customers and their wagons are shown in front of the store. The TEXAS sign on the store's front suggests Southern sympathies or was placed there to give that impression. (Courtesy Kansas State Historical Society)

tapped the barrels and replaced the liquor used with fresh water from some spring or stream.

The merchant had to hustle with business customers all day, and then entertain them royally at night; for some of them came hundreds of miles to trade, and the business house had to furnish many of them with sleeping quarters, place to cook their meals, corrals in which to keep their stock, and open access to the corn cribs.... Plainsmen, hunters, trappers, wagon bosses, soldiers, bullwhackers, broncho [*sic*] busters, long lines of prairie schooner, and heads of horses, mules and cattle, were the attractions of the passing day.

The frontier merchant had to take some interest in the local horse races, and have some money in the purse, and set them up all around whether he won or not. It was his duty to prepare and finance the Fourth of July celebration; pay for the music at the Indian dances when he visited their villages near by, and interest himself in the welfare of all of his customers of whatever grade. It was "How are you,

John and Jim?" "How are all the folks getting along?" "Been thinking of you every day, wondering why you didn't come to town"—and he asked them all in a cheerful, wholesouled manner, especially about wife and children. If they were with the father, many compliments had to be made, and the wife of the local settler in the valley had to be favored in all things. It would have been an insult to tell a woman that her butter was not good or that she had sold ancient eggs the last time in town; but the merchant had to take her merchandise even if he did lose out on these articles and had to consign them to the rubbish heap in the back yard as soon as she was out of town.[7]

Another Council Grove merchant, Seth M. Hays, the first permanent settler in the town, also operated a saloon. By 1865, he was prominent in the community and owned considerable property. Several church ladies in the town wanted a room where they could hold a festival. When they found none, Hays offered his saloon, promising to keep all of the liquor out of sight. Some of the women were horrified, but one woman knew Hays would keep his promise and convinced the others to accept his

Council Grove, Kansas, about 1901. This photo was taken from near the top of Belfry Hill, close to where Matteo Boccalini made his home under a rock overhang. (Author's Collection)

offer. When festival time came, the bar was curtained with wagon covers and the room was nicely decorated. In fact, Hays himself was present at the door and ushered guests to tables covered with good things to eat. The affair was both a social and a financial success for the ladies of the church.[8]

One Civil War traveler who stayed longer than most was an Italian named Matteo Boccalini, who arrived in town in the spring of 1863 walking beside a wagon train. Soon after his arrival he climbed the eastern face of Belfry Hill on the western edge of town, near where townspeople had erected a large bell to be rung in the event of an Indian attack. Several yards north of the bell Boccalini apparently found an overhang in the stone outcroppings and there made his home. Aside from the clothing on his back, the newcomer's belongings consisted of a few religious articles, a half-dozen well-thumbed books, and an old mandolin. During the evenings that followed, many residents could hear the sound of mandolin music floating down over their town.

Some residents tried to learn more about Boccalini. Tradition has it that he had been a Catholic priest and may have fallen out of favor with the church. He spoke Italian and Spanish. On the stone walls of his makeshift home he carved his name, a cross, and the words GESU MARIA and CAPRI. He ate no meat or bread, only uncooked cornmeal mixed with milk or water. Each day he would sit in front of his makeshift home and read, regularly taking time to survey the town as though he were looking for something or someone.

After many days he became friends with a few residents of Council Grove. In time they learned that Boccalini had been born on the island of Capri about 1808 and lived there until he was eighteen, when he was sent to Rome to study for the priesthood. At the age of twenty-one, he was ordained and became Father Francesco. He was an eloquent and bold speaker and soon came to the attention of the Pope, who named him one of his secretaries. At first, members of the Congregation for the Propagation of the Faith refused to confirm his appointment, because they considered him too outspoken. But Boccalini defended himself so eloquently that he was confirmed and assumed his Vatican duties.

Still, some of his colleagues did not like Boccalini and plotted his downfall. During the 1830s his enemies supposedly saw to it that a dark-haired young lady befriended him. He fell in love with the young girl and was immediately charged, prosecuted, and denounced. Before he could be sentenced, Boccalini fled Rome and, fearing for his life, became a wanderer. He made his way to America during the 1850s, and after the Civil War began he traveled west, continuing to practice his religion. While in Council Grove, a Mexican teamster was stabbed in an argument with another driver in a wagon train. The Mexican knew he was dying and said he wanted a priest. Boccalini hurried to the man's side and administered the Last Sacraments in Spanish, much to the satisfaction of the dying Mexican.

Five months after Boccalini arrived in Council Grove, he saw a man dressed in clerical garb, and his old fears surfaced. Believing the man was looking for him, he hurriedly returned to his home on the side of Belfry Hill, gathered his belongings, and early the next morning quietly joined a caravan bound for New Mexico. Although invited to ride in one of the wagons, Boccalini refused and instead walked next to the wagons. Only when he was hard pressed for food would he accept a meal from the Mexican teamsters.

When the caravan neared Santa Fe, Boccalini thanked the wagon master and left the caravan. For nearly a year he reportedly wandered the countryside. Early in 1865, while walking along the eastern edge of the Sangre de Cristo Mountains northwest of modern Las Vegas, New Mexico, he came upon a cave near the summit of Rincón de Tecolote (The Owl's Corner), a mountain peak more than nine thousand feet high, not far south of the headwaters of the Mora River. There Boccalini made his new home, again carving his name, a cross, and the words GESU MARIA and CAPRI on the cave's walls. He divided his time between solitude in the cave or among nearby piñon trees and religious work among the poor Mexicans who lived in the valley below. For nearly four years he lived a peaceful life helping the depressed and ill. One day in 1869, he failed to appear as usual among the local people. After he had been absent for more than a week, a search party was sent from the valley into the mountains, and it found his body near the entrance to his cave home, a knife stuck in his heart. To this day, no one knows if Boccalini's death was suicide or murder. But people near Las Vegas still refer to the nearby mountain as Hermit's Peak, and to the east on the Santa Fe Trail in Council Grove, Kansas, a rock overhang is still referred to as the "Hermit Priest's Cave."[9]

WHILE COUNCIL GROVE was unaffected by the Civil War directly, that was not the case for many travelers who passed through the town on the Santa Fe Trail. Alexander Caldwell got a contract to carry military freight from Fort Leavenworth to Fort Union. He hired a well-known teamster, Tom Atkins, to organize a caravan and hire bullwhackers to drive the wagons. Caldwell later wrote:

The employees of this train were citizens of the western border of Missouri, and as soon as they learned of the fall of Sumter, were restless to return and join the Rebel army. During the journey they conceived the idea of stealing the entire train and its cargo. Their plan was to run it into Texas, dispose of it for cash, and join the Confederacy. All except Atkins, his assistant, and one other, were engaged in the conspiracy. It was agreed that if Atkins opposed the plan he should be killed. One night, in the Raton mountains, soon after getting into camp, and when within a few miles of a military post, the plan was submitted. Atkins suggested that after supper they would gather around the camp fire and talk it over. He so managed as to get them seated some distance from the wagon and their weapons, and listened to their proposals. Suddenly springing to his feet, he and his assistants covered the party with their revolvers, while the extra man was dispatched to the fort for assistance. The mutineers were taken to the fort as prisoners, while soldiers were sent to take the train through to its destination. Thus did the courage and decision of Tom Atkins save to our company, and to the United States, thousands of dollars of valuable property.[10]

Troubles along the Santa Fe Trail discouraged some traders, freighters, and travelers from traveling the trail, but not Charles Raber. He became a teamster in 1860 and two years later formed a partnership with Martin Keck. They bought two wagons and teams, bought loads of groceries from Charles E. Kearney at Westport, and headed west on the Santa Fe Trail. They intended to go to Colorado Territory and trade with the miners, but when they reached the Arkansas River they fell in with some Mexican freighters who persuaded Raber and Keck to go with them to New Mexico. The Mexicans assured the new traders that they would find a better market there for their goods. Aware that the Confederates from Texas had left New Mexico, Raber recalled why he and Keck decided to take the Mexicans' advice:

When we got to William Kroening's ranch at La Junta [Colorado Territory], we stopped and commenced selling to the settlers. I took part of a load, consisting of bacon, lard, soap, candles, tobacco and whisky to Loma Parda, a small Mexican town three miles from Fort Union, where soldiers did most of their trading. I found ready sale and sold out in a short time. At the time the government was issuing legal tender and the Mexicans thought they were better than demand notes. The only way they could tell the difference was by their backs. It tickled me to see them turn them over and pick out demand notes to pay for the goods. I knew they were at a premium in the states. We sold out in a short time and cleaned up with a good profit on our first venture. We returned to Westport and bought another team and loaded the three wagons with groceries. When our friends learned of our good luck, some of them got the fever and wanted to go along. George and Jake Wiedman, William Eisele and George Keck each rigged up one team and loaded them with groceries and went with us. When we reached Fort Larned a friend of mine, formerly from Independence, Mo., at that time in charge of the state station at Larned, came to camp and bought a large barrel of whisky. But as whisky was a contraband article, it had to be smuggled into the post. So we arranged for him to send a hay wagon to our next camp, near a haymaking camp, where the whisky was put in the bottom of the wagon and the hay on top. In this manner food for man and beast was taken into the fort to be removed to a safe place after dark. On my return I called on my friend. I asked him how he got along with the contraband goods?

"Oh fine," he replied. He said it helped clear the alkali dust from many a weary traveler's throat and was highly appreciated by friends at the fort.[11]

THE WEST CHANGED during the early 1860s. Gold-seekers and others who had gone to far western Kansas Territory, which reached the summit of the Rocky Mountains, complained that going east to the territorial capital at Lecompton, more than five hundred miles away, was too far to travel to conduct business. When Kansas Territory became a state early in 1861, the western third of the territory was lopped off and became part of Colorado Territory, which was created on February 28, 1861. Another change occurred when the Homestead Act of 1862 permitted any person to file for 160 acres of federal land if he or she was an American citizen or had filed his or her intention papers. To file, one had to be at least twenty-one years old or the head of a family or have served fourteen days in the U.S. Army or Navy, and he or she could never have fought against the United States. In many areas of eastern Kansas along the Santa Fe Trail, people began claiming homesteads, and in a few places, by the end of the Civil War, the course of the trail changed as caravans had to travel around fields of corn, wheat, or other crops planted by homesteaders.

To the southwest, the Territory of New Mexico, which stretched westward to California, was carved up in 1863 when the Territory of Arizona was created. But these actions had little effect on the war or the Santa Fe Trail. Commerce in Kansas City and Westport remained crippled, especially after Quantrill and more than 100 men raided and burned Lawrence, Kansas, several miles north of the Santa Fe Trail, on August 21, 1863, and killed at least 143 people. Outraged and in apparent retaliation for the attack, Union general Thomas Ewing Jr. at Kansas City, Missouri, issued Special Orders No. 11, which directed all persons living in Jackson, Bates, and Cass counties and those living more than a mile from military posts in Vernon County—all in Missouri—to leave within fifteen days.

With Union forces in control along Missouri's border with Kansas, Kansas City and Westport began to gain back much of the private freighting business to New Mexico by early 1864. By the fall of that year, however, a new threat was rumored on the horizon. Word reached Kansas City that Confederate general Sterling Price was planning a raid into Kansas. The state militia was called out and ordered to several points along the eastern border of Kansas. From the east came General Price with perhaps fifteen thousand Confederate troops. On October 20, 1864, a small engagement occurred near the Santa Fe Trail crossing on the Little Blue River. The following day there was a battle along the Little Blue with most of Price's men engaged and closing on the Big Blue, within six miles of Kansas City. On October 22, Union forces won the battle on the Big Blue, and the next day the Union troops beat Price in the battle of Westport, often called the "Gettysburg of the West." General Price and his men retreated south, making their last stand on the Marmaton River many miles south of Kansas City, Missouri, where they were beaten.

To THE WEST along the Santa Fe Trail, there were more Indians and soldiers. Soon after the Civil War began, many regular army troops had been replaced by volunteers, most of them untrained and ignorant of Indian tactics. Then, too, the Indians took advantage of whites fighting whites and increased their harassment and raids on caravans traveling the Santa Fe Trail. In one instance, Indians had camped near Fort Larned, which was manned by volunteer soldiers. The Indians decided to steal the military horses and mules at the post. They got the commanding officer drunk, and then the women entertained the soldiers with a dance while the men silently moved in and stole 240 horses and mules. In the investigation that followed, the Indian Bureau accused the soldiers of selling whiskey to the Indians and demoralizing their women.

The soldiers maintained control along the trail until the spring of 1864, when Indians renewed hostilities against the whites. On April 20, Indians robbed wagon trains near Fort Larned. More troops were requested by the post commander, but they were not immediately available. After a new commander, Captain J. W. Parmetar, Twelfth Kansas Volunteer Infantry, took over, he sent a dispatch to Washington warning that if more troops were not sent the Santa Fe Trail would be closed. Some troops were sent from Fort Riley, and then ten companies of Colorado volunteers came to protect the trail west of Larned. Still other soldiers were stationed at Council Grove and elsewhere. The troops stationed at Council Grove would escort caravans westward toward Fort Larned. The wagons would trickle in from the east, establish camps, and wait several days until at least a hundred wagons had gathered. The caravan would then leave on its westward journey escorted by the troops. Troops from Fort Larned would then pick up the wagons and escort them down the trail. At one point in the spring of 1864, Fort Larned was suddenly swamped by hundreds of loaded freight wagons heading west. Because supplies at the fort soon dwindled, the military ordered the wag-

This painting by the early Kansas artist Henry Worrall shows Fort Zarah about 1864 or 1865. (Courtesy Kansas State Historical Society)

ons to be formed up, four abreast, and leave under escort. More than a thousand wagons then moved westward over the Santa Fe Trail, a sight never again seen.

By July 1864, Indians raids were continuing not only on caravans but even on Fort Larned, where Kiowas took 172 animals owned by the military. The Indian threat was so serious that Major General Samuel R. Curtis took a battalion of about four hundred volunteer troops from Fort Riley to push the Indians off the Santa Fe Trail. The soldiers arrived at the Walnut Creek crossing near present-day Great Bend, Kansas, in late July, and Curtis established another military post, Fort Zarah. The new post was named for General Curtis's son, Major Zarah Curtis, who had been killed earlier in the war. It was built out of sandstone and consisted of a single building 120 feet long and 52 feet wide, with towers at two diagonally opposite corners. Before the post was completed, Curtis continued west to Fort Larned, where he divided his command into three detachments and went in pursuit of Indians. None were found, and the Santa Fe Trail now appeared to be safe. Curtis returned east as General Price and his Confederate forces were approaching Kansas City and Westport, and after he left, the Indian raids resumed. Soon General James Blunt marched west from Fort Larned and found on September 25, 1864, more than three thousand Cheyennes, Kiowas, and Arapahos camped about seventy-five miles away. Blunt and his troops pursued the Indians, killing nine and wounding many more. Two of Blunt's soldiers were killed and seven wounded. The military's actions plus the approach of winter saw a reduction of Indian raids in Kansas, but to the west in Colorado, hostilities increased. They all but stopped after Colonel John M. Chivington, Third Colorado Volunteer Cavalry, and his troops surprised a sleeping camp of Cheyenne and Arapaho Indians on Sand Creek, November 29, 1864. More than two hundred Indians, including many women and children, were killed. The Cheyenne soon retaliated and sacked Julesburg, Colorado, on two occasions and closed travel across the plains to Denver. The "Sand Creek Massacre," as it came to be called, drew government investigations. Chivington escaped punishment, but he was condemned by the investigating groups.

Anticipating renewed Indian hostilities in the spring of 1865, the military in 1864 began to plan to improve the security of caravans that would be traveling the Santa Fe Trail. Three new military posts were established: Camp Nichols, located northwest of Wheeless in the Oklahoma Panhandle; Fort Dodge, situated just east of present-day Dodge City, Kansas; and Fort Aubrey (first called Camp Wynkoop), west of present-day Syracuse, Kansas. The army then established a simple sched-

The Kansas artist Carl P. Bolmar drew this scene of Indians attacking a corralled caravan of freighters on the Santa Fe Trail. (Courtesy Kansas State Historical Society)

ule for caravan escorts whereby on the first and fifteenth day of each month, troops would escort caravans from Council Grove, Fort Larned, and other military posts on the trail. The military prohibited any wagon train from leaving between these dates, and made it mandatory to wait for the military escorts. Although simple, the plan reduced the number of Indian raids on the Santa Fe Trail.

Aside from the Confederate guerrilla raids on some caravans early in the Civil War at the eastern end of the trail, nearly all attacks to the west were conducted by Indians. In one exception, the Mexican trader Don Antonio Manuel Otero left Santa Fe for Missouri in late May 1864 following the mountain route. Near Raton Pass, his caravan was robbed by a group of men who claimed they were Texans. All of the caravan's animals and a large amount of money were carried off, but none of the men in the caravan was harmed. A Santa Fe newspaper, in reporting the robbery, observed: "The story of the robbers being Texans is discredited. They are supposed to be men who knew the value of the train and who put on the guise of Texans to escape detection and punishment. Gen'l Carleton has taken all the steps within his powers to have the guilty par-

Fort Dodge, Kansas, in 1867, about two years after the military post was established to improve security for traders and other travelers on the Santa Fe Trail.
(Courtesy Beeson Museum, Dodge City, Kansas)

ties arrested, and if they have made their way in the direction of Texas, there is scarcely a possibility of their being able to escape."[12]

In April 1865, the Civil War ended. William Darnell, a mule skinner driving a team of six mules hitched to a government wagon, was approaching Fort Zarah on the trail as word reached the post that Lee had surrendered. Darnell recalled that the soldiers decided to celebrate the good news. He wrote:

Dragging out their small brass cannons, they loaded them with a good charge of powder and crammed them to the muzzle with wet gunny sacks. As soon as the lead wagon of our train came within shouting distance of the outpost the gunners pointed their cannons up into the air and fired. The firing alone possibly would not have frightened our mules, but when those gunny sacks hurtled up into the air, were caught by the wind and opened up and then went floating off, they were enough to startle the dead. Not knowing we were going to be treated to a reception like this, we were not prepared for what followed. Before anything could be done to quiet them, the lead-wagon team ducked away at a right angle and went stampeding across the prairie, the driver finding he was unable to manage them and hopping off his mount to "save his bacon." The next shots following in quick succession caused the next team to follow suit. And no sooner had it left the beaten tracks than the next and the next, down the line, followed suit—each following as soon as the one in front had got out of the way. Seeing what was happening I decided to try preventing my team doing as the others had done.

Jumping off my horse, I made my way hurriedly to the leaders, and grasping them by the bits, firmly held back, and just as the wagon in front of me left the road and went ricocheting across the prairie like a toy vehicle dragged by a frightened team, I yelled a command to my wheelers to "back." This they did. I held back on my leaders, and with some little difficulty prevented my team from joining in the mad stampede.[13]

There is little question that the Santa Fe Trail carried the heaviest traffic in its history during the Civil War years. The *Weekly Western Journal of Commerce* published at Kansas City, Missouri, reported in its December 16, 1865, issue that Charles Withington, who had the toll bridge at 142 Mile Creek, counted 4,472 wagons crossing his bridge between May 20 and November 26 of that year. Twenty-one years later, in 1886, Alexander Caldwell spoke about the task of transporting 50 million pounds of freight by wagons. He said,

Usually trains were composed of twenty-six teams, each wagon loaded with about 6,000 pounds, and drawn by six yoke of cattle or four to six mules. Oxen were generally used, because the first cost was less than that of mules, and they could subsist on grass alone, while mules or horses required grain to keep them in serviceable condition. Another advantage in the use of cattle was, that when they became foot-sore or disabled, they could be left at stations to recruit for use in succeeding trains, or killed for beef, as the occasion might require. With each train of twenty-five wagons, there were three hundred head of cattle, twenty-five drivers, a captain, (or, as we then called him, a wagon-master), an assistant, and three extra men; in all, thirty men. To transport 50,000,000 pounds in this manner required 10,000 wagons, 12,000 men, and 120,000 head of stock. . . . Had they been formed into one continuous line, in the ordinary way of travel, we should have had a column more than 1,000 miles long. This was an expensive mode of transportation. The investment in a single train of twenty-six wagons was about $35,000, and the means of transportation necessary to carry 50,000,000 pounds would cost more than $5,000,000. The cost of subsisting and moving these caravans was enormous, and therefore large rates of transportation were paid. . . . As late as 1865 the Government paid $2.25 per 100 pounds per 100 miles.[14]

The U.S. Army quartermaster general reported in 1865 that his department had no statistics to show the extent of overland freighting in the number of wagons that were engaged, but he noted that the total cost of transporting stores to Fort Union, posts along the Santa Fe Trail, and New Mexico was $1,439,538. Wagon freighting was expensive, and this was one reason why the approaching iron horse was more than welcome.

FIFTEEN

◆◆◆

The Slow Death of the Trail, 1866-1880

*The gods conceal from men the happiness
of death, that they may endure life.*

—*Lucan*

THE LAST DAY of November 1859 was unusually warm at St. Joseph, Missouri. The afternoon sun was still high in the sky as the Hannibal and St. Joseph Railroad train from the east pulled into the station, the westernmost point in the nation then served by any railroad. The tall and lanky man in the stovepipe hat appeared tired as he stepped down from the coach. The man was Abraham Lincoln, heading to Kansas Territory on a visit, less than a year before he would be elected president of the United States. Lincoln's train had traveled over part of thirty thousand miles of track then crisscrossing much of the nation, with more than three thousand of those miles west of the Mississippi. Compared to the twenty-four miles of track that existed in 1830, the growth of railroads had been tremendous until the panic of 1857 slowed further expansion.

As railroads expanded in the East during the early 1830s, people realized that they were a more reliable means of transportation than steamboats and canal boats, and they were faster. Calls for a transcontinental rail line began in 1836, part of the sweeping nationalism or idea of manifest destiny then infecting the nation. The demand for such a line increased after the United States acquired California and Oregon in the late 1840s. Congress came to accept the idea by the early 1850s, and in

1853 it authorized the army to survey all feasible routes between the Mississippi and the Pacific Ocean. When the results of the surveys were released in 1855, four routes were recommended, two across the South and two across the North. But the sectional differences that led to the Civil War made it impossible for Congress to agree on one of the routes. Only after Northerners gained control of Congress in 1861 did agreement come. Congress then ignored the four recommended routes and selected a fifth, a central route, that ran west from Omaha, Nebraska Territory, to California. The Central Pacific Railroad of California began building eastward in 1862, while the Union Pacific Railroad did not begin to build west from Omaha, Nebraska Territory, until 1864.

A year earlier, the Union Pacific Railway, Eastern Division, began laying tracks west of the Missouri River in Kansas, opposite Kansas City, but construction was delayed and the line did not reach Lawrence, Kansas, forty miles away, until late in 1864. Lawrence, only a few miles north of the Santa Fe Trail, rapidly became the trail's eastern terminal. Forwarding and commission houses from Kansas City established offices in Lawrence, where freighters and Santa Fe traders saved forty miles of slow wagon travel by picking up their goods shipped by rail from the Missouri River. On September 18, 1865, the *Rocky Mountain News* at Denver reported that a correspondent of the *New York Tribune,* who had crossed the plains to Denver from Kansas City, had seen "at least two thousand wagons" between Lawrence and Junction City, Kansas, near Fort Riley. That same year the rails reached Topeka, twenty miles west of Lawrence, and the trail's eastern terminal shifted to Topeka. This pattern of a shifting railhead and trailhead would continue as the railroad built westward along the Kansas River valley.

Traffic on the Santa Fe Trail about fifty miles to the south was heavy. East of Council Grove, 2,692 men, 1,183 wagons, 736 horses, 2,904 mules, 15,855 oxen, and 56 carriages crossed the bridge at 142 Mile Creek between May 12 and July 12, 1865. The following year Colonel J. F. Meline on a western tour estimated that between 5,000 and 6,000 wagons would traverse the trail. "The trains are remarkable . . . each wagon team consisting of ten yokes of fine oxen, selected and arranged not only for drawing but for pictorial effect, in sets of twenty, either all black, all white, all spotted or otherwise marked uniformly."[1]

When the railroad reached Junction City in mid-1866, the forwarding and commission houses followed. The weekly *Junction City Union,* August 4, 1866, published the route that could be followed by wagons heading westward from there over what became known as the Smoky Hill route to Santa Fe. The route had been used in 1859 by gold-seekers

A late-nineteenth-century view of Santa Fe, New Mexico. (Author's Collection)

This wagon train, presumably from the Santa Fe Trail, is being unloaded on San Francisco Street on the south side of the Plaza in Santa Fe. Nicholas Brown made this photo about 1867 or '68. (Courtesy Museum of New Mexico, negative no. 70437)

heading for far western Kansas Territory (now Colorado). It was far more direct than the Santa Fe Trail since it followed a course due west of Kansas City, Missouri, along the Kansas River to near Fort Riley, where the Smoky Hill River flowed into the Kansas. From there it followed the Smoky Hill west to near the Colorado border. It was over this route that stagecoaches belonging to the Leavenworth and Pike's Peak Express Company carried passengers from the Missouri River west to Denver and back. When the line's first coaches left Leavenworth, Kansas, on April 18, 1859, Horace Greeley, editor of the *New York Tribune*, was a passenger going west to inspect the goldfields. In his letters sent east and published in his paper, Greeley makes no reference to seeing freight wagons, which did not begin to use the route until after the Union Pacific Railway, Eastern Division, pushed west to Junction City, Kansas.

How much freight was transported west over this route from Junction City is not known, nor have any records been located to indicate the division between trading goods bound for Santa Fe and government stores bound for military posts to the west. Both were apparently significant, but Junction City was short-lived as a terminal for wagon freighting. The

This drawing by Thomson Willing shows the Palace of the Governors in Santa Fe as it looked late in the nineteenth century. The drawing appeared in Henry Inman's The Old Santa Fe Trail *(1897).* (Author's Collection)

This illustration from Harper's New Monthly Magazine, April 1880, *shows the construction in Santa Fe during the late 1860s of Saint Francis Cathedral around the existing La Parroquia, an early adobe church. This was the first Roman Catholic cathedral to be built between Durango, Mexico, and St. Louis, Missouri.* (Author's Collection)

following year the Union Pacific, Eastern Division, reached the town of Salina and then Fort Ellsworth, thirty-four miles to the west. In 1868 the line reached Hays City. Colorado newspaper editors carefully scanned exchange papers from Kansas advising their readers of the railroad's westward progress toward Denver. A Central City paper, the *Daily Colorado Herald,* May 25, 1868, reprinted an item from the weekly *Hays City Advance* that reported that five miles along the creek, prairie schooners were packed as close as steamers at a Mississippi levee. W. E. Webb of Topeka visited Hays City and later wrote that since it was then the eastern terminus "for the great Santa Fe trade, the town was crowded with Mexicans and speculators. Large warehouses along the track were stored with wool awaiting shipment east, and with merchandise to be taken back with the returning wagons [to Santa Fe]."[2]

As the Union Pacific Railway, Eastern Division, pushed westward toward Colorado, the *Daily Colorado Tribune* at Denver reported on June 27, 1867, that the business of freighting was changing: "Consequently those forty or fifty wagon trains are things of the past, the freighting business is now being done by mule or horse train instead of oxen." Shorter and quicker trips meant merchants had a longer season to receive goods, and on September 5, 1867, the same newspaper observed that merchants no longer had to buy six months' or a year's supply of goods at one time.

After Hays City, Kansas, the tiny settlement of Coyote became the western terminal of the railroad for a few months but then disappeared as track was laid to Monument, another town born with the arrival of the railhead. By July 1868, the tracks had reached a point only forty-one miles from the Colorado border and about six miles from Fort Wallace, a military post first called Camp Pond Creek when it was established in 1865. The laying of tracks westward came to a stop because the railroad had used up its government subsidies, and where it stopped the town of Phil Sheridan boomed almost overnight. Named for the famous Civil War general, Sheridan, as the town was called, had two hundred residents within two weeks and about sixty-five businesses. Like the earlier terminals, Sheridan became a major transfer point for freight and passengers, but because everyone knew the railroad was stalled, more permanent buildings were constructed, some by the Union Pacific Railway, Eastern Division. The railroad brought passengers, who would then transfer to stagecoaches for a ride of thirty or more hours to Denver or Pueblo, or of three days to Santa Fe. When freight arrived by rail, it was either stored temporarily in Sheridan or transferred to ox-drawn wagons for the much slower journey to Denver or Pueblo or Santa Fe. Wagons coming east from these points often carried wool, buffalo hides, ore, and lumber that was either sold, stored, or transferred to rail cars and taken to eastern markets. Much of the lumber brought to Sheridan from Colorado was sold in Sheridan, where a thousand board feet of pine cost a hundred dollars.

Other goods were just as expensive at Sheridan. A reporter for the *Junction City Union* who visited Sheridan in late July 1868 reported that a hundred pounds of winter-wheat flour was selling for $14, a bushel of corn brought $2.50, butter was 75 cents per pounds, and eggs were 60 cents per dozen. Milk cost 25 cents a quart, while whiskey was 24 cents per drink. At the same time, ordinary laborers were being paid only $2.50 a day. Most of the larger business houses in Sheridan were built of wood, including a few hotels and several buildings belonging to the railroad. There were also tents, crude shacks, and even houses made of sod cut from the nearby prairie. A flat-shared plow cut the sod two inches thick and about two feet in length. The bricks were then piled up into walls that were two to three feet thick. Timbers were laid across the top, and sod was placed on the timbers to form a roof. Such structures were cool in the summer and warm in the winter, unlike the many tents that dotted the Sheridan town site.

During 1868, the wagon master who claimed the record—eleven and a half days—for taking freight from Sheridan to Denver, a distance of 230 miles, said he used eighteen teams of ten to twelve yoke of oxen drawing two wagons in tandem loaded with twelve thousand pounds of freight. Aside from himself, his crew consisted of an assistant, eighteen drivers, a day herder, and a night herder. His cook drove the lead wagon and received extra pay for doing so.[3]

In its day Sheridan was one of the toughest and wildest towns in the West. Nathan Meeker, a reporter for the *New York Tribune*, visited the town and wrote:

> Sheridan is at present the most remarkable place in America, or in the world . . . where legitimate business centers, and where the most reckless of men and women gather, in order that in the absence of law and in the unprotected state in which property necessarily is placed, they may reap a harvest of plunder. It will remain to a great extent unchanged until the road advances, when they will move on. . . .
>
> Sheridan is composed of two half streets, some 300 feet apart, the railroad track being in the center. There are large commercial houses engaged in the Santa Fe trade. . . . Some of the stores are as much as 150 feet long, and wide in proportion, and I saw one where tons of Mexican wool were stored waiting shipment. . . . Beside these houses there are a few hotels and several buildings belonging to the railroad, and the rest are saloons and gambling establishments, more than 50 in number, all open and apparently doing good business. In almost every one are women. Fiddles and accordions are playing, glasses jingling, and there are billiard and roulette tables and other gambling devices. The men are able-bodied and strong; few are more than 35; the majority are less than 30 years old. . . . Of course they are well armed and ready at any moment for attack or defense; but I saw none who were either offensive or aggressive, although I have every reason to believe that they would commit murder on what we would call the slightest provocation, for they have been so audacious and bold that men of property have been obliged to resolve themselves into a Vigilance Committee and hang fifteen or twenty. Back of the town is a small graveyard, where they have been buried, and only a few days

Kit Carson, for whom Kit Carson, Colorado, is named, made several trips over the Santa Fe Trail, the first in 1826. Carson was first a mountain man, then a hunter at Bent's Fort, a scout, and a guide for the explorer John C. Frémont's three expeditions into the West. Carson ranched near Taos, New Mexico, starting in 1849, served as an Indian agent during the late 1850s, and as a Union officer during the Civil War. (Courtesy Kansas State Historical Society)

before I arrived one of them was hanged to the trestlework a little out of town. For some time past the engineer has been in the habit of moving the morning train slowly over this spot, in order that the passengers might have a chance to see if any one was hanged by the neck. . . . Among the aggressive acts of these men it is related that at a hotel one asked a gentleman sitting opposite for the butter, and as he was not heard, he presented a small pocket pistol at the head of the gentleman, and, with his finger on the trigger, said, "Pass the butter."[4]

Even before Meeker visited Sheridan, the beginning of the end for the town had occurred. To raise money to complete the line to Denver, Congress let the Union Pacific's officials mortgage the road and its land between Sheridan and Denver at $32,000 a mile. With this money, the railroad, which changed its name to the Kansas Pacific on March 3, 1869, resumed construction westward, but Sheridan remained the line's western terminal until the tracks crossed into Colorado and reached Kit Carson in March 1870. Nearly all of Sheridan then moved west to Kit Carson, named for the trailblazer who had died two years earlier. Buildings—including shacks—were dismantled, tents were taken down, and just about everything was shipped west over the line to Kit Carson. By early July 1870, only about eighty people remained in Sheridan, and after its post office closed early the following year, what remained was a

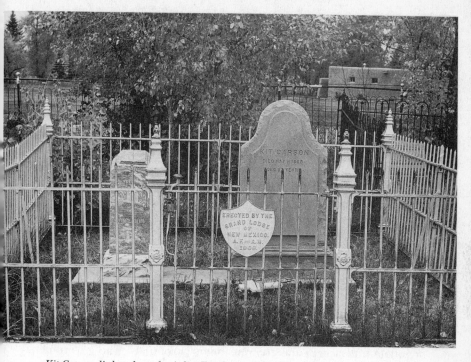

Kit Carson died and was buried at Fort Lyon, Colorado, on May 23, 1868, at age fifty-nine. Later his remains were removed and reburied at Taos, New Mexico, where this photo was taken. Carson's tombstone is on the right. (Author's Collection)

ghost town. Today nothing remains except a few depressions in a pasture in Logan County, Kansas.

SOON AFTER the Union Pacific Railway, Eastern Division, pushed west of Junction City, the railroad and caravans began to be plagued by occasional Indian raids, which increased as the road pushed farther west. In March 1867, General W. S. Hancock left Fort Leavenworth with artillery and six companies of infantry. At Fort Riley, General George Custer joined him with four companies of the Seventh Cavalry and one company of the Thirty-seventh Infantry. From Fort Riley this large body of troops marched ninety miles up the Smoky Hill River to Fort Harker, where two more troops of cavalry joined the group and marched west to Fort Larned, seventy miles to the southwest on the Santa Fe Trail. The large body of soldiers arrived there on April 7. General Hancock had selected Fort Larned because many Cheyennes and Sioux were camped on the Pawnee Fork about thirty miles away. When Hancock asked the Indians to come to Fort Larned to make a treaty, they refused, so he decided to go to the Indians.

Approaching their camp he was met by Indian emissaries, including Roman Nose, who carried a white flag and said he wanted peace. Hancock and his men then made camp within half a mile of the three hundred lodges or so in the Indians' villages. Soon the chiefs visited Hancock and informed him that the soldiers had frightened the Indian women and children and that they had fled. That night the chiefs also fled, and Hancock sent General Custer and some cavalry in pursuit, but the Indians were not found. They had crossed the Smoky Hill River, destroyed several stage stations, and murdered several whites. Troopers went in pursuit but failed to find them.

Meantime, in the spring of 1867, a peace commission came west to make peace with the Indians. While the military had little faith in peace treaties, the soldiers had no choice but to go along, and a treaty conference was held on Medicine Lodge Creek near present-day Medicine Lodge in southern Kansas. More than five thousand Comanches, Kiowas, Arapahos, and Cheyennes attended and appeared willing to negotiate and accept the commissioners' proposals. The government abandoned the one-reservation concept and assigned each tribe its own reservation in what is now western Oklahoma, forbidding them to occupy territory outside their own reservations. The Indians were directed to move immediately to the new reservations, where, whether they wanted them or not, there would be schools and resident farmers to teach them the white man's agricultural and cultural practices.

Before the Indians left, the commissioners plied them with gifts, including food, clothing, and ammunition for their weapons. As one historian observed, "The piles of goods were enormous. Even the Indians were astounded at the liberality—prodigality—of the Great Father. They could not carry away all that was given them; much was left lying on the prairies to rot. And when the food and clothing had been disposed of, the greatest gift of all was brought out—it was the ammunition. The Indians had used up their entire supply along the frontier killing settlers and ranchmen and railroad workmen, and it was good of the Great Father to load them up for another campaign. The Indians were not to be blamed for believing the government liked to have them drench the border in blood; to them it was evident that the fiercer the attacks on the settlements, the greater would be their compensation."[5]

When they left with their gifts, the commissioners undoubtedly thought the Indians were going to their new reservations to the south, but most of the warriors refused to abandon their hunting grounds and the only way of life they knew, and soon resumed their attacks on the whites pushing into the Saline and Solomon River valleys. In November 1867, General Phil Sheridan decided to put an end to the Indians' usual pattern of having war in the summer and peace in the winter. He and his troops converged from three different directions on what is now northwest Oklahoma. Scouts soon found a large Indian village, and at dawn on November 27, 1868, Brevet Major General George Armstrong Custer led the Seventh Cavalry in an attack on the village, which was actually on the territory of the tribe's reservation near modern Cheyenne, Oklahoma. Within ten minutes he had captured the village, killed more than a hundred Indians, and slaughtered about eight hundred of their horses. One of the warriors killed was Black Kettle, a peaceful chief. It took Sheridan's troops nearly another year to stop the Indians permanently. The end came in the battle of Summit Springs, Colorado, July 11, 1869, when Tall Bull, chief of the Dog Soldiers, a Cheyenne warrior society, was killed in an attack on his village.

Charles E. Campbell, an army officer in western Kansas between 1869 and 1872 who worked in Indian service with the Kiowa, Comanche, Wichita, Arapaho, and Cheyenne agencies, wrote in 1928: "The origin of nearly every war with Indians can be traced to some offense on the part of the white man. Stock belonging to the Indians is stolen by renegade whites, followed by swift pursuit and the killing of a few of the depredators. The affair is generally magnified into an unwarranted attack by the Indians, followed by calling out the military power to pursue and punish the offenders. Often the vengeance of the Indians has been visited on innocent whites who happened to be in the vicinity of the original depredation, as the Indians never sought to find the actual guilty parties, but classing all white men as equally responsible, killed without discrimination. This is the testimony of all the leading Indian fighters from the earliest times and practically has no exception."[6]

In mid-May 1869, the Central Pacific and Union Pacific linked up at Promontory near present-day Ogden, Utah, but the completed transcontinental line had little affect on the Santa Fe Trail far to the south. Traffic along the western portion of the trail remained heavy. Exactly how many men, wagons, oxen, and mules carried goods from the

This 1868 photo looks east on San Francisco Street in Santa Fe. The Plaza is to the left. The building right of center was the Spiegelberg Brothers store. The ox-drawn freight wagons probably were unloaded just before the photo was taken. (Courtesy Museum of New Mexico, negative no. 11329)

end of the railroad to Santa Fe and other points in the West during the late 1860s is not known, but it appears the majority was military stores for Fort Union and other posts along the trail in Kansas, Colorado, New Mexico, and beyond. By then some freighters had adopted the practice of hooking two or more wagons in tandem, like the wagon master in 1868 who claimed a record in traveling from Sheridan to Denver. This required modifications to the wagon. The overhangs at the front and rear of these wagons were eliminated, and the tongue of the wagon that was to be towed was shortened so that it could be attached to the wagon in front. If three wagons were to be hitched together, they were not uniformly loaded. The lead and second or swing wagon might each carry 6,500 pounds, but the third or trail wagon only carried about 4,500 pounds. One teamster, P. G. Scott, wrote in his diary during 1870 at Trinidad, Colorado, that "Trains [were] passing and repassing every year. Oxen and mules en route to Fort Union. Most were military personnel, the hardest looking set of soldiers I ever saw, dirty and ragged, their toes sticking through their boots."[7]

Five years after the Union Pacific Railway, Eastern Division, began building westward across Kansas, another line was starting across Kansas. The Atchison, Topeka and Santa Fe Railroad, first chartered in 1859, began its construction in 1868, laying track from Topeka south to Emporia, reaching there in 1870. It then pushed westward and three years later reached Granada, Colorado, just west of the Kansas border. The line seemed to be in a position to capture the Santa Fe trade that until then had been dominated by the Kansas Pacific, formerly the Union Pacific Railway, Eastern Division. But the Kansas Pacific quickly built a branch line to Las Animas, located on the Arkansas River, about fifty miles west of Granada. Las Animas became a boomtown and the eastern terminus for the Santa Fe trade. Within days of the railroad's arrival, several wooden buildings were constructed, including two general stores, three restaurants, two hotels, several saloons, a number of frame houses, and even two lumber yards whose goods were largely freighted from the

Steamboat traffic on the Mississippi River at St. Louis was heavy when this illustration was made in the late 1870s. By this time the railroad had crossed Missouri and was pushing across Kansas, transporting much of the Santa Fe–bound merchandise to the end of the line. There wagons met the trains and transported the goods the rest of the way to New Mexico. This illustration appeared in Switzler's Illustrated History of Missouri, *published in St. Louis in 1881.* (Author's Collection)

About five months after the railroad reached Santa Fe in 1880, these men posed with a wagon train in camp near the old statehouse building in Santa Fe. The photographer, Ben Wittick, probably sensed that the days of long caravans of freight wagons on the Santa Fe Trail were over. (Courtesy School of American Research Collections in the Museum of New Mexico, negative no. 15817)

Once the railroad arrived, freighting goods over the Santa Fe Trail faded. The only need for freight wagons was to carry goods from the railroad terminal to local businesses. The ox-drawn wagon in this 1876 photo was used for local hauling in Topeka, Kansas. (Courtesy Kansas State Historical Society)

This view of the city of Chihuahua, Mexico, was made by William Henry Jackson about 1883 from the Casa de Moneda. (Courtesy Museum of New Mexico, negative no. 74699)

Rocky Mountains to the west. Two forwarding houses, Prowers and Hough and Kihlberg and Bartels, were established. But because Las Animas was close to the range of the hostile Kiowas and Comanches, townspeople kept their weapons handy.

By this time the pattern of wagon-freighting in the region was changing. Because the distances to be covered were not as long, the initial investment needed to become a freighter was smaller. More and more men entered the business of hauling freight from rail terminals to places not served by the railroads. For instance, in 1874, a newcomer to freighting, Pat Shanley, carried 38,000 pounds of freight including 32,000 pounds of mining machinery from Las Animas, Colorado, to Silver City, New Mexico, in less than two months.[8]

The Kansas Pacific at Las Animas and the Atchison, Topeka and Santa Fe at Granada competed for the Santa Fe trade until 1875, when both lines pushed farther west to La Junta, Colorado. There the Kansas Pacific moved toward Denver. The Atchison, Topeka and Santa Fe pushed its tracks into Pueblo in early 1876, connecting with the Denver

These wagons and carts are parked on Guadalupe Street in the city of Chihuahua, Mexico, in this 1883 photograph taken by William Henry Jackson. Traders continued to take wagon trains loaded with merchandise from New Mexico to Chihuahua after the railroad arrived in Santa Fe. (Courtesy Museum of New Mexico, negative no. 54088)

and Rio Grande line that ran south from Denver to El Moro near Trinidad, Colorado, at the foot of Raton Pass. In 1879, however, the Santa Fe laid its own controversial line from Pueblo to Trinidad and won control of Raton Pass by 1880, when its terminal was moved to Otero and then to Las Vegas, New Mexico, in early July 1879. As track was laid south from Las Vegas, it was evident that the main line could not go through Santa Fe because of the terrain. So after crossing Glorieta Pass, instead of swinging northwest to Santa Fe, plans called for the road to follow the easiest terrain and to swing south toward Albuquerque. Concerned townspeople in Santa Fe voted to pay for an eighteen-mile spur line to Santa Fe from Lamy, a stop on the main line named for Archbishop Jean-Baptiste Lamy. Early in February 1880 the first engine puffed along the spur line south of the Santa Fe River, which ended about a mile south of the Plaza. Its arrival fulfilled the railroad's name—the Atchison, Topeka and Santa Fe. The headline in Santa Fe's *New Mexican* read: THE OLD SANTA FE TRAIL PASSES INTO OBLIVION. The glory days of the trail as a highway for freight-hauling had come to an end.

SIXTEEN

❖❖❖

The Legacy of the Trail, 1880-2000

When a land forgets its legends, sees but falsehoods in its past,
When a nation views its sires in the light of fools and liars—
'Tis a sign of its decline, and its glories cannot last.

—*J. Fairfax-Blakesborough*

THE RAILROAD'S ARRIVAL in Santa Fe in 1880 marked the end of the grand old highway and symbolically marked the beginning of an era in which steam engines shrank time and distance in the West. By 1890 only portions of the old trail were used for local traffic along its route. Much of the rest was overgrown and rapidly fading from the nation's memory until the late 1890s, when Henry Inman, a Kansas writer, took up his pen and wrote the first book devoted entirely to the Santa Fe Trail since Josiah Gregg's *Commerce of the Prairies* was published more than half a century earlier.

Inman, a New York City native, served as a captain in the Union Army during the Civil War and then joined the regular army and was ordered west to Kansas, where he served as quartermaster at Fort Harker during the late 1860s. Careless with paperwork, he was dismissed from military service during the mid-1870s. He remained in Kansas, entered the newspaper business, and soon established the weekly *Larned (Kansas) Enterprise* in 1878. There, at the age of forty-one, he began to write of the Old West he had known. His first book, *Stories of the Old Santa Fe Trail*, was printed in Kansas City, Missouri, in 1881, a year after the need for the Santa Fe Trail ended. Inman's book contained fifteen adventure stories

The ruts of the Santa Fe Trail are still visible in this 1938 photo made by S. L. Schoff in Cimarron County, Oklahoma, over the Cimarron or dry route of the trail. (Courtesy Western History Collections, University of Oklahoma Libraries)

tied to the trail and was well received in Kansas. It went into a second printing and a paperback edition that was hawked by news butchers in railroad stations and on trains crossing the state. But while the book attracted some attention as popular reading, it did not receive the national attention of Inman's *The Old Santa Fe Trail: The Story of a Great Highway,* published in New York seventeen years later, in 1897. The book was soon reprinted by Crane and Company, a Kansas publishing house in Topeka that, to capitalize on the popularity of the work, also brought out Inman's *Tales of the Trail: Short Stories of Western Life* (1898), which contained some of the stories about the trail taken from his 1881 book plus some new ones. This book was popular, too, and also went through several printings. Inman's books contain some errors in fact, but they were written with passion and for a popular audience, capitalizing on the nostalgia many people were then feeling for the old trail. They created new interest in the Santa Fe Trail almost twenty years after its glory years ended.

Inman's books caught the fancy of the Kansas socialite Fannie Geiger Thompson, and she suggested at a 1902 state conference of the Daugh-

Henry Inman (1837–1899), soldier turned writer. His 1897 book The Old Santa Fe Trail, the Story of a Great Highway, *caused renewed interest in the history of the old trail.* (Author's Collection)

ters of the American Revolution (D.A.R.) that the Old Santa Fe Trail should be marked before it became obliterated. Other women agreed, and with the help of the Kansas State Historical Society, a committee of Kansas D.A.R. members obtained old maps of the trail and paid Roy Marsh $7.50 to map the trail across Kansas. Committee members also gained the cooperation of club women in towns along the trail. A thousand dollars was obtained from the Kansas legislature in 1905 to mark the trail between Kansas City, Missouri, and the Colorado line. By then other D.A.R. chapters in Colorado, New Mexico, and Missouri were joining in the task of marking the trail. In late 1907 the Kansas State Historical Society reported that fifty-nine markers had been erected by the state, six by local D.A.R. chapters, and thirty by the Kansas D.A.R. A total of ninety-five stone markers were placed along the route of the old trail, and most can still be seen in Kansas today. Other markers include twenty-seven erected along the mountain and Cimarron routes and one at the end of the trail on the southeast corner of the Plaza in Santa Fe.[1]

WHEN THE ATCHISON, Topeka and Santa Fe Railroad reached Santa Fe early in 1880, the town's six thousand residents expected an economic boom. A real-estate promoter arrived and was not impressed with the old

This marker, erected by the Daughters of the American Revolution and the Territory of New Mexico in 1910, stands near the southeast corner of the Plaza in Santa Fe, marking the end of the Santa Fe Trail. (Author's Collection)

Plaza in the center of town. He decided to promote a new city center near the new railroad depot, which was located about a mile south of the Plaza, but Santa Fe businessmen did not support the idea. Since the railroad could now deliver things that wagons did not carry and do so more quickly and cheaply, many businessmen ordered building materials from the East to build new buildings or remodel old ones on or near the Plaza. The materials delivered by train included "inexpensive cast-iron columns and pressed-metal cornices and window hoods, loosely patterned after Renaissance palazzi." Many of Santa Fe's commercial buildings took on the Italianate style.[2]

Other entrepreneurs who arrived in Santa Fe found property values and rents too high in and around the Plaza and moved on to Albu-

Santa Fe about 1886. (Courtesy Western History Collection, University of Oklahoma Libraries)

querque or other railroad towns. The anticipated boom from the railroad's arrival did not occur, and the economy began to stagnate. In 1887, seven years after the Santa Fe Railroad arrived, a second boom failed to materialize after the Denver and Rio Grande Railroad reached Santa Fe from the north. In fact, Santa Fe's population had declined by more than four hundred people in ten years when the 1890 census figures were released. City leaders decided to incorporate Santa Fe in hopes of making the town more attractive to business while at the same time relying on the fact that Santa Fe was the territorial capital. When there was talk across New Mexico of moving the territorial capital to Albuquerque, business leaders in Santa Fe feared the worst. They relaxed when the U.S. Congress made Santa Fe the permanent capital in 1887, and three years later a new capitol building was constructed along with new commercial buildings, schools, a county courthouse, and other structures. Still, the town's economy did not boom, and the town's leaders continued to try to make Santa Fe look like any other American town of the same size.

This illustration of San Francisco Street in Santa Fe appeared in Harper's New Monthly Magazine *in April 1880, soon after the Santa Fe Railroad reached the town.* (Author's Collection)

This 1885 view of Santa Fe looks east on San Francisco Street from the Plaza (left). (Courtesy Western History Collections, University of Oklahoma Libraries)

This photo made by the author during the 1970s shows the adobe house in Santa Fe reputed to be the oldest structure still standing in the United States. (Author's Collection)

Even though the faces of many commercial buildings were changed by 1900, Santa Fe still retained much of its earlier charm. Soon after 1900, a Massachusetts native, Clifton Johnson, went west to Santa Fe because it is the oldest community in America next to St. Augustine, Florida. Of his visit, Johnson later wrote that Santa Fe

> has much the character of a big lazy village. Its people like to loiter on the shadowy, green-turfed Plaza and on the corridor-like sidewalks, across which the older buildings have extended pillared porticos. There has apparently never been any regular plan in the building of the city, and the streets wind, and zigzag, and jerk around corners in a most unexpected fashion. As a somewhat garrulous visitor whom I fell in with remarked: "You walk along and think you are going somewhere only to find you are going somewhere else. Oh, it's jiggety job; but, by gracious! I like it."

The speaker was a gray old man, who had been a captain in the

Gold's Old Curiosity Shop on "Burro Alley" in Santa Fe late in the nineteenth century. (Courtesy Kansas State Historical Society)

A wood peddler making his rounds in Santa Fe, as shown in an 1880 illustration from Harper's New Monthly Magazine. (Author's Collection)

Civil War. Santa Fe's reputation as a health resort had drawn him thither, and he was delighted with its climate, its quaintness and the friendliness of its inhabitants. He had a cheerful greeting for everyone we met. Often he paused to shake hands with this one or that—to sympathize with a sick man, to pat a child on the head, to discuss history and religion with some priest.

"You couldn't use street cars here," the old man said in commenting on the character of the town, "unless they were made on an angle and a circle, because the streets are so crooked. Why, there isn't a square corner in the city. You go along one street, and you run right up ag'in' a house. You try another and it takes you into a dooryard; and I was in one that ended like a wedge so I just had to turn around and come back.

"See those little burros with the loads of wood on their backs," said the captain pointing down the street with his cane. "The wood is all cut up ready for the stove, and the driver in charge peddles it from house to house. Each burro carries about two wheelbarrow loads, and they've come from five to twenty miles. A man or boy follows behind and tickles them up with a switch—any old way to get there."[3]

As many residents of Santa Fe looked for ways to rejuvenate the local economy, someone hit upon the idea of promoting the city with its dry mountain air as a tuberculosis health resort. Some people came for their health, but more came as tourists, not to see the progressive little American town as it was portrayed by Santa Fe's business leaders and the Territorial Bureau of Immigration, but to capture its image of rich history and romance that had been portrayed by writers in the East and depicted in engraved illustrations published in *Harper's Weekly* and elsewhere. That image included Indians and pueblos near Santa Fe. To accommodate the influx of tourists, local photographers offered stereograph photos and postcards of Indians and pueblos, which were sold through curio dealers in Santa Fe. Those dealers also tried to satisfy the wants of tourists with Indian and Mexican crafts. The residents of Santa Fe, however, including some old-timers who had traveled the Santa Fe Trail, were reluctant to accept tourism. Many residents probably saw little romance in their town and may have wondered why anyone would want to visit.

By then the Santa Fe Railroad was recognizing the value of its railcars running through Indian country. Railroad officials found that the Indians who lived near the railroad were an attraction for passengers, who stopped at stations where Harvey House restaurants provided appetizing

A late-nineteenth-century view of part of Santa Fe and the mountains east of town.
(Courtesy Western History Collections, University of Oklahoma Libraries)

ESTABLISHED IN 1825.

THE **MURPHY WAGON,**

No. 1401 BROADWAY,

St. Louis, *July 21, 1887*

J. MURPHY & SONS,

SOLD TO

Mr M. H. Kamp

One 3 inch wagon Broke
seat complete $ 42.00

Rec'd Payment

J. Murphy & Sons

J. Murphy & Sons in St. Louis, which began making freight wagons in 1825 and produced the large Murphy wagon to carry freight over the trail, did not die after wagons ceased to travel the Santa Fe Trail in 1880. The firm continued to prosper by turning its attention to manufacturing wagons designed for farm and agricultural use, like the one pictured on this 1887 receipt. (Courtesy Smithsonian Institution, Washington, D.C.)

meals in a comfortable setting and an opportunity to see the Indians. Fred Harvey, who came to America from England in 1850, opened his first restaurant in Topeka, Kansas, in 1876, and soon a relationship developed between Harvey and the Santa Fe Railroad. More Harvey Houses were built along the line, and Harvey hired young, single women from the Middle West and the East to serve as waitresses. These "Harvey girls," as they were called, gave passengers a sense that the restaurants were safe and clean, and to add a touch of adventure for the tourists, the restaurant decor included images of Indians. By the turn of the century there were about twenty-six Harvey House restaurants located at depots and hotels along the Santa Fe line and twenty more aboard railroad dining cars.

After a young man named Herman Schweizer became manager of the Harvey House at Coolidge, Arizona, he began buying blankets, jewelry, and other items from the Navajo people and selling them to travelers. The idea caught on, and the Harvey House firm added an Indian Department and began offering Indian items for sale. But in Santa Fe, many residents still did not recognize the value of their town's history and traditions in attracting tourists. They were reluctant to accept the idea that tourism might be the answer to their economic woes.[4]

One man who knew the value of local history and traditions was Charles Fletcher Lummis, a Massachusetts native educated at Harvard (where one of his classmates was Theodore Roosevelt). After graduation, Lummis worked for a newspaper in Chillicothe, Ohio, and pursued his interests in hunting, fishing, archaeology, photography, and poetry. He produced a tiny book of poetry that was printed on birch bark. In 1884, Lummis struck a deal with Colonel Harrison Gray Otis of the *Los Angeles Times*. Lummis would walk to California and write a weekly report for the *Times*, for which he would be paid five dollars per letter and be guaranteed a job at the paper once he reached Los Angeles. As he walked west he wrote of his experiences and what he saw, and when he reached New Mexico he was fascinated with the beauty of the region. Lummis walked 3,507 miles in 163 days, and upon his arrival in Los Angeles he was given his promised job. Two years later he was sent to Fort Bowie, Arizona Territory, to cover the Apache wars. After three months he returned to Los Angeles, where he suffered a stroke. To recuperate, he returned to New Mexico and spent the next five years living in the Indian pueblo at Isleta, along the Rio Grande, where he learned much of the language and customs of the people. It was there he met Adolph Bandelier and made many trips with him throughout the Southwest. During this time he wrote three books: *A New Mexico David and*

Wagon ruts on the Santa Fe Trail near Fort Union, New Mexico, in 1905. Ruts are still visible in the Fort Union area. (Courtesy Museum of New Mexico, negative no. 12845)

Other Stories and Sketches of the Southwest (1891), *A Tramp Across the Continent* (1892), and *The Land of Poco Tiempo* (1893).

In 1894, Lummis left Isleta Pueblo and returned to Los Angeles, where, to make a living, he sold prints of photographs taken on his trips with Bandelier. The same year Lummis became editor of the *Land of Sunshine*, a 24-page tourist-oriented magazine that was renamed *Old West* in 1902. The magazine studied and promoted life in the Southwest, a name that he coined for the region. Before he returned to California, Lummis had seen how the Santa Fe Railroad was capitalizing on the history and rich Indian culture of the Southwest, and it apparently confirmed his belief that art could also shape and sustain emerging social currents and institutions while providing moral uplift. Having traveled, observed, and experienced life in the Southwest, especially New Mexico, Lummis wanted to make the rest of the nation as proud of the region as he was. He sought the help of western writers and painters to produce art, poetry, history, and ethnography for boosterism, and published their works in his magazine.

The *Land of Sunshine* gained much popularity not only in California but also in the East, where Lummis's former classmate, President Theodore Roosevelt, claimed it was the only magazine he had time to read. Roosevelt asked Lummis for advice on Indians, and Lummis helped Roosevelt produce a background paper that was used in the formation of the government's Indian policy. Lummis also wrote other books on the history and folklore of New Mexico, including *Spanish Pioneers* (1893), *Pueblo Indian Folk-Stories* (1894), *Delight Makers* (1890), *The King of the Broncos and Other Stories of New Mexico* (1897), and nearly a dozen more books dealing with the culture and way of life in the Indian-Spanish Southwest.[5]

A year after Lummis took over as editor of *The Land of Sunshine*, the Santa Fe Railroad established an advertising department in its Chicago office to come up with ways to increase ridership, and Lummis helped the railroad develop a plan to attract tourists to the Southwest, especially to New Mexico. Lummis's plan, which promoted local history and the Indian cultures of the Southwest, was adopted by boosters in New Mexico who began to rework its image. The first and most noticeable change occurred at the Louisiana Purchase Centennial Exposition, which began April 30, 1904, in St. Louis, where the New Mexico building was constructed in a semblance of the California mission style. There was also a Pueblo village of wood frame and plaster that was staffed by Pueblo Indians. These exhibits were well received, and convinced many leaders in Santa Fe that they should take another look at their town's local history and traditions.

As a result, the early twentieth century saw more tourists visit Santa Fe, some planning to visit the Museum of New Mexico, which was founded in 1909. The museum soon helped to promote Santa Fe through the excavation of Anasazi ruins and the preservation of existing Pueblo villages. Between 1909 and 1912, the Palace of the Governors on the Plaza was restored, with its exterior reflecting Spanish architecture and a more informal style based on the missions of New Mexico and its pueblos. More photographs were taken of historic sites, especially by the Colorado native Jesse Nusbaum, who became fascinated by Santa Fe and New Mexico. Many of his photos appeared in magazines, on postcards, in railroad travel brochures, and in *Palacio,* a new publication of the museum. A museum official sent a packet of Nusbaum's photos to the advertising office at the Santa Fe Railroad in Chicago with a letter advising that "it seems to be the general opinion among the Chamber of Commerce [in Santa Fe] that we can well dispense with views of ordinary business blocks and residences which might be found anywhere in order to emphasize the quaintness of old doors ways, interiors, etc." A Santa Fe Railroad official responded that he liked the idea of "playing up more strongly the picturesqueness of old Santa Fe," and that's what the railroad did.

The Santa Fe Railroad began offering reduced tourist rates to visit Santa Fe during summer months at about the time New Mexico became a state, early in 1912. Chris Wilson, whose fine book *The Myth of Santa Fe* (1997) examines the manmade image of Santa Fe, wrote: "Once statehood was achieved and Santa Fe resolved its contending identities, the romantic image of the city became the central vehicle for economic resurgence and the blueprint for its physical transformation."[6]

During the years that followed statehood, the mission style that reflected the architecture found throughout the Southwest began to give way to a style based more on the missions of New Mexico and on the Pueblo villages, and the Santa Fe Railroad began to adopt this style in structures built along its line, even west of New Mexico. The Hopi House at the Grand Canyon, the interior of the railroad's Harvey House restaurants, and the El Ortiz Hotel in Lamy near Santa Fe were designed to reflect what became known as the "Santa Fe style."

The archaeologist Sylvanus Morley and a group of concerned citizens deplored the gaudy Victorian excessiveness that was beginning to appear in Santa Fe. In a 1915 article published in *Old Santa Fe,* Morley outlined what he perceived as appropriate for New Mexico. It was based on a survey of the features and furniture of historical structures. Morley's article provided the basis for restoring the Plaza in Santa Fe and much of the town's center to what it looked like during the Spanish colonial period, requiring that new buildings employ the Santa Fe style. Buildings had to be one-story for the most part; two-story structures were the exception, and there were no three-story buildings save the church towers. In 1919, a fine tourist hotel, La Fonda, that adapted Pueblo and Spanish forms was built on the southeast corner of the Plaza. The Santa Fe of today was taking shape, and businessmen began to discover profit in playing up its colorful past.

EARLY IN THE twentieth century the railroad was the primary means for travelers to reach Santa Fe because cross-country roads were poor. Road building was a local responsibility, but as the use of automobiles increased across the nation, state governments became more interested in road building, especially after farmers began calling for better roads. Before the arrival of rural mail delivery in the 1890s, farmers had to go to their nearest post office to pick up their mail, and because of work or the weather, they often were unable to get their mail for weeks. The Kansas legislature passed a good-road bill in 1907 calling for certain counties to construct hard-surfaced roads, the expense of which was to be borne in part by the county, in part by the township, and in part by residents in a special benefit district adjoining the road. Kansas was the first state to have such a law, and it provided for county roads but ignored the need for state roads. Other states followed this pattern.

With Santa Fe promoted as a tourist attraction and following the marking of the Santa Fe Trail by the D.A.R., business leaders in some Kansas towns along the trail sought to capitalize on the historic nature of their communities. For example, Joseph S. Vernon of the Tucker-Vernon Company at Larned and Cimarron, Kansas, produced the 190-page book *Along the Old Trail: A History of the Old and a Story of the New Santa Fe Trail* (1910). It contained historic information but also focused heavily on the growth and prosperity of modern towns along the route with words and photographs, emphasizing what was called the New Santa Fe Trail. The following year, businessmen from towns in eight counties through which the old trail crossed met at Herington, Kansas, and organized the Old Santa Fe Trail Association. The group met again in 1912 in Hutchinson, to talk about how to promote their towns using the Santa Fe Trail as a theme. Many people at that meeting agreed that better roads were needed before more tourists would come, and as a group they called for such improvements. Nearly three years later, Kansas governor Arthur Capper proclaimed April 18, 1915, "Good Roads Day." Across the state many citizens went out and used horse teams dragging skids to scrape the roads in an effort to improve them. That same month a car whose occupants were marking what they called the National Old Trail from Los Angeles crossed Kansas on the Santa Fe Trail. The publicity associated with the drive gave the Santa Fe Trail another boost.

Meantime in Missouri, the marking of the Santa Fe Trail and a growing interest in better roads to accommodate automobiles attracted the attention of businessmen in Lexington, Missouri, during the summer of 1911. They met and organized the Santa Fe Trail and Boone's Lick Road Association and adopted bylaws that urged the construction of a modern highway across Missouri between St. Louis and Kansas City. In another meeting later that summer, they organized the Missouri Old Trails Road Association and called for a new Old Trails Road to parallel the old Santa Fe and Boone's Lick Trails. Support from leaders in other communities, who were largely guided by economic motives, led to the establishment of the National Old Trails Road Association at Kansas City, Missouri, in 1912.

As the use of automobiles increased, Congress passed the Federal-Aid Road Act in 1917 to encourage the building of state highways, which would be linked into a national system. Every state using the federal fund had to spend an equal amount raised by taxation within the state. In Kansas, a state highway department was created, but the actual construction of highways was left to the counties. The state highway engineer was little more than an adviser with no power to build highways from one part of the state to another, except as counties agreed to cooperate with each other. Then, in 1921, Congress approved the Federal Highway Act, and soon other states were providing unified systems of state highways. Gradually a national highway system was built.

On October 11, 1922, Dodge City, Kansas, residents celebrated their town's fiftieth anniversary and the centennial of the beginning of the Santa Fe Trail and William Becknell's first successful trading venture from Missouri to Santa Fe. About three years later, in August 1925, the citizens of Council Grove, Kansas, held a seven-day centennial celebration to mark the 1825 arrival of George Sibley and other government commissioners surveying the trail. Sibley's party, of course, had named the place Council Grove after the grove of trees where they met with chiefs from the Osage tribe. U.S. Highway 56 goes through Council Grove following the Santa Fe Trail from Missouri westward. After that two-lane highway was completed, it attracted more attention to the old trail. World War II reduced all traffic, but beginning in the late 1940s, business leaders all along the highway began touting it as "The Santa Fe Trail, the shortest diagonal to the Southwest." In towns like Council Grove that once catered to wagon caravans, businesses began to capitalize on their towns' historic sites in an effort to attract visitors in automobiles.

The renewed interest in the Santa Fe Trail spread to Hollywood and Tin Pan Alley. In 1940, Errol Flynn, Ronald Reagan, and Olivia De Havilland were among the stars in *Santa Fe Trail*, a Warner Brothers film that sought to capture the public's new interest in the old trail. But the film had little to do with the trail, unlike *Santa Fe Passage*, a 1955 Republic film starring John Payne, Rod Cameron, and Slim Pickens that dealt with a scout traveling the trail between Missouri and New Mexico. Radio performers, too, sought to capitalize on the trail through songs like *Down on the Santa Fe Trail*, released in 1939, and the more popular *Along the Santa*

The renewed interest in the Santa Fe Trail during the 1930s was captured in popular music. Here is the sheet-music cover to Down on the Santa Fe Trail, *with words by Edward A. Tinkham and music by Merle St. Leon. Written in pencil on the cover is Tinkham's permission to use the song on radio or any way desired. (Author's Collection)*

Fe Trail, performed by Glenn Miller and his orchestra and other music groups that offered nostalgic relief during World War II.

Between 1928 and 1948 the National Old Trails Road Association, for a time under the leadership of the Missourian Harry S. Truman, a future president, paid the cost of erecting twelve monuments across the entire United States, three of which were located along the Santa Fe Trail: one at Lexington, Missouri; another at Council Grove, Kansas; and a third at Lamar, Colorado. The monuments depicted a pioneer mother and two children, sometimes called the "Madonna of the Trail," sculpted by August Leimbach of St. Louis. A fourth monument was to have been placed in Santa Fe, but a dispute over its artistic merit resulted in it being erected at Albuquerque. In 1948 the National Old Trails Road Association gave way to the American Pioneer Trail Association, and some of the organization's new chapters marked portions of old trails, especially the Santa Fe Trail. The end of World War II also saw the National Park Service resume a survey of historic sites started during the 1930s. Ray H. Mattison started a field survey of the Santa Fe Trail in 1958, two years after the federal government created the Highway Trust Fund establishing the Interstate Highway System. New highways soon made it easier for motorists traveling across the nation to reach sites along the route of the Santa Fe Trail.

During the 1960s into the 1980s, interest in the history of the Santa Fe Trail grew as Americans became more fascinated with the American West. More professional historians and history buffs became interested in the people, places, and events that occurred along the trail, and their work resulted in an increased number of articles, monographs, and books dealing with one aspect or another of the trail's history. As momentum grew to save not only the Santa Fe Trail but its history, the Colorado Historical Society held a symposium at Trinidad, Colorado, in September 1986. The historians, buffs, and others organized the Santa Fe Trail Council, later renamed the Santa Fe Trail Association, and urged passage of pending legislation to make the Santa Fe Trail a National Historic Trail. The group held its organizational meeting the following year at Hutchinson, Kansas, adopting bylaws and program goals that included the quarterly publication of a newsletter called *Wagon Tracks.*

That same year, 1987, Congress passed the legislation, and on May 15, President Ronald Reagan signed the bill. The National Park Service was directed to administer the Santa Fe Trail as a National Historic Site on a partnership basis with other federal, state, and local governments, who today manage individual sites and segments along the trail, plus private landowners, local historical societies, and other trail interest groups such as the Santa Fe Trail Association, which annually holds a symposium at some point along the trail. Local chapters of the Santa Fe Trail Association also hold periodic meetings. In 1990, the final plan for the Santa Fe National Historic Trail was completed, detailing how the trail was to be administered to provide for protection of its historic and natural resources, and for the public use and enjoyment. The plan also called for the marking of it as a National Historic Trail, which has since occurred with the assistance of the states of Missouri, Kansas, Oklahoma, Colorado, and New Mexico.

As the nation moves into a new century, the attraction and appeal of the Santa Fe Trail continue unabated because of the romance and color of its history and the role it played in opening the American West. Its attraction, however, is closely tied to its named destination, Santa Fe, with its image of a different culture and implied different way of life, one often envisioned to be slower and more peaceful than that lived by most Americans. The late Texas writer J. Frank Dobie wrote in 1943:

> Look at it in one way, Santa Fe was a mud village. In another way, it was the solitary gem in an empire of vacancy. Like that of Athens, though of an entirely different quality, its fame was out of all proportion to its size. . . . No other town of its size in America has been the subject and focus for as much good literature as Santa Fe. Pittsburgh and dozens of other big cities all put together have not inspired one tenth of the imaginative play that Santa Fe has inspired. Some of the transcontinental railroads probably carry as much freight in a day as went over the Santa Fe Trail in all the wagons in all the years they pulled over the Santa Fe Trail. But the Santa Fe Trail is one of the three great trails of America that, though plowed under, fenced across and cemented over, seem destined for perennial travel—by those happily able to go without tourist guides. To quote Robert Louis Stevenson, "The greatest adventures are not those we go to seek."[7]

While the early attraction of the trail was the dream of profit, the picture of life on the trail and in Santa Fe had been painted in words even while the trail was alive with bullwhackers, mule-skinners, traders, and other travelers. Josiah Gregg's two-volume *Commerce of the Prairies* (1844) remains a classic of the Santa Fe trade and trail. It is, as Dobie observed, "one of the classics of bedrock Americana." If Dobie were still alive, he might agree that the second work of the six top classics is George Frederick Ruxton's *Adventures in Mexico and the Rocky Mountains* (1848). Like Gregg's work, it helped to mold the image of Santa Fe and the trail, and it offers the perspective of a civilized man fascinated with the wilderness. The four other works that can be considered classics are D. W. H. Davis's *El Gringo; or, New Mexico and Her People* (1857), providing insights on the manners and customs of New Mexicans; Philip St. George Cooke's *Scenes and Adventures in the Army; Or, Romance of Military Life* (1857), conveying the military side of escorting Santa Fe traders; Lewis Hector Garrard's *Wah-To-Yah and the Taos Trail; or, Prairie Travel and Scalp Dances, with a Look at Los Rancheros from Muleback and the Rocky Mountain Campfire* (1850), relating the author's experiences traveling from Westport, Missouri, to

Santa Fe and back in 1846 and 1847; and Susan Shelby Magoffin's diary, first published in 1926 as *Down the Santa Fe Trail and into Mexico: The Diary of Susan Shelby Magoffin, 1846–1847.*

These works and many others that have helped to capture and convey the life, customs, romance, and excitement of the trail are included in the bibliography and in the late Jack D. Rittenhouse's *The Santa Fe Trail: A Historical Bibliography* (1971), which lists more than 350 books, 250 articles, and 100 congressional documents containing information on the trail during its glory years.

But its literature is only one aspect of the trail's legacy. It was the absence of an Anglo-American history in Santa Fe and the Southwest that eventually led Americans to turn the region's Hispanic past into their own history. Putting aside their old cultural prejudices toward the "Spanish," Americans now saw what they once thought of as backward mud huts with piñon logs burning in corner fireplaces as sturdy adobe homes with flowers in pots on hand-molded windowsills. These Americans included Charles Lummis, Sylvanus Morley, the Santa Fe Railroad officials, members of the Fred Harvey Company, and others who have reinterpreted and romanticized the trail's destination of Santa Fe and all of New Mexico as something that seems bigger than life, something that receives more attention today than it ever did during those years when caravans of slowly moving wagons rolled over the Santa Fe Trail.

Glossary

Terms and Place Names Associated with the Santa Fe Trail

Allison and Booth's Ranch located near the Walnut Creek crossing about two miles east of Great Bend, Kansas, and south of U.S. Highway 56. Allison and Booth (sometimes spelled Boothe) established a trading ranch here in 1855. Booth was killed in 1857, and after Allison died in 1859, George Peacock operated the ranch until he was killed in 1860. Charles Rath then ran the trading ranch until 1867.

Apache Canyon located at the western end of Glorieta Pass on modern I-25, it was once a narrow wagon gap on the trail. During the Civil War, Union and Confederate forces fought here in the battle of Apache Canyon on March 26, 1862.

Arkansas River Crossing located at present-day La Junta, Colorado.

Arrow Rock name of a bluff on the west side of the Missouri River that was used as a landmark, later the site of the town of Arrow Rock, founded in 1829. About 1811 a ferry was established here.

Arrow Rock Landing located near the town of Arrow Rock and used from about 1811 until 1827, when the town was washed away. Ruts of the road from the landing to the town site still exist.

Aubry's Crossing a crossing on the Arkansas River for a new route, the Aubry Cutoff, opened in 1850 by Francis X. Aubry. It became an important route because water was more plentiful, and it avoided a dry portion of the Cimarron route. The crossing is located about three miles downstream from the site of Fort Aubrey west of Syracuse, Kansas.

Barclay's Fort located on the south bank of the Mora River, west of I-25 at Watrous. The private post was established in 1849.

Bent's Fort the name of two forts. The first, often called Bent's Old Fort, was located eight miles northeast of La Junta, Colorado, on the north side of the

Arkansas River. Active from 1833 until 1849, the trading post has been reconstructed and is open to the public. In 1852, William Bent destroyed the first fort and constructed a new one nearly sixty miles to the east—known as Bent's New Fort—which he operated until 1860, when the site was leased to the U.S. Army. Only the foundation ruins of the second fort remain.

Big Blue River Crossing located between Independence and Westport, Missouri, near old U.S. Highway 40. The crossing is no longer visible.

Big Timbers located along the Arkansas River near Bent's New Fort and Old Fort Lyon. In early years the stand of large, old trees, including many cottonwoods, extended for thirty miles along the river. As whites arrived, many of the trees were cut down.

Blue Mound the larger and more prominent of two hills located three miles south of Lawrence, Kansas. Travelers on the Santa Fe Trail used it as a landmark.

Boone's Lick a salt lick or natural saltwater spring that was a primary source of salt for settlements along the Missouri River from 1805 until the 1830s. Nathan and Daniel Morgan Boone, sons of Daniel Boone, developed its economic potential. Now a Missouri state historic site, it is located north of Petersburg.

buffalo chips dried bison dung or manure picked up on the prairie and plains and used as fuel for fires in areas where wood was not available.

bullion silver or gold shaped into bars instead of coins.

bull train a caravan of wagons pulled by oxen. They were called bulls because oxen are simply castrated bulls.

bullwhacker the driver of a wagon who walked on the left side of the lead oxen, controlling them through yells and with a bullwhip.

cache a manmade hole in the ground where goods or provisions were stored or hidden.

"Caches" well-known pits dug by James Baird and Samuel Chambers in 1822–23 to hide supplies and trading goods after their animals died. Bound for New Mexico, the traders' pack train was caught by a blizzard. They later returned and dug up their cache. The site of the "Caches" was a few miles west of present-day Dodge City, Kansas, but nothing remains of the pits.

Camp Mackay see Fort Atkinson.

Camp Nichols located three and a half miles northwest of Wheeless, Oklahoma, it was established by Kit Carson and occupied for only a few months in 1865. This is the only military site on the trail in Oklahoma and was briefly home to Marian Sloan Russell, who wrote of her experiences as an army officer's wife in her book *Land of Enchantment*. Cedar Spring and Carrizozo Creek are located nearby.

Camp Wynkoop see Fort Aubrey.

caravan a group of traders and their wagons traveling together. Sometimes called a train.

Carrizozo Creek see Camp Nichols.

Cedar Spring see Camp Nichols.

Chouteau's Island was located southwest of Lakin, Kansas, in the Arkansas River.

While it no longer exists, the island got its name in 1815 after Auguste P. Chouteau and a party of trappers were attacked by Pawnee Indians. The Chouteau party took cover on the island.

Cimarron Plaza located in Cimarron, New Mexico, one block east of New Mexico Highway 21. A stopping point on the trail's mountain route. A mansion built in 1864 by Lucien Maxwell once stood on the plaza, but it was destroyed by fire in 1885.

Cold Spring located on the Cimarron route about six miles west and eight miles north of Boise City, in the Oklahoma Panhandle. Rock at this site contains the engraved names of many travelers beginning in the 1840s. A stage station may have been located here.

Concord coach a stagecoach manufactured by Abbott, Downing and Company, Concord, New Hampshire, beginning about 1827. It was the Cadillac of stagecoaches.

Conestoga a large covered wagon first made in Lancaster or Pittsburgh, Pennsylvania.

contraband goods not legally allowed to be exported or imported into another country.

Cottonwood Creek Crossing the site of a major campsite located on Cottonwood Creek about one mile west of Durham, Kansas. The site of a trading ranch and stage station beginning about 1856.

Cow Creek Crossing an important campsite and crossing where a trading ranch and stage station were constructed in 1858. It is located four miles west of Lyons, Kansas, on U.S. Highway 56 and then one mile south and west.

Dearborn a light carriage, usually covered and curtained, named for General Henry Dearborn. Frequently used for transportation by traders on the trail.

Diamond Spring a favored campsite because of the good springwater located about fifteen miles west of Council Grove.

draft animals animals, usually horses, mules, or oxen, used to pull wagons. On the trail, oxen and mules were used almost exclusively to pull freight wagons.

dragoon an infantry soldier trained to fight on horseback.

Dragoon Creek Crossing a natural rock crossing named after a troop of dragoons who traveled the trail during the 1850s. It is located three miles northwest of Burlingame, Kansas, and north of state highway 31.

dry goods goods such as cloth, clothing, and manufactured items.

Duncan's Crossing see Pawnee Fork Crossing.

Elm Grove see Lone Elm Campground.

estanco the Spanish word for a government trading post or store in the Southwest.

fandango a lively Spanish or Spanish American dance in triple time; held in New Mexico.

Flag Spring see Upper Spring.

follow the tongue when making camp at night, freighters would spot the North Star and point the tongue of the lead wagon to it in order to move in the right direction the following morning.

Fort Atkinson originally established as Camp Mackay in 1850 to control Indians and protect trail traffic, it was renamed Fort Atkinson in 1851. The post, located about two miles west of Dodge City, Kansas, was abandoned in 1854.

Fort Aubrey located four miles west of Syracuse, Kansas. The military post was built in 1864 and first called Camp Wynkoop. It was renamed Fort Aubrey in 1865 but abandoned in 1866.

Fort Dodge located about four miles east of Dodge City, Kansas, the military post was established in 1864 and remained active until 1882. Many of its buildings still stand and have been used by the State Soldiers Home.

Fort Ellsworth see Fort Harker.

Fort Harker first established as Fort Ellsworth in 1866, and located four miles from Ellsworth, Kansas, the post was moved. Its new site is now the town of Kanopolis. It was renamed Fort Harker later in 1866. Several of its buildings are now private residences in Kanopolis. The post remained active until 1873.

Fort Larned located about six miles west of Larned, Kansas, this military post was active from 1859 until 1878. It was first called Camp Alert and then Camp on Pawnee Fork. The parade ground and many of the original buildings still exist and are maintained by the National Park Service.

Fort Leavenworth although not located on the main Santa Fe Trail, this post, established in 1827, housed military troops sent to protect caravans on the trail. Situated on the Missouri River, northwest of present-day Kansas City, Missouri, it was the command headquarters for all the troops serving along the trail from the Mexican War until the trail closed in 1880. Supplies were unloaded from steamboats and taken by wagons to the post's warehouses before being transported over several routes to the main Santa Fe Trail. The post remains an active military installation.

Fort Lyon name of two forts. The first, called Old Fort Lyon or Fort Wise, was located less than a mile from Bent's New Fort. The post was built by the army in 1860. In 1867, Fort Lyon was relocated to just east of Las Animas, Colorado, and was active until 1889. It is now a veterans hospital.

Fort Mann established in 1847 as a military repair station midway between Fort Leavenworth and Santa Fe, it was never a regular military post and was abandoned in 1848. The site is located about a mile west of Dodge City, Kansas, on U.S. Highway 50.

Fort Marcy constructed on a hill overlooking Santa Fe in 1846. Some features still may be seen. U.S. troops were headquartered here until Fort Union was built in 1851.

Fort Osage built in 1808 to fulfill one of the provisions of a treaty between the Osage Indians and the United States. Constructed on a high bluff on the south bank overlooking the Missouri River, the fort was the westernmost fur-trading factory of the United States and later was the westernmost military post. It was a trading center for Indians and a rendezvous for trappers, mountain men, and explorers. The restored fort is located on the north side of Sibley, Missouri, about fourteen miles northeast of Independence.

Fort Union located eight miles northwest of the town of Watrous on New Mexico Highway 161, near the junction of the Cimarron and mountain routes of the trail. Between 1851 and 1891, it was the largest American military fort in the Southwest. The remains are now a National Monument, and extensive trail ruts may be seen.

Fort Wise see Fort Lyon.

Fort Zarah post located at Walnut Creek Crossing that provided protection for travelers on the trail. There were actually two posts, the first established in 1864. A second and more improved post was erected in 1867 a half mile north of the first. It was abandoned in 1869.

Franklin the town where William Becknell and his party started out for Santa Fe in 1821 following the Osage Trace. The town's site is north of the Missouri River and about a half mile west of the Boonville Bridge on Missouri Highway 87. The town itself was washed away by the Missouri River in 1828.

Glorieta Pass a mountain pass between Glorieta Mesa and the Sangre de Cristo Mountains, just west of Glorieta, New Mexico. It was a major feature of the mountain route and the place where the Confederate troops were defeated in their drive west by Union forces under Colonel John Chivington.

goddam an Indian term for a freighting wagon, because bullwhackers frequently used the expression in moving their ox-drawn wagons.

greaser a word often used by Anglos to describe Mexican bullwhackers and teamsters. Although considered a derogatory Anglo term today for any Mexican, it was not always used in that context. The term appears to have come into use in Texas during the 1830s to describe any Mexican male of the lower class. Tradition has it that the appellation originated when a Mexican would walk alongside a mule-drawn cart and constantly grease the axle.

Hermit's Peak located between La Cueva and Las Vegas, New Mexico, the peak was named in honor of Giovanni Maria Augustini (Matteo Boccalini), after whom Hermit Priest's Cave in Council Grove, Kansas, is also named. The peak can be viewed from either New Mexico 518 or I-25.

Indian Mound natural landmark on the trail that was located about five miles southwest of Lakin, Kansas.

Inscription Rock see Cold Spring.

Jarvis (Chávez) Creek Crossing located in Rice County, Kansas, west of the Little Arkansas River. Here Antonio José Chávez, a Mexican trader, was murdered in 1843.

Johnson's Ranch a trading ranch on the trail established by A. P. Johnson in 1858. It is located on the western side of Glorieta Pass at the town of Canoncito, north of I-25. Confederate forces used the ranch as their headquarters during the battle of Glorieta Pass. Only the ranch site remains.

Jornada a portion of the Cimarron branch of the Santa Fe Trail known as the "Journey of Death." It refers to an area of the trail where little water was available.

jumping-off point the beginning of a trail where a wagon train began its journey.

La Jornade del Muerto translated as "The Day's Journey of the Dead Man"; used to describe the trail that threaded the great Pass of the North (El Paso) and crossed a vast desert before reaching Chihuahua City in Mexico.

Las Vegas Plaza located in the town of Las Vegas, New Mexico, which began as a stop on the trail in 1835. General Stephen W. Kearny claimed New Mexico Territory for the United States in 1846 while standing on the top of the flat-roofed adobe structure on the north side of the plaza.

Last Chance Store a store constructed on the west side of Council Grove, Kansas, in 1857. As the name implies, for many years it was the last chance for west-bound travelers to buy supplies before reaching New Mexico.

leaders the draft animals, oxen or mules, that are hitched at the front of a team.

Lexington a town in Missouri on the Santa Fe Trail. Located on U.S. Highway 24, there are several warehouses and other buildings that served the trail. The Santa Fe trade outfitters James and Robert Aull outfitted caravans in Lexington.

Little Arkansas River Crossing actually two crossings of the river located on the present-day McPherson-Rice County, Kansas, line. Areas on both sides of the river were popular campsites.

Little Blue River Crossing located about midway between Fort Osage and Independence, Missouri, this crossing of the Little Blue River was difficult until a bridge was constructed in 1857.

Lone Elm Campground located three miles south of present-day Olathe, Kansas, it was originally known as Round Grove or Elm Grove because of a stand of trees. But travelers on the Santa Fe Trail eventually cut down all the trees except one for firewood. It became known as "Lone Elm" even after the last tree was cut down.

Lost Spring a valuable source of water for travelers located about forty-five miles west-southwest of Council Grove, Kansas.

Lower Cimarron Spring located about eleven miles south-southwest of Ulysses, Kansas, this crossing on the Cimarron route provided travelers with the first reliable water supply since leaving the Arkansas River. It also was a favorite campground. Because of a spring, it also became known as Lower Spring until about 1847, when someone sank a wooden wagon bed in the spring to collect water. After that it was called Wagon Bed Spring.

Lucien Maxwell House located in Rayado, twelve miles south of Cimarron, New Mexico. On the mountain route of the trail, Maxwell developed a campsite at Rayado in 1848 and later built a home. A military camp was located here during the early 1850s to help protect travelers.

McNees' Crossing named for a young trader killed by Indians in 1828, the crossing on Corrumpa Creek is three and a half miles west of the Oklahoma state line, and one and a half miles south on New Mexico Highway 406. Travelers often camped at the crossing.

mess a group of men within a caravan or wagon train who ate meals together. Usually each mess had a cook. Other men in a mess would share the tasks of gathering fuel, hunting, carrying water, and cleaning up.

Middle Crossing of the Arkansas River extending from about two to twenty-four miles west of Dodge City. Wagons could cross the river at just about any point because of the stream's shallow flow.

Middle Spring located eight miles north of Elkhart, Kansas, and about thirty-six miles from Lower Spring (later Wagon Bed Spring). This spring afforded travelers a reliable water supply and a good campground.

mountain branch or route a portion of the Santa Fe Trail that runs from present-day western Kansas through La Junta, Colorado, and then turns south over Raton Pass into New Mexico. This route follows the Arkansas River and then runs along the edge of the Sangre de Cristo Mountains to Santa Fe.

mud wagon a poor man's Concord coach, open-sided, light and low, and simply constructed.

mule-skinner the driver of one or more mule teams. Like a bullwhacker, he yelled and used a whip to control the animals.

Murphy wagon a large freight wagon crafted by Joseph Murphy in St. Louis for use on the trail.

Narrows a ridge of land on the Santa Fe Trail running from near present-day Baldwin City, Kansas, nine miles west to Willow Spring. Wagons had to stay on this ridge to avoid rough terrain and muddy ravines.

Neosho River Crossing an important river crossing located in what is now Council Grove, Kansas. The crossing was about where a bridge on U.S. Highway 56 now crosses the river.

nigh an old term for left. Bullwhackers walked on the nigh side of their lead pair of oxen.

nooning taking a midday stop on the trail. It was not uncommon on the Santa Fe Trail for teamsters to noon or take a break during which both breakfast and a noon meal were served before a caravan or train continued on its way.

norther a sudden winter storm with freezing temperatures blowing in from the north.

notions trading items related to sewing including needles, thread, buttons, and ribbons.

142 Mile Creek located about twenty miles east of Council Grove. During the early 1850s, Charles Withington operated a store where the trail crossed the creek. In 1855, he moved the store a few miles west to the community of Allen on Duck Creek.

110 Mile Creek first known as Oak Creek in the 1820s, it became known by its present name after the trail was surveyed in 1825. It is located just south of the intersection of U.S. Highway 56 and U.S. Highway 75 between Overbrook and Scranton, Kansas. The site of a stage station is just southwest of the intersection.

Osage Trace a trail established by the Osage Indians along the north side of the Missouri River.

ox train a series of wagons pulled by oxen (as opposed to wagons pulled by mules). Ox trains were sometimes called grass freight because oxen could survive by eating grass alone.

Pawnee Fork Crossing located about five and a half miles north of U.S. Highway 156 in Hodgeman County, Kansas. A trading ranch and bridge were established about 1869 by John O'Laughlin and later owned by George Duncan.

Pawnee Rock one of the better-known natural landmarks along the trail in Kansas.

It is located a half mile north of U.S. Highway 56 on the northern edge of the town of Pawnee Rock, Kansas.

Peacock Trading Ranch see Allison and Booth's Ranch.

Pennsylvania wagon a Conestoga wagon manufactured in Pennsylvania.

Pigeon's Ranch located about three and a half miles southeast of the Glorieta exit on I-25, on the eastern side of Glorieta Pass. The battle of Glorieta Pass was fought a half mile west of the ranch house established by Alexander Valle.

Pitt schooner a Conestoga wagon manufactured in Pittsburgh, Pennsylvania.

Plum Buttes several very large sand dunes covered with plum bushes. Although the dunes no longer exist because of wind erosion, the site is located four miles west of present-day Chase, Kansas, on U.S. Highway 56, one mile north, and then one mile west. Travelers often stopped for their noon meal here.

Point of Rocks name of four trail landmarks. One, a low rounded hill with a rocky face on the south side, was located just west of Dodge City, Kansas. The second was located eight miles north of Elkhart, Kansas, near Middle Spring. The third was located in Colfax County, New Mexico. A fourth is located about two and a half miles west of Pierceville, Kansas.

post a word meaning a fort or trading post.

prairie schooner a nickname for a Conestoga wagon, because of its shiplike profile.

proprietor a term used early in the trail's years to describe a trader in a caravan or train who had obtained merchandise to trade or sell.

Rabbit Ears actually two peaks located about seven miles northwest of Clayton, New Mexico. This trail landmark is believed to have been named for a Cheyenne Indian called Rabbit Ears, who was killed nearby.

Rabbit Ears Creek Camp located about six miles north of Mount Dora, New Mexico, this spot provided springwater, grass, wood, and game for food, and was a favorite campground on the trail.

railhead the last point where railroad tracks were laid during the construction of a railroad.

ration the amount of food provided for one person.

Raton Pass located on the Colorado–New Mexico border and now crossed by I-25, the pass was difficult to cross until the army made improvements during the Mexican War. The pass, however, was not widely used until "Uncle Dick" Wootton began improving it in 1864 and charged travelers a toll.

relief people of a wagon train who guard the train from dangers such as Indians and buffalo stampedes.

Rock Crossing of the Canadian River a crossing on the Cimarron route located two miles south of U.S. Highway 56 in Colfax County, New Mexico. This river crossing provided a natural stone floor. For travelers, this spot was considered to be the real entry into Mexico, and Mexican troops were sometimes sent this far to escort traders to Santa Fe.

Round Grove see Lone Elm Campground.

Round Mound a significant landmark on the trail located about four miles south of Grenville, New Mexico. Today the site is known as Mount Clayton.

running gear the parts underneath a wagon.

Santa Fe tea made from the leaves of *Alstonia theaeformis*.

scoop wagon used to describe a Conestoga wagon with a scoop-shaped wagon bed.

skin to skin mules is to drive them.

sowbelly bacon preserved with salt, sometimes called salt pork.

span a pair of two draft animals that work together.

Spanish Peaks located west-northwest of present-day Trinidad, Colorado. They served as landmarks for travelers on the trail.

Studebaker wagon a large freight wagon first built by the Studebaker Brothers in 1852 and used on the Santa Fe Trail.

sutler a merchant who sets up a store at a fort to sell supplies to soldiers.

swingers the pair of draft animals that are hitched just ahead of the wheelers.

tandem two or more wagons hitched together and pulled by one team of draft animals.

Taos lightning a rough brew distilled in Taos, New Mexico.

terrain land types, such as hilly, rolling, level, or mountainous.

trailhead the beginning of a trail. The Santa Fe Trail had different trailheads at different points of time. These were also called jumping-off points.

Upper Crossing a popular crossing on the Arkansas River, stretching from about a mile east of present-day Lakin, Kansas, to Chouteau's Island.

Upper Spring located nine miles north and one and a half miles west of Boise City, in the Oklahoma Panhandle. Situated on a high rocky hill, the spring formed a pond and provided a view of the Cimarron Valley. The spot was often used as a campground and was also called "Flag Spring." Upper Spring was about eighteen miles from Middle Spring.

wagon bed the body of a wagon, sometimes called a wagon box, where cargo is carried.

Wagon Bed Spring see Lower Cimarron Spring.

wagon box see wagon bed.

wagon master the leader of a caravan of wagons or wagon train. Sometimes called the trail boss.

Wagon Mound one of the best-known landmarks on the trail, so named because it looks like a covered wagon being pulled by oxen. It is located next to the town of Wagon Mound, New Mexico.

Walnut Creek Crossing name of two crossings. One was located about two miles east of present-day Great Bend, Kansas, and south of U.S. Highway 56. Near the crossing was a trading ranch and toll bridge. Fort Zarah was located nearby between 1864 and 1869. The second crossing with the same name was located in Rush County, Kansas. There a bridge and trading ranch were established about 1870.

Watrous Store a trading post established in 1849. It is located north of the Mora River on U.S. Highway 161 at Watrous. What was the store became the Doolittle Ranch house.

Westport Landing established in 1832, it was located on the south bank of the Missouri River in what is now Kansas City, Missouri. The town of Westport, also now part of Kansas City, was four miles south.

wheelers the pair of draft animals directly hitched to a wagon.

Willow Bar a crossing on the Cimarron River located eleven miles north and eleven miles east of Boise City, in the Oklahoma Panhandle. Water was usually available, and travelers camped on the site near Wolf Mountain.

Willow Springs located at the south end of Raton Pass in present-day Raton, New Mexico. Travelers on the trail frequently camped at the site.

Wolf Mountain a prominent landmark on the Cimarron route located between Willow Bar and Upper Spring about nine miles north of Boise City, in the Oklahoma Panhandle, and then northeast. Branches of the trail passed on both sides of the mountain.

Wootten Ranch located near I-25 at the northern entrance to Raton Pass, it was the home of Richens Lacy "Uncle Dick" Wootton, who owned and operated the Raton Pass toll road.

yoke a large wooden bar or frame attached to the heads of two oxen for working together. Freighters often used the term to mean two oxen (i.e., a three-yoke team).

Notes

ONE: FROM CONQUEST TO DE OÑATE, 1492–1610

Much has been published on the early Spanish exploration and settlement of the New World. A fine overview is David J. Weber's *The Spanish Frontier in North America* (New Haven, Conn.: Yale University Press, 1992), which has an excellent bibliography. A good source for the recollections of Álvar Núñez Cabeza de Vaca is *Cabeza de Vaca's Adventures in the Unknown Interior of America,* translated and edited by Cyclone Covey (New York: Crowell-Collier, 1961). This work relates Cabeza de Vaca's story as it was first published in Zamora, Spain, in 1542, and is similar to Morris Bishop's *The Odyssey of Cabeza De Vaca* (New York: Century, 1933), which also describes Cabeza de Vaca's life after his journey to the New World. The best source on Juan de Oñate is Marc Simmons's biography, *The Last Conquistador: Juan de Oñate and the Settling of the Far Southwest* (Norman: University of Oklahoma Press, 1991). Other works consulted include Abraham P. Nasatir, *Borderland in Retreat: From Spanish Louisiana to the Far Southwest* (Albuquerque: University of New Mexico Press, 1976); Marc Simmons, *Spanish Government in New Mexico* (Albuquerque: University of New Mexico Press, 1968); and Louise Barry, *The Beginning of the West: Annals of the Kansas Gateway to the American West 1540–1854* (Topeka: Kansas State Historical Society, 1972). The quote describing carts came from Nick Eggenhofer, *Wagons, Mules and Men* (New York: Hastings House, 1961), pp. 72–3. A scholarly review of Spanish wheeled vehicles in New Spain can be found in Marc Simmons, *"Carros y Carreta:* Vehicular Traffic on the Camino Real," in *Hispanic Arts and Ethnohistory in the Southwest,* ed. Marta Weigle (Santa Fe: Ancient City Press, 1983), pp. 324–34.

TWO: THE ATTRACTION OF SANTA FE, 1610–1672

1. "A Trade Invoice of 1638," *New Mexico Historical Review* 10, no. 3 (July 1937): 242–6.
2. Carl P. Russell, *Guns of the Early Frontiers* (Berkeley: University of California Press, 1957), pp. 6–7. See also Geoffrey Boothroyd, *Guns Through the Ages* (New York: Sterling Publishing, 1962).

3. Franciscans belonged to the religious order of Friars Minor founded early in the thirteenth century by Saint Francis of Assisi. Later in that century the Jesuit (Society of Jesus) religious order was founded in the Roman Catholic church to spread the church's teachings by preaching, or to do whatever else urgently needed to be done for the church. Franciscans accompanied Columbus to the New World, and both orders were represented in New Spain. The Jesuit order, devoted to the papacy, however, suffered steadily increasing prejudice. At one time or another the order was expelled from every country in Europe, and in 1773, a few years after the Jesuits' expulsion from New Spain, the Pope suppressed the order, but he reestablished it in 1814.

4. Ramón A. Gutiérrez, *When Jesus Came, the Corn Mothers Went Away: Marriage, Sexuality, and Power in New Mexico, 1500–1846* (Stanford, Calif.: Stanford University Press, 1991), pp. 301–2.

5. Noel M. Loomis and Abraham P. Nasatir, *Pedro Vial and the Roads to Santa Fe* (Norman: University of Oklahoma Press, 1967), pp. 48–9.

6. Donald J. Blakeslee, *Along Ancient Trails: The Mallet Expedition of 1739* (Niwot: University Press of Colorado, 1995). This study provides a wealth of information about the Mallets and their expedition of 1739, plus appendixes containing copies of documents relating to the Mallets' 1739 expedition and the Fabry expedition.

THREE: TRAILS TO SANTA FE, 1762–1807

1. W. F. Switzler, *Switzler's Illustrated History of Missouri* (St. Louis: C. R. Barns, 1881), pp. 144–50. Laclede, founder of St. Louis, died on the Mississippi near the mouth of the Arkansas River on June 20, 1778, while returning from a business trip to New Orleans. He was buried nearby.

2. Noel M. Loomis and Abraham P. Nasatir, *Pedro Vial and the Roads to Santa Fe* (Norman: Univ. of Oklahoma Press, 1967), pp. 376–7.

3. Ibid., pp. 400–1.

4. Alfred B. Thomas, "The First Santa Fe Expedition, 1792–1793," *Chronicles of Oklahoma* 9, no. 2 (June 1931): 195–208.

5. When the United States purchased Louisiana Territory, President Thomas Jefferson was concerned about the constitutionality of the purchase, since the U.S. Constitution did not seem to empower the government to engage in such a transaction. But since the Constitution did give the president treaty-making power, the Louisiana Purchase was ratified into law as a treaty by the U.S. Senate.

6. Elihu H. Shepard, *The Early History of St. Louis and Missouri, to Which Is Appended the Author's Autobiography* (St. Louis: privately printed, 1870), p. 35.

7. Z. M. Pike, *An Account of Expeditions to the Sources of the Mississippi, and through the Western Parts of Louisiana, to the Sources of the Arkansaw, Kans, La Platte, and Pierre Juan, Rivers . . .* (Philadelphia: C. & A. Conrad, 1810), p. 145.

8. Stephen E. Ambrose, *Undaunted Courage: Meriwether Lewis, Thomas Jefferson, and the Opening of the American West* (New York: Simon and Schuster, 1997), pp. 406–10. See also Reuben Gold Thwaites, ed., *Original Journals of the Lewis*

and Clark Expedition 1804–1806 (New York: Arno Press, 1969), vol. 5, pp. 391–5. This is a reprint of the 1904 edition in seven volumes plus atlas.

9. Pike, *Account of Expeditions*, p. 195. Pike was commissioned a brigadier general at the beginning of the War of 1812. He was killed when a powder magazine exploded on April 27, 1813, as he was leading American troops in an assault on York, the capital of Upper Canada (now Toronto, Ontario).

Four: Destination Santa Fe, 1807–1822

1. A. P. Nasatir, "Jacques Clamorgan," in *The Mountain Men and the Fur Trade of the Far West*, ed. LeRoy R. Hafen (Glendale, Calif.: Arthur H. Clark, 1965), pp. 81–94.
2. Reuben Smith, "Reuben Smith," in *Mountain Men*, ed. Hafen, vol. 7 (1969), pp. 261–79.
3. Richard E. Oglesby, "Manuel Lisa," in *Mountain Men*, ed. Hafen, vol. 5 (1968), pp. 179–201. See also Hiram Martin Chittenden, *The American Fur Trade of the Far West: A History of the Pioneer Trading Posts and Early Fur Companies of the Missouri Valley and the Rocky Mountains and of the Overland Commerce with Santa Fe* (Stanford, Calif.: Academic Reprints, 1954), vol. 1, pp. 125–36.
4. Rex W. Strickland, "James Baird," in *Mountain Men*, ed. Hafen, vol. 3 (1966), pp. 27–37.
5. Janet Lecompte, "Jules De Nun," in *Mountain Men*, ed. Hafen, vol. 8 (1971), pp. 98–100.
6. Ibid. See also Janet Lecompte, "Auguste Pierre Chouteau," in *Mountain Men*, ed. Hafen, vol. 9 (1972), pp. 63–90.
7. Ezra Delos Smith, "Jedediah S. Smith and the Settlement of Kansas," *Collections of the Kansas State Historical Society, 1911–1912, Vol. XII* (Topeka: State Printing Office, 1912), pp. 254–5. Jedediah Smith was the author's great-uncle.
8. Walter Williams and Floyd Calvin Shoemaker, *Missouri, Mother of the West* (Chicago and New York: American Historical Society, 1930), vol. 1, p. 190.
9. Albert Watkins, ed., *Publications of the Nebraska State Historical Society, Vol. XX* (Lincoln: Nebraska State Historical Society, 1922), pp. 19, 22.
10. Ibid., pp. 20–2.
11. John Charles Frémont, *The Exploring Expedition to the Rocky Mountains, Oregon and California* (Buffalo, N.Y.: Geo. H. Derby; and Cleveland, Ohio: Smith, Knight, 1850), pp. 5–152. This popular work, with its then new material on the discovery of gold in California, contains Frémont's official report printed by order of the U.S. Senate, 27th Cong., 3rd sess., 1843, S. Doc. 243, serial 416, which was also consulted.
12. *Missouri Historical Society Collections*, 4, no. 2 (St. Louis: Missouri Historical Society, 1913), pp. 194–208. Ezekiel Williams is the hero in David E. Coyner's *The Lost Trappers: A Collection of Interesting Scenes and Events in the Rocky Mountains* (Philadelphia: Carey and Hart, 1847), a somewhat fictitious account of the beginnings of the American fur trade. See also Frederic E. Voelker's biographical sketch "Ezekiel Williams," in *Mountain Men*, ed. Hafen, vol. 9 (1972), pp. 393–409.

13. William Becknell's *Journal* reproduced from notes excerpted from the *Missouri Historical Review* in David A. White, ed., *News of the Plains and Rockies 1803–1865. Original Narratives of Overland Travel and Adventure Selected from the Wagner-Camp and Becker Bibliography of Western Americana* (Spokane, Wash.: Arthur H. Clark, 1996), vol. 2, p. 62.

14. Ibid., p. 63.

15. Ibid., p. 64.

16. Ibid., p. 65.

17. Robert L. Duffus, *The Santa Fe Trail* (New York: Longmans, Green, 1930), pp. 68–9. Duffus credits George P. Morehouse with obtaining the quote from H. H. Harris. It is known that the Harris family owned property next to Becknell's property in Franklin. Harris may have witnessed the event as a boy or heard his father describe it. As for Morehouse, his home was Council Grove, Kansas, a stopping point on the Santa Fe Trail. A civic leader and politician, he also was an avid researcher and writer on such subjects as the Santa Fe Trail and the Kansas Indians.

FIVE: THE SANTA FE TRAIL, 1822–1825

1. Thomas James, *Three Years among the Indians and Mexicans* (St. Louis: Missouri Historical Society, 1916), a reprint of the rare first edition published at Waterloo, Illinois, in 1846. James was about sixty-four years old when he dictated his reminiscences to Nathan Niles, an attorney. Just after they were published in a 130-page book, the work was quickly withdrawn from circulation and destroyed by Niles because of James's characterizations of men prominent in the fur and Indian trade. The 1916 edition, edited by Walter B. Douglas, was limited to 365 numbered copies. Although the work is somewhat of a classic, James's memory for dates apparently was faulty. For instance, he dated his arrival in Santa Fe as December 1, 1821, about two weeks after William Becknell arrived, yet neither man mentions the other in his recollections. See also "Thomas James," by Frederic E. Voelker, in *The Mountain Men and the Fur Trade of the Far West*, ed. LeRoy R. Hafen, vol. 4 (Glendale, Calif.: Arthur H. Clark, 1966), pp. 158–62. Details on the keelboat may be found in Hiram Martin Chittenden, *The American Fur Trade of the Far West: A History of the Pioneer Trading Posts and Early Fur Companies of the Missouri Valley and the Rocky Mountains and of the Overland Commerce with Santa Fe* (Stanford, Calif.: Academic Reprints, 1954), vol. 1, pp. 32–4.

2. Justus H. Rogers, *Colusa County, Its History Traced from a State of Nature through the Early Period of Settlement and Development, to the Present Day . . .* (Orland, Calif.: privately printed, 1891), p. 353. This work contains the "Autobiography of Major Stephen Cooper," written in 1888, pp. 351–61. The frontispiece is a photograph of Stephen Cooper as he appeared before his death in California on May 16, 1890.

3. Elliott Coues, ed., *The Journal of Jacob Fowler, Narrating an Adventure from Arkansas Through the Indian Territory, Oklahoma, Kansas, Colorado, and New Mex-*

ico, to the Sources of Rio Grande del Norte, 1821–22 (New York: Francis P. Harper, 1898), p. 167.

4. Ezra Delos Smith, "Jedediah S. Smith and the Settlement of Kansas," *Collections of the Kansas State Historical Society, 1911–1912, Vol. XII* (Topeka: State Printing Office, 1912), pp. 254–5.

5. William Becknell's *Journal* as excerpted from the *Missouri Historical Review,* cited in David A. White, ed., *News of the Plains and Rockies 1803–1865. Original Narratives of Overland Travel and Adventure Selected from the Wagner-Camp and Becker Bibliography of American History* (Spokane, Wash.: Arthur H. Clark, 1996), vol. 2, p. 66.

6. Ibid., p. 67.

7. Ibid.

8. Rex W. Strickland, "James Baird," in *Mountain Men,* ed. Hafen, vol. 3 (1966), pp. 27–37. This article includes an appendix listing the chattels and goods in Baird's possession at the time of his death.

9. *Niles Weekly Register,* Dec. 13, 1823.

10. Floyd F. Ewing, Jr., "The Mule as a Factor in the Development of the Southwest," *Arizona and the West* 5, no. 3 (1963): 316.

11. Walter Williams and Floyd Calvin Shoemaker, *Missouri, Mother of the West* (Chicago and New York: American Historical Society, 1930), vol. 1, pp. 585–6, 619–20. See also John Ashton, *History of Jack Stock and Mules in Missouri* (Jefferson City: Missouri State Board of Agriculture, 1924).

12. *Missouri Intelligencer,* Sept. 2, 1825. See also "The Santa Fe Trail: M. M. Marmaduke Journal," in *Missouri Historical Review* 6 (St. Louis: Missouri Historical Society, 1911): 1–10. Marmaduke's journal is also reproduced in White, *Plains and Rockies,* vol. 2, pp. 71–5.

13. Ibid.

14. Duncan Emrich, *It's an Old Wild West Custom* (New York: Vanguard Press, 1949), pp. 178–9.

15. James O. Pattie, *The Personal Narrative of James O. Pattie, the 1831 Edition, Unabridged* . . . (Philadelphia and New York: J. B. Lippincott, 1962), pp. 11–230.

16. Thomas Hart Benton was born on March 14, 1782, at Hart's Mill, near Hillsborough, North Carolina. After his education, Benton moved with his family to the Cumberland Valley of Tennessee in 1801. There he helped to farm, taught school, and studied law. Benton was licensed to practice law in 1806 and became a state senator in Tennessee in 1809. He served as a colonel of the Tennessee militia and as an aide to Andrew Jackson during the War of 1812. In 1818, he became editor of the *St. Louis Enquirer,* a position he held until 1826. The newspaper helped Benton advance his political career; he was elected a U.S. senator in 1820, after Missouri became a state. He entered the Senate in August 1821 and served there continuously until March 1851. Benton died on April 10, 1858.

17. White, "Augustus Storrs, 1825," in *Plains and Rockies,* vol. 2, pp. 91–2. Augustus Storrs was born in New England in 1791. He came west and served as post-

master and justice of the peace at Franklin, Missouri Territory, in 1819, before statehood, and again as postmaster from 1821 to 1823. In 1824 he was a member of the LeGrand-Marmaduke trading caravan to Santa Fe. He died in Refugio County, Texas, in 1850.

18. *Missouri Intelligencer,* Apr. 22, 1823, as quoted in White, *Plains and Rockies,* vol. 2, pp. 60–1, 65. See also Augustus Storrs and Alphonso Wetmore, *Santa Fe Trail. First Reports: 1825* (Houston, Tex.: Stagecoach Press, 1960), pp. 3–69, which contains the complete text of the original documents.

19. *Plains and Rockies,* vol. 2, pp. 101–103.

20. Buford Rowland, ed., "Report of the Commissioners on the Road from Missouri to New Mexico, October 1827," *New Mexico Historical Review* 14, no. 3 (July 1939): 213–5. Congressional support for roads was nothing new when the survey of the Santa Fe Trail was approved. In 1802, Congress stated that highways should be freely available to all travelers, and work on a national road began in 1811 and finally reached Illinois in 1838. Its route follows closely present-day U.S. Highway 40.

SIX: SURVEYING THE ROAD TO SANTA FE, 1825–1827

1. Ora Brooks Peake, *A History of the United States Indian Factory System, 1795–1822* (Denver: Sage Books, 1954), pp. 19 ff. See also Kate L. Gregg, ed., *The Road to Santa Fe. The Journal and Diaries of George Champlin Sibley and Others Pertaining to the Surveying and Marking of a Road from the Missouri Frontier to the Settlements of New Mexico, 1825–1827* (Albuquerque: University of New Mexico Press, 1952), pp. 8–20.

2. Ibid.

3. Ibid., p. 27.

4. Washington Irving's *Adventures of Captain Bonneville; or, Scenes beyond the Rocky Mountains of the Far West* was first published (1837) in three volumes by Richard Bentley in London. The work has since been reprinted many times. Benjamin Louis Eulalie de Bonneville was born in France in 1796 and came to America as a child. He graduated from West Point in 1815. Seventeen years later he obtained leave from the army and, with a group of more than a hundred men, engaged in the Rocky Mountain fur trade. He returned to military life in 1835 and won a promotion to lieutenant colonel for gallantry during the Mexican War. Bonneville retired from the military in 1861 and spent his last years at Fort Smith, Arkansas. Irving's work contains a long account of the expedition led by Joseph Walker, whom Bonneville sent west to California in 1833 to search for new fur sources. The ten-volume work *The Mountain Men and the Fur Trade of the Far West,* ed. Le Roy R. Hafen (Glendale, Calif.: Arthur H. Clark, 1965–1972) contains biographical sketches of Williams S. "Old Bill" Williams (vol. 8) and Joseph R. Walker (vol. 5).

5. A copy of the contract is in the collections of Lindenwood College at St. Charles, Missouri, an institution started in 1831 by Major George C. and Mary Easton Sibley. The collections include many of George C. Sibley's diaries and papers and those of others involved in the first survey of the Santa Fe Trail.

After retiring from government service, Sibley lived out his life at St. Charles, where he died in 1863.

6. Kate L. Gregg, longtime professor of English and literature at Lindenwood College, St. Charles, Missouri, custodian of the Sibley papers cited in note 5, conducted a search for other documents relating to George C. Sibley and the first survey of the Santa Fe Trail. During the search, in 1938, an employee of the National Archives located Sibley's unpublished journal and other documents. Gregg edited the material, but World War II delayed publication until 1952, when *The Road to Santa Fe* was published by the University of New Mexico Press. By then Gregg had retired and was living in Chehalis, Washington.

7. "Indian Treaties and Councils Affecting Kansas," *Collection of the Kansas State Historical Society, 1923–1925, Vol. XVI* (Topeka: State Printing Office, 1925), pp. 751–2.

8. Gregg, *Road to Santa Fe,* pp. 57–8. See also "Indian Treaties and Councils Affecting Kansas," p. 752.

9. Frederic A. Culmer, "Marking the Santa Fe Trail," *New Mexico Historical Review,* 9, no. 1 (Jan. 1934): 78–93.

10. Gregg, *Road to Santa Fe,* pp. 66–74.

11. *Eighteenth Biennial Report of the Board of Directors of the Kansas State Historical Society* (Topeka: State Printing Office, 1913), p. 121. This work contains the full field notes of Joseph C. Brown, surveyor, 1825–1827.

12. Gregg, *Road to Santa Fe,* p. 93.

13. Ibid., pp. 105–6.

14. Ibid., p. 113.

15. Ibid., p. 234.

16. Max L. Moorhead, *New Mexico's Royal Road: Trade and Travel on the Chihuahua Trail* (Norman: University of Oklahoma Press, 1958), p. 96.

SEVEN: THE BUSINESS OF TRADE, 1821–1829

1. *Missouri Intelligencer,* May 2, 1828.

2. Jonas Viles, "Old Franklin: A Frontier Town of the Twenties," *Mississippi Valley Historical Review* 10, no. 4 (Mar. 1923): 269–82.

3. Charles J. Latrobe, *The Rambler in North America* (London: R. B. Seeley and W. Burnside, 1836), vol. 1, p. 128.

4. Lewis E. Atherton, "James and Robert Aull—a Frontier Missouri Mercantile Firm," *Missouri Historical Review* 30, no. 1 (Oct. 1935): 3–9.

5. Elvid Hunt and Walter E. Lorence, *History of Fort Leavenworth, 1827–1937* (Fort Leavenworth, Kans.: Command and General Staff School Press, 1937), pp. 12–22. See also F. F. Stephens, "Missouri and the Santa Fe Trade," *Missouri Historical Review,* 10, no. 4 (July 1916): 245–9.

6. Louise Barry, *The Beginning of the West: Annals of the Kansas Gateway to the American West, 1540–1854* (Topeka: Kansas State Historical Society, 1972), p. 142.

7. *Missouri Intelligencer,* Sept. 12, 1828.

8. The account of Milton E. Bryan's adventures is based on his reminiscences written in pencil and given to the author many years ago by James Stuppy,

Bryan's great-great-great-grandson. An undated newspaper clipping from an unidentified Seneca, Kansas, newspaper provided by Mr. Stuppy suggests that the reminiscences were prepared and presented as a speech by Bryan in May 1885 at Wathena, Kansas. Bryan's remarks were the basis for a newspaper story titled "The Flight of Time. Adventures on the Plains, Sixty Years Ago," published in the *Kansas Chief,* Troy, June 9, 1887. Bryan was married in 1833 and settled down near St. Joseph, Missouri, but the discovery of gold in California saw him go to California in 1852, where he panned more than two thousand dollars in gold dust before returning to Missouri in the fall of 1853. When Kansas Territory was opened in 1854, Bryan settled at Wathena, a new settlement across the Missouri River from Missouri. There he lived until his death on March 27, 1892, at the age of eighty-five. Bryan was a great-nephew of Daniel Boone's wife, Rebecca Bryan, and a great-nephew of James Wilson of Pennsylvania, one of the signers of the Declaration of Independence and later a U.S. Supreme Court justice.

9. Philip St. George Cooke, "A Journey on the Santa Fe Trail," ed. William E. Connelley, *Mississippi Valley Historical Review* 12, no. 1 (June 1925): 72–98; 12, no. 2 (Sept. 1925): 227–55.

10. Stephens, "Missouri and the Santa Fe Trade," pp. 253–4.

11. Otis E. Young, *The First Military Escort on the Santa Fe Trail, 1829: From the Journal and Reports of Major Bennet Riley and Lieutenant Philip St. George Cooke* (Glendale, Calif.: Arthur H. Clark, 1952), pp. 146–8.

EIGHT: THE GROWTH OF TRADE, 1830–1835

1. William E. Connelley, *A Standard History of Kansas and Kansans* (Chicago and New York: Lewis Publishing, 1918), vol. 1, p. 140.

2. *Western Monitor,* Mar. 31 and Apr. 7, 1830. Josiah Gregg, *Commerce of the Prairies; or, The Journal of a Santa Fe Trader* (New York: Henry G. Langley, 1844), vol. 2, p. 160.

3. Ibid., vol. 1, pp. 35–6.

4. *Missouri Intelligencer,* Oct. 15, 1831. See also Gregg, *Commerce of the Prairies,* vol. 1, pp. 47–8.

5. The best source of information on Jedediah Smith is Dale L. Morgan, *Jedediah Smith and the Opening of the West* (Indianapolis and New York: Bobbs-Merrill, 1953). For Jackson, see Carl D. W. Hays, "David E. Jackson" in *The Mountain Men and the Fur Trade of the Far West,* ed. LeRoy R. Hafen, vol. 9 (Glendale, Calif.: Arthur H. Clark, 1972), pp. 215–44. For Sublette, see John E. Sunder, *Bill Sublette Mountain Man* (Norman: University of Oklahoma Press, 1959).

6. Ezra Delos Smith, "Jedediah S. Smith and the Settlement of Kansas," *Collections of the Kansas State Historical Society, 1911–1912. Vol. XII* (Topeka: State Printing Office, 1912), pp. 254–5.

7. Albert Pike, *Prose Sketches and Poems, Written in the Western Country* (College Station: Texas A&M Press, 1987), p. xii.

8. Ibid. pp. 38–9.

9. Susan Calafate Boyle, *Los Capitalistas: Hispano Merchants and the Santa Fe Trade* (Albuquerque: University of New Mexico Press, 1997), pp. 60–1. See also

Max L. Moorhead, *New Mexico's Royal Road: Trade and Travel on the Chihuahua Trail* (Norman: University of Oklahoma Press, 1958), pp. 65–6.

10. W. F. Switzler, *Switzler's Illustrated History of Missouri, from 1541 to 1881* (St. Louis: C. R. Barns, 1881), pp. 223–7.

11. Gregg, *Commerce of the Prairies*, vol. 1, p. 160.

12. J. Evarts Greene, *The Santa Fe Trade: Its Route and Character* (Worcester, Mass.: Press of Charles Hamilton, 1893), pp. 11–12.

13. *Missouri Republican*, Mar. 3, 1833. The story is also cited in Gregg, *Commerce of the Prairies*, vol. 2, pp. 49–53; in Hiram Martin Chittenden, *The American Fur Trade of the Far West: A History of the Pioneer Trading Posts and Early Fur Companies of the Missouri Valley and the Rocky Mountains and the Overland Commerce with Santa Fe* (Stanford, Calif.: Academic Reprints, 1954), vol. 2, p. 550; and Louise Barry, *The Beginning of the West: Annals of the Kansas Gateway to the American West, 1540–1854* (Topeka: Kansas State Historical Society, 1972), pp. 224–5.

14. Barry, Beginning of the West, pp. 247–8.

15. Marian Meyer, *Mary Donoho, New First Lady of the Santa Fe Trail* (Santa Fe: Ancient City Press, 1991), pp. 17–82.

16. David Lavender tells this story in his fine book *Bent's Fort* (Garden City, N.Y.: Doubleday, 1954), pp. 120–2. Samuel P. Arnold repeats it in "William W. Bent," a biographical sketch in ed. Hafen, *Mountain Men*, vol. 6 (1968), pp. 66–7.

17. George Bird Grinnell, "Bent's Old Fort and Its Builders," *Collections of the Kansas State Historical Society, 1919–1922*, Vol. XV (Topeka: State Printing Office, 1923), pp. 38–42.

Nine: Over the Trail, 1835–1840

1. The late-nineteenth-century account appears in Howard Louis Conrad, *"Uncle Dick" Wootton: The Pioneer Frontiersman of the Rocky Mountain Region* (Chicago: W. E. Dibble, 1890), p. 36. Gregg's figures appear in his *Commerce of the Prairies; or, The Journal of a Santa Fe Trade* (New York: Henry G. Langley, 1844), vol. 1, p. 160.

2. Conrad, *"Uncle Dick" Wootton*, pp. 35–8.

3. Ibid., pp. 39–40.

4. George Bird Grinnell, "Bent's Old Fort and Its Builders," *Collections of the Kansas State Historical Society, 1919–1922*, Vol. XV (Topeka: State Printing Office, 1923), pp. 52–4.

5. *Missouri Argus*, July 4, 1837, as cited in F. F. Stephens, "Missouri and the Santa Fe Trade" (second article), *Missouri Historical Review* 11, no. 4 (July 1917): 311.

6. Gregg, *Commerce of the Prairies*, vol. 2, p. 131.

7. Ibid., pp. 11–2.

8. Ibid., pp. 25–6.

9. Ibid., pp. 114–6.

10. Louise Barry, *The Beginning of the West: Annals of the Kansas Gateway to the American West, 1540–1854* (Topeka: Kansas State Historical Society, 1972), pp. 369–71.

11. John E. Sunder, ed., *Matt Field on the Santa Fe Trail* (Norman: University of Oklahoma Press, 1995), p. 100.

12. Ibid., pp. 160–1.

13. Ibid., p. 208.

14. Susan Calafate Boyle, *Los Capitalistas: Hispano Merchants and the Santa Fe Trade* (Albuquerque: University of New Mexico Press, 1997), pp. 60–1.

15. George Shumway and Howard C. Frey, *Conestoga Wagon 1750–1850* (York, Pa.: George Shumway, 1964), pp. 14–22. See also Jerome H. Wood Jr., *Conestoga Crossroads, Lancaster, Pennsylvania, 1730–1790* (Harrisburg: Pennsylvania Historical and Museum Commission, 1979), p. 109.

16. Emily Ann O'Neil Bott, "Joseph Murphy's Contribution to the Development of the West," *Missouri Historical Review* 47, no. 1 (Oct. 1952): 22.

17. Henry P. Walker, *The Wagonmasters: High Plains Freighting from the Earliest Days of the Santa Fe Trail to 1880* (Norman: University of Oklahoma Press, 1966), pp. 96–8.

18. William F. Cody, *The Life of Hon. William F. Cody Known as Buffalo Bill the Famous Hunter, Scout and Guide* (Hartford, Conn.: Frank E. Bliss, 1879), p. 66.

TEN: YEARS OF CHANGE, 1840–1845

1. Josiah Gregg, *Commerce of the Prairies; or, The Journal of a Santa Fe Trader* (New York: Henry G. Langley, 1844), vol. 2, p. 160. See also Louise Barry, *The Beginning of the West: Annals of the Kansas Gateway to the American West, 1540–1854* (Topeka: Kansas State Historical Society, 1972), pp. 410, 412–3, 415.

2. *Missouri Daily Argus,* July 9 and 29, 1840.

3. *Daily Missouri Republican,* June 12, 1840.

4. "Bypaths of Kansas History, Santa Fe and the West in 1841," *Kansas State Historical Quarterly, Vol. VIII* (Topeka: Kansas State Historical Society, 1939), pp. 104–5. The letter is reproduced in full as it was taken from the Evansville, Ind., newspaper (n.d.) and reprinted in the weekly *New York Tribune*, Nov. 13, 1841.

5. Barry, *Beginning of the West*, pp. 435–6.

6. George Wilkins Kendall, *Narrative of the Texan Santa Fe Expedition . . .* (New York: Harper and Brothers, 1844), vol. 1, pp. 281–316.

7. Barry, *Beginning of the West*, p. 440.

8. Ibid., p. 449. Christopher Houston "Kit" Carson was born in Richmond, Kentucky, in 1809. He moved with his family to St. Louis in 1812, where he was apprenticed to a saddler at age fourteen. In 1826, at age seventeen, he fled his apprenticeship and joined a company of traders at Fort Osage bound for Santa Fe. He then traveled to Taos, met and worked with many mountain men, and between 1828 and 1831 joined the trapper Ewing Young in travels across Arizona and California, learning to trap beaver. During the 1830s he explored much of the West, and with the mountain man Jim Bridger he attended the 1835 rendezvous on the Green River. In the early 1840s he worked as a hunter at Bent's Fort before a chance meeting with John C. Frémont, whom he then guided on three expeditions. He ranched near Taos beginning in 1849 and served as an Indian agent in northern New Mexico

during the late 1850s. After fighting as a Union officer during the Civil War, Carson served briefly as commander of Fort Garland in southern Colorado and then settled with his family at Boggsville, near Las Animas, Colorado. He died at Fort Lyon, Colorado, on May 23, 1868.

9. Thomas Falconer, *Letters and Notes on the Texan Santa Fe Expedition* (New York: Dauber and Pine, 1930), p. 40. This work was first printed by the *New Orleans Picayune* in 1842 and later published in London.

10. Barry, *Beginning of the West*, p. 455.

11. Many newspaper accounts and books, beginning with Gregg's *Commerce of the Prairies* (vol. 2, pp. 166–9), published in 1844, the year after Chávez was killed, contain references to Don Antonio José Chávez's murder, and many disagree on the facts and events and whether Chávez had buried a treasure before being killed. Even the testimony by John McDaniel and his men in a Missouri court leaves unanswered questions, including that of credibility. The early secondary accounts have been repeated, sometimes with embellishment and change, since they were published. The present author published one version in his *True Tales of Old-time Kansas* (Lawrence: University Press of Kansas, 1984), which related the tradition that Chávez did bury much of the money he was carrying before he was killed. The most recent scholarly version, that by Marc Simmons—*Murder on the Santa Fe Trail: An International Incident, 1843*, published in 1987—ignores the possibility of a buried treasure.

12. Barry, *Beginning of the West*, pp. 486–7.

13. Ibid., p. 504. See also Gregg, *Commerce of the Prairies*, vol. 2, p. 177; and William R. Bernard, "Westport and the Santa Fe Trade," *Transactions of the Kansas State Historical Society, 1905–1906, Vol. IX* (Topeka: State Printing Office, 1906), p. 556. The latter article includes Philip St. George Cooke's account of the Snively-Warfield event as published by the *Army and Navy Journal* during the summer of 1882.

14. Barry, *Beginning of the West*, pp. 512, 519.

15. Josiah Gregg's *Commerce of the Prairies* was first published in 1844 in New York City. It remains one of the classic accounts of the nineteenth-century American West, not only because the author was a participant but because, as the late historian Reuben Gold Thwaites observed, Gregg "judiciously mingles history, description, and narrative in such proportions that the interest is retained throughout." Born on July 19, 1806, in Tennessee, Gregg set out for Santa Fe in 1831 to recover his health. He soon became an active trader on the Santa Fe Trail. He took part in the Mexican War as a government agent and interpreter, and then in 1850 led a small exploration party to California. While suffering from hunger in trying to reach the Sacramento Valley, Gregg fell from his horse and died of starvation. Companions dug a hole with sticks, buried the body, and then covered the grave with stones.

16. James Josiah Webb, *Adventures in the Santa Fe Trade 1844–1847*, ed. Ralph P. Bieber (Glendale, Calif.: Arthur H. Clark, 1931), pp. 47–9.

17. Barry, *Beginning of the West*, p. 527.

18. Ibid., p. 528.

19. Ibid., pp. 536–8, 545.

20. Ibid., pp. 539–47, 556, 359–60. See also Westport Improvement Association, *Westport, 1812–1912* (Kansas City, Mo.: Press of Franklin Hudson Publishing, 1912), pp. 19–24. This scarce booklet is a contribution to the history of Westport.

Eleven: The Mexican War and the Santa Fe Trade, 1846–1848

1. There are several good histories of the Mexican War, including Robert W. Johannsen, *To the Halls of the Montezumas: The Mexican War in the American Imagination* (1985); John H. Schroeder, *Mr. Polk's War: American Opposition and Dissent, 1846–1848* (1973); and John E. Weems, *To Conquer a Peace: The War between the United States and Mexico* (1988).

2. Edwin Bryant, *What I Saw in California: Being the Journal of a Tour . . .* (New York and Philadelphia: D. Appleton, 1848), p. 14.

3. *New York Tribune*, Dec. 4, 1847, quoting the *St. Louis New Era*. See also David Dary, *Entrepreneurs of the Old West* (New York: Alfred A. Knopf, 1986), p. 132.

4. Susan Shelby Magoffin, *Down the Santa Fe Trail and into Mexico: The Diary of Susan Shelby Magoffin, 1846–1847*, ed. Stella A. Drumm (New Haven, Conn.: Yale University Press, 1926), pp. 42–3.

5. Ibid., p. 48.

6. Louise Barry, *The Beginning of the West: Annals of the Kansas Gateway to the American West, 1540–1854* (Topeka: Kansas State Historical Society, 1972), p. 626.

7. Magoffin, *Down the Santa Fe Trail*, pp. 60–1.

8. Ibid., p. 72.

9. Ralph Emerson Twitchell, *Dr. Josiah Gregg, Historian of the Santa Fe Trail* (Santa Fe: Historical Society of New Mexico, 1924), p. 11.

10. Magoffin, *Down the Santa Fe Trail*, pp. 72–3. Her quote from Gregg is from *Commerce of the Prairies; or, The Journal of a Santa Fe Trader* (New York: Henry G. Langley), vol. 1, pp. 99–100.

11. Barry, *Beginning of the West*, pp. 642–3.

12. Ibid., pp. 647, 648, 650.

13. Ibid., p. 652.

14. George Frederick Augustus Ruxton, *Adventures in Mexico and the Rocky Mountains* (New York: Harper & Brothers, 1848), p. 190.

15. Bryant, *What I Saw in California*, pp. 13–5.

16. Barry, *Beginning of the West*, pp. 671–2. See also Lilla Maloy Brigham, *The Story of Council Grove and the Santa Fe Trail* ([Council Grove]: privately printed, 1921), pp. 8, 12.

17. The most scholarly study of Francis X. Aubry is Donald Chaput's *Francois X. Aubry: Trader, Trailmaker and Voyageur in the Southwest, 1846–1854* (Glendale, Calif.: Arthur H. Clark, 1975). Many of Aubry's journals are reprinted in this work.

Twelve: Forts, Emigrants, and Freighting, 1849–1852

1. Louise Barry, *The Beginning of the West: Annals of the Kansas Gateway to the American West, 1540–1854* (Topeka: Kansas State Historical Society, 1972), p. 794.

2. Ibid., pp. 807–8.

3. Ibid., pp. 802–3. The printing plant of the *Santa Fe Republican* was owned by the U.S. Army. Soldiers were assigned to the paper as printers. Hovey seems to have been a civilian hired to edit the paper. The first regular issue of the *Republican* appeared on September 10, 1847, but the army decided not to subsidize it indefinitely. In late November 1849, the army sold the printing plant to the *Santa Fe New Mexican.*

4. H. M. T. Powell, *The Santa Fe Trail to California, 1849–1852* (New York: Sol Lewis, 1981), p. 29.

5. Ibid., p. 45.

6. Ibid., p. 74.

7. Robert M. Utley, *Fort Union National Monument* (Washington, D.C.: National Park Service, 1962), p. 9.

8. Barry, *Beginning of the West,* p. 853.

9. Ibid., p. 873.

10. Walker Wyman, "Freighting: A Big Business on the Santa Fe Trail," *Kansas Historical Quarterly* 1 (1931): 19. See also Donald Chaput, *Francois X. Aubry: Trader, Trailmaker and Voyageur in the Southwest* (Glendale, Calif.: Arthur H. Clark, 1975), pp. 83–6.

11. Barry, *Beginning of the West,* p. 890.

12. Wyman, "Freighting," pp. 19–20, citing the *Missouri Republican,* Sept. 28, 1850.

13. Morris F. Taylor, *First Mail West: Stagecoach Lines on the Santa Fe Trail* (Albuquerque: University of New Mexico Press, 1971), pp. 13, 28–30. See also Barry, *Beginning of the West,* p. 950; and Frank A. Root and William E. Connelley, *The Overland Stage to California* (Topeka, Kans.: privately printed, 1901), p. 5. Adhesive postage stamps were first approved and issued in 1847 by the U.S. Post Office.

14. Barry, *Beginning of the West,* pp. 890, 908.

15. Kenneth L. Holmes, ed., *Covered Wagon Women: Diaries and Letters from the Western Trails, 1840–1890,* vol. 2 (Glendale, Calif.: Arthur H. Clark, 1983), pp. 36–7. The massacre of the express mail party does not refer to David Waldo's mail service, which did not begin until July 1, 1850.

16. Ibid., pp. 39–40.

17. Ibid., pp. 19, 41.

18. Barry, *Beginning of the West,* pp. 999, 1042.

19. Stephen L. Massey, *James's Traveler's Companion* (Cincinnati, Ohio: J. A. & U. P. James, 1851), as cited by Barry, *Beginning of the West,* p. 1054.

20. Barry, *Beginning of the West,* pp. 1005, 1120–1.

21. Ibid., pp. 1005–6, 1037–8.

22. Ibid., p. 1051.

23. David Dary, "Storied Silver, Fabled Gold: Buried Treasure Legends along the Santa Fe Trail," *The Santa Fe Trail New Perspectives: Essays in Colorado History* (Denver: Colorado Historical Society, 1987), pp. 102–3. Other buried-treasure legends relating to the Santa Fe Trail are included.

24. Leola Howard Blanchard, *Conquest of Southwest Kansas* (Wichita, Kans.: Wichita Eagle Press, 1931), pp. 36–7.

25. Marian Russell, *Land of Enchantment: Memoirs of Marion Russell along the Santa Fe Trail* (Albuquerque: University of New Mexico Press, 1981), p. 13.
26. Ibid., pp. 11–30.
27. David Dary, "The Crazy Bet of F. X. Aubry," in *True Tales of Old-time Kansas* (Lawrence: University Press of Kansas, 1984), pp. 36–7. See also Donald Chaput, *Francois X. Aubry: Trader, Trailmaker and Voyageur in the Southwest 1846–1854* (Glendale, Calif.: Arthur H. Clark, 1975), pp. 157–9.

Thirteen: New Tensions and Trade, 1853–1860

1. George Bird Grinnell, "Bent's Old Fort and Its Builders," *Collections of the Kansas State Historical Society 1919–1922,* Vol. XV (Topeka: State Printing Office, 1923), pp. 81–2.
2. W. F. Pride, *The History of Fort Riley* (Fort Riley, Kans.: privately printed, 1926), pp. 61–3.
3. Louise Barry, *The Beginning of the West: Annals of the Kansas Gateway to the American West, 1540–1854* (Topeka: Kansas State Historical Society, 1972), p. 1150.
4. Percival G. Lowe, *Five Years a Dragoon ('49 to '54) and Other Adventures on the Great Plains* (Kansas City, Mo.: Franklin Hudson Publishing, 1906), pp. 128–9.
5. Barry, *Beginning of the West,* p. 1159.
6. Bernard Bryan Smyth, *The Heart of the New Kansas: A Pamphlet Historical and Descriptive of Southwestern Kansas* (Great Bend, Kans.: B. B. Smyth, 1880), pp. 61–8.
7. C. C. Spaulding, *Annals of the City of Kansas* (Kansas City, Mo.: Van Horn & Abeel's Printing House, 1858), pp. 74–81.
8. Raymond W. Settle and Mary L. Settle, *Empire on Wheels* (Stanford, Calif.: Stanford University Press, 1949), p. 28.
9. Randolph B. Marcy, *The Prairie Traveler: A Hand-book for Overland Expeditions* (New York: Harper & Brothers, Publishers, 1859), pp. 71–4.
10. Jane Lenz Elder and David J. Weber, eds., *Trading in Santa Fe: John M. Kingsbury's Correspondence with James Josiah Webb, 1853–1861* (Dallas: Southern Methodist University Press, DeGolyer Library, 1996). The letters reprinted in this work provide many insights into the volume and value of merchandise shipped over the Santa Fe Trail during the 1850s.
11. William H. Davis, *El Gringo; or, New Mexico and Her People* (New York: Harper & Brothers, 1857), pp. 272–3.
12. Morris F. Taylor, *First Mail West: Stagecoach Lines on the Santa Fe Trail* (Albuquerque: University of New Mexico Press, 1971), pp. 39–40.
13. James Alexander Little, *What I Saw on the Old Santa Fe Trail* (Plainfield, Ind.: Friends Press, 1904), pp. 3–27.
14. Barry, *Beginning of the West,* p. 1210.
15. David K. Clapsaddle, "Toll Bridges on the Santa Fe Trail," *Wagon Tracks* 13, no. 2 (1999): 15–7.
16. Mamie Stine Sharp, "Home-coming Centennial Celebration at Council Grove, June 27 to July 2, 1921," *Collections of the Kansas State Historical Society*

1923–1925, Vol. XVI (Topeka: Kansas State Printing Plant, 1925), p. 556. See also Lilla Maloy Brigham, *The Story of Council Grove on the Santa Fe Trail* ([Council Grove]: privately printed, 1921), p. 20; and Mark L. Gardner, "Malcolm Conn: Merchant on the Trail," *Wagon Tracks* 1, no. 2 (1987), pp. 7–8.

17. Heinrich Balduin Mollhausen, "Over the Santa Fe Trail Through Kansas in 1858," *Kansas Historical Quarterly* 16, no. 4 (1948): 374–5. The diary was translated from German by John A. Burzle and edited by Robert Taft.

18. David Dary, *Entrepreneurs of the Old West* (New York: Alfred A. Knopf, 1986), pp. 161–3.

19. "The Santa Fe Trail in Johnson County, Kansas," *Collections of the Kansas State Historical Society, 1909–1910*, Vol. XI (Topeka: State Printing Office, 1910), pp. 457–8.

20. David Dary, "The First White Woman to Climb Pike's Peak," *True Tales of Old-time Kansas* (Lawrence: University Press of Kansas, 1984), pp. 274–77.

21. *Kansas City Star*, Aug. 6, 1905.

22. Theo. S. Case, *History of Kansas City, Missouri* (Syracuse and New York: D. Mason, 1888), p. 33.

23. John D. Cruise, "Early Days on the Union Pacific," *Collections of the Kansas State Historical Society, 1909–1010*, Vol. XI (Topeka: State Printing Office, 1910), p. 533.

24. William E. Unrau, *History of Fort Larned* ([Larned, Kans.]: [Tiller and Toiler], [1950s]), p. [4]. Although no publisher or place of publication appears in this twenty-four-page pamphlet, it probably was published by the *Tiller and Toiler*, Larned's newspaper. An introductory note tells readers that the material was taken from the author's master's thesis at the University of Wyoming. Essentially the same material was later published under the title "The Story of Fort Larned" in the *Kansas Historical Quarterly* 13, no. 3 (autumn 1957).

25. *Westport (Missouri) Border Star*, July 14, 1860.

FOURTEEN: THE CIVIL WAR, 1861–1865

1. Walker D. Wyman, "Kansas City, Mo., a Famous Freighter Capital," *Kansas Historical Quarterly* 6, no. 1 (1937): 10–2.

2. Don E. Alberts, *The Battle of Glorieta, Union Victory in the West* (College Station: Texas A&M University Press, 1998), pp. 3–173.

3. William E. Connelley, *Quantrill and the Border Wars* (Cedar Rapids, Iowa: Torch Press, 1910), pp. 196–204, 236–47, 254–8.

4. D. Hubbard, "Reminiscences of the Yeager Raid, on the Santa Fe Trail, in 1863," *Transactions of the Kansas State Historical Society, 1903–1904, Vol. III* (Topeka: Geo. A. Clark, State Printer, 1904), pp. 168–71.

5. Alexander Majors, *Seventy Years on the Frontier* (Chicago: Rand McNally, 1893), p. 105.

6. Ibid., pp. 71–193. See also Raymond W. Settle and Mary L. Settle, *Empire on Wheels* (Stanford, Calif.: Stanford University Press, 1949), pp. 27–32.

7. William F. Shamleffer, "Merchandising Sixty Years Ago," *Collections of the Kansas State Historical Society, 1923–1925, Vol. XVI* (Topeka: Kansas State Printing Plant, 1925), pp. 567–8.

8. R. M. Armstrong, "Sixty Years in Kansas and Council Grove," *Collections of the Kansas State Historical Society, 1923–1925, Vol. XVI* (Topeka: Kansas State Printing Plant, 1925), pp. 552–7.

9. This story of Matteo Boccalini is included in my *True Tales of Old-time Kansas* (Lawrence: University Press of Kansas, 1984), pp. 220–4. John Maloy first told the story in the *Council Grove Republican*, Feb. 7, 1890, after having interviewed old-timers in Council Grove who remembered Boccalini, who is identified as Juan Maria Agostini in T. M. Pearce, *New Mexico Place Names* (Albuquerque: University of New Mexico Press, 1965), p. 70.

10. Alexander Caldwell, "Address of Alexander Caldwell . . . ," *Transactions of the Kansas State Historical Society, Vol. III* (Topeka: Kansas Publishing House, 1886), pp. 453–4.

11. Charles Raber, "Personal Recollections of Life on the Plains from 1860 to 1868," *Collections of the Kansas State Historical Society, 1923–1925, Vol. XVI* (Topeka: Kansas State Printing Plant, 1925), pp. 321–2.

12. *Santa Fe Gazette,* June 11, 1864.

13. George A. Root, "Reminiscences of William Darnell," *Collections of the Kansas State Historical Society, 1926–1928, Vol. XVII* (Topeka: Kansas State Printing Plant, 1928), pp. 508–9.

14. Caldwell, "Address," pp. 452–3.

FIFTEEN: THE SLOW DEATH OF THE TRAIL, 1866–1880

1. Walker Wyman, "Freighting: A Big Business on the Santa Fe Trail," *Kansas Historical Quarterly,* 1, no. 1 (1931): 26.

2. W. E. Webb, *Buffalo Land: An Authentic Account of the Discoveries, Adventures, and Mishaps of a Scientific and Sporting Party in the Wild West* (Cincinnati, Ohio, and Chicago: E. Hannaford, 1872), p. 142. Although this work contains much fiction, Webb's descriptions are generally accurate.

3. *Daily (Denver) Colorado Tribune,* May 12 and 24, 1868.

4. *New York Tribune,* Dec. 11, 1869.

5. William E. Connelley, "The Treaty Held at Medicine Lodge," *Collections of the Kansas State Historical Society, 1926–1928, Vol. XVII* (Topeka: Kansas State Printing Plant, 1928), pp. 603–4.

6. Charles E. Campbell, "Down among the Red Men," *Collections of the Kansas State Historical Society, 1926–1928, Vol. XVII* (Topeka: Kansas State Printing Plant, 1928), p. 633.

7. P. G. Scott, "Diary of a Freighting Trip from Kit Carson to Trinidad in 1870," *Colorado Magazine* 8 (July 1931): 154.

8. *La Animas (Colorado) Leader,* Feb. 13, 1874.

SIXTEEN: THE LEGACY OF THE TRAIL, 1880–2000

1. T. A. Cordry, *The Story of the Marking of the Santa Fe Trail by the Daughters of the American Revolution in Kansas and the State of Kansas* (Topeka, Kans.: Crane, 1915), pp. 13–135.

2. Chris Wilson, *The Myth of Santa Fe Creating a Modern Regional Tradition* (Albuquerque: University of New Mexico Press, 1997), p. 71.

3. Clifton Johnson, *Highways and Byways of the Rocky Mountains* (New York: Macmillan, 1910), pp. 115–7.

4. Kathleen L. Howard and Diana F. Pardue, *Inventing the Southwest: The Fred Harvey Company and Native American Art* (Flagstaff, Ariz.: Northland Publishing, 1996), pp. 9–22.

5. Dan L. Thrapp, *Encyclopedia of Frontier Biography* (Glendale, Calif.: Arthur H. Clark, 1988), vol. 2, pp. 884–5.

6. Wilson, *Myth of Santa Fe*, p. 95.

7. J. Frank Dobie, *Guide to Life and Literature of the Southwest* (Austin: University of Texas Press, 1943), pp. 50–1.

Bibliography

BOOKS

Adler, Jeffrey S. *Yankee Merchants and the Making of the Urban West: The Rise and Fall of Antebellum St. Louis.* Cambridge U.K.: Cambridge University Press, 1991.

Alberts, Don E. *The Battle of Glorieta, Union Victory in the West.* College Station: Texas A&M University Press, 1998.

Allyn, Joseph Pratt. *West by Southwest, Letters of Joseph Pratt Allyn, a Traveller along the Santa Fe Trail, 1863.* Dodge City: Kansas Heritage Center, 1984.

Ambrose, Stephen E. *Undaunted Courage: Meriwether Lewis, Thomas Jefferson, and the Opening of the American West.* New York: Simon and Schuster, 1997. The most definitive treatment of the Lewis and Clark expedition to date.

Arnold, Samuel P. *Eating up the Santa Fe Trail.* Niwot: University Press of Colorado, 1990. A delightful work on what people on the trail ate and how it was prepared.

Audubon, John James. *The Life of John James Audubon, the Naturalist.* New York and London: G. P. Putnam's Sons, 1902. Edited by Audubon's widow.

Bannon, John Francis. *The Spanish Borderlands Frontier, 1513–1821.* New York: Holt, Rinehart and Winston, 1963.

Barry, Louise. *The Beginning of the West: Annals of the Kansas Gateway to the American West, 1540–1854.* Topeka: Kansas State Historical Society, 1972. An invaluable reference work on events relating to the Santa Fe Trail before 1854.

Bishop, Morris. *The Odyssey of Cabeza de Vaca.* New York: Century, 1933.

Blakeslee, Donald J. *Along Ancient Trails: The Mallet Expedition of 1739.* Niwot: University Press of Colorado, 1995.

Blanchard, Leola Howard. *Conquest of Southwest Kansas.* Wichita, Kans.: Wichita Eagle Press, 1931.

Bolton, Herbert Eugene. *Coronado, Knight of Pueblos and Plains.* New York and Albuquerque: Whittlesey House and University of New Mexico Press, 1949.

Bolton, Herbert Eugene, ed. *Spanish Exploration in the Southwest, 1542–1706.* New York: Barnes & Noble, 1959. A reprint of the 1908 first edition. This work contains original narratives.

Boothroyd, Geoffrey. *Guns Through the Ages.* New York: Sterling Publishing, 1962.

Boyle, Susan Calafate. *Los Capitalistas: Hispano Merchants and the Santa Fe Trade.* Albuquerque: University of New Mexico Press, 1997.

Branch, E. Douglas. *Westward, the Romance of the American Frontier.* New York: Cooper Square Publishers, 1969. A reprint of the 1930 first edition.

Brandon, William. *Quivira: Europeans in the Region of the Santa Fe Trail, 1540–1820.* Athens: Ohio University Press, 1990.

Brigham, Lilla Maloy. *The Story of Council Grove on the Santa Fe Trail.* ([Council Grove]): privately printed, 1921.

Brown, William E. *The Santa Fe Trail.* St. Louis: Patrice Press, 1988. This is a reprint of the National Park Service 1963 Historic Sites Survey.

Bryant, Edwin. *What I Saw in California: Being the Journal of a Tour. . . .* New York and Philadelphia: D. Appleton, 1848.

Cabeza de Vaca. *Cabeza de Vaca's Adventures in the Unknown Interior of America.* Trans. and ed. Cyclone Covey. New York: Crowell-Collier, 1961.

Carr, Lucien. *Missouri: A Bone of Contention.* Boston and New York: Houghton, Mifflin, 1888.

Case, Theo. S. *History of Kansas City, Missouri.* Syracuse and New York: D. Mason, 1888.

Chalfant, William Y. *Cheyennes and Horse Soldiers: The 1857 Expedition and the Battle of Solomon's Fork.* Norman: University of Oklahoma Press, 1989.

Chalfant, William Y. *Dangerous Passage: The Santa Fe Trail and the Mexican War.* Norman: University of Oklahoma Press, 1994.

Chaput, Donald. *Francois X. Aubry: Trader, Trailmaker and Voyageur in the Southwest 1846–1854.* Glendale, Calif.: Arthur H. Clark, 1975.

Chittenden, Hiram Martin. *The American Fur Trade of the Far West: A History of the Pioneer Trading Posts and Early Fur Companies of the Missouri Valley and the Rocky Mountains and of the Overland Commerce with Santa Fe.* 2 vols. Stanford, Calif.: Academic Reprints, 1954. A reprint of the 1902 first edition.

Clark, Calvin Perry. *Two Diaries: The Diary and Journal of Calvin Perry Clark Who Journeyed by Wagon Train from Plano, Illinois to Denver and Vicinity over the Santa Fe Trail in the Year 1859, Together with the Diary of His Sister Helen E. Clark Who Made a Similar Journey by the Northern Route in the Year 1860.* Denver, Colo.: Denver Public Library, 1962.

Cody, William F. *The Life of Hon. William F. Cody Known as Buffalo Bill the Famous Hunter, Scout and Guide.* Hartford, Conn.: Frank E. Bliss, 1879.

Collections Missouri Historical Society 4, no. 2 (1913).

Connelley, William E. *A Standard History of Kansas and Kansans.* 5 vols. Chicago and New York: Lewis Publishing, 1918.

Connelley, William E. *Quantrill and the Border Wars.* Cedar Rapids, Iowa: Torch Press, 1910.

Connor, Seymour V., and Jimmy M. Skaggs. *Broadcloth and Britches, the Santa Fe Trade.* College Station: Texas A&M University Press, 1977.

Conrad, Howard Louis. *"Uncle Dick" Wootton, the Pioneer Frontiersman of the Rocky Mountain Region.* Chicago: W. E. Dibble, 1890.

Cooke, Philip St. George. *Scenes and Adventures in the Army; Or, Romance of Military Life.* Philadelphia: Lindsay & Blakiston, 1857. Cooke's military career began in 1829, when he was assigned as a lieutenant in the military escort commanded by Major Bennett Riley to guard the Santa Fe traders from depredations.

Copeland, Fayette. *Kendall of the* Picayune, *Being His Adventures in New Orleans, on the Texan Santa Fe Expedition, in the Mexican War, and in the Colonization of the Texas Frontier.* Norman: University of Oklahoma Press, 1943.

Cordry, T. A. *The Story of the Marking of the Santa Fe Trail by the Daughters of the American Revolution in Kansas and the State of Kansas.* Topeka, Kans.: Crane, 1915.

Coues, Elliott, ed. *The Journal of Jacob Fowler, Narrating an Adventure from Arkansas Through the Indian Territory, Oklahoma, Kansas, Colorado, and New Mexico, to the Sources of the Rio Grande del Norte, 1821–22.* New York: Francis P. Harper, 1898.

Coyner, David E. *The Lost Trappers: A Collection of Interesting Scenes and Events in the Rocky Mountains.* Philadelphia: Carey and Hart, 1847.

Dale, Edward Everett. *The Indians of the Southwest. A Century of Development Under the United States.* Norman: University of Oklahoma Press, 1949. Published in cooperation with the Huntington Library, San Marino, Calif.

Dary, David. *Entrepreneurs of the Old West.* New York: Alfred A. Knopf, 1986.

Dary, David. *True Tales of Old-time Kansas.* Lawrence: University Press of Kansas, 1984.

Davis, Walter Bickford, and Daniel S. Durrie. *An Illustrated History of Missouri.* St. Louis: A. J. Hall and Company, 1876. Contains biographical sketches of many early Missourians.

Davis, William H. *El Gringo; or, New Mexico and Her People.* New York: Harper & Brothers, 1857. Davis traveled from Independence to Santa Fe in 1853.

Dobie, J. Frank. *Guide to Life and Literature of the Southwest.* Austin: University of Texas Press, 1943.

Douglas, Walter B. *Manuel Lisa.* New York: Argosy-Antiquarian, 1964. First published in 1911, this reprint edition includes hitherto unpublished material annotated and edited by Abraham P. Nasatir.

Duffus, Robert L. *The Santa Fe Trail.* New York: Longmans, Green, 1930.

Eggenhofer, Nick. *Wagons, Mules and Men.* New York: Hastings House, 1961.

Eighteenth Biennial Report of the Board of Directors of the Kansas State Historical Society. Topeka: State Printing Office, 1913. This work contains the full field notes of Joseph C. Brown, surveyor, 1825–1827.

Elder, Jane Lenz, and David J. Weber, eds. *Trading in Santa Fe: John M. Kingsbury's Correspondence with James Josiah Webb, 1853–1861.* Dallas: Southern Methodist University Press, DeGolyer Library, 1996.

Elliott, Richard Smith. *Notes Taken in Sixty Years.* St. Louis: R. P. Studley, 1883.

Emrich, Duncan. *It's an Old Wild West Custom.* New York: Vanguard Press, 1949.

Falconer, Thomas. *Letters and Notes on the Texan Santa Fe Expedition.* New York: Dauber and Pine, 1930.

Farnham, Thomas Jefferson. *Travels in the Great Western Prairies, the Anahuac and Rocky Mountains, and in the Oregon Territory.* Poughkeepsie, N.Y.: Killey and Lossing, 1841. Includes Farnham's account of travel over the Santa Fe Trail from Independence, Missouri, to Bent's Fort in 1839.

Franzwa, Gregory M. *The Santa Fe Trail Revisited.* St. Louis: Patrice Press, 1989. A handy guide to the trail.

Frémont, John Charles. *The Exploring Expedition to the Rocky Mountains, Oregon and California.* Buffalo, N.Y.: Geo. H. Derby; and Cleveland, Ohio: Smith, Knight, 1850.

Froebel, Julius. *Seven Years' Travel in Central America, Northern Mexico, and the Far West of the United States.* London: Richard Bentley, 1859. Froebel, a German, traveled to Chihuahua and returned east by way of the Santa Fe Trail in 1852, 1853, and 1854.

Gardner, Mark L., and Marc Simmons, eds. *The Mexican War Correspondence of Richard Smith Elliott.* Norman: University of Oklahoma Press, 1997.

Garrard, Lewis Hector. *Wah-To-Yah and the Taos Trail; or, Prairie Travel and Scalp Dances, with a Look at Los Rancheros from Muleback and the Rocky Mountain Campfire.* Cincinnati, Ohio: H. W. Derby, 1850. Garrard traveled from Westport to Santa Fe early in the fall of 1846 and returned to St. Louis during the summer of 1847.

Greeley, Horace. *An Overland Journey, from New York to San Francisco in the Summer of 1859.* New York: C. M. Saxton, Barker, 1860.

Greene, J. Evarts. *The Santa Fe Trade: Its Route and Character.* Worcester, Mass.: Press of Charles Hamilton, 1893.

Greene, Max. *The Kanzas Region.* New York: Fowler and Wells, Publishers, 1856. Provides a history of the Santa Fe trade and descriptions of the Santa Fe trail. Greene was a tramp printer sent west by the *Hollidaysburg (Pennsylvania) Register.*

Gregg, Josiah. *Commerce of the Prairies; or, The Journal of a Santa Fe Trader.* 2 vols. New York: Henry G. Langley, 1844. A classic. The first book devoted entirely to the Santa Fe Trail.

Gregg, Kate L., ed. *The Road to Santa Fe: The Journal and Diaries of George Champlin Sibley and Others Pertaining to the Surveying and Marking of a Road from the Missouri Frontier to the Settlements of New Mexico, 1825–1827.* Albuquerque: University of New Mexico Press, 1952.

Gutiérrez, Ramón A. *When Jesus Came, the Corn Mothers Went Away: Marriage, Sexuality, and Power in New Mexico, 1500–1846.* Stanford, Calif.: Stanford University Press, 1991.

Hafen, LeRoy R., ed. *The Mountain Men and the Fur Trade of the Far West.* 10 vols. Glendale, Calif.: Arthur H. Clark, 1965–1972. A definitive work including detailed biographical sketches of mountain men and fur traders in the West.

Hafen, LeRoy R., and Ann W. Hafen. *Old Spanish Trail: Santa Fe to Los Angeles with Extracts from Contemporary Records and Including Diaries of Antonio Armijo and Orville Pratt.* Glendale, Calif.: Arthur H. Clark, 1954.

Hayes, Augustus Allen. *New Colorado and the Santa Fe Trail.* New York: Harper & Brothers, 1880.

Hermann, Binger. *The Louisiana Purchase and Our Title West of the Rocky Mountains with a Review of Annexation by the United States.* Washington, D.C.: Government Printing Office, 1900. Hermann was commissioner of the General Land Office.

Holmes, Kenneth L., ed. *Covered Wagon Women: Diaries and Letters from the Western Trails, 1840–1890.* 11 vols. Glendale, Calif.: Arthur H. Clark, 1983–1993.

Houck, Louis. *The Spanish Regime in Missouri, a Collection of Papers and Documents*

Relating to Upper Louisiana Principally within the Present Limits of Missouri . . . 2 vols. Chicago: W. E. Donnelley & Sons, 1902.

Howard, Kathleen L., and Diana F. Pardue. *Inventing the Southwest: The Fred Harvey Company and Native American Art.* Flagstaff, Ariz.: Northland Publishing, 1996.

Hunt, Elvid, and Walter E. Lorence, *History of Fort Leavenworth, 1827–1937.* Fort Leavenworth, Kans.: Command and General Staff School Press, 1937. Revised and expanded edition of the 1926 first edition.

Inman, Henry. *The Old Santa Fe Trail, the Story of a Great Highway.* New York: Macmillan, 1897.

Inman, Henry. *Stories of the Old Santa Fe Trail.* Kansas City, Mo.: Ramsey, Millett & Hudson, 1881.

Inman, Henry. *Tales of the Trail, Short Stories of Western Life.* Topeka, Kans.: Crane, 1898.

Irving, Washington. *Adventures of Captain Bonneville: or, Scenes Beyond the Rocky Mountains of the Far West.* 3 vols. London: Richard Bentley, 1837.

Irving, Washington. *The Crayon Miscellany . . . a Tour on the Prairies.* Philadelphia: Carey, Lea & Blanchard, 1835.

Jackson, W. Turrentine. *Wagon Roads West, a Study of Federal Road Surveys and Construction in the Trans-Mississippi West, 1846–1869.* Lincoln: University of Nebraska Press, 1979. A reprint of the 1964 first edition published by Yale University Press.

James, General Thomas. *Three Years among the Indians and Mexicans.* St. Louis: Missouri Historical Society, 1916. A reprint of the rare 1846 first edition published at Waterloo, Illinois.

Johnson, Clifton. *Highways and Byways of the Rocky Mountains.* New York: Macmillan, 1910.

Kendall, George Wilkins. *Narrative of the Texan Santa Fe Expedition . . .* 2 vols. New York: Harper and Brothers, 1844.

Kroh, Dorothy Hart. *Morris 1821–1997, a Community on the Ft. Leavenworth Military Road to the Santa Fe Trail.* Kansas City, Kans.: Morris Association for Family and Community Education, 1997.

Lamar, Howard R. *The Trader on the American Frontier, Myth's Victim.* College Station: Texas A&M University Press, 1977.

Latrobe, Charles Joseph. *The Rambler in North America.* 2 vols. London: R. B. Seeley and W. Burnside, 1836. Latrobe accompanied Washington Irving on his tour of the prairies.

Laut, Agnes Christian. *Pilgrims of the Santa Fe.* New York: Frederick A. Stoke, 1931.

Lavender, David. *Bent's Fort.* Garden City, N.Y.: Doubleday & Co., 1954.

Little, James Alexander. *What I Saw on the Old Santa Fe Trail.* Plainfield, Ind.: Friends Press, 1904.

Loomis, Noel M., and Abraham P. Nasatir. *Pedro Vial and the Roads to Santa Fe.* Norman: University of Oklahoma Press, 1967.

Lowe, Percival G. *Five Years a Dragoon ('49 to '54) and Other Adventures on the Great Plains.* Kansas City, Mo.: Franklin Hudson Publishing, 1906.

Magoffin, Susan Shelby. *Down the Santa Fe Trail and into Mexico: The Diary of Susan*

Shelby Magoffin, 1846–1847. Ed. Stella A. Drumm. New Haven, Conn.: Yale University Press, 1926.

Majors, Alexander. *Seventy Years on the Frontier.* Chicago: Rand McNally, 1893.

Marcy, Randolph B. *The Prairie Traveler. A Hand-book for Overland Expeditions.* New York: Harper & Brothers, 1859.

Massey, Stephen L. *James's Traveler's Companion.* Cincinnati, Ohio: J. A. & U. P. James, 1851.

McWilliams, Carey. *North from Mexico: The Spanish-Speaking People of the United States.* New York: Greenwood Press, 1968. This work first appeared in 1949.

Meyer, Marian. *Mary Donoho, New First Lady of the Santa Fe Trail.* Santa Fe: Ancient City Press, 1991.

Morgan, Dale L. *Jedediah Smith and the Opening of the West.* Indianapolis and New York: Bobbs-Merrill, 1953.

Moorhead, Max L. *New Mexico's Royal Road: Trade and Travel on the Chihuahua Trail.* Norman: University of Oklahoma Press, 1958.

Nasatir, Abraham. *Borderland in Retreat: From Spanish Louisiana to the Far Southwest.* Albuquerque: University of New Mexico Press, 1976.

Noyes, Stanley. *Los Comanches: The Horse People, 1751–1845.* Albuquerque: University of New Mexico Press, 1993.

Parkison, Jami. *Path to Glory: A Pictorial Celebration of the Santa Fe Trail.* Kansas City, Mo.: Highwater Editions, 1996.

Parkman, Francis, Jr. *The California and Oregon Trail: Being Sketches of Prairie and Rocky Mountain Life.* New York: George P. Putnam; and London: Putnam's American Agency, 1849. Parkman traveled the Santa Fe Trail from Bent's Fort to Independence on his return east.

Pattie, James O. *The Personal Narrative of James O. Pattie, the 1831 Edition, Unabridged . . .* Philadelphia and New York: J. B. Lippincott, 1962. A reprint edition with an introduction by William H. Goetzmann.

Peake, Ora Brooks. *A History of the United States Indian Factory System, 1795–1822.* Denver, Colo.: Sage Books, 1954.

Pearce, T. M. *New Mexico Place Names.* Albuquerque: University of New Mexico Press, 1965.

Perkins, James H. *Annals of the West: Embracing a Concise Account of Principal Events which Have Occurred in the Western States and Territories.* Cincinnati, Ohio: James R. Albach, 1847.

Pike, Albert. *Prose Sketches and Poems, Written in the Western Country.* Boston: Light & Horton, 1834. Includes a narrative of Pike's experiences and those of Aaron B. Lewis on the Santa Fe Trail. Reprinted by Texas A&M Press in 1987.

Pike, Z. M. *An Account of Expeditions to the Sources of the Mississippi, and through the Western Parts of Louisiana, to the Sources of the Arkansaw, Kans, La Platte, and Pierre Juan, Rivers. . . .* Philadelphia: C. & A. Conrad, 1810.

Powell, H. M. T. *The Santa Fe Trail to California, 1849–1852.* New York: Sol Lewis, 1981. Powell's journal was first printed by the Grabhorn Press for the Book Club of California in an edition of three hundred copies in 1931.

Pride, W. F. *The History of Fort Riley.* Fort Riley, Kan.: privately printed, 1926.

Rathbone, Perry T., ed. *Westward the Way, the Character and Development of the*

Louisiana Territory as Seen by Artists and Writers of the Nineteenth Century. St. Louis: City Art Museum of St. Louis in collaboration with the Walker Art Center, Minneapolis, Minnesota, 1954.

Riddle, Kenyon, *Records and Maps of the Old Santa Fe Trail.* Raton, N. Mex.: published by the author, 1949. With maps in pocket at back of book. This work was reprinted in a revised and enlarged edition by Riddle's son in 1963 at West Palm Beach, Florida.

Rittenhouse, Jack D. *The Santa Fe Trail: A Historical Bibliography.* Albuquerque: University of New Mexico Press, 1971. Contains 718 entries describing 350 books, 250 articles from scholarly journals, and more than 100 congressional documents. Nearly half were written by people who traveled the trail. A great reference work.

Robinson, Jacob S. *A Journal of the Santa Fe Expedition under Colonel Doniphan.* Princeton, N.J.: Princeton University Press, 1932. Robinson's account of the journey from Fort Leavenworth to Santa Fe in 1846.

Rogers, Justus H. *Colusa County, Its History Traced from a State of Nature through the Early Period of Settlement and Development, to the Present Day . . .* Orland, Calif.: privately printed, 1891. This work includes the "Autobiography of Major Stephen Cooper," written in 1888. Cooper was a trader on the Santa Fe Trail in 1822.

Root, Frank A., and William E. Connelley, *The Overland Stage to California.* Topeka, Kans.: privately printed, 1901.

Russell, Carl P. *Guns of the Early Frontiers.* Berkeley: University of California Press, 1957.

Russell, Marian. *Land of Enchantment: Memoirs of Marion Russell along the Santa Fe Trail.* Albuquerque: University of New Mexico Press, 1981.

Ruxton, George Frederick Augustus. *Adventures in Mexico and the Rocky Mountains* (New York: Harper & Brothers, Publishers, 1848). In his essay "Ruxton of the Rocky Mountains" published in the *Bulletin* of the Missouri Historical Society (Jan. 1949), F. E. Voelker wrote that in traveling through Mexico to the Rocky Mountains, Ruxton "was acting in the dual capacity of roving commercial attaché of the British diplomatic service and commercial agent of the Mexican government," apparently seeking to reestablish the Santa Fe Trade that had been interrupted by the Mexican War.

Ryus, William H. *The Second William Penn. A True Account of Incidents that Happened along the Old Santa Fe Trail in the Sixties.* Kansas City, Mo.: Frank T. Riley Publishing, 1915.

Sanchez, Joseph P. *Explorers, Traders, and Slavers, Forging the Old Spanish Trail, 1678–1850.* Salt Lake City: University of Utah Press, 1997.

Segale, Sister Blandina. *At the End of the Santa Fe Trail.* Milwaukee, Wisc.: Bruce Publishing, 1948. This work spans 1850 to 1941.

Settle, Raymond W., and Mary L. Settle. *Empire on Wheels.* Stanford, Calif.: Stanford University Press, 1949.

Shepard, Elihu H. *The Early History of St. Louis and Missouri, to Which Is Appended the Author's Autobiography.* St. Louis: privately printed, 1870.

Shumway, George, and Howard C. Frey. *Conestoga Wagon 1750–1850.* York, Pa.: George Shumway, 1964.

Simmons, Marc. *Coronado's Land: Essays on Daily Life in Colonial New Mexico.* Albuquerque: University of New Mexico Press, 1991.

Simmons, Marc. *Following the Santa Fe Trail: A Guide for Modern Travelers.* Santa Fe: Ancient City Press, 1986. A handy guide to anyone traveling the trail.

Simmons, Marc. *The Last Conquistador: Juan de Oñate and the Settling of the Far Southwest.* Norman: University of Oklahoma Press, 1991.

Simmons, Marc. *Murder on the Santa Fe Trail: An International Incident, 1843.* El Paso, Texas: Texas Western Press, 1987.

Simmons, Marc. *Spanish Government in New Mexico.* Albuquerque: University of New Mexico Press, 1968.

Simmons, Marc, ed. *On the Santa Fe Trail.* Lawrence: University Press of Kansas, 1986. A collection of narratives and reports.

Spaulding, C. C. *Annals of the City of Kansas.* Kansas City, Mo.: Van Horn & Abeel's Printing House, 1858.

Storrs, Augustus, and Wetmore, Alphonso. *Santa Fe Trail. First Reports: 1825.* Houston, Texas: Stagecoach Press, 1960. Contains complete text of two original documents published by the U.S. Senate during the Eighteenth Congress, Second Session, in 1825. The two documents are Senate Document 7, which comprises answers written by Storrs to questions posed by Senator Thomas Hart Benton, and Senate Document 79, containing a petition from citizens of Missouri and a letter from Wetmore.

Sunder, John E. *Bill Sublette Mountain Man.* Norman: University of Oklahoma Press, 1959.

Sunder, John E., ed. *Matt Field on the Santa Fe Trail.* Norman: University of Oklahoma Press, 1960. Collected by Clyde and Mae Reed Port, this work contains a series of articles written by Matt Field for the *New Orleans Picayune.* The work includes his previously unpublished journal relating his experiences on the Santa Fe Trail.

Switzler, W. F. *Switzler's Illustrated History of Missouri, from 1541 to 1881.* St. Louis: C. R. Barns, 1881.

Taylor, Morris F. *First Mail West: Stagecoach Lines on the Santa Fe Trail.* Albuquerque: University of New Mexico Press, 1971.

Thomas, Alfred Barnaby, ed. *After Coronado, Spanish Exploration Northeast of New Mexico, 1696–1727. Documents from the Archives of Spain, Mexico, and New Mexico.* Norman: University of Oklahoma Press, 1935.

Thomas, Alfred Barnaby, ed. *Forgotten Frontiers. A Study of the Spanish Indian Policy of Don Juan Bautista de Anza, Governor of New Mexico, 1777–1787. From the Original Documents in the Archives of Spain, Mexico, and New Mexico.* Norman: University of Oklahoma Press, 1932.

Thrapp, Dan L., *Encyclopedia of Frontier Biography.* 4 vols. Glendale, Calif.: Arthur H. Clark, 1988.

Thwaites, Reuben Gold, ed. *Original Journals of the Lewis and Clark Expedition 1804–1806.* New York: Arno Press, 1969. A reprint of the 1904 edition in seven volumes plus atlas.

Vernon, Joseph S., et al. *Along the Old Trail: A History of the Old and a Story of the*

New Santa Fe Trail. Larned and Cimarron, Kans.: Tucker-Vernon Co. Publishers, 1910.

Villagra, Gaspar Perez de. *History of New Mexico.* Trans. Gilberto Espinosa. Los Angeles: Quivira Society, 1933. This history was originally published in 1610, the year Santa Fe was founded.

Walker, Henry P. *The Wagonmasters: High Plains Freighting from the Earliest Days of the Santa Fe Trail to 1880.* Norman: University of Oklahoma Press, 1966.

Waters, L. L. *Steel Trails to Santa Fe.* Lawrence: University of Kansas Press, 1950.

Watkins, Albert, ed. *Publications of the Nebraska State Historical Society, Vol. XX.* Lincoln: Nebraska State Historical Society, 1922.

Webb, James Josiah. *Adventures in the Santa Fe Trade 1844–1847.* Ed. Ralph P. Bieber. Glendale, Calif.: Arthur H. Clark, 1931.

Webb, W. E. *Buffalo Land: An Authentic Account of the Discoveries, Adventures, and Mishaps of a Scientific and Sporting Party in the Wild West.* Cincinnati, Ohio, and Chicago: E. Hannaford, 1872.

Weber, David J. *The Spanish Frontier in North America.* New Haven, Conn.: Yale University Press, 1992.

Weigle, Marta, ed. *Hispanic Arts and Ethnohistory in the Southwest.* Santa Fe: Ancient City Press, 1983. Its value in relation to the Santa Fe Trail is Marc Simmons's *"Carros y Carretas:* Vehicular Traffic on the Camino Real," pp. 325–46.

West, Elliott. *Contested Plains, Indians, Goldseekers, and the Rush to Colorado.* Lawrence: University Press of Kansas, 1998.

White, David A., compiler. *News of the Plains and Rockies 1803–1865. Original Narratives of Overland Travel and Adventure Selected from the Wagner-Camp and Becker Bibliography of Western America.* Spokane, Wash.: Arthur H. Clark, 1996, vol. 2 containing "Santa Fe Adventures, 1818–1843," and "Settlers, 1819–1865."

White, John Barber. *The Missouri Merchant One Hundred Years Ago.* Columbia: State Historical Society of Missouri, 1919.

Williams, Walter, and Floyd Calvin Shoemaker. *Missouri, Mother of the West.* 5 vols. Chicago and New York: American Historical Society, 1930.

Wilson, Chris. *The Myth of Santa Fe Creating a Modern Regional Tradition.* Albuquerque: University of New Mexico Press, 1997.

Wilson, Richard Lush. *Short Ravelings from a Long Yarn; or, Camp and March Sketches, of the Santa Fe Trail.* Chicago: Geer & Wilson, Daily Journal Office, 1847. Wilson joined a Santa Fe caravan headed by Solomon Houck in the spring of 1841 at Independence, Missouri.

Wood, Dean Earl. *The Old Santa Fe Trail from the Missouri River, Documentary Proof of the History and Route of the Old Santa Fe Trail.* Kansas City, Mo.: E. L. Mendenhall [1951].

Wood, Jerome H., Jr. *Conestoga Crossroads, Lancaster, Pennsylvania, 1730–1790.* Harrisburg: Pennsylvania Historical and Museum Commission, 1979.

Works Projects Administration. *Missouri: A Guide to the "Show Me" State.* New York: Hastings House, 1954.

Young, Otis E. *The First Military Escort on the Santa Fe Trail, 1829: From the Journal and Reports of Major Bennet Riley and Lieutenant Philip St. George Cooke.* Glendale, Calif.: Arthur H. Clark, 1952.

NEWSPAPERS

Daily Colorado Herald
Daily Colorado Tribune
Junction City Union
Kansas Chief
Kansas City Star
Kansas Press
Missouri Argus
Missouri Commonwealth
Missouri Intelligencer
Missouri Republican
New Era
New Orleans Weekly Picayune
New York Tribune
Niles National Register
Niles Weekly Register
Public Ledger
Rocky Mountain News
Santa Fe Gazette
Santa Fe Republican
Weekly Western Journal of Commerce
Western Dispatch
Western Expositor
Western Monitor

PAMPHLETS AND BOOKLETS

Ashton, John. *History of Jack Stock and Mules in Missouri.* Jefferson City: Missouri State Board of Agriculture, 1924.

Broadhead, Edward. *Ceran St. Vrain, 1802–1870.* Pueblo, Colo.: Pueblo County Historical Society, 1982.

Gardner, Mark L. *The Santa Fe Trail: National Historic Trail.* Tucson, Ariz.: Southwest Parks and Monuments Association, 1993.

Hall, Thomas B. *Medicine on the Santa Fe Trail.* Dayton, Ohio: Morningside Bookshop, 1971.

Hamilton, Jean Tyree. *Arrow Rock Where Wheels Started West.* Centralia, Mo.: Guard Printing & Publishing, 1963.

Long, Jim. *Herbal Medicines on the Santa Fe Trail.* Oak Grove, Ark.: published by the author, 1996.

Oliva, Leo E. *Fort Larned.* Topeka: Kansas State Historical Society, 1982.

Perkins, Margaret. *Echoes of Pawnee Rock.* Wichita, Kans.: Woman's Kansas Day Club, 1908.

Riley, James Francis. *Recollections of James Francis Riley, 1838–1918.* Independence, Mo.: John R. James, 1949.

[Scarborough, Asia]. *Diary of a Member of the First Pack Train to Leave Fort Smith for California in 1849.* Canyon, Tex.: Palo Duro Press, 1969. A separate reprint from the *Panhandle-Plains Historical Review* 42 (1969).

Smyth, Bernard Bryan. *The Heart of the New Kansas: A Pamphlet Historical and Descriptive of Southwestern Kansas.* Great Bend, Kans.: B. B. Smythe, 1880.

State Historical Society of Colorado. *Bent's Fort on the Arkansas.* Denver: State Historical Society of Colorado, 1954.

Twitchell, Ralph Emerson. *Dr. Josiah Gregg, Historian of the Santa Fe Trail.* Santa Fe: Historical Society of New Mexico, 1924. No. 26 in the society's publications.

Unrau, William E. *History of Fort Larned.* [Larned, Kans.]: [Tiller and Toiler], [1950s].

Utley, Robert M. *Fort Union National Monument.* Washington, D.C.: National Park Service, 1962.

Walter, Paul A. F., Jr. *Old Santa Fe and Vicinity: Points of Interest and Convenient Trips.* Santa Fe: Historical Society of New Mexico, 1933.

Westport Improvement Association. *Westport, 1812–1912.* Kansas City, Mo.: Press of Franklin Hudson Publishing, 1912.

Wilson, Chris. *The Myth of Santa Fe: Creating a Modern Regional Tradition.* Albuquerque: University of New Mexico Press, 1997.

Wilson, Richard Lush. *Short Ravelings from a Long Yarn; or, Camp March Sketches of the Santa Fe Trail.* Santa Ana, Calif.: Fine Arts Press, 1936.

GOVERNMENT DOCUMENTS

Frémont, John Charles. *A Report on an Exploration of the Country Lying between the Missouri River and the Rocky Mountains, on the Line of the Kansas and Great Platte Rivers.* 27th Cong., 3d sess., 1843. S. Doc. 243. Serial 416.

President. "American Citizens Captured Near Santa Fe. Message from the President of the United States, Transmitting the Information Required by the Resolution of the House of Representatives of the Fourteenth Instant, in Relation to American Citizens Captured Near Santa Fe, &C. January 20, 1842. Referred to the Committee on Foreign Affairs." 27th Cong., 2d sess., 1842. H. Doc. 49. Serial 402. Inquiries made by the United States concerning George W. Kendall and Franklin Coombs, who were captured by Mexico during the Texan expedition to Santa Fe.

President. "Message from the President of the United States, in Compliance with a Resolution of the Senate Concerning the Fur Trade, and Inland Trade to Mexico. February 9, 1832. Referred to the Committee on Indian Affairs. March 5, 1832." 22d Cong., 1st sess., 1832. S. Doc. 90. Serial 213. This document contains a brief history of the Santa Fe trade by Alphonso Wetmore, with extracts from his diary of a journey on the Santa Fe Trail in 1828.

President. "Message from the President of the United States, in Reply to a Resolution of the Senate, and Relating to the Protection of the Trade between Missouri and Mexico, February 8, 1830. Read, and Ordered to be Referred to the Committee on Military Affairs, and Printed." 21st Cong., 1st sess., 1830. S. Doc. 46. Serial 192. Contains a report of Major Riley's escort of a caravan of traders bound for Santa Fe in 1829.

President. "Message from the President of the United States, Transmitting in
Compliance with a Resolution of the House of Representatives of the Tenth
Instant, Information Relative to the Arrest and Imprisonment of Certain
American Citizens at Santa Fe, by Authority of the Government of Spain.
April 15, 1818. Read, and Ordered to Lie Upon the Table." 15th Cong., 1st
sess. 1818. H. House Doc. 197. Serial 12. Washington, D.C.: Printed by E. de
Krafft, 1818. This document concerns the 1812 party of James Baird, Robert
McKnight, Benjamin Shreve, and Michael McDonough plus five other men
and an interpreter, and the 1817 party of Auguste Chouteau and Julius De
Mun.

Storrs, Augustus. *Answers of Augustus Storrs, of Missouri, to Certain Queries upon the
Origin, Present State, and Future Prospect, of Trade and Intercourse, Between Missouri
and the Internal Provinces of Mexico, Propounded by the Hon. Mr. Benton. January 3,
1825.* 18th Cong., 2d sess., 1825. S. Doc. 7. Serial 108. Washington, D.C.:
Printed by Gales & Seaton, 1824. Storrs, who joined a trading expedition to
Santa Fe during the summer of 1824, answers questions from Senator Benton
regarding the route, country, trade, conditions in New Mexico, and Indian
attacks on traders.

U.S. Congress. Senate. *Appendix to the Report of the Commissioner of Indian Affairs.*
30th Cong., 1st sess., 1847. S. Doc. 1. Serial 503. The appendix is a letter written by at Bent's Fort by Thomas Fitzpatrick, Indian agent on the Upper Platte
and Arkansas Rivers, dated Sept. 18, 1847.

ARTICLES

Armstrong, R. M. "Sixty Years in Kansas and Council Grove." *Collections of the
Kansas State Historical Society, 1923–1925,* Vol. XVI. Topeka: Kansas State
Printing Plant, 1925.

Atherton, Lewis E. "Business Techniques in the Santa Fe Trade." *Missouri Historical Review* 34, no. 3 (Apr. 1940).

Atherton, Lewis E. "James and Robert Aull—a Frontier Missouri Mercantile
Firm." *Missouri Historical Review* 30, no. 1 (Oct. 1935).

Bernard, William R. "Westport and the Santa Fe Trade." *Transactions of the Kansas
State Historical Society, 1905–1906,* Vol. IX. Topeka: State Printing Office,
1906.

Bott, Emily Ann O'Neil. "Joseph Murphy's Contribution to the Development of
the West." *Missouri Historical Review* 47, no. 1 (Oct. 1952).

"Bypaths of Kansas History, Santa Fe and the West in 1841." *Kansas State Historical Quarterly,* Vol. VIII Topeka: Kansas State Historical Society, 1939.

Caldwell, Alexander. "Address of Alexander Caldwell . . . " *Transactions of the
Kansas State Historical Society, Vol. III.* Topeka: Kansas Publishing House, 1886.

Campbell, Charles E. "Down Among the Red Men," *Collections of the Kansas State
Historical Society, 1926–1928,* Vol. XVII. Topeka: Kansas State Printing Plant,
1928.

Clapsaddle, David K. "Toll Bridges on the Santa Fe Trail." *Wagon Tracks* 13, no. 2
(1999).

Connelley, William E. "The Treaty Held at Medicine Lodge." *Collections of the*

Kansas State Historical Society, 1926–1928, Vol. XVII. Topeka: Kansas State Printing Plant, 1928.

Cooke, Philip St. George. "A Journey on the Santa Fe Trail." Ed. William E. Connelley. *Mississippi Valley Historical Review* 12, no. 1 (June 1925): 72–98; 12, no. 2 (Sept. 1925): 227–55.

Cruise, John D. "Early Days on the Union Pacific." *Collections of the Kansas State Historical Society, 1909–1910,* Vol. XI. Topeka: State Printing Office, 1910.

Culmer, Frederic A. "Marking the Santa Fe Trail." *New Mexico Historical Review* 9, no. 1 (Jan. 1934).

Dary, David. "Storied Silver, Fabled Gold: Buried Treasure Legends along the Santa Fe Trail." In *The Santa Fe Trail New Perspectives: Essays in Colorado History,* ed. Denver: Colorado Historical Society, 1987. David N. Wetzel, editor.

Ewing, Floyd F., Jr. "The Mule as a Factor in the Development of the Southwest." *Arizona and the West* 5, no. 3 (1963).

Gardner, Mark L. "Malcolm Conn: Merchant on the Trail." *Wagon Tracks* 1, no. 2 (1987).

Grinnell, George Bird. "Bent's Old Fort and Its Builders." *Collections of the Kansas State Historical Society, 1919–1922,* Vol. XV. Topeka: State Printing Office, 1923.

Hubbard, D. "Reminiscences of the Yeager Raid, on the Santa Fe Trail, in 1863." *Transactions of the Kansas State Historical Society, 1903–1904,* Vol. III. Topeka: Geo. A. Clark, State Printer, 1904.

"Indian Treaties and Councils Affecting Kansas." *Collections of the Kansas State Historical Society, 1923–1925,* Vol. XVI. Topeka: Kansas State Printing Plant, 1925.

Krakow, Jere L. "Preservation Efforts on the Santa Fe Trail." *Journal of the West,* 28, no. 2 (Apr. 1989).

Marmaduke, M. M. "The Santa Fe Trail: M. M. Marmaduke Journal." *Missouri Historical Review* 6 (1911).

Mollhausen, Heinrich Balduin. "Over the Santa Fe Trail Through Kansas in 1858." *Kansas Historical Quarterly* 16, no. 4 (1948).

Raber, Charles. "Personal Recollections of Life on the Plains from 1860 to 1868." *Collections of the Kansas State Historical Society, 1923–1925,* Vol. XVI. Topeka: Kansas State Printing Plant, 1925.

Root, George A. "Reminiscences of William Darnell." *Collections of the Kansas State Historical Society, 1926–1928,* Vol. XVII. Topeka: Kansas State Printing Plant, 1928.

Rowland, Buford, ed. "Report of the Commissioners on the Road from Missouri to New Mexico, October 1827." *New Mexico Historical Review* 14, no. 3 (July 1939): 213–5.

"The Santa Fe Trail in Johnson County, Kansas." *Collections of the Kansas State Historical Society, 1909–1910,* Vol. XI. Topeka: State Printing Office, 1910.

Scott, P. G. "Diary of a Freighting Trip from Kit Carson to Trinidad in 1870." *Colorado Magazine,* July 1931.

Shamleffer, William F. "Merchandising Sixty Years Ago." *Collections of the Kansas State Historical Society, 1923–1925,* Vol. XVI. Topeka: Kansas State Printing Plant, 1925.

Sharp, Mamie Stine, "Home-coming Centennial Celebration at Council Grove, June 27 to July 2, 1921." *Collections of the Kansas State Historical Society, 1923–1925,* Vol. XVI. Topeka: Kansas State Printing Plant, 1925.

Smith, Ezra Delos. "Jedediah S. Smith and the Settlement of Kansas." *Collections of the Kansas State Historical Society, 1911–1912,* Vol. XII. Topeka: State Printing Office, 1912.

Stephens, F. F. "Missouri and the Santa Fe Trade." *Missouri Historical Review* 10, no. 4 (July 1916). First article.

Stephens, F. F. "Missouri and the Santa Fe Trade." *Missouri Historical Review* 11, no. 4 (July 1917). Second article.

Thomas, Alfred B. "The First Santa Fe Expedition, 1792–1973." *Chronicles of Oklahoma* 9, no. 2 (June 1931).

"A Trade Invoice of 1638." *New Mexico Historical Review* 10, no. 3 (July 1937).

Unrau, William E. "The Story of Fort Larned." *Kansas Historical Quarterly* 13, no. 3 (autumn 1957).

Viles, Jonas. "Old Franklin: A Frontier Town of the Twenties." *Mississippi Valley Historical Review,* Vol. 10, no. 4, March 1923.

Voelker, Frederic E. "Thomas James." *The Mountain Men and the Fur Trade of the Far West.* Glendale, Calif.: Arthur H. Clark, 1966.

Wyman, Walker D. "Freighting: A Big Business on the Santa Fe Trail." *Kansas Historical Quarterly* 1 (1931).

Wyman, Walker D. "Kansas City, Mo., a Famous Freighter Capital." *Kansas Historical Quarterly* 6, no. 1 (1937).

THESES AND DISSERTATIONS

Askins, Arthur D. "The History of the Santa Fe Trail." Ohio State University, 1930.

De Liniere, Virginia. "The Santa Fe Trail." Washington University, 1923.

Langefeld, Wilfred C. "The Santa Fe Trail, 1850–1854." Washington University, 1950.

Newton, Dwight B. "Techniques of Overland Freighting in the Trans-Missouri West." University of Missouri, Kansas City, 1942.

Oliva, Leo E. "Soldiers on the Santa Fe Trail, 1829–1860." University of Denver, 1964.

Ramsey, Helen G. "The Historical Background of the Santa Fe Trail." University of California, 1941.

Smith, Eileen Z. "The Santa Fe Trail during the Civil War, 1861–1866." Washington University, St. Louis, 1947.

Vaughan, Martha L. "The Old Santa Fe Trail." Oklahoma State University, 1939.

Walker, Henry P. "The Rise and Decline of High Plains Wagon Freighting, 1822–1880." University of Colorado, 1965.

Wyman, Walker D. "Freighting on the Santa Fe Trail, 1829–1860." University of Iowa, 1931.

Young, Otis E., Jr. "The Military Escort of the 1829 Santa Fe Caravan." University of Indiana, 1949.

Index

FOR THE BEST IN PAPERBACKS, LOOK FOR THE (P)

In every corner of the world, on every subject under the sun, Penguin represents quality and variety—the very best in publishing today.

For complete information about books available from Penguin—including Puffins, Penguin Classics, and Compass—and how to order them, write to us at the appropriate address below. Please note that for copyright reasons the selection of books varies from country to country.

In the United Kingdom: Please write to *Dept. EP, Penguin Books Ltd, Bath Road, Harmondsworth, West Drayton, Middlesex UB7 0DA.*

In the United States: Please write to *Penguin Putnam Inc., P.O. Box 12289 Dept. B, Newark, New Jersey 07101-5289* or call 1-800-788-6262.

In Canada: Please write to *Penguin Books Canada Ltd, 10 Alcorn Avenue, Suite 300, Toronto, Ontario M4V 3B2.*

In Australia: Please write to *Penguin Books Australia Ltd, P.O. Box 257, Ringwood, Victoria 3134.*

In New Zealand: Please write to *Penguin Books (NZ) Ltd, Private Bag 102902, North Shore Mail Centre, Auckland 10.*

In India: Please write to *Penguin Books India Pvt Ltd, 11 Panchsheel Shopping Centre, Panchsheel Park, New Delhi 110 017.*

In the Netherlands: Please write to *Penguin Books Netherlands bv, Postbus 3507, NL-1001 AH Amsterdam.*

In Germany: Please write to *Penguin Books Deutschland GmbH, Metzlerstrasse 26, 60594 Frankfurt am Main.*

In Spain: Please write to *Penguin Books S. A., Bravo Murillo 19, 1° B, 28015 Madrid.*

In Italy: Please write to *Penguin Italia s.r.l., Via Benedetto Croce 2, 20094 Corsico, Milano.*

In France: Please write to *Penguin France, Le Carré Wilson, 62 rue Benjamin Baillaud, 31500 Toulouse.*

In Japan: Please write to *Penguin Books Japan Ltd, Kaneko Building, 2-3-25 Koraku, Bunkyo-Ku, Tokyo 112.*

In South Africa: Please write to *Penguin Books South Africa (Pty) Ltd, Private Bag X14, Parkview, 2122 Johannesburg.*